CHINA'S NAVAL OPERATIONS IN
THE SOUTH CHINA SEA

**RENAISSANCE BOOKS
ASIA PACIFIC SERIES**

Managing Editor
Roger Buckley

VOLUME 3 ISSN 2396-8877

The titles published in this series are listed at
www.renaissancebooks.co.uk/series

China's Naval Operations in the South China Sea

EVALUATING LEGAL, STRATEGIC AND MILITARY FACTORS

By

Bruce A. Elleman

William V. Pratt Professor of International History
U.S. Naval War College

RENAISSANCE BOOKS

Renaissance Books Asia Pacific series, Vol. 3 ISSN 2396-8877

CHINA'S NAVAL OPERATIONS IN THE SOUTH CHINA SEA
EVALUATING LEGAL, STRATEGIC AND MILITARY FACTORS

First published 2018 by
RENAISSANCE BOOKS
P O Box 219
Folkestone
Kent CT20 2WP

Renaissance Books is an imprint of Global Books Ltd

ISBN 978-1-898823-67-4 Hardback
     978-1-898823-68-1 e-Book

© Bruce A. Elleman 2018

All rights reserved. No part of this publication may be reproduced, translated, stored in a retrieval system, or transmitted in any form or by any means, electronic, mechanical, photocopying, recording, or otherwise, without prior written permission from the publisher.

British Library Cataloguing in Publication Data
A catalogue record for this book is available from the British Library

Set in Garamond 11 on 12.0 pt by Dataworks
Printed and bound in England by CPI Antony Rowe Ltd., Chippenham, Wilts

*To Anna Virginia Elleman,
for preparing me to handle the complexities of life*

Contents

―――――o―――――

Preface	*ix*
Acknowledgements	*x*
List of Maps and Graph	*xiii*
List of Acronyms	*xv*

Introduction: Evaluating China's Maritime Strategy
in the South China Sea ... xvii

1. The Early History of the South China Sea Disputes ... 1
2. China's Maritime Territorial Disputes with Vietnam ... 31
3. China's Spratly-KIG Maritime Dispute with the Philippines ... 54
4. China's Continental Shelf Dispute with Malaysia ... 75
5. China's Energy Resources Dispute with Brunei ... 85
6. China's Natuna Island Fishing Dispute with Indonesia ... 93
7. China's Sovereignty Disputes with Taiwan ... 105
8. The United States as the South China Sea
Maritime Arbiter ... 127

Conclusions: China's Contemporary and
Future Maritime Strategy in the SCS ... 161

Appendix A: Timeline ... 195

SUPPORTING DOCUMENTS: ... 209

Document 1: Sino-French Tonkin Treaty, 26 June 1887 ... 209
Document 2: Cairo Declaration, 1 December 1943 ... 213
Document 3: Potsdam Proclamation, 26 July 1945 ... 214
Document 4: Treaty of Peace with Japan, 8 September 1951 ... 216
Document 5: Treaty of Peace between the Republic of
China and Japan, 28 April 1952 ... 218
Document 6: U.S.-ROC Mutual Defense Treaty,
2 December 1954 (ratified 1955) ... 222

Document 7:	Formosa Resolution, 1955	225
Document 8:	Declaration on China's Territorial Sea, 4 September 1958	227
Document 9:	Prime Minister Pham Van Dong's Letter, 14 September 1958	229
Document 10:	Shanghai Communiqué, 28 February 1972	230
Document 11:	Joint Communiqué on the Establishment of Diplomatic Relations between the People's Republic of China and the United States of America, 16 December 1978	235
Document 12:	Taiwan Relations Act, 10 April 1979	236
Document 13:	Joint Communiqué on the Question of Arms Sales to Taiwan, 17 August 1982	248
Document 14:	Law on the Territorial Sea and the Contiguous Zone, 25 February 1992	250
Document 15:	1992 ASEAN Declaration on the South China Sea, 22 July 1992	255
Document 16:	United Nations Convention on the Law of the Sea, PART V, Exclusive Economic Zone, in force since 14 November 1994	257
Document 17:	A concurrent resolution expressing the sense of Congress regarding missile tests and military exercises by the People's Republic of China, 21 March 1996.	271
Document 18:	Law on the Exclusive Economic Zone and the Continental Shelf of the PRC, 26 June 1998	274
Document 19:	2002 Declaration on the Conduct of Parties in the South China Sea, 4 November 2002	278
Document 20:	Anti-Secession Law adopted by NPC, 14 March 2005	281
Document 21:	Cross-Straits Economic Cooperation Framework Agreement, 29 June 2010	284
Document 22:	In the Matter of the South China Sea Arbitration, 12 July 2016	292

Selected Bibliography   *301*

Index   *312*

Preface

―――o―――

THIS BOOK EXAMINES the evolving strategy of the People's Republic of China (PRC) toward the South China Sea (SCS). In addition to long-standing territorial disputes over the islands and waters of the SCS, the PRC and the other claimant governments – Vietnam, the Philippines, Malaysia, Brunei, Indonesia, and Taiwan – have growing and often mutually exclusive interests over the region's offshore energy reserves and fishing grounds.

Meanwhile, many other countries outside of the region worry about the protection of sea lines of communication (SLOC) for military and commercial traffic – oil tankers in particular. These differences have been reflected in the increasing frequency and intensity of maritime incidents, involving both naval and civilian vessels, sometimes working in coordination against an opponent's naval or civilian targets.

This book has endeavored to provide a comprehensive history of the SCS conflict and lay out the stakes for each of the bordering states, including focused chapters on Vietnam, the Philippines, Malaysia, Brunei, Indonesia, and Taiwan. It also examines the U.S. government's role as the maritime arbiter in the region.

Each chapter on the various claimant states offers an in-depth overview of that state's territorial claims to the islands and waters of the SCS, its primary economic and military interests in these areas, its views on the sovereignty disputes over the entire sea, its strategy to achieve its objectives, and its views on the U.S. involvement in any of these issues.

The conclusions consider four different strategic scenarios – indirect, unilateral, bilateral, and multilateral – that might impact the future of this highly volatile region. With the almost daily changes occurring throughout the SCS, however, any scenario is mere speculation.

Supporting the main text is a detailed Timeline of SCS events, commencing in the second century B.C.E. and continuing up to the present period. Twenty-two supporting documents, referenced in the text, appear in the appendices.

ACKNOWLEDGEMENTS

The author would like to thank all those former naval officers who shared their insights and expertise during personal, telephone, and email interviews, including Joseph W. Prueher, Lyle Bien, Michael Mullen, and James P. Wisecup. At the NWC, I benefited from the support of Jeffrey A. Harley, Lewis Duncan, Phil Haun, and Timothy Schultz. When discussing the intricacies of the South China Sea territorial disputes, I made extensive use of both unpublished dissertations and published books and articles by Esmond Douglas Smith, Stephen Kotkin, Clive Schofield, Ramses Amer, Ian Storey, I Made Andi Arsana, Vivian Louis Forbes, and Lowell Batista. David Rosenberg, Middlebury College, kindly allowed me to make use of his extensive collection of South China Sea maps, and William A. Callahan gave me permission to reprint the Chinese 1927 "National Humiliation" map.

This book was based on extensive archival research. At the Naval Historical Center (now Naval History and Heritage Command), John Hodges helped me gain access to the U.S. Navy archives, John Greco located biographies, while Edward J. Marolda and Jeff Barlow helped me locate essential documents. At the U.S. Army Center of Military History, Mason Schaefer and Frank Shirer assisted my research. At the Air Force History Division, John Q. Smith answered all my questions. At the Marine Corps History Division, Annette Amerman was helpful, as were Rachel Kingcade and Lindsay Kleinow in the U.S. Marine Corps Research Library. Professor Andrew Lambert, King's College, gave me advice on the UK National Archives, Kew Garden, and how to access the Julian Corbett papers at the National Maritime Museum, Greenwich, UK. Ben Primer assisted me in using the John Foster Dulles Papers at the Seeley G. Mudd Manuscript Library, Princeton University. In the NWC Security Office, Lenny Coleman and Sandra Blogette helped me obtain clearances to use materials at the National Archives, where I was supported by Alan Lipton, Don Mcilwain, and Paula Ayres. Thanks to Evelyn M. Cherpak and

Dara Baker for help using the NWC Naval Historical Collection. I am also indebted to the many reference librarians and archival specialists at the Harry S. Truman Presidential Library in Independence, Missouri, the Dwight D. Eisenhower Presidential Library in Abilene, Kansas, and the Lyndon Baines Johnson Presidential Library in Austin, Texas. All American and British sources with a classification designation have been declassified in accordance with standard procedures in that country.

I also owe a considerable debt to Alice Juda, Wayne Rowe, Robin Lima, and Bob Schnare for assistance at the NWC Library, as well as to Andrew Marshall, former director of the Office of Net Assessment, for his incredible support for this and other China-related projects.

Thanks to Garth Schofield for clarifying that the South China Sea Arbitration was issued by an arbitral tribunal as administered by the Permanent Court of Arbitration pursuant to Annex VII to the United Nations Convention on the Law of the Sea, and that the final decision is known as "South China Sea Arbitration (Philippines v. China), Award of 12 July 2016."

Particular thanks go to Roger Buckley, who I first met when a language student at International Christian University almost twenty-five years ago, for accepting this book as part of his Renaissance Books Asia Pacific Series, and to Paul Norbury, Publisher, and David Blakeley, Copy Editor, at Renaissance Books, plus to the skilled typesetting staff at Dataworks.

Finally, I want to thank Sarah C.M. Paine for reading and commenting on the manuscript. All mistakes, however, remain mine and mine alone.

Bruce Elleman
Portsmouth, Rhode Island
September 2017

Maps and Graph

———o———

Map 1:	Conflicting South China Sea Maritime Claims	xviii
Map 2:	The Republic of China's 11-Dash Map of the SCS	9
Map 3:	SCS Oil and Natural Gas Resources	14
Map 4:	Vietnam's SCS Claim	33
Map 5:	Oil Exploration Blocks off Vietnam	46
Map 6:	The PRC "nine-dash" Map of the SCS	61
Map 7:	The Joint Seismic Survey Area	67
Map 8:	Sovereignty Claims in the South China Sea	76
Map 9:	A Taiwanese stamp showing the connected U-shaped line	109
Map 10:	Location of PRC Missiles Tests during 1995–1996	117
Map 11:	Nationalist China's Territorial Claims in 1927	123
Map 12:	SCS Oil and Natural Gas Proved and Probable Reserves	137
Map 13:	The SCS Maritime Claims	151
Map 14:	Complex Nature of the SCS Claims	162
Map 15:	Major Oil Deliveries through the SCS SLOC	164
Map 16:	The SCS resembles a "Weiqi" board	168
Map 17:	China's Malacca Dilemma	171
Graph 1:	Chinese arms imports from Russia, 1992–2010	155

Acronyms

―――o―――

ADIZ	Air Defense Identification Zone
ARATS	Association for Relations Across the Taiwan Straits
ARF	ASEAN Regional Forum
ASEAN	Association of Southeast Asian Nations
ASM	Anti-Ship Missile
Bbls	billion barrels
CARAT	Cooperation Afloat Readiness And Training
CBM	Confidence Building Measure
CIA	Central Intelligence Agency
CoC	Code of Conduct
CLCS	Commission on the Limits of the Continental Shelf, UN
CNOOC	China National Offshore Oil Company
CVN	Aircraft Carrier Nuclear
DDG	Guided Missile Destroyer
DoC	Declaration of Conduct
DPP	Democratic Progressive Party
DRV	Democratic Republic of Vietnam [North Vietnam]
ECS	Extended Continental Shelf
EDCA	Enhanced Defense Cooperation Agreement
EEZ	Exclusive Economic Zone
EoL	Exchange of Letters
EU	European Common Market
FON	Freedom of Navigation operation
GNP	Gross National Product
ICCOC	Indonesia-China Centre for Ocean and Climate
ICJ	International Court of Justice
IUU	Illegal, Unreported, and Unregulated fishing activities

JMSU	Joint Marine Seismic Undertaking
JOAC	Joint Operational Access Concept
KIG	Kalayaan Island Group
km/km²	Kilometers, Square Kilometers
MMAF	Ministry of Marine Affairs and Fishing
NAFTA	North American Free Trade Agreement
NATO	North Atlantic Treaty Organization
nm/nm²	Nautical Miles, Square Nautical Miles
PCA	Permanent Court of Arbitration
PETROVIETNAM	Vietnam Oil and Gas Corporation
PLA	People's Liberation Army
PLAN	People's Liberation Army Navy
PNOC	Philippine National Oil Company
PRC	People's Republic of China
RBAF	Royal Brunei Armed Forces
RBN	Royal Brunei Navy
RCEP	Regional Comprehensive Economic Partnership
ROC	Republic of China
ROV	Republic of Vietnam [South Vietnam]
SCS	South China Sea
SEF	Straits Exchange Foundation
SLOC	Sea Lines of Communication
SRBM	Short Range Ballistic Missile
Tcf	Trillion cubic feet
TNI	Indonesian National Army
UN	United Nations
UNCLOS	United Nations Convention on the Law of the Sea
UNESCO	United Nations Educational, Scientific and Cultural Organization
WPP	*Wilayah Pengelolaan Perikanan* [Indonesian Regulation]

INTRODUCTION

Evaluating China's Maritime Strategy in the South China Sea

―――○―――

THE PEOPLE'S REPUBLIC of China (PRC) is just one of the many nations claiming sovereignty over the widespread groups of tiny islets, reefs, and atolls in the Pratas islands (Dongsha in Chinese), Scarborough Shoal (Huangyan Dao), Macclesfield Bank (Zhongsha), Paracel islands (Xisha), and Spratly islands (Nansha), known collectively as the South China Sea (SCS) (see Map 1 below). This territorial dispute has become a major concern to the nations of Southeast Asia and a potential threat to regional security. As such, it also poses serious legal, strategic, and military questions for the United States government.

This book seeks to examine both the historical creation of China's sea borders with its SCS neighbors and provide critical analysis of contemporary border problems and military tensions. In those cases where these maritime boundaries have been settled it will discuss exactly how these disputes have been solved, as well as examine possible strategies for resolving any further conflicts. In July 2016, a UN tribunal "rejected the PRC's argument that it enjoys historic rights over most of the South China Sea."[1] Given this recent UN decision, each chapter will also discuss how this ruling might impact China's economic, diplomatic, and cultural policies with these neighboring countries so as to evaluate Beijing's overall maritime strategy in the SCS.

---

[1] Jane Perlez, "Tribunal Rejects Beijing's Claims in South China Sea," *New York Times*, 12 July 2016, http://www.nytimes.com/2016/07/13/world/asia/south-china-sea-hague-ruling-philippines.html [accessed 9 November 2016].

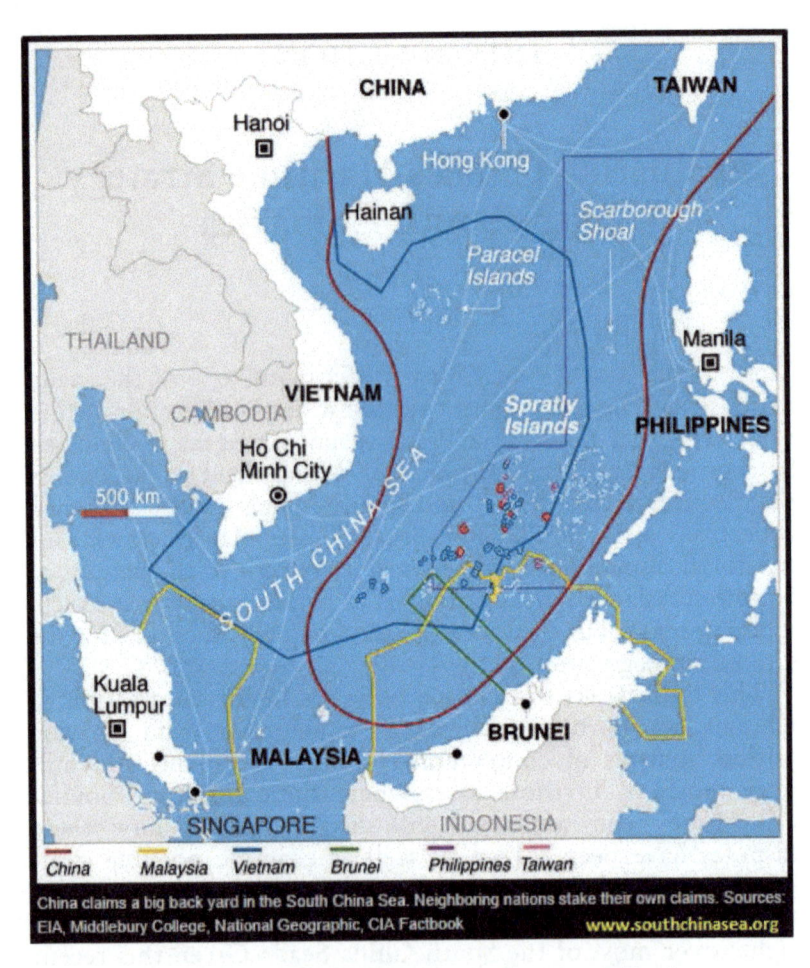

Map 1: Conflicting South China Sea Maritime Claims[2]

Several SCS countries including China have resorted to force to uphold their claims. These operations resulted in the occupation of many islands by small military garrisons, thus making the area potentially volatile and a major security concern for many other nations in the region. Developments in mili-

---

[2] SCS map courtesy of David Rosenberg www.southchinasea.org.

tary technology, including the recent availability of modern, high-tech aircraft, ships, and missiles – many acquired from Russia after the collapse of the Soviet Union – are giving the People's Liberation Army Navy (PLAN) new capabilities for sea, undersea, air, and shore combat that make it possible for the first time for the Chinese to attack, overwhelm, and thereby neutralize key non-Chinese held islands in the SCS. A reexamination of China's maritime strategy is particularly important in light of the momentous developments that have occurred in the SCS over the past two decades.

***

Historically, the SCS did not lie within any country's territorial waters, and the islands themselves were long thought to contain few resources of economic value. They were most often cited as dangers to navigation. Despite their tiny size – Itu Aba, the largest island in the Spratlys, is only .166 square miles (.43 square kilometers), while Spratly Island is just .0579 square miles (.15 km^2) – and apparent limited economic worth, the SCS is today at the center of a territorial dispute that could have major implications for regional security in Southeast Asia. The potential conflict over the Spratlys, in particular, is complicated by the fact that many nations have claims in the southern and southwestern portion of the SCS, including China, Vietnam, the Philippines, Malaysia, Brunei, and – as the PRC argues at least – Indonesia, not to mention Taiwan. The SCS's critical strategic location, adjacent to the principal international shipping lanes from the Indian Ocean to the Pacific, also makes this dispute a legitimate concern to all maritime states, such as the United States, Japan, and South Korea, as well as regional states, including Australia, Singapore, and India, which depend on sea lanes for a substantial percentage of their trade.

Beijing's first major use of naval expeditionary warfare to back up its sovereignty claims dates to 1974, when the PRC used its navy to defeat South Vietnamese troops and resolve its claim to the Paracel islands by force. Shortly after their defeat in the Paracel islands, Vietnamese troops moved south and occupied several of the Spratly islands. Following the unification of North and South Vietnam, further clashes occurred during March 1988 over the Spratlys. Since that time, there has been a "scramble" by all of the claimants to consolidate and, in many cases, expand their outposts.

In addition to these historic factors, dynamic political and military changes have occurred in Southeast Asia in the late 1980s, throughout the 1990s, and into the current century. These included the withdrawal of Soviet (now Russian) naval forces from Vietnam, the departure of American military forces from the Philippines, and the Asian financial collapse of 1998. Meanwhile, the 1 April 2001 EP-3 incident between the United States and China revealed just how quickly relations could become tense over these disputed waters. Since 9-11, the United States and its allies have arguably been preoccupied with the Middle East, and only in recent years has U.S. policy "pivoted" back to Asia. This makes a fuller understanding of the outstanding territorial disputes of even greater contemporary importance.

***

The SCS dispute grew out of its geography, history, and strategic position. According to one expert: "The maritime strategic geography of East Asia makes it one of the most complex geostrategic regions in the world with the chain of narrow seas along the east coast of Asia, the offlying archipelagos and islands, overlapping exclusive economic zones (EEZs), and a proliferation of maritime boundary disputes and conflicting claims to sovereignty over offshore islands and reefs."[3] Among the factors that make this area unique are its relative geographic isolation, dearth of natural resources – in particular an almost total lack of fresh water – and so almost zero indigenous population. Until recently, the hundreds of islands, reefs, and atolls that comprise the Paracel and Spratly island chains were largely uninhabited except by the

---

[3] Sam Bateman, "Maritime security: regional concerns and global implications," in William T. Tow, ed., *Security Politics in the Asia-Pacific: A Regional-Global Nexus?* (New York: Cambridge University Press, 2009), 249.

occasional fisherman. Even today, the only people that could be said to live on most of these islands permanently are military personnel manning the small outposts of the various claimant nations.

The big change came when oil was discovered in the 1960s. Many of the tensions in the SCS are linked to exploiting untapped energy sources. Developments in resource exploitation have created pressures on China and its neighbors to gain control of these disputed waters to locate oil, natural gas, and other minerals. The influence of new technologies is striking, particularly with regard to new forms of offshore oil drilling. Modern drilling technology has made previously insignificant islands potentially valuable and thereby created an imperative for further Chinese action. Realistic options to resolve the dispute peacefully appear to be limited because of the complex and varied nature of the claims as well as the intransigence of the PRC, the most powerful claimant.

All of the nations that claim sovereignty to some or all of the Paracel and Spratly islands need new energy resources to fuel their own industrial development. This is particularly true of China. The PRC's economy has been growing at an impressive rate, with Gross National Product (GNP) increasing by an average of Annual Growth Rate that averaged 9.76% from 1989 until 2016, reaching an all time high of 15.40% in the first quarter of 1993; even the current 6.8% "low" rate is higher than most industrial economies.[4] China's rapid industrial growth has put a severe strain on its domestic oil supplies. While current Chinese offshore oil production continues to increase, China's oil imports have skyrocketed to 64.4% in 2016.[5] These factors could underlie Beijing's recent efforts to accelerate foreign investment and participation in Chinese oil exploration and gas development projects, particularly in the potentially resource-rich SCS. At the same time, advances in drilling technology

---

[4] China GDP Annual Growth Rate, 1989–2017, *Tradingeconomics.com*, http://www.tradingeconomics.com/china/gdp-growth-annual [accessed 10 April 2017].

[5] Irina Slav, "China's Oil Import Dependency Deepens," *OilPrice.com*, 13 January 2017, http://oilprice.com/Latest-Energy-News/World-News/Chinas-Oil-Import-Dependency-Deepens.html [accessed 10 April 2017].

have made it economically feasible to explore and then exploit deep undersea natural gas resources in the Spratlys region, giving this area a value not recognized earlier.

**

Why are SCS relations so complicated? Government-to-government negotiations combined with a broad array of bilateral and multinational security mechanisms are now widely available to assist in resolving international problems. The growth of an international maritime regime that establishes and codifies norms of international behavior is exemplified by the 1982 United Nations Convention on the Law of the Sea (UNCLOS). This convention came into force on 14 November 1994, and as of June 2016 had 167 countries plus the European Union as members. New concepts of international law, largely based on the UNCLOS agreement have changed how countries perceive the oceans as well as give legitimacy to expanding national territorial claims. But as the map above shows, each of the adjoining countries' claims over the SCS differs widely with China.

UNCLOS was based on the assumption that all states have equal rights, and that they would be treated as equals in any maritime dispute. In case of a dispute, third party adjudication could be called in to settle disputes based on internationally accepted legal norms and precedence. While the final convention has not been formally ratified by all nations – most notably by the United States government – the provisions have been generally adhered to in practice, indicating a near universal *de facto* acceptance by the international community. China, which has signed and ratified UNCLOS, has promised to follow its provisions but has so far refused to agree to the July 2016 UNCLOS ruling as issued by the UN Permanent Court of Arbitration (PCA) (see Document 22).

The various conflicting sovereignty claims to the SCS are complex. Most studies have focused on China's geopolitical concerns, seeking to analyze the respective policies of the PRC and the other claimants from a political, legal, or economic perspective. China's total control over the Paracels since 1974 makes significant territorial changes in this island group unlikely. However, the recent establishment, reclamation, and expansion of PRC military outposts in the Spratlys significantly changed the *status quo*, since there are a number of states competing for control of the Spratly islands.[6]

Meanwhile, an ever growing Chinese military presence in these disputed islands has serious regional, as well as international, implications. Although diplomacy has resulted in several border treaties, including the partial resolution of the Gulf of Tonkin (Beibu Gulf) disputes, there are three reasons why the Spratly island dispute is not likely to be resolved by a legal settlement, including: 1) the complex nature of the dispute; 2) the extreme sensitivities of Asian countries to territorial issues; 3) a general reluctance of Asian states to rely on contemporary international law.[7]

The framework of this book is both historical and geographical. Chapter one focuses on the early history of the Paracel and Spratly islands disputes; Chapter two discusses China's complex maritime territorial disputes with Vietnam; Chapter three examines China's Spratly- Kalayaan Island Group (KIG) maritime dispute with the Philippines; Chapter four discusses China's ongoing continental shelf dispute with Malaysia; Chapter five looks at China's energy resources dispute with Brunei; Chapter six examines China's Natuna islands fishing dispute with Indonesia; Chapter seven summarizes China's sovereignty disputes with Taiwan; while Chapter eight provides an analysis of the United States as the SCS maritime arbiter.

After examining the historic and geographic background of the SCS dispute, the conclusions will discuss China's likely contemporary and future maritime strategy and will offer several possible future scenarios that could affect the policies of China and the other claimants. It will assess future prospects for resolving these disputes, either through peaceful means such as diplomacy, which might include bilateral or multinational agreements to develop

---

[6] For a discussion of exactly which islands comprise the Spratly archipelago see Daniel J. Dzurek, "Boundary and Resource Disputes in the South China Sea," in *Ocean Yearbook 5* (Chicago: University of Chicago Press, 1985), 259.

[7] Choon-Ho Park, "The South China Sea Disputes: Who Owns the Islands and the Natural Resources?" *Ocean Development and International Law* 5 (1978): 33.

the SCS's natural resources jointly, or, if diplomacy fails, through military force. It will also examine how China's recent island reclamation program might impact its neighbors' military responses. Finally, it will conclude by arguing that the U.S. government should publicly renew its support for the 1899 Open Door Policy, and that this policy should be applied throughout East Asia to guarantee equal opportunity access to the contested waters of the SCS.

CHAPTER ONE

The Early History of the South China Sea Disputes

———*———

CHINA IS ONE of seven countries, including Vietnam, the Philippines, Malaysia, Brunei, and – in China's view at least – Indonesia, plus Taiwan, claiming sovereignty over all or part the widespread group of tiny islands, reefs, and atolls in the SCS. These territorial disputes have become a major concern to the Association of Southeast Asian Nations (ASEAN), which includes Brunei, Cambodia, Indonesia, Laos, Malaysia, Myanmar, the Philippines, Singapore, Thailand, and Vietnam, and thus represent a threat to regional security. As such, they also pose serious strategic challenges for the United States and its Asian allies. This chapter will examine the early history of maritime conflict over the Paracel and Spratly islands, especially from the nineteenth century down to the early 1990s, with a special emphasis on China's maritime actions, including its 1974 expeditionary campaign to the Paracels and the 1988 clash over the Spratlys.

The Paracel islands, a group of 130 islands and reefs located about 190 nm (350 km) southeast of Hainan, are currently under sole Chinese control, and unlike the situation in the Spratlys this does not appear to be subject to change. By contrast, both the islands and the waters surrounding the Spratly islands remain highly disputed. The Spratly islands correspond generally with the area that the Chinese call Nansha Qundao, and the Vietnamese call Truong Sa. At one point, Japan specified that its claim included all of the area from 7° to 12° north and then from 111°30' to 117°00' east. Several western geographers describe the area as bounded by latitudes 4° to 11°30' north and longitudes

109°30' to 117°50' east.[8] The area that the Philippine government calls "Kalayaan" or "Freedomland" generally includes only those Spratly islands that lie west of Palawan and north of 7°40' North latitude.[9] China has an even larger claim encompassing 3°37' to 11°55' north latitude and 109°43' to 117°47' east longitude.[10] The point here is that there is not even a common definition of where the Spratlys are located.

A similar problem exists with regard to how many islands are located in this region. The Spratly Island archipelago is a widespread group of approximately 170 small islands, shoals, and reefs, including some that are barely above water level at low tide. Under the best of circumstances, only a dozen of these could be called islands. These formations are scattered over an area variously estimated from 52,413–69,883 square nautical miles (about 180,000 to 240,000 square kilometers) in the southeastern part of the SCS. Some estimates of this area's size are much greater, with one Western claim of 154,000 nm^2 (528,000 km^2) and a Chinese claim of 232,000 nm^2 (800,000 km^2).[11] Although the water area of the Spratly islands is enormous, the dozen or so habitable islands represent less than 2 square miles (5 km^2) of dry land. The dearth of large islands should not diminish the strategic value placed on control of the SCS.

STRATEGIC IMPORTANCE OF THE SOUTH CHINA SEA

The SCS is of great strategic importance, especially because the sea lines of communication (SLOCs) for commercial ships transiting between the Indian and Pacific Oceans lie just to the west of the Spratly islands and just to the east of the Paracels.

---

[8] Marwyn S. Samuels, *Contest for the South China Sea* (New York: Methuen, 1982), 188; this agrees with Dieter Heinzig, *Disputed Islands in the South China Sea* (Wiesbaden: Harrassowitz, 1976), 17.
[9] Douglas M. Johnston and Mark J. Valencia, *Pacific Ocean Boundary Problems: Status and Solutions* (Boston: Martin Nijhoff Publishers, 1991), 123.
[10] Daniel J. Dzurak, *The Spratly Islands Dispute: Who's On First*, Maritime Briefing, Vol. 2, No. 1, International Boundaries Research Unit (IBRU), 1996, 3.
[11] Dzurak, The Spratly Islands Dispute, 1n4

There are a large number of potential maritime tensions over control of these SLOCs between Beijing and its Southeast Asian neighbors. Open conflict erupted in 1974, when Chinese forces drove South Vietnamese troops out of the Paracel islands, and again in 1988 when China fought with Vietnamese troops over the Spratlys. The PRC's official policy is that only China has the right to claim sovereignty over the SCS.

The SCS region is a highly strategic gateway due to its geographic position as a chokepoint between the Pacific and the Indian oceans. Beijing's perspective on the significance of the Paracel and Spratly islands was stated in a 24 November 1975 article from the Chinese newspaper *Guangmin Ribao*:[12]

> As it lies between the Indian Ocean and the Pacific, the SCS is a vital strategic area. It acts as a gateway to the outside world for the mainland and offshore islands of China. The [Paracel and Spratly] archipelagos occupy a position central to the shipping lanes connecting Canton [modern day Guangzhou], Hong Kong, Manila and Singapore. [Hence] their geographic position is extremely important.

While both Beijing and Taipei agree on China's claim to the SCS, Beijing disputes Taipei's control over the Pratas islands and Itu Aba, the largest island in the Spratly group.

Despite its potential strategic importance, the Spratly islands were historically avoided. The Spratly's northernmost areas are labeled on most nautical charts as "dangerous ground" because of the many reefs, shoals, and other hazards to navigation. While the number of islands, shoals, reefs, and cays comprising the Spratlys is in dispute, it is generally agreed that only a few are capable of sustaining human life or economic enterprise – the generally agreed upon criteria for distinguishing islands from rocks in international maritime boundary claims. Indeed, before Itu Aba was seized by the Japanese as a base for submarine operations in World War II, these islands were never permanently occupied, but only visited seasonally – if at all – by fishermen. Even today, the only people that can be said to live in the Spratly islands permanently are military personnel manning small national outposts on a temporary basis.

---

[12] Samuels, *Contest for the South China Sea*, 139.

There is disagreement about how many islands are in the Spratlys. Low estimates state that there are 33 islands, cays, and rocks that stand permanently above sea level. But the five claimant nations have now fortified dozens of island bases in the archipelago. Chang Pao-Min's estimate of "more than 230 barren islets, reefs, sand bars and atolls, about 180 of which have been named," is probably one of the larger numbers.[13] The distinction between rocks and islands is important, since a rock generates a 452 nm^2 maritime zone but an island generates 125,600 nm^2. The wide range of estimates is due to variations in the definition of what comprises a rock, island, or reef and the fact that some are unnamed and others are underwater at high tide.[14] Only seven features are larger than 0.1 square kilometers in size: Itu Aba, Spratly, Thitu, West York, North East Cay, Southwest Cay, and Sand Cay. Meanwhile; the highest is Namyit Island at 6.1 meters.[15] As a result of the small size of all of these islands, the July 2016 UN tribunal determined they were all "too small . . . to claim control of economic activities in the waters around them."[16] This ruling, albeit authoritative, is largely being ignored by all of the claimants.

The UNCLOS ruling is especially relevant to China's claim over the SCS and the southern islands, which it claims are part of its "historic waters." Beijing cites extensive maritime trade throughout the region beginning as early as the Han dynasty (206 B.C.E.-220). Later, during the Ming dynasty (1368-1644), Chinese expeditions regularly traveled through these waters on the way to Malacca. Zheng He's treasure fleets may have even visited some of the larger islands. By the mid-nineteenth century, the Qing dynasty (1644-1911) had established throughout the SCS a "flourishing" trade between East and West and

---

[13] Chang Pao-Min, "A New Scramble for the South China Sea Islands," *Contemporary Southeast Asia*, 12 (June 1990), 20-21.
[14] Joseph P. Morgan and Mark J. Valencia, eds., *Atlas for Marine Policy in Southeast Asian Seas* (Los Angeles: University of California Press, 1983), 35.
[15] Jon M. Van Dyke, "Disputes Over Islands and Maritime Boundaries in East Asia," in Seoung- Yong Hong and Jon M. Van Dyke, eds., *Maritime Boundary Disputes, Settlement Processes, and the Law of the Sea* (Leiden: Martinus Nijhoff Publishers, 2009), 68.
[16] Perlez, "Tribunal Rejects Beijing's Claims in South China Sea."

"Chinese trading junks and Western merchantmen dominated the region's economy."[17]

Even though Chinese certainly visited these islands, there was as yet no topographical tradition in China of making detailed maps or marking maritime territory. Therefore, the archipelago is named after Richard Spratly, the captain of a British whaling ship, who reportedly explored the islands in the early 1840s.[18] Bill Hayton puts the exact date of discovery as 29 March 1843.[19] Spratly Island itself is located along the southwest edge of the chain, and is only 13 hectares in size, or just over 30 acres. Due to their discovery by an English ship, England was the first Western country to claim the Spratly islands officially in 1864, and it later renewed its claims in 1877 and 1889.[20] The claiming of obscure islands was considered standard operating procedure for British ships. In fact, the Spratlys were simply a few of the more than one hundred Pacific islands claimed by Britain as potential fueling stations during these years, many of which were later turned over to New Zealand after World War I.[21]

The intervention of European states into Southeast Asia complicated the ownership disputes. As a result of the Sino-French conflict in 1884–1885, France made Annam (Vietnam) a protectorate and later a colony. A treaty delimiting borders in the Gulf of Tonkin signed by France and China in 1887 stated: "The isles which are to the east of the meridian of 105° 43' longitude east of Paris, which is to say of the north-south line passing through the eastern point of the island of Chagu [Tch'a-Kou or Ouan-chan (Tra-co)] and

---

[17] Robert J. Antony, *Like Froth Floating on the Sea; The World of Pirates and Seafarers in Late Imperial South China* (Berkeley, CA: China Research Monograph, 2003), 9.
[18] British researcher R. Haller-Trost located two British captains named Spratly in the Lloyd's Captains Register of 1869. Only the first, Richard Spratly, was active in the 1840s, the generally accepted date of the discovery of these islands by the British. See R. Haller-Trost, *Occasional Paper No. 14 - The Spratly Islands: A Study on the Limitations of International Law* (Canterbury: University of Kent Centre of South-East Asian Studies, 1990), 4.
[19] Bill Hayton, *The South China Sea: The Struggle for Power in Asia* (New Haven: Yale University Press, 2014), 91.
[20] Corazon Siddayao, *The Off-Shore Petroleum Resources of South-East Asia* (New York: Oxford University Press, 1978), 84
[21] James Truslow Adams, *Empire on the Seven Seas: The British Empire, 1784–1939* (New York: Charles Scribner's Sons, 1940), 264.

forming the border, are similarly assigned to China. The Jiutou [Go-tho] islands and other islands which are to the west of this meridian belong to Annam" (see Document 1). China lost other islands to foreign powers. During the first Sino-Japanese War of 1894–1895, Japan took possession of Taiwan away from Qing China, which also included various island chains like the Pescadores (Penghus).

These setbacks prompted Qing China to pay more attention to the SCS. Faced with what China considered to be illegal mining operations on several phosphorite and guano-rich islands in the Pratas and Spratly islands, in 1907 Sa Zhenbing, one of the most famous leaders of China's Navy, commanded a naval expedition to reclaim these islands for China. In September 1909 the Qing government renamed the Naval Reorganization Council the Ministry of the Navy and China's newly modernized navy conducted several operations in the SCS. Subsequently, in 1909 and 1910 China formally annexed many of these islands to Guangdong province. For example, on 6 June 1909, Admiral Li Xun raised a Chinese flag over Duncan Island in the Paracels.[22] China also sent a ship every year to the SCS "to maintain contact with overseas Chinese on these islands."[23] There are reliable reports that as late as 1922, the British Embassy in Beijing urged that "China should be encouraged to assert her sovereignty" over the Paracels.[24]

But Beijing was in no position to assert its sovereignty. Following the collapse of the Qing dynasty in early 1912, China experienced the beginning of what would become almost forty years of on-again off-again civil war. In 1926, the Nationalist Navy did build a radio station on Pratas Island, but in 1928, a Chinese commission authorized by the new Nationalist government determined that the southernmost territory of the Chinese state were the Paracel islands. This meant that Mainland China's claim to the Spratlys dates to 1988, when it built a "marine observatory" on Fiery Cross Reef.[25]

---

[22] Anthony Carty, "The South China Sea Disputes Are Not Yet Justiciable," in Wu Shicun and Keyuan Zou, eds., *Arbitration Concerning the South China Sea: Philippines versus China* (Surrey: Ashgate, 2016), 28–29.
[23] Bruce Swanson, *Eighth Voyage of the Dragon: A History of China's Quest for Seapower* (Annapolis, MD: Naval Institute Press, 1982), 119–120.
[24] Carty, "The South China Sea Disputes Are Not Yet Justiciable," 29.
[25] Nalanda Roy, *The South China Sea Disputes: Past, Present, and Future* (New York: Lexington Books, 2016), 4.

In response to a French claim to the Paracel islands in 1931, a Chinese protest referred to France's implied recognition of Chinese sovereignty over the Paracels when a French delegate to the 1930 Hong Kong Far Eastern Meteorological Conference agreed to a request that Beijing build a weather station on one of the Paracel islands. In response to China's protest, the French claimed a year later that the conference in question was scientific and did not deal with political questions.[26] Taking advantage of China's domestic chaos, French Indochina annexed the Paracel islands in 1932. The first effective occupation of the Spratlys was also by the French, who claim to have exercised *de facto* control over six of the Spratly islands, including Spratly Island itself, from 1930 to 1939.

Following Japan's invasion of China, Tokyo began to make its own claims to the Pratas, Paracel, and Spratly islands. During 1937, Japan seized Pratas Island, captured about two dozen Nationalist soldiers, and fortified the island. France, in response to this military threat, sent an expedition to the Paracels, officially claiming it as part of its colony of Annam (Vietnam) on 3 July 1938. Immediately, both the Nationalist government in Chongqing and the Japanese government protested France's action; Japan even stated in its own 8 July 1938 protest that France was violating Chinese sovereignty when it occupied the Paracel islands.

France next claimed the Paracel islands as part of the French Union in 1939. In response to this attempt to add the islands to the French empire, on 31 March 1939 Japan made a parallel claim on behalf of the Governor General of Taiwan, which at that point was considered an integral part of the Japanese empire. When France withdrew its forces the next year, however, Japan occupied the Paracels during February 1939, but this time not on behalf of Taiwan but as Japanese territory based on an earlier territorial claim dating to 1917. On 4 April 1939, Japan made the Paracels a protectorate. During 1941, it did shift sovereignty over "Shinnan Gunto" (New South Archipelago) to the Takao-shu (Kaohsiung district), Taiwan.[27]

---

[26] Hungdah Chiu and Choon-Ho Park, "Legal Status of the Paracel and Spratly Islands," *Ocean Development and International Law* 3 (1975), 12–13.

[27] "Sovereignty over the Spratly Islands," *National Policy Foundation*, 10 July 2009, http://www.npf.org.tw/printfriendly/6120 [accessed 9 November 2016].

Between 1939 and 1945, the Japanese also occupied Itu Aba in the Spratlys, building a fuel depot, submarine base, and a radio station.

During World War II, the Allies agreed that Japan would have to give back all territory it took by force. According to the Cairo Declaration of 1 December 1943 the Japanese were to be "stripped of all the islands in the Pacific which she has seized," plus give back "all the territories . . . stolen from the Chinese," but the SCS was not specifically mentioned (see Document 2). Two years later, the Potsdam Declaration of 26 July 1945 further stated that Japan's sovereignty was restricted to its main islands (see Document 3). According to one scholar, if only China had "demanded the 'return' of the South China Sea islands in the Cairo Declaration," then there would not have been any doubt in later years that they belonged to China.[28] Near the end of the war, therefore, the Japanese were forced to withdraw from the SCS but without ceding control to any other nation.

POST-WORLD WAR II SCS CLAIMS

Soon after the end of World War II, the Nationalist government retook Pratas Island and once again set up a radio station there. The Nationalists also initially set up a base on Woody Island in the Amphitrite group in the northeastern Paracels. Meanwhile, France stationed Annamese marines further to the West on Pattle Island in the Crescent group of the Paracels. In the Spratlys, the Chinese Nationalists also occupied the former Japanese held island of Itu Aba, which they called Taiping Island, from 1948 to 1950. In 1947, the Nationalist government put forward its claim to virtually all of the South China Sea, as outlined by eleven dotted lines on a Nationalist Chinese-produced map (see Map 2 below). On 1 December 1947, the Chinese Ministry of the Interior calculated that the SCS included a total of 162 distinct island "units."[29] The entire SCS was administered by Guangdong province.

China's access to the SCS was limited. Prior to World War II, Chinese governments had largely ignored Hainan Island, although

---

[28] David Lai, *Asia-Pacific: A Strategic Assessment* (Carlisle: Army War College Press, 2013), 60.
[29] Ting Tsz Kao, *The Chinese Frontiers* (Aurora, Ill: Chinese Scholarly Publishing Company, 1980), 289.

there was a naval station at Haikou in the early 1900s. The Nationalist forces under Chiang Kai-shek did not take control of Hainan away from the Guangdong warlord until 1926. But Hainan was

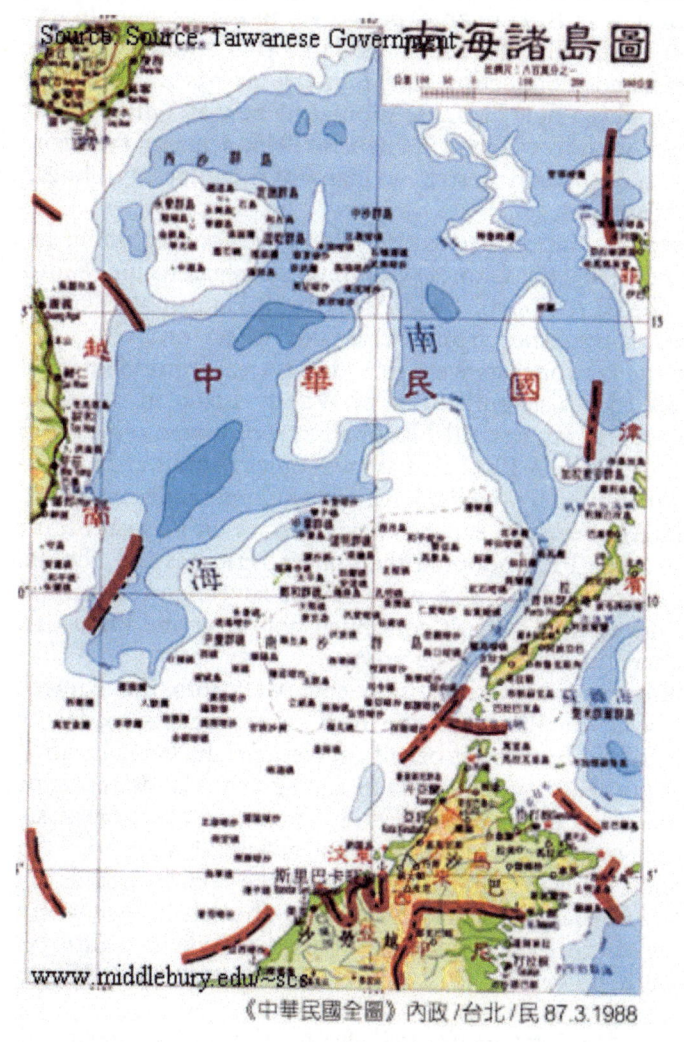

Map 2: The Republic of China's 11–Dash Map of the SCS[30]

---
[30] SCS map courtesy of David Rosenberg www.southchinasea.org.

not used as a military base or even exploited industrially until the Chinese puppet government under Wang Jingwei allowed Japan to fortify it in February 1939. During the Japanese occupation in World War II, Hainan experienced an extensive military and industrial buildup. This included large coal mines as well as the first railroads connecting to a military air base, a navy base at Haikou, plus a new Japanese submarine base at Yulin. When the Japanese withdrew from Hainan in 1945, a major typhoon the next year reportedly destroyed many of the mines, rail lines, and naval structures.

After the Nationalist troops left the region beginning in late 1949, however, the Chinese Communists began to move into the SCS. The PLA Fourth Field Army took Hainan after overcoming heavy resistance from Nationalist forces on 1 May 1950.[31] When the Nationalists were forced to retreat from Hainan Island in 1950, they also pulled out of Woody Island in the Paracels. Some reports say that all Nationalist troops were removed from Itu Aba as well. A PRC air base was quickly built at Haikou and was inaugurated by the PLA Air Force Commander in June 1952. The PLAN began to expand their facilities on Hainan beginning in 1957. The PRC adopted the same position as the Nationalist government that the SCS was Chinese sovereign territory, even while disputing Taiwan's continued hold over the Pratas islands and, later, Itu Aba in the Spratlys.

Following the Nationalist withdrawal from the Paracels in 1950, both the PRC and the ROC governments made official claims, as did France on behalf of Vietnam. In 1951, Japan abandoned any claim over the Paracel and Spratly islands as part of the San Francisco peace treaty. On 8 September 1951, Japan signed the peace treaty in San Francisco, and article 2(f) stated that "Japan renounces all right, title, and claim to the Spratly Islands and to the Paracel Islands" (see Document 4). This left France with tacit control of the Paracels. Once Vietnam was divided into North and South, however, the islands remained part of South Vietnam's

---

[31] He Di, "The Last Campaign to Unify China: The CCP's Unrealized Plan to Liberate Taiwan, 1949–1950," in Mark A. Ryan, David M. Finkelstein, and Michael A. McDevitt, eds., *Chinese Warfighting: The PLA Experience Since 1949* (Armonk, NY: M.E. Sharpe, 2003), 83.

territory, because they were located just south of the dividing line between South and North Vietnam.

Although the PRC and Taiwan were not invited to sign the peace treaty with Japan, the PRC insisted on its rights in the SCS. In a preemptive move, on 15 August 1951, three weeks before the San Francisco peace conference convened, PRC Foreign Minister Zhou Enlai declared that all islands in the SCS, including the Paracels and Spratlys, "have always been Chinese territory," and that while they were "occupied by Japan for some time during the war of aggression waged by Japanese imperialism, they were all taken over by the then Chinese government following Japan's surrender."[32] Woody Island appears to have remained uninhabited through the mid-1950s, however, when a PRC base was set up with about 200 occupants.

On 4 September 1958, during the midst of the second Taiwan Strait crisis, and perhaps also responding to South Vietnam's decision to send troops to the Paracels, China issued a *Declaration on Territorial Waters*. It unequivocally stated that the Xisha (Paracel) and Nansha (Spratly) islands were Chinese territory (see Document 8). The Communist government of North Vietnam, which relied on military support from the PRC, appeared to accept Chinese sovereignty over the Paracel and Spratly islands. On 14 September 1958, in a note to Chinese Premier Zhou Enlai, North Vietnamese Premier Pham Van Dong expressed his government's support and recognized China's declaration, stating "the Government of the Democratic Republic of Viet Nam recognizes and supports the Declaration of the Government of the People's Republic of China on China's territorial sea made on September 4, 1958"[33] (see Document 9). After Vietnam's unification in 1975, however, Hanoi denied that it had recognized

---

[32] Chi-kin Lo, *China's Policy Towards Territorial Disputes: The Case of the South China Sea Islands* (New York: Routledge, 1989), 31.

[33] A photograph of the original Vietnamese letter accompanies this Chinese document: "Declaration. Prime Minister Pham Van Dong, Democratic Republic of Vietnam, Hanoi, to Secretary of State Zhou Enlai, People's Republic of China, Beijing, 14 September 1958." A copy of this letter appears on Wikipedia at https://commons.wikimedia.org/wiki/File:1958_diplomatic_note_from_phamvandong_to_zhouenlai.jpg.

China's claim, even though their 1958 letter appeared to acknowledge the PRC's complete sovereignty.

Meanwhile, even as this diplomatic exchange was being conducted between North Vietnam and China, South Vietnam made a point of ignoring Beijing's Declaration on Territorial Waters by increasing its military forces in the Paracel islands. This activity culminated in early 1959 with a South Vietnamese naval invasion of Duncan Island, which was occupied at the time by Chinese fishermen. China protested South Vietnam's actions. However, due to internal turmoil linked to the PRC's Great Leap Forward, Beijing did not retaliate. Instead, it gradually increased its military and economic support to North Vietnam. However, Beijing's interest in controlling the SCS increased once significant energy resources were discovered there.

SPRATLY ISLAND NATURAL RESOURCES

Looking beyond strategic considerations, until recently the SCS was considered to have a highly limited intrinsic economic value – stemming principally from guano deposits and coconut palms. Of course, the SCS had long been a traditional fishing ground for all of the coastal states in the region, and a yearly catch of 5 million tons equals 10% of the entire global fish catch.[34] But all this changed with the purported discovery of vast natural resource deposits, including petroleum and natural gas. Sovereignty over the islands could confer legal rights to develop and control the area's resources. There are six nations – the PRC, Vietnam, Malaysia, Brunei, the Philippines, plus Taiwan – that currently claim ownership to all or part of this area's resources, plus the PRC argues that the fishing grounds off of Indonesia's Natuna islands are also within China's proclaimed historic waters.

The Spratly islands' primary importance today is the potential for significant deposits of oil, natural gas, and minerals located on and under the surrounding seabeds. The promise of large natural gas and oil fields in the SCS has been generally accepted since

---

[34] Chien-peng Chung, *Domestic Politics, International Bargaining and China's Territorial Disputes* (New York: RoutledgeCurzon, 2004), 140.

the late 1960s, when a seismic survey was conducted under the sponsorship of the United Nations Committee for the Coordination of Joint Prospecting in Asian Off-shore areas. The UN survey indicated the presence of oil and gas in exploitable quantities. It was not until the mid-1970s, however, that technological advances in offshore oil exploration and production made it economically feasible to consider drilling in these hitherto inaccessible offshore sites.

The U.S. Energy Information Administration has concluded that the SCS may contain significant deposits of petroleum and natural gas. USGS estimated anywhere between 0.8 and 5.4 (mean 2.5) billion barrels of oil and between 7.6 and 55.1 (mean 25.5) Tcf of natural gas (see Map 3 below). Evidence suggests that the bulk of these resources were located in the contested Reed Bank at the northeast end of the Spratlys, which is claimed by China, Taiwan, Vietnam, and the Philippines.[35] All of the SCS nations are eager to exploit new sources of energy and so: "It is also a prime factor in the lingering sovereignty disputes over the Spratly Islands and other features in the South China Sea."[36]

In sharp contrast to these conservative EIA figures, Chinese estimates for oil and gas reserves in the SCS are enormous, at one point reaching 213 billion barrels (bbl) for the first and 2,000 trillion cubic feet (tcf) for the second, although later estimates reduced this to 125 bbl and 500 tcf, respectively. Such estimates may be inflated, but they still represent five times more than China's "proven reserves."[37] Although one can dispute the numbers, "China's belief in these estimates is more important than their dubious accuracy, and Beijing's high expectations strengthen its determination to protect its sovereignty claims in the Spratly Islands."[38] Meanwhile, China calls the SCS a "second Persian Gulf."[39] China is not the only country to believe the SCS is full of oil. Eugenio Bito-onon,

---

[35] http://www.eia.gov/countries/regions-topics.cfm?fips=SCS [accessed 9 April 2013].
[36] Bateman, "Maritime security: regional concerns and global implications," 249.
[37] Clarence J. Bouchat, *Dangerous Ground: The Spratly Island and U.S. Interests and Approaches* (Carlisle, PA: U.S. Army War College Press, 2013), 5.
[38] Bernard Cole, *The Great Wall at Sea: China's Navy Enters the Twenty-first Century* (Annapolis, MD: Naval Institute Press, 2001), 55–60.
[39] Roy, *The South China Sea Disputes*, 16.

the mayor of the Philippine-claimed islands, also stated "We call our island group the submerged Saudi Arabia of the Philippines."[40]

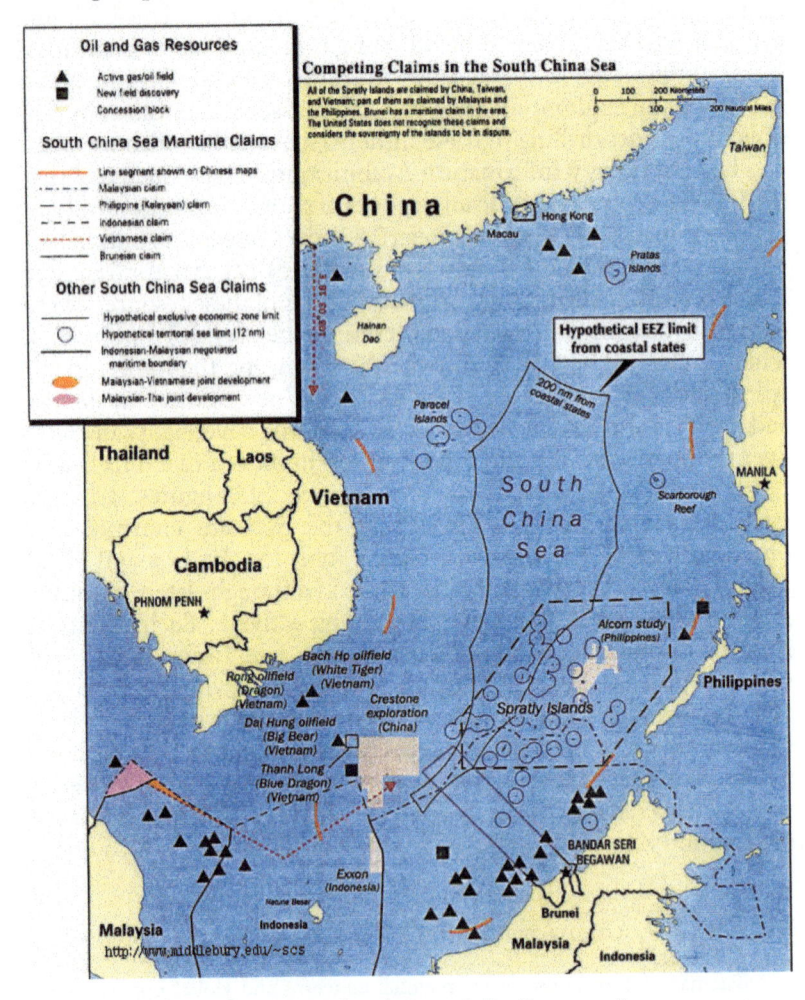

Map 3: SCS Oil and Natural Gas Resources[41]

[40] "Spratly Islands: Foreign Correspondent Visits Remote Reef Flashpoint Where Filipino Marines Hold Out Against Chinese Navy," *Australian Broadcasting Corporation*, 14 May 2014, http://www.abc.net.au/news/2014-05-20/oil-key-in-spratly-islands-dispute-south-china-sea/5463080 [accessed 13 March 2017].

[41] SCS map courtesy of David Rosenberg www.southchinasea.org.

Prior to the 1960s, underwater oil and gas reserves were difficult to exploit. Significant advances in the technology of deep sea offshore oil and gas exploitation have made it possible to tap into the petroleum-bearing sediment believed to be in the deep waters surrounding the islands. As a result, this has made regional initiatives to determine legal ownership of the Spratlys even more important. Immediately prior to the forcible unification of North and South Vietnam in 1975, Beijing took advantage of Hanoi's preoccupation to further extend its control over the disputed Paracel islands.

THE BATTLE FOR THE PARACEL ISLANDS, 19 JANUARY 1974

The PRC assisted North Vietnam both economically and militarily during the 1960s and 1970s, which played a crucial role in Hanoi's victory during 1975. Not only did China send troops to North Vietnam to help maintain supply lines, but Beijing's estimate of its military and economic support for Hanoi from 1950 to 1978 exceeded $20 billion.[42] Beijing was understandably upset, therefore, about improving relations between Moscow and Hanoi. In an action that closely paralleled the USSR's behavior at the end of World War II, when Moscow took advantage of China's preoccupation to annex Tannu Tuva outright and coerce China into recognizing the independence of Outer Mongolia, the PRC decided to use force to take possession of the Paracel islands away from South Vietnam. This action occurred immediately before North Vietnam could unify the country and claim the islands as Vietnamese territory.

Beijing argues that it was forced to take action. In September 1973, the Spratly islands were incorporated by South Vietnam into Phuoc Tuy province. According to one source, this was done at the urging of the National Petroleum Board, which "in turn was the result of granting oil concessions to a number of international oil companies and consortia for exploration off the shores of South Vietnam in July 1973." China responded to South Vietnam's expansionism on 11 January 1974. Chinese fishermen

---

[42] King C. Chen, *China's War with Vietnam, 1979* (Stanford, CA, Hoover Institution Press, 1987), 27.

were reported to be operating on three islands of the Paracels, and "South Vietnamese vessels and troops were subsequently sent to the Paracels, where they soon confronted Chinese gunboats."[43]

On 19 January 1974, the PLAN seized the Paracel islands from South Vietnam, even though the islands were also in theory claimed by China's supposed ally North Vietnam. The Chinese name for this naval expedition is *Xisha Ziwei Fanjizhan* (西沙自衛反擊戰), or "Counterattack in Self-Defense in the Paracel Islands."[44] Deng Xiaoping was chief of the PLA general staff at the time and oversaw the operation. The main conflict occurred during the morning of 19 January, when four Vietnamese vessels encountered an equal number of Chinese ships. The battle lasted less than an hour, but resulted in the sinking of one Vietnamese ship, and damage to the other three. While the Chinese ships also sustained damage, none of them sank. A total of 71 died from both sides.[45]

Beijing's view is that it was forced to take action and, according to the Chinese version of these events, the conflict occurred when the South Vietnamese illegally arrested Chinese fishermen during November 1973, prompting the Chinese foreign ministry to announce on 11 January 1974 that South Vietnam had invaded its sovereign territory. However, another, much more critical, view of the Chinese action has stated: "Two unarmed Chinese fishing boats were sent into an area patrolled by the Vietnamese to precipitate a hostile act so that subsequent Chinese actions could be viewed as 'defense against Vietnamese aggression'."[46] Another author concludes South Vietnam was set up: "They were

---

[43] Lo, *China's Policy Towards Territorial Disputes*, 55–56.
[44] 杨志本 [Yang Zhiben, ed.], 中国海军百科全书 [China Navy Encyclopedia], vol. 2 (Beijing: 海潮出版社 [Sea Tide Press], 1998), 1747.
[45] Ralph Jennings, "Vietnam Taking Long-Term Hard Line Toward China on Maritime Claims," *Asia*, 28 November 2016, http://www.voanews.com/a/vietnam-taking-long-term-hard-line-toward-china-on-maritime-claims/3614214.html [accessed 28 November 2016].
[46] John W. Garver, "China's Push Through the South China Sea: The Interaction of Bureaucratic and National Interests," *The China Quarterly* 131 (Sept 1992): 1009–1013.

provoked and then defeated by well-prepared Chinese naval and air forces in the area."[47]

The 1974 Sino-Vietnamese conflict over the Paracel islands must also be put into the context of the problems undermining Sino-Soviet relations. Following their formal "split" in 1960, Sino-Soviet relations through the late 1960s were marred not only by sharp disagreement over the status of Outer Mongolia, but also by numerous territorial disputes along their mutual border. The 1969 border clashes gave the PLA's confidence that it could counter the Red Army, opening an opportunity during 1971 for China to adopt a new foreign policy initiative by promoting friendly relations with the United States.

The PRC's diplomatic shift from the USSR to the USA culminated in President Richard Nixon's historic 21–28 February 1972 trip to Beijing. Nixon signed the *Shanghai Communiqué*, essentially backing China against the USSR, when he agreed "that it would be against the interests of the peoples of the world for any major country to collude with another against other countries, or for major countries to divide up the world into spheres of interest" (see Document 10). Thus, China's "geopolitical interests" in taking the Paracels included "the central question of how to contain the influence of the Soviet Union in the region."[48] As one expert opines: "By 1974, China's leaders must have concluded that if they did not act, they would be increasingly vulnerable in the South China Sea, especially if the Soviet Union assumed control over the Paracels as a forward base for operations against China."[49] There were also valid concerns that if the USSR established a naval base in Vietnam, as it later did at Cam Ranh Bay in 1979, this might block China's access to the Malacca Strait.

What is most notable is that the U.S. Navy did not actively intervene on behalf of its ally South Vietnam, but stood by passively. One American civilian named Gerald Kosh was taken

---

[47] Lo, *China's Policy Towards Territorial Disputes*, 185.
[48] Lo, *China's Policy Towards Territorial Disputes*, 189.
[49] M. Taylor Fravel, *Strong Borders Secure Nation: Cooperation and Conflict in China's Territorial Disputes* (Princeton: Princeton University Press, 2008), 287.

prisoner by Chinese forces, but he was released unharmed about two weeks later. Reportedly, the U.S. government "ordered Seventh Fleet ships, operating nearby in the Tonkin Gulf and South China Sea, to stay clear of the Paracels area."[50] Considering the distances involved and the time it took to deploy the PLAN ships to the area, the date of the 19 January battle – on exactly the 24th anniversary of the PRC's recognition of the North Vietnamese government – was clearly not a coincidence. This timing was perhaps intended to send a signal to Hanoi that taking the islands was partial payback for PRC aid as well as punishment for its decision to form closer ties with the USSR.

On 20 January, these islands were officially annexed by the PRC, and were made an integral part of Guangdong province. Supporting Hanoi's claim to these islands, the USSR immediately denounced China's actions in the 1 February 1974 edition of *Novoe Vremya*.[51] This diplomatic incident was almost unique during the Cold War, therefore, with the U.S. government declining to support its ally South Vietnam in favor of China, while the Soviet government was in fact diplomatically supporting its arch-enemy the South Vietnamese government in opposition to its supposed socialist ally China.

The PRC wasted no time militarizing the Paracel islands. As one Vietnamese scholar has clarified, the Paracels were "strategically important" to China, since they are "located on one of the world's most important sea-lanes."[52] During the Sino-Vietnamese conflict in 1979, the PLAN's South Sea Fleet deployed 2 missile destroyers, 4 missile escort destroyers, 27 patrol boats, 20 submarines, and 604 other vessels throughout the region. In addition to stationing patrol boats around the Paracels, a 1,000–man garrison was established with defensive anti-aircraft guns. Two dozen Vietnamese fishermen were captured by the Chinese Navy and

---

[50] David G. Muller, *China as a Maritime Power* (Boulder: Westview Press, 1984), 153.
[51] Kimie Hara, *Cold War Frontiers in the Asia-Pacific: Divided Territories in the San Francisco System* (London: Routledge Press, 2007), 156.
[52] Nguyen Van Canh, *Vietnam Under Communism, 1975–1982* (Stanford, CA: Hoover Institution Press, 1983), 242.

kept imprisoned for over a year. Thus, the Paracels served both as a buffer area between the PRC and Vietnam, and also potentially as a strategic area to stage "punitive naval strikes against the Vietnamese."[53] The strategic position held by the Paracels almost guaranteed future military tensions.

FURTHER CHINESE MILITARY ENCROACHMENT

Momentous political changes occurred during the last decade of the Cold War that significantly altered the military and political balance of power in East Asia. The SCS had long been a center of superpower interaction. For much of the twentieth century, American military bases in the Philippines provided the logistical support necessary to maintain American naval and air deployments throughout Southeast Asia and into the Indian Ocean. Meanwhile, Soviet bases in Vietnam pitted the U.S. Navy against the Soviet Navy over the waters in the SCS. But this all changed in the early 1990s. As one scholar observed: "The end of the Cold War gave littoral states, and China, the political space to press their conflicting maritime territorial claims in the South China Sea."[54]

The construction of a Soviet naval base at Cam Ranh Bay in Vietnam began in March 1979. This Soviet base provided a counterbalance not just to China, but also to America's military presence in the region. Perhaps most importantly, it was a symbol of Soviet political support for Vietnam. To offset this alliance, China was willing to use force. During April 1987, a PRC statement protested the recent Vietnamese occupation of a small island in the Spratlys, claiming that "Vietnam's purpose in illegally dispatching troops to Bojiao island is to occupy the continental shelf nearby to pave the way for its future exploitation of oil."[55] During 1988, the

---

[53] Steven J. Hood, *Dragons Entangled: Indochina and the China-Vietnam War* (Armonk, N.Y.: M.E. Sharpe, 1992), 129.

[54] J.N. Mak, "Maritime Security and the ARF: Why the focus on dialogue rather than action," in Jurgen Haacke and Noel M. Morada, eds., *Cooperative Security in the Asia-Pacific: The ASEAN Regional Forum* (New York: Routledge 2010), 172.

[55] Quoted in "Continued Border Tension with China – Re-emergence of Spratly Islands Dispute as Source of Sino-Vietnamese Conflict," *Keesing's Record of World Events* 34 (1988): 35902.

PRC established its first outpost in the Spratlys, on Fiery Cross Reef (in Chinese Yongshu Jiao).

The PRC's decision to take action was perhaps indirectly a result of a 1987 request by the United Nations Educational, Scientific, and Cultural Organization (UNESCO) to establish a marine weather observation station in the Spratlys. The Chinese responded quickly to this request in early 1988, which suggests that they may have arranged the UNESCO request behind the scenes. After surveying the Spratlys with research ships accompanied by navy destroyers, the Chinese eventually drew up a plan to establish the oceanic observation station on Fiery Cross Reef, strategically located in the geographic center of the Spratlys. As part of this plan, China forcibly occupied six reefs.[56]

News of these plans upset Vietnam, which reportedly "sent troops to plant its national flag on the island."[57] On 14 March 1988, the PRC and Vietnam fought over ownership of Johnson South Reef (Chigua in Chinese), near Fiery Cross Reef. The March event was actually the third incident, after two previous clashes in January and February. Chinese forces fired on the Vietnamese naval vessels, sinking one, damaging two others and taking several Vietnamese prisoners. Chinese naval forces, including three missile-equipped frigates, then drove Vietnamese troops from Johnson South Reef. This battle reportedly resulted in 64 Vietnamese deaths and many injuries. Rejecting a Vietnamese protest, Beijing warned:[58]

> Vietnam has no right to interfere with Chinese vessels patrolling their territorial waters. It is Vietnam that has occupied illegally islands and reefs in China's Nansha [Spratly] islands. If the Vietnamese side ignores the consistent stand of the Chinese government and hinders our legitimate activities in these areas, it will have to bear the responsibility and the consequences.

---

[56] Min Gyo Koo, *Island Disputes and Maritime Regime Building in East Asia: Between a Rock and a Hard Place* (New York: Springer, 2009), 153.
[57] Christopher L. Daniels, *South China Sea: Energy and Security Conflicts* (Lanham: The Scarecrow Press, Inc., 2014), 9.
[58] Roy, *The South China Sea Disputes*, 41.

After this conflict, China established garrisons on at least seven islands. Since Taiwan controlled Itu Aba, and some reports also say Zhongzhou Reef, part of Tizard Bank, there were as many as nine PRC-ROC features.[59]

Global events at the end of the 1980s were destined to impact the SCS. The fall of the Berlin Wall in 1989 and the end of the Cold War, followed only two years later by the dissolution of the former USSR in 1991, resulted in the withdrawal of Russian naval forces, military advisors, and support from Vietnam. This left Vietnam without a superpower sponsor. During the early 1990s the American military also conducted a phased withdrawal from its former naval and air bases in the Philippines after the Mount Pinatubo eruption and Washington's failure to negotiate new terms with Manila for the continued use of the bases.

After these momentous changes, U.S. forces were pulled back to Okinawa, Guam, and Singapore, leaving the SCS region devoid of any U.S. naval bases. Vice Admiral Stanley Arthur, Commander of the U.S. Seventh Fleet, stated at the time: "As for our overseas commitments [in Southeast Asia] ... we are going to protect our ability to be forward deployed in the Pacific for as long as we can."[60] The U.S. Navy has conducted freedom of navigation (FON) missions since 1979, but its military presence was limited to periodic naval and air deployments, a major reduction from the former "permanent" military presence. Guam largely replaced the Philippines as the major U.S. base in the region, but it is located much further from the SCS.

In response to the collapse of the USSR, the PRC quickly filled the vacuum by stepping up the scope and nature of its own military deployments into the region. It also expanded economic ties with many of the littoral states. The PRC, along with Taiwan, claimed Chinese sovereignty over the entire Spratly archipelago based on historical grounds. But Beijing began to establish and

---

[59] According to Alexander Vuving, Taiwan only occupies one feature – Itu Aba – and he claims that reports that Taiwan erected structures on Ban Than Reef were incorrect. Alexander L. Vuving, "South China Sea: Who Occupies What in the Spratlys? A closer look at a basic yet poorly understood question," *The Diplomat*, 6 May 2016.

[60] Susumu Awanohara, "Washington's Priorities: US Emphasizes Freedom of Navigation," *Far Eastern Economic Review*, 13 August 1992, 18–19.

consolidate its physical presence in the Spratlys only beginning in 1988. Prior to this time, the PRC seemed content to repeat its claim to the islands and to protest activity in the islands by other states. The on-again off-again Taiwanese presence in the islands was apparently considered sufficient to uphold China's claims of sovereignty. PRC maps from the 1950s onward are directly based on the Nationalist map from 1947, therefore, showing China's national boundary line extending into the SCS around all of the Spratlys islands.[61]

From 1988 to the present, China has taken a more active role in establishing its own permanent military presence in the Spratly archipelago and now occupies seven of the islands with its own military forces. Despite the tiny size of the various reefs and islands in the Spratlys – the largest, Itu Aba, is just under one-half km^2 in size and rises only 8 feet above sea level at its highest point – new outposts have continued to be established. Many of these outposts are built on raised platforms secured to the coral reefs and are highly vulnerable to weather and high seas. While several of these fortified bases have their own sources of fresh water, the ability of these tiny garrisons to sustain themselves for any length of time without supplies from the mainland is questionable.

For all of the other claimants, however, Chinese activities spurred a final rush to establish territorial claims before Beijing decided to resolve the dispute over sovereignty through military force. To date, China's military activities in the Spratlys have focused mainly on Vietnam, but this could easily spread to involve the military forces of the other claimants or even non-belligerent merchant shipping transiting through the nearby sea lanes. A number of regional initiatives, such as by ASEAN, have attempted to defuse tensions throughout the SCS. The exponential growth of Chinese power and influence in the SCS worries all of the other countries throughout Southeast Asia, as well as many extra-regional states concerned with maintaining freedom of the seas.

---

[61] Chinese national maritime boundaries are illustrated in *Zhonghua Renmin Gongheguo Ditu* (Map of the People's Republic of China), 6th ed. (Beijing: The Cartographic Publishing House, 1971).

REGIONAL INITIATIVES TO RESOLVE THE SCS CONFLICTS

Due to concerns about future Chinese expansion in the SCS, regional efforts to defuse the situation and allow for joint development of resources in the area have increased. One of the earliest of these initiatives was undertaken by Indonesia, which during January 1990 sponsored a series of workshops on managing potential conflicts in the SCS. Partly as a result of Indonesian initiatives, the Spratly islands dispute was the focus of the annual ASEAN foreign minister's meeting in July 1992. The resulting ASEAN declaration then called for the peaceful resolution of the Spratly dispute (see Document 15). In 1996, China opened dialogue with ASEAN and during 32 meetings from 1990 to 1998 this group developed what some scholars have called an "epistemic community" to help manage maritime conflicts.[62]

Subsequent claims were made that the ASEAN meetings had resulted in a "shelving of territorial claims" and an agreement to "pursue joint development projects." A more careful reading of the Chinese foreign minister's statements indicates, however, that China sought to negotiate a series of bilateral treaties to the Spratly dispute, and so suggested that all discussions should be held in private. The Chinese domestic radio service *Xinhua* even quoted a spokesman for the Chinese delegation as saying:[63]

> The basic principles expounded in the ASEAN Declaration on the South China Sea are identical or similar to what China stands for. The Chinese government has consistently advocated a peaceful settlement on territorial disputes over the Nansha (Spratly) islands through negotiation and has been opposed to resorting to armed force. China has put forward a proposal for laying disputes aside and undertaking joint development. China is willing to hold negotiations with countries concerned when conditions are ripe or to lay disputes aside for the time being when conditions are not ripe.

---

[62] Brantly Womack, *China and Vietnam: The Politics of Asymmetry* (New York: Cambridge University Press, 2006), 219.
[63] Xiaong Changyi, "Peaceful Settlement Advocated," *Xinhua*, translated and transcribed in *Daily Report: China*, 23 July 1992, 2.

Despite all assertions of their peaceful intent, however, right after this meeting ended, Vietnam claimed that China had occupied yet another atoll in the Spratlys. This action appeared to belie the Chinese representative's assurances of peaceful intent.

Backing the ASEAN declaration was not a new policy for the Chinese, therefore, even though some analysts interpreted it to mean that Beijing might be willing to come to some kind of accommodation over the Spratlys. Since that time, China has consistently rejected efforts to "internationalize" the Spratlys dispute by allowing it to be resolved by multinational negotiations. One Chinese editorial summarized the situation as follows: "The reason why the Spratly issue should not be internationalized is quite simple and clear: The Spratlys have since ancient times been Chinese territory. This being the case, the possibility of internationalization does not exist."[64] China's intransigence has had an enormous impact on the SCS, making it more likely additional territory will change hands by force.

ACQUISITION OF TERRITORY UNDER INTERNATIONAL LAW

The conflicting claims to the Spratlys are complex.[65] Regardless of the legal rationale that each country has developed for its claim, one must accept that this is basically a dispute over territory. This is best shown by the PRC's foreign ministry response to the July 2016 U.N. tribunal decision, calling it "invalid . . . China does not accept or recognize it."[66] At the core of this dispute are control, ownership, and sovereignty over hundreds of tiny islands, reefs, and atolls, as well as rights to the surrounding waters, water columns, and subsurface ocean floor. Resolution of these basic territorial issues is required before the questions of ocean boundaries, economic zones, and other resource-related issues can be fully addressed. Despite the apparent futility of judicial

---

[64] "Session on the Spratlys and China's Stand," Hong Kong *Wen Wei Pao*, translated in *Daily Report: China*, 18 July 1992, 2.
[65] This section is based on Esmond Douglas Smith, "China, technology and the Spratly Islands: The Geopolitical impact of new technologies," PhD dissertation (1994), Salve Regina University, 98–102.
[66] Perlez, "Tribunal Rejects Beijing's Claims in South China Sea."

measures, the claimants have all attempted to establish a legal basis for their claims. There are some well-established and generally agreed upon principles in international law that pertain to the acquisition of territory. For example, there are three main types of territory recognized in international law: 1) territory that belongs to some state; 2) territory that belongs to no state (*terra nullius*); and 3) territory that belongs to all states (*terra communis*).[67] There are also at least five ways in which territory can be acquired by a state: 1) occupation, 2) prescription, 3) accretion, 4) cession, and 5) conquest.

Throughout history, simple occupation is the principal means of acquiring territory not belonging to another state (*terra nullius*) and of exercising or demonstrating sovereignty over territory acquired by other means. To show that a country's SCS claim is valid, occupation must show a continuous display of state authority over the claimed territory. Mere discovery that is not immediately followed by effective occupation gives the discoverer only temporary title, called an inchoate title. Unless the occupation is followed by effective jurisdiction within a reasonable time it is subject to appropriation by another state. In other words, the "mere discovery of a *terra nullius* is not sufficient to obtain a valid title based on occupation. Such involves effective control by the state."[68]

Historically, title by discovery is the most common method to claim sovereignty. Discovery usually resulted in a proclamation notifying other countries of this discovery. The concept of *terra nullius* is complicated by the fact that this term "covers, in addition to areas which have never been the object of any appropriation, those which have been successively appropriated and abandoned."[69] For example, the Philippines claim to have "discovered" several of the unoccupied Spratly islands abandoned by Japan in the 1950s and so they employ the legal term *terra nullius* to claim

---

[67] B.A. Hamzah, "Jurisdictional Issues and the Conflicting Claims in the Spratlys," *The Indonesian Quarterly* 18, no. 2 (1990): 143–154.
[68] Haller-Trost, *The Spratly Islands*, 44.
[69] Santiago Torres Bernadez, "Territory, Acquisition, *in Encyclopedia of Public International Law* (North Holland: Max Planck Institute, 1988), Volume 10, 500.

the area that they call Kalayaan under the right of discovery of unoccupied and unclaimed territory. Considering how long various nations have been fighting over ownership of the Spratlys, however, it seems unlikely that these more recent discovery claims will be upheld. In January 2013, the Philippines Foreign Secretary Albert del Rosario announced that Manila had exhausted "almost all political and diplomatic avenues," and it became the first country to submit its case to U.N. arbitration.[70]

Once the fact of discovery had been announced, other states by courtesy are supposed to respect the notification. If discovery was then followed by settlement of a state, it constituted a perfect title. Two additional elements are thus involved in establishing a valid claim to *terra nullius* by occupation: annexation and settlement, with settlement demonstrating "actual physical possession of the territory." Discovery and annexation usually provided an inchoate – partial or incomplete – title which may "serve as a temporary bar to occupation by any other state."[71] To validate such an inchoate title, the country has to display activity on the discovered territory so as to show effective occupation. This could include establishing a military garrison, a civilian settlement, or by performing some other act indicating sovereignty, such as by building a lighthouse.

The importance of effective occupation in establishing a valid claim to sovereignty has led one expert to state that "some writers have even suggested that all of the above modes of acquisition be reduced to last one: effective occupation."[72] Beginning in the 1990s, many states with claims in the SCS began to occupy shoals and reefs within the Spratlys. This will probably end only when all of the islets are occupied or the claimants exhaust them-

---

[70] Amrutha Gayathri, "Philippines to Take South China Sea Dispute to International Court," 22 January 2013, http://www.ibtimes.com/philippines-take-south-china-sea-dispute-international-court-1029508 [accessed 23 March 2017].

[71] John K. T. Chao, "South China Sea: Boundary Problems Relating to the Nansha and Hsisha islands," *Chinese Yearbook of International Law and Affairs*. Vol 9 (1989-19901, 66-156. Reprint, Taipei: Chinese Society of International Law, 1991, 78, 79.

[72] Bernadez, "Territory, Acquisition," 497, 504.

selves by establishing outposts on every conceivable projection of coral. China and Vietnam have shown themselves to be particularly adept of constructing outposts even on tiny reefs. Several of the various national "outposts" in the Spratlys consist of small, man-made structures built on coral outcroppings. A handful of them are even now being enlarged so that airfields can be added.

Prescription as a mode of territorial acquisition also requires effective occupation to be valid, but differs from occupation because it applies to land lawfully claimed by another state: "Title through prescription is effective only through a sufficient period of uninterrupted occupation . . . and by the acquiescence of the other claiming party."[73] In essence, prescription "is based on a peaceful, unopposed and continuous manner of governance by one state, while the territory actually belongs to another."[74] This principle is perhaps applicable in the Spratly dispute in the sense that North Vietnam assumed the territorial claims of South Vietnam in both the Paracels and Spratlys when the two merged in the mid-1970s; a second possible application would be if Taiwan were to allow the PRC to land troops or make use of territory that it claims, such as Itu Aba Island.

The principle of accretion, on the other hand, may have even greater relevance in this dispute. Accretion is considered to occur when new territory is formed through the operation of nature. This could occur when a coastline recedes or a river changes course and exposes new territory, or due to the emergence of a new island in the territorial sea or the EEZ of a state. The *Encyclopedia of Public International Law* states that, "Accretion may also appear to be involved when a state extends its territory by carrying out operations there-on which modify its physical nature (artificial accretion) at the expense of either the international community . . . or of a neighbor state."[75]

The current island-building efforts in the SCS largely fit this definition. Examples of "artificial accretion" might include the semi-permanent structures built on many of the reefs and atolls

---

[73] Hamzah, "Jurisdictional Issues and the Conflicting Claims in the Spratlys," 144.
[74] Haller-Trost, *The Spratly Islands*, 44.
[75] Bernadez, "Territory, Acquisition," 501.

in the Spratlys. These bases would otherwise not be considered islands as defined in article 121 of the Law of the Sea, which states in part that: "Rocks which cannot sustain human habitation or economic life of their own shall have no exclusive economic zone or continental shelf."[76] Man-made structures on reefs and islets that could not normally be used as a basis for measuring territorial waters or economic zones might be considered to be "artificial accretion," changing them into legitimate territorial entities. Even if this were the case, however, "it would seem logical in such cases to require some kind of recognition or acquiescence [by other nations] to consolidate acquisition of title."[77]

The opposite of accretion is also likely in the SCS, in particular considering the apparent impact of global climate change on weather patterns. The tenuous nature of the man-made structures in the SCS make them highly vulnerable to typhoons and rough seas common in this area. If global warming really does lead to rising water levels then these low-lying man-made islands could also be gradually submerged. China could thus end up spending millions of defense dollars building articifical bases that could be completely destroyed at any time by the region's unpredictable weather or by rising waters.

Cession is defined as the voluntary or forced transfer of territory from one state to another. It is generally carried out by means of a treaty or formal agreement whereby one state renounces its legal title in favor of another. In the Spratly case, Japan can be considered to have voluntarily relinquished its interests when it withdrew from the islands in August 1945 and then forfeited them in the 1951 San Francisco Peace Treaty. Unfortunately, there is a great deal of ambivalence regarding to which state Japan ceded these interests. Both the PRC and Taiwan claim that these interests reverted to China, but they disagree on which China. Meanwhile, other countries in the SCS argue that Japan gave up its sovereign claims to the SCS without ceding them to any particular nation, thus making the SCS region open for other claimants.

---

[76] *The Law of the Sea* (New York: United Nations, 1983), 39.
[77] Bernadez, "Territory, Acquisition," 501.

Finally, conquest differs in fundamental ways from cession. It is the acquisition of territory through the threat or use of force. In the past, most borders changed due to conquest. During the Cold War, conquest was often considered a legitimate means of acquiring territory, and so this concept continues to have some relevance to the Spratlys dispute. Chinese military conquests in 1974 and in 1988 are two good examples where conquest has led to what appears to have become permanent occupation by the PRC. In the modern era, conquest is not considered a valid mode of acquiring territory since it is considered to be incompatible with sovereignty, territorial integrity, and the political independence of states. Russia's 2014 invasion of the Crimea, however, is an example of how territorial conquest is still a very real concern.

CONCLUSIONS

The intransigence of the various Southeast Asian governments through the early 1990s precluded a peaceful resolution to the SCS dispute, regardless of the efforts of the other regional states to bring the claimants together for serious negotiations. The PRC, Taiwan, and Vietnam contest each other's claims to full sovereignty over the Paracel islands. In the Spratlys, the PRC, Taiwan, and Vietnam claim the entire group, while the Philippines, Malaysia, and Brunei have more limited claims. Except for Brunei, all these Southeast Asian nations have at one time or another supported military action, and there were numerous reported conflicts during the 1990s (see Appendix A).

After years of trying to convince Beijing to open talks, the Philippines broke with the rest of ASEAN by putting the Spratlys dispute before the United Nation. The findings of the UN tribunal were unacceptable to China, which promotes bilateral negotiations over multinational arbitration. But such bilateral negotiations worry many maritime nations:[78]

> A glance at a chart shows what Chinese control of the Spratly Islands would mean to the maritime interests of the United States

---

[78] Esmond D. Smith, Jr., "The Dragon Goes to Sea," *Naval War College Review*, 44, No. 3 (Summer 1991): 44.

and our Asian friends. Naval bases capable of supporting submarines and surface combatants in the Spratlys would provide China with a capability to monitor and potentially to interdict shipping of any nationality transiting the South China Sea.

As the foremost military power in the region, the PRC undoubtedly fears that the very process of opening multilateral negotiations might imply that the other claimants have legitimate rights in the islands, an implication that might undermine China's own claim. Beijing's policy statements have consistently indicated that the issue of sovereignty is non-negotiable.

Of all of the SCS countries, Vietnam has the most to fear of domination of the region by an expansionist China. The Sino-Vietnamese territorial disputes in the SCS are particularly complex. Like China, Vietnam cites historical ownership and argues that French sovereignty over the Paracel and Spratly islands devolved to Vietnam after World War II with the breakup of the French Colonial Empire in Indochina. Of all the countries that have claims to these waters, only the PRC and Vietnam have attempted to build fully functional military bases in the South China Sea that might allow these two countries to one day obtain their strategic goals through force.

CHAPTER TWO

China's Maritime Territorial Disputes with Vietnam

---*---

OF ALL OF China's maritime neighbors to the south, the Sino-Vietnamese border relations are the most complex, since they include both land and sea boundaries. In the early 1990s, when the Cold War ended, 88 square miles (227 km^2) remained in dispute along the two countries' mutual border. In 1999, the two countries agreed to divide up these areas, with Hanoi receiving just under 44 square miles (113 km^2) and Beijing getting just over 44 square miles (114 km^2).[79] The maritime disputes, however, are more complex, encompassing large areas in the Gulf of Tonkin and competing sovereignty claims over the Paracel and Spratly islands in the SCS.

Since 1988, Vietnam has actively pressed its own claim to the entire Spratly area while increasing the number of islands under its occupation. Despite this expansion, Vietnam fears Beijing will attempt to repeat its successful takeover of the Paracel islands in 1974 and expansion into the Spratlys in 1988. But Hanoi might agree to a negotiated settlement in the Spratlys. In July 1992, for example, Vietnam endorsed the ASEAN declaration calling for the peaceful resolution of the Spratly dispute without the use of military force. In recent years, Vietnam has tried to foster better relations with the U.S. government, plus is actively purchasing large amounts of military equipment – much of it from Russia – to put pressure on China.

---

[79] Ramses Amer, "Sino-Vietnamese Border Disputes," in Bruce Elleman, Stephen Kotkin, and Clive Schofield, eds., *Beijing's Power and China's Borders: Twenty Neighbors in Asia* (Armonk, NY: M.E. Sharpe, 2013), 295.

The situation is not all negative, therefore, and China is Vietnam's largest trade partner, with over $60 billion in annual trade. Some progress has been made negotiating maritime boundaries. In 2000, a Sino-Vietnamese agreement was signed dividing the Gulf of Tonkin into Chinese and Vietnamese zones, but other maritime disputes–including delimiting the mouth of the gulf – remained unresolved. In particular, China's nine-dashed map of the SCS overlap with Vietnam's claims to an EEZ and continental shelf areas to the east of Vietnam's coastline. During 2009–2012, bilateral tensions increased dramatically, culminating in China's announcement during July 2012 that it would station a special Sansha garrison in the disputed Paracel islands to help defend its maritime claims. Since that time, the PRC has undertaken a massive reclamation project to increase the size of its Spratly bases, reportedly reclaiming 3,200 acres of land compared to Vietnam's 80 acres.[80] Vietnam's claim will be examined first.

THE VIETNAMESE CLAIM

At the conclusion of a 51–nation conference held in San Francisco in 1951 to mark the end of the war with Japan, a Vietnamese delegate to the conference announced Vietnam's ownership of both the Spratly and Paracel island groups. The Vietnamese stated: "We affirm our rights to the Spratly and Paracel Islands, which have always belonged to Vietnam."[81] Vietnam's claim to these islands was uncontested by the other nations at the San Francisco conference, mainly because of the absence of any Chinese representatives from either the PRC or the ROC. The Vietnamese claim was later rejected, however, by both China and Taiwan. After the conference ended, the Vietnamese government made no immediate effort to back up its declaration with action. It was not until 1956 that the South Vietnamese government established a permanent presence in the Spratlys. Vietnam's proclaimed SCS waters are huge (see Map 4 below).

---

[80] Tim Huxley and Benjamin Schreer, "Standing up to China," *Survival*, Volume 57, Number 6 (December 2015–January 2016), 127–143; 129.
[81] Chao, "South China Sea: Boundary Problems Relating to the Nansha and Hsisha islands," 88.

South China Sea Claims

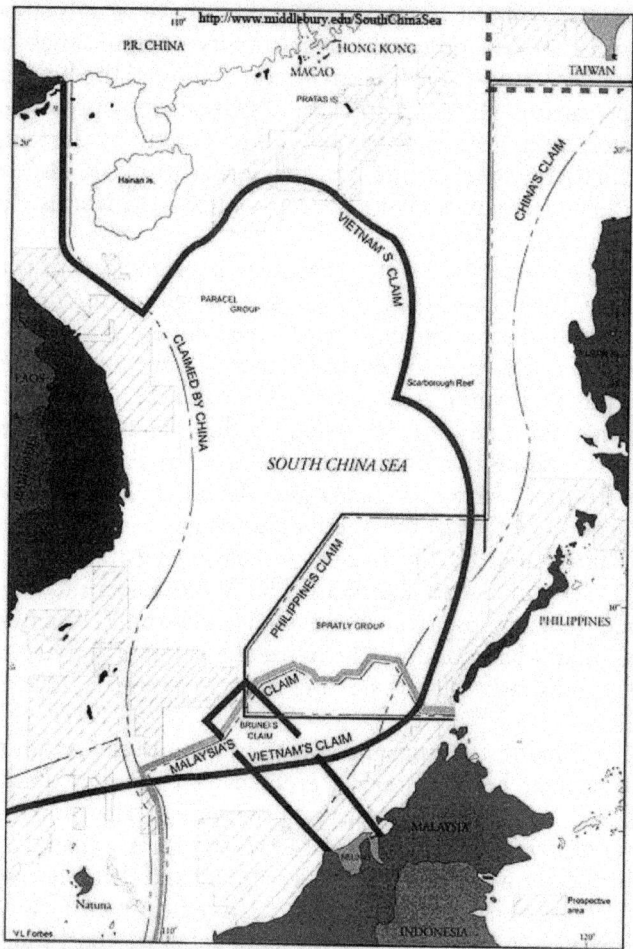

Source: Vivian Louis Forbes, *Conflict and Cooperation in Managing Maritime Space in Semi-enclosed Seas* (Singapore: Singapore University Press, 2001), p. 136. (Reproduced with the kind permission of Dr Vivian Louis Forbes)
Source: Buszynski, Leszek, and Iskandar Sazlan. Maritime Claims and Energy Cooperation in the South China Sea. Contemporary Southeast, map 3

Map 4: Vietnam's SCS Claim[82]

---

[82] SCS map courtesy of David Rosenberg www.southchinasea.org.

Vietnam's historical claim to the Paracels and the Spratlys is based on its own exploration and exploitation of the islands since the eighteenth century and on the later activity of the French in the area. The 1887 Sino-French Convention delimited the boundary between Annam (Vietnam) and China's Guangdong province, plus made an implicit reference to the Gulf of Tonkin by drawing a straight line that extended the maritime border from the eastern end of the Sino-Vietnamese land border southward towards the Gulf of Tonkin.

Although the convention states that islands located east of this line belong to China and islands lying west of it belong to Annam, there are apparent discrepancies between the Chinese and French versions as to whether the line divides just the islands or whether it separates the SCS water area as well. The Chinese text reportedly states that the line applies "so far as the islands in the sea are concerned," while the French text defines the line as "making up the frontier" between China and Annam.[83] Immediately before unification, details of the Vietnamese claim were published in a 1975 White Paper by the Ministry of Foreign Affairs of the Republic of Vietnam (South Vietnam). This White Paper included historic documents, maps, and other evidence that the Vietnamese were aware of and had conducted extensive economic activity in the Paracel and Spratly islands starting as early as the eighteenth century.[84]

In 1956, following the announcement by Philippine national Tomas Cloma that he was staking a claim to a number of the Spratly islands, the South Vietnamese government also put forward their competing claim that in the 1930s the Spratlys had been under the jurisdiction of the French government and that Vietnam had jurisdiction by virtue of inheriting sovereignty from France. This was initially contested by the French. In 1956, the French government claimed to have ceded the Paracels to Vietnam, but not the Spratlys. A Vietnamese spokesman argued that the Spratlys had been officially incorporated into the Vietnamese province

---

[83] Pao-Min Chang, *The Sino-Vietnamese Territorial Dispute* (New York: Praeger, 1986), 12.
[84] Republic of Vietnam Ministry of Foreign Affairs, *White Paper on the Hoana Sa (Paracell and Truona Sa) Spratly Islands* (Saigon: 1975), 32.

of Baria in 1929, thereby pre-dating the French occupation of some of the islands in 1933, and so was automatically included in the French transfer of sovereignty to Vietnam. This point was apparently conceded by the French government, because no further claim to the islands was made by Paris.

The French occupation of several of the Spratlys during 1933–1939 is considered by Vietnam to be the main proof for its legal claim to the islands. France's "invasion" of the islands was officially protested at the time by the Chinese government. The French did acknowledge that Chinese nationals were living in the Spratlys, which undermined its sovereignty claim, since it indicated that the islands were not *terra nullius*. The Japanese government also refused to recognize these early French claims when the Japanese took them by force in 1939. These arguments may all be moot, however, as Martin Katchen has pointed out:[85]

> Whether or not France occupied the Spratly Islands as *terra nullius*, or whether or not the Chinese presence on the islands raises doubts about the legality of the French occupation, the fact is that the French did occupy the Spratlys and conquest is still a valid method of transferring territory under international law. However, the Japanese conquered the Spratlys from France, and then yielded them after World War II, without any specification to whom the islands were to be yielded.

If the French possession of the Spratlys in 1933 constituted a valid claim of sovereignty, then the Japanese conquest of the islands in 1939 must also be considered valid, despite French diplomatic protests. On the other hand, if France's occupation did not constitute valid title, then Vietnam's subsequent claim is weakened: "if France never owned the Spratlys, Vietnam, as a successor state, cannot claim it inherited the islands."[86] Since the French claim to the Spratlys is ambiguous, the Vietnamese claim to the islands is also equally questionable. Unlike with the Paracels case, there is no evidence that France handed over the Spratlys to South

---

[85] Martin Katchen, "The Spratly Islands and the Law of the Seas," *Asian Survey*, 17 (December 1977): 1179–1180.
[86] Haller-Trost, *The Spratly Islands*, 45.

Vietnam upon dissolution of the French Empire. Therefore Vietnam's claim that it inherited the islands from France may be incorrect.

But Vietnam's claims do not rest just on historic grounds, cession from France, or public declarations; Hanoi also bases its sovereignty on physical occupation. Since 1956, Vietnam has aggressively established and expanded a physical presence in the islands. In August 1956, the South Vietnamese government reportedly occupied Spratly Island (Truona Sa Dao in Vietnamese) and annexed the Spratlys to Phuoc Tuy province. It then began to make regular naval patrols in the area, sparking protests from both China and Taiwan.

Meanwhile, perhaps because it needed material support from the PRC, North Vietnam appears to have accepted Chinese sovereignty over the Paracel and Spratly islands. As mentioned above, on 4 September 1958, Beijing issued a declaration proclaiming both a 12 nm territorial sea and stated that this limit applied to all Chinese territories, including the Paracel (Xisha) and Spratly (Nansha) Islands. Ten days later, in a note to Chinese Premier Zhou Enlai, North Vietnamese Premier Pham Van Dong expressed his government's support and recognition of China's declaration, stating "the Government of the Democratic Republic of Vietnam has noted and supports the September 14, 1958 declaration by the People's Republic of China regarding territorial waters of China" (see Document 9).

This Vietnamese statement has been cited by the Chinese as proof that the Democratic Republic of Vietnam acknowledged China's sovereignty over the Paracel and Spratly islands. While not denying that the letter was sent, the Vietnamese government issued a statement in August 1979 clarifying that, "the spirit and letter of the note were strictly confined to recognition of China's 12-mile territorial waters."[87] By recognizing China's declaration without specifying this reservation, however, Vietnam appears to have legally accepted all of its provisions, including sovereignty over the Spratlys. The fact that a senior official of the North Vietnamese government wrote in support of a Chinese declaration that

---

[87] "Vietnam-China: Background to the Conflict," *Keesing's Contemporary Archives* 25 (October 1979): 29870.

explicitly mentioned the Chinese claim of sovereignty over the Paracel and Spratly islands would normally be considered valid recognition of that claim and thus weaken subsequent Vietnamese counterclaims.

While this diplomatic exchange between North Vietnam and China was taking place, the government of South Vietnam ignored the PRC's Declaration on Territorial Waters by stepping up its military activity in the Paracel islands during 1956. This culminated in early 1959 with a South Vietnamese naval invasion of Duncan Island in the Paracels, occupied at the time by Chinese fishermen. South Vietnam's move was protested by the Chinese. The resulting sovereignty dispute between China and South Vietnam over the Paracels waxed and waned for over a decade, eventually resulting in the well-orchestrated and successful attack in January 1974 by Chinese forces to push the South Vietnamese completely out of the Paracels. Soon after North and South Vietnam reunified, however, Hanoi assumed control over six Spratly island bases formerly occupied by the South, and protested Beijing's claim to both the Paracels and the Spratlys.

THE CHINESE CLAIM

China, which in this case includes both the PRC and the ROC, already controls the Pratas, Paracels, many of the Spratlys, and has the longest-standing claim to the SCS as historic waters. According to geographer Marwyn Samuels, the oldest written reference to this region is found in Chinese chronicles dating from the third century, although he considers it likely that the area known today as the SCS was explored by the Chinese much earlier.[88] Certain Chinese scholars argue China's situation is unique, and that it should enjoy "historic rights with tempered sovereignty" over the SCS.[89]

Although China is certainly a major claimant to sovereignty over the islands, its adoption of a "Sino-centric version of history" completely overlooks the rights of the other regional states and in particular "ignores the fact that ethnic Malay seafarers, the

---

[88] Samuels, *Contest for the South China Sea*, 10.
[89] Roy, *The South China Sea Disputes*, 13.

ancestors of today's Malaysians, Indonesians, Filipinos and the Chams of Vietnam, dominated commerce in those waters centuries before the Chinese."[90] The Chinese were simply the first to document on paper their early presence: "From the foregoing, it is true that the weight of the evidence appears in the present case to be on the Chinese side, although this may reflect mainly the greater industry of traditional Chinese authors in keeping geographical and historical records."[91]

Despite the historical claims of the Vietnamese and Chinese, it has been argued that only those events since the 1930s are relevant to determining the present dispute. Following the Japanese occupation of the islands in the late 1930s, valid claims of sovereignty through effective occupation could be made for the first time. While Chinese historical claims to the islands might establish an inchoate or incipient right to sovereignty, therefore, such a right must be followed up with *de facto* occupation of the territory to establish legal sovereignty. Permanent occupation was not attempted by China until after World War II. Since Nationalist troops were the first to occupy one of the Spratly islands after the Japanese withdrawal in 1945, the joint PRC-ROC claim to the Spratlys is theoretically stronger than that of the Vietnamese.

However, a Vietnamese or Chinese claim based only on discovery and historical usage of the islands, "is not a sufficient but only a necessary condition [for claiming sovereignty] because it must be sustained by continuous and uninterrupted exercise of sovereignty. On this point neither side appears to be sufficiently persuasive."[92] In particular, historical claims notwithstanding, Japan took possession of most of these islands by conquest in 1939, but due to the 1951 San Francisco Peace Treaty renounced its claims. From that time on, all subsequent claims and counterclaims have

---

[90] Ian Jeffries, *Contemporary Vietnam: A guide to economic and political developments* (New York: Routledge Press, 2011), 58; citing two 2010 opeds by Philip Bowring.

[91] Chao, "South China Sea: Boundary Problems Relating to the Nansha and Hsisha Islands," 113.

[92] Choon-Ho Park, "The South China Sea Disputes: Who Owns the Islands and the Natural Resources?" *Ocean Development and International Law* 5 (1978): 33.

not been so simple to assess. This issue is further complicated by a Vietnamese military presence, which cannot be ignored. China's legal position on the islands, based on applicable international law, is not only weak *de jure*, therefore, but also *de facto*, principally because China did nothing to exercise its jurisdiction over the Spratly islands until it established its own outposts in the area in 1988. By contrast, Taiwan has a more airtight claim to Itu Aba, particularly since it has effectively held and developed it. However, "Taiwan cannot deduce from this any claim to the whole archipelago (which is, after all, an arbitrary definition in regard to insular affiliation and dimension) just because it occupies one feature of the group."[93]

There is also some uncertainty regarding the exact length of time that the Chinese military occupied Itu Aba during this period. Most authorities agree that Nationalist forces left the Spratly islands in May 1950 due to losing the civil war in Mainland China and only returned in July 1956, possibly in response to activity in the area by Philippine nationals. During an interview in Taipei in March 1993, the absence of a Chinese military presence in the island for several years was apparently confirmed by Vice Admiral Liu Ta-Tsai, a retired ROC Navy officer, who was a member of the Society for Strategic Studies in Taiwan. But Pao-Min Chang accepts a Chinese study indicating that a "small contingent of Taiwanese troops remained on the largest island Itu Aba (Taipingdao) in the Spratly group" during this period.[94]

A CLOSER EXAMINATION OF CHINESE HISTORICAL DOCUMENTS

In the aftermath of the Sino-Vietnamese War of 1979, China's Ministry of Foreign Affairs published a document entitled *China's Indisputable Sovereignty over the Xisha and Nansha Islands*, which detailed China's historical claims to the Paracel and Spratly Island groups. This document indicated that as early as the reign of Emperor Wu Di of the Han Dynasty in the second century B.C.E., the Chinese began sailing through the South China Sea.

---

[93] Haller-Trost, *The Spratly Island*, 59–69.
[94] Chang, *Sino-Vietnamese Territorial Dispute*, 18.

After many years, they discovered the Paracels and Spratlys: "The geographical features of these islands are described in *Nan Zhou Yi Wu Zhi* (*Strange Things of the Southern Provinces*) by Wan Zhen and *Fu Nan Zhuan* (*An Account of Fu Nan*) by Kang Tai, both of which were written in the Three Kingdoms period (220–265 [A.D.])."[95]

The Paracel islands are located on the major north-south sea lanes extending from the East China Sea to the Malacca Strait, so were certainly familiar to Chinese sailors. China's historical claim has been succinctly summarized by Pao-Min Chang:[96]

> Beijing contended that the Chinese discovered the two archipelagos in the second century B.C. and had begun to inhabit them as early as the seventh century. By the tenth century, Chinese naval patrols had reached the Paracel (Xisha) islands and placed them under Chinese jurisdiction. In the ensuing centuries, the Chinese government continued to conduct surveys around the islands and dispatch naval patrols to their adjacent areas.

By contrast, early references to what we now call the Spratly islands were considered unusual since the islands were outside of the regular trading routes, and so Chinese contact with the islands was usually accidental. The lack of detailed information on the Spratlys can be attributed to the fact that so few "managed to survive the encounter."[97]

However, there can be little doubt that the Chinese knew of the presence and general location of the Spratly islands by the eleventh century, even if only to avoid them. The great maritime expansion of China under the Song, Yuan, and Ming Dynasties from the eleventh to the fifteenth centuries provided ample opportunities for Chinese mariners to explore and examine these islands. During May 2012, PRC government Foreign Ministry officials announced that Beijing's claim to the SCS could be dated precisely to a 1279

---

[95] "China's Indisputable Sovereignty Over the Xisha and Nansha Islands" (Beijing: Ministry of Foreign Affairs of the People's Republic of China, 30 January, 1980), trans. in *Beijing Review* 23 (18 February 1980): 15–24.
[96] Chang, *The Sino-Vietnamese Territorial Dispute*, 135.
[97] Samuels, *Contest for the South China Sea*, 11.

survey "commissioned by Emperor Kublai Khan," a Mongol leader during China's Yuan dynasty, who controlled most of Eurasia at that time.[98]

China's reference back to the Mongol Yuan dynasty did not necessarily mean the Chinese government promoted full-time occupation. The Confucian literati who made up the bulk of the Chinese government did not value small islands, and the islands were probably considered as simply navigational hazards interfering with China's maritime access to the southern SCS. But Chinese scholars have argued that by the application of the doctrine of intertemporal law – meaning the legality of an act being determined by the law at the time of the act – that "discovery alone in the second century B.C. may be considered to found a good title."[99]

Although such an argument might provide the basis for an incipient or partial title, this claim would have to be followed up by positive steps, such as occupation. China does not appear to have met the criteria for effective occupation, since it did not have a continuous presence in the Spratlys before the Japanese occupation of the islands in 1939, which appears to be the first time that the Spratlys were effectively occupied in modern history. The occupation of several of the islands by France in the early 1930s might have met the legal criteria for occupation but there is no hard evidence that France physically governed the Spratlys, even if they did include them pro forma into their colonial administration. France also did not make any official claim to the Spratlys in the Treaty of San Francisco in September 1951, at which time the Japanese relinquished control of the islands.

After the Japanese defeat in 1945, the former Japanese naval base on Itu Aba was occupied by Nationalist troops from the ROC. The occupation was reportedly interrupted in 1950 during the Chinese civil war and the subsequent relocation of the Nationalist Chinese government to Taiwan. But a permanent military presence on Itu Aba was reestablished by Taiwan in 1956 and has

---

[98] Jane Perlez, "Beijing Exhibiting New Assertiveness in South China Sea," *New York Times*, 31 May 2012.

[99] Chao, "South China Sea: Boundary Problems Relating to the Nansha and Hsisha islands," 110.

continued to the present. According to one Taiwanese source, three flotillas were sent to the Spratlys beginning in June 1956, including landing marines, and "Taipei decided to station a [permanent] marine platoon on Taiping at the end of 1956."[100]

The PRC and ROC can thus claim to have both discovered the Spratly islands in the distant past as well as effectively occupied and controlled what is the largest and arguably the "principal island" in the archipelago since at least 1956. This gives the joint PRC-ROC claim greater weight than many of the other claimants. While Itu Aba is only one island, there is also precedent in International Court of Justice(ICJ) rulings to conclude that, "the occupation of the principal islands of an archipelago must also be deemed to include the occupation of islets and rocks in the same archipelago, which have not actually been occupied by another state."[101]

China's first post-World War II claim to the Spratlys was prompted by the international conference convened in 1951 in San Francisco to conclude the war with Japan. While neither the PRC nor the ROC on Taiwan was represented at the conference, Communist China's Foreign Minister Zhou Enlai declared in a statement before the conference opened that the Paracel and Spratly islands had always been China's territory. In 1980, the PRC's Ministry of Foreign Affairs called attention to additional evidence of Japan's intention to cede the Paracel and Spratly islands to China: "Although the [1951] ... peace treaty with Japan did not mention the ownership of these islands [the Paracels and Spratlys], in 1952, the year after the San Francisco Peace Treaty with Japan was signed, the 15th map, Southeast Asia, of the Standard World Atlas, which was recommended by the signature of the then Japanese Foreign Minister Katsuo Okazaki, marks as part of China all the Xisha [Paracels] and Nansha [Spratly] Islands."[102]

---

[100] "Sovereignty over the Spratly Islands," National Policy Foundation, 10 July 2009, http://www.npf.org.tw/printfriendly/6120 [accessed 9 November 2016].

[101] Chao, "South China Sea: Boundary Problems Relating to the Nansha and Hsisha islands," 85.

[102] "China's Indisputable Sovereignty," 20.

In general, Taiwan's claim to the entire SCS bolsters the PRC's case. Beijing cites an October 1955 event as evidence that Taiwan's and therefore China's joint claim to the Spratly islands was recognized by other states. During an international conference on aviation safety, "the British delegation and the delegation of the International Aviation Transport Association jointly submitted an official proposal requesting the government of the Republic of China [Taiwan] to establish a meteorological post on one island in the Nansha [Spratly] archipelago."[103] Since this was a scientific conference, however, it is unclear what the political implications – assuming there are any – might be.

To sum up, China's legal claim to the SCS islands is arguably based upon discovery, annexation, and occupation, as well as past recognition of their claim by other states. These events would seem to give China a strong case to sovereignty over the Spratlys after World War II, particularly since Taiwan had effectively occupied the principal island in the Spratly. As pointed out by Taiwanese commentator Peter Kien-hong Yu, however, the subsequent occupation of several of the other Spratly islands by military forces from mainland China since 1987–1988 means that "the burden of defending [the Chinese claim to] the Spratly archipelago has been shifted from the ROC [Taiwan] to the PRC [Communist China]."[104]

PRC-VIETNAMESE TENSIONS OVER THE SCS

By the end of January 1974, the PLAN had consolidated full control over the Paracel islands. China accomplished this naval action despite Soviet protests on behalf of their Vietnamese ally. Some of the South Vietnamese military forces departing the Paracels reportedly moved south and established new garrisons on several unoccupied islands in the Spratlys. After the fall of the Saigon regime in April 1975, six of these Spratly garrisons were taken over by North Vietnamese forces, thus

---

[103] Chao, "South China Sea: Boundary Problems Relating to the Nansha and Hsisha islands," 89.
[104] Peter Kien-hong Yu, *The Four Archipelagoes in the South China Sea* (Taipei: Council for Advanced Policy Studies, 1991), 73.

maintaining continuity in the Vietnamese presence on these islands. A month later, Hanoi's military newspaper, *Quan Dao Nham Dan*, published "a map depicting the Spratly Islands as part of Vietnam's territory."[105] The six bases, plus several additional islands subsequently occupied by Vietnam in the Spratlys, provide Vietnam's strongest evidence of a territorial claim based on occupation.

When the North Vietnamese invaded and forcibly unified North and South Vietnam, Hanoi immediately renewed its claim over other Spratly islands and, in particular, over the Paracels islands, by adopting the diplomatic position of the defeated South Vietnamese government. On 1 July 1976, the day before the national election on 2 July 1976 that reunified Vietnam, Hanoi announced that the Paracels were Vietnamese territory. In response, the PRC pointed to Premier Pham Van Dong's September 1958 recognition of China's maritime borders as proof that the government of the Democratic Republic of Vietnam had already acknowledged China's sovereignty over the Paracel and Spratly islands, but Hanoi rejected this interpretation.

Rising tensions over the SCS were related to increasingly poor Sino-Soviet relations. Growing Chinese discontent with the USSR by the mid-1970s resulted in increased troop strength of over a million Russian troops along the Sino-Soviet border. Meanwhile, over seventy Soviet ships and some seventy-five submarines were stationed in the Pacific and were capable of coming to Vietnam's aid. After unification, Vietnam began to turn away from China and shifted more toward the Soviet Union for aid. According to one Vietnamese official, Hanoi also hoped to use the USSR to limit China's power: "There is a tangibly strong Soviet interest coinciding with Vietnamese interests – to reduce Chinese influence in this part of the world."[106]

Fearful of a two front war, the Sino-Vietnamese war of 1979 was fought by China in part to prove that the Soviet government would not uphold its promises to assist Vietnam. But there

---

[105] Koo, *Island Disputes and Maritime Regime Building in East Asia*, 149.
[106] Chang Pao-min, *Kampuchea Between China and Vietnam* (Singapore, Singapore University Press, 1985), 46–47.

were important boundary issues as well in which the SCS figured prominently. For example, when it appeared that a Chinese naval force might participate in China's 1979 invasion, and perhaps take even more territory, four Soviet warships intervened on Vietnam's behalf.[107] During March 1979, Vietnam also agreed to let the Soviet Navy operate out of the former American naval base at Cam Ranh Bay.

Soon after the end of the 1979 war, the Vietnamese government issued a statement during August 1979 condemning China's 1958 declaration. Tensions throughout the SCS continued, resulting in other Sino-Vietnamese clashes during 1988. On 13 April 1988, China incorporated both the Paracels and the Spratly islands into a new Chinese province it called Hainan province. In May 1992, China signed an agreement with the Crestone Energy Corporation to explore in a 10,000 square mile area in the SCS, but Vietnam protested this area was part of its continental shelf (see Map 5 below). In September 1992, Vietnam protested again when China undertook drilling operations in a disputed section of the Gulf of Tonkin.

Despite periodic protests from China, Vietnam has gradually taken physical possession of more Spratly islands than any other claimant. By 1992, the Vietnamese military had reportedly occupied 21 of the SCS features and currently it occupies 33 different outposts in the SCS. The fact that Vietnam has *de facto* control of these islands and reefs is effective occupation, which is considered useful in determining territorial sovereignty under contemporary international law. Taking a page out of China's playbook, in 1994 Hanoi granted exploration rights to Mobil Oil in a concession area claimed by Beijing.[108] This arrangement worked well and by 2000, Vietnam was exporting 20% of its total oil production to China.[109] The legal rights accruing to Vietnam by its extensive physical presence in the Spratlys is likely one of the principal

---

[107] Chang, *The Sino-Vietnamese Territorial Dispute*, 86.
[108] Carlyle A. Thayer, Ramses Amer, eds., *Vietnamese Foreign Policy in Transition* (New York: St. Martin's Press, 1999), 229.
[109] Womack, *China and Vietnam*, 29.

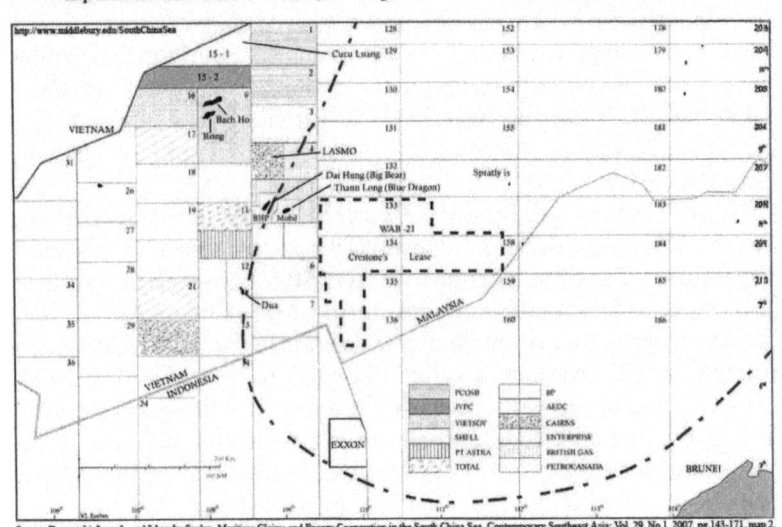

Map 5: Oil Exploration Blocks off Vietnam

reasons that China has refused to consider international arbitration of the dispute.[110]

VIETNAMESE MILITARY PREPARATIONS IN THE SCS

China and Vietnam have made many statements supporting "peaceful means" to resolve disputes, yet both countries are preparing to back their claims by military force if necessary. On 25 February 1992, China enacted a new law on territorial waters entitled *Law on the Territorial Sea and the Contiguous Zone* that claimed sovereignty over all of the Spratlys. The law restated its earlier law published in 1958 by reiterating China's claim to all offshore islands, which included the Paracel and Spratly islands, and defining China's territorial waters as extending 12 nm with a "contiguous area" extending a further 12 nm offshore (see

---

[110] Johnston and Valencia, *Pacific Ocean Boundary Problems*, 128.

Document 14). China has also claimed an Exclusive Economic Zone (EEZ) of 200 nm.[111]

Vietnam was arguably the single most powerful military power in Southeast Asia before they lost their major ally and source of military equipment following the 1991 disintegration of the Soviet Union. The withdrawal of Soviet Naval forces from Cam Ranh Bay left Vietnam without a northern pincer on China. Unable to come to a mutually satisfactory agreement for basing rights in the Philippines, in 1992 the U.S. Seventh Fleet departed Subic Bay, hitherto its largest base in the Western Pacific, and relocated to Guam. The departure of both superpowers from Southeast Asia occurred during a time of increased naval development in China that many analysts see as geared specifically to expanding Chinese control over the Spratly islands.[112]

In May 1992, despite talk of shelving the disputes over sovereignty to allow for joint development of resources in the SCS, Sino-American oil exploration began in a contested area within Vietnam's declared 200 nm EEZ and near a Vietnamese offshore oil field. Ignoring Vietnamese protests over their oil exploration contract, China occupied two additional islands in the Spratlys in June 1992, bringing the total number of islands occupied by China at that time to seven. The Vietnamese, either in response to these Chinese moves or as part of a planned expansion, also increased the number of islands under their control to 21 in 1992.

Any armed conflict between the small military units stationed on these tiny islands, often within sight of each other, could easily escalate into a full-scale naval battle between China and Vietnam. From the mid-1990s on, the PLAN has been incorporating modern military technology, much of it purchased from Russia. Moscow is more than willing to play both sides against the other, however, and has sold Vietnam six *Kilo*-class submarines, reportedly for $2 billion, in addition to 24 advanced *Su*-30MK2 maritime bombers,

---

[111] "Law on Territorial Waters, Adjacent Areas," *Daily Report: China*, 28 February 1992, 2–3; later published in United Nations *Law of the Sea Bulletin* No. 21 (August 1992): 24–27.

[112] Tai Ming Cheung "Fangs of the Dragon," *Far Eastern Economic Review*, 13 August 1992, 19–20.

and "up to four *Gepard* frigates."[113] In addition, Vietnam bought two batteries of Russian shore-based anti-ship missiles, plus can produce its own version of the the Russian Uran anti-ship missile. The ongoing military competition in the SCS is accelerating quickly, forcing China to adopt a layered defense.

THE PRC'S LAYERED DEFENSE

When it comes to a Chinese layered defense, the Paracel islands are second in importance only to Hainan for their electronic support systems. China has expanded the capabilities of the airfield on Woody Island to support high performance fighter and reconnaissance aircraft. In 1990, China constructed a 1,200-foot runway on Woody Island that was suitable for jet fighter aircraft. In 1998, the runway was extended to 7,300 feet and finally to 8,100 feet for heavier aircraft such as H-6 bombers or large transports for resupply. During the early 1990s, the Chinese purchased Russian high performance strike/interceptor aircraft such as SU-27 "Flanker" fighters. Meanwhile, a longer pier augmented the island's single jetty, and fuel storage has been added. In June 2001, HY-2 antiship cruise missiles were reportedly added.[114]

On 4 December 2007, China announced that all of its claimed territory in the SCS would be administered as a separate district within Hainan Province. Called Sansha, this huge new city administered an estimated 700,000 nm^2 (2.4 million km^2) of sea that included the Paracels, Spratlys, and Macclessfield Bank. According to news reports, "Shock waves were felt immediately throughout the region: both Vietnam and Indonesia formally protested China's unilateral and preemptive move."[115] Spontaneous and "passionate" demonstrations also broke out on 9 December 2007 in front of the Chinese Embassy in Hanoi, as approximately 250 demonstrators, mainly students, gathered to chant "Down

---

[113] Jonathan Holslag, *Trapped Giant: China's Military Rise* (Abingdon: Routledge, 2010), 105.
[114] Bill Gertz, "Woody Island Missiles," *The Washington Times*, 15 June 2001.
[115] Vu Duc Vuong, "Between a Sea and a Hard Rock," *Asian Week*, 8 January 2008.

with China."[116] On 26 July 2012, China announced that Senior Colonel Cai Xihong would command a newly created Sansha garrison, located on Woody island, to help defend China's SCS claims.

China has also sponsored massive island reclamation operations. Although dispersed over an enormous area, many islands in the Spratly group have now been turned into Chinese bases with significant airfields of their own. Johnson South Reef (Chigua) or Kennan Reef, Subi or Zamora Reef, and Mischief Reef or Panganiban were developed during the 1990s. During 2016, China reclaimed an estimated 3,200 acres of land on these three different islands, plus on Johnson Reef (Mabini), Gaven Reef, Calderon or Cuarteron Reef, and Fiery Cross Reef or Kagitingan. Reclamation allowed for new airfields to be built on Subi Reef and Mischief Reef. While these changes will not necessarily give China any new territorial rights, it will "significantly enhance" China's position in the SCS by improving "China's ability to detect and challenge activities by rival claimants or third parties, widen the range of capabilities available to China, and reduce the time required to deploy them."[117]

All of these developments potentially help provide air support to Chinese naval operations in the Spratlys. Beginning in December 2016, daily civilian flights began from Hainan Island to Woody Island. In January 2017, Chinese strategic bombers circled the contested Spratlys twice in a show of force. All of these trends – increasing interest in the development of offshore resources in the region; a scramble to occupy islands in the Spratlys; and developing Chinese naval and air capabilities that appear to be tailored to the Spratlys situation – may indicate that China intends to resolve the Spratly dispute by military means, possibly in the near future. In the meantime, bilateral negotiations have led to some compromises.

---

[116] Bill Hayton, *Vietnam: Rising Dragon* (New Haven: Yale University Press, 2010), 192.
[117] "China has reclaimed 3,200 acres in the South China Sea, says Pentagon," *The Guardian*, 13 May 2016.

THE SUCCESS OF SINO-VIETNAMESE NEGOTIATIONS

Multilateral solutions to the SCS dispute appear to be impossible. China objected to ASEAN caucusing as a group prior to discussions with Chinese officials, and Beijing's policy adopted in the 1990s was that all outstanding territorial problems should only be discussed bilaterally. In addition, Taiwan was not invited to participate in any discussions, even though Taipei has previously stated that it would not abide by any agreement to which it was not a member. Considering that Taiwan retains physical control over some of the largest islands, including Itu Aba, any lasting resolution would have to take Taiwan into account.

PRC-Vietnamese relations remained tense throughout the 1990s, but negotiations did produce results. During November 1994, Jiang Zemin visited Vietnam and the two countries agreed to form a group of experts to "consider the dispute over the Spratly Islands."[118] On 28 July 1995, Vietnam joined ASEAN, becoming its seventh member. Thereafter, during 2002, China and the countries belonging to ASEAN signed a Declaration of Conduct (DoC) agreeing to try to resolve all outstanding disputes peacefully; a Code of Conduct (CoC) is still being discussed. The DoC is designed to manage rather than resolve the SCS problem and reduce tensions and build trust through the implementation of cooperative confidence building measures (CBMs). Yet since the DoC was signed, not a single CBM has been effectively carried out. Chinese assertiveness led to President Nguyen Minh Triet stating "we will not let anyone infringe on our territory. We will not make concessions, even an inch of ground to anyone."[119]

There have been selective breakthroughs in Sino-Vietnamese diplomacy, however. In 1999, a joint Sino-Vietnamese working group met to delimit the Gulf of Tonkin. On 25 December 2000, these talks led to the signing of a Delimitation Agreement stipulating the exact coordinates of the maritime boundary in the Gulf of Tonkin. In these negotiations, Vietnam advocated using the

---

[118] Ian Jeffries, *Vietnam: A guide to economic and political developments* (New York: Routledge, 2006), 9.
[119] Holslag, *Trapped Giant: China's Military Rise*, 104.

Sino-French Agreement of 1887. But China opposed using this treaty, arguing it did not apply to the water and the seabed in the gulf. So, both sides agreed to ignore it. Fishing rights were also discussed. On 25 December 2000, an Agreement on Fishing Cooperation in the Gulf of Tonkin was signed, including regulations for establishing joint fishing areas, cooperation in preserving and sustainably exploiting the aquatic resources in the gulf, and regulations for furthering fishing cooperation and scientific research. Later, on 29 April 2004 a Supplementary Protocol to the Fishery Agreement was signed in Beijing.

Vietnam also made separate agreements with Malaysia and Indonesia at about the same time. During 1992, Vietnam and Malaysia agreed to "engage in joint development in areas of overlapping claims to continental shelf areas to the south-west of Vietnam and to the east-north-east off the east coast of Peninsular Malaysia and the Gulf of Thailand." In 2003, Vietnam and Indonesia signed an agreement delimiting continental shelf boundaries just to the north of the Natunas, which are controlled by Indonesia.[120] On 15 June 2004, the ratification of the Sino-Vietnamese Delimitation Agreement was made by the National Assembly of Vietnam. From 21 to 25 June 2004 final ratification was granted by the 10th Standing Committee of the National People's Congress of China. Both agreements entered into force on 30 June 2004.

The Sino-Vietnamese agreement did not determine borders at the mouth of the Gulf of Tonkin, which could result in further tensions. For example, in 2014, Vietnamese and Chinese ships rammed each other in the Gulf of Tonkin in response to a Chinese-run offshore oil rig being placed in disputed waters. A Chinese state oil company official referred to this $840 million oil rig as "our mobile national territory," since if "China can drill an oil well on some other country's seabed, they can then claim

---

[120] Ramses Amer and Nguyen Hong Thao, "Vietnam's Border Disputes – Assessing the Impact on its Regional Integration," in Stephanie Balme and Mark Sidel, eds., *Vietnam's New Order: International Perspectives on the State and Reform in Vietnam* (New York: Palgrave Macmillan, 2007), 72–73.

that it was China's territory all along."[121] At one point the oil rig was protected by as many as 120 Chinese vessels, including 17 PLAN warships, 36 Chinese marine police vessels, and 14 freighters.[122] These ships were arranged in three strategic rings, with the PLAN in the inner ring, the middle ring composed of large patrol boats, and the outermost ring made up of smaller patrol boats and fishing trawlers.[123] On 28 May 2014, a Vietnamese fishing boat was surrounded by 40 Chinese fishing boats and was deliberately rammed; when the ship sank, however, all ten Vietnamese crew members were rescued.[124]

CONCLUSIONS

Vietnam and China are constantly vying to increase their control over the small islands and surrounding waters in the SCS. To obtain its objectives, China has demonstrated a willingness to use force to support its territorial claims. In January 1974, for example, elements of the PLAN attacked and defeated South Vietnamese forces in the Paracel islands, forcing their withdrawal from that contested archipelago. The Sino-Vietnamese war of 1979 was also fought over boundary issues in which the SCS islands figured prominently. Almost exactly a decade later, China used force again during the 1988 conflict to expand its control over the Spratlys.

---

[121] David Archibald, "China's 'Mobile National Territory'," *American Thinker*, 19 May 2014, http://www.americanthinker.com/2014/05/chinas_mobile_national_territory.html [accessed 9 March 2017].

[122] "Vietnamese Vessels Approaching Chinese Oil Rig at New Location," *Touitre News*, 28 May 2014, https://sites.google.com/a/usnwc.edu/weekly-maritime-news/home/november-25-30/vietnamesevesselsapproachingchineseoilrigatnewlocation [accessed 9 March 2017].

[123] Mai Thanh Hai, "China sends armored fishing boats to ram Vietnamese ships near illegal rig," *Thanhnien News*, 19 May 2014, http://www.thanhniennews.com/politics/china-sends-armored-fishing-boats-to-ram-vietnamese-ships-near-illegal-rig-26458.html [accessed 13 March 2017].

[124] "Tensions Rise as (Vietnamese) Fishing Vessel Sinks," *China Daily*, 28 May 2014, http://usa.chinadaily.com.cn/china/2014-05/28/content_17545460.htm [accessed 13 March 2017].

The media mainly focuses on the PRC, but it is often overlooked that by 1992 Vietnam had already started building 33 military outposts on 21 separate islands, which is more than any other country. These outposts are also spread out more widely than those of China or the other claimants. In total, they span 400 nm from their northern-most garrison on Southwest Cay (Song Tu Tay Dao in Vietnamese) to Vanguard Bank (Bai Tu Chinh) in the southwest and are fairly evenly distributed in between. While China's reclamation efforts are large and so have brought more international attention, Vietnam has "already done landfill work on 27 South China Sea islets, more than any other claimant," and so its physical presence on so many features should give it some rights under international law.[125]

Vietnam's historical claim to ownership of the Spratly islands is challenged by China, even though Vietnam's position there is arguably much stronger. By contrast, China has established only eight garrisons and the PLA maintains troops on at least seven of the islands since 1988. Most of these features are also claimed by Vietnam, including: (1) Fiery Cross Reef (Yongshu Jiao or Da Chu Thap); (2) Cuarteron Reef (Huayang Jiao or Da Chau Vien); (3) Johnson South Reef (Chigua Jiao or Da Gac Ma); (4) Hughes Reef (Dongment Jiao or Da Hu-go); (5) Gaven Reef (Nanxun Jiao or Da Gaven); (6) Subi Reef (Zhubi Jiao or Da Su-bi); and (7) Mischief Reef (Meiji Jiao). To make this situation even more complicated, Filipino claims to the SCS are in many cases parallel to those of Vietnam, and Manila has also backed up its claims in the Spratlys with a physical presence.

---

[125] Ralph Jennings, "Vietnam Taking Long-Term Hard Line Toward China on Maritime Claims," *Asia*, 28 November 2016, http://www.voanews.com/a/vietnam-taking-long-term-hard-line-toward-china-on-maritime-claims/3614214.html [accessed 28 November 2016]; Alexander L. Vuving, "South China Sea: Who Occupies What in the Spratlys" A closer look at a basic yet poorly understood question," *The Diplomat*, 6 May 2016, http://thediplomat.com/2016/05/south-china-sea-who-claims-what-in-the-spratlys/ [accessed 12 December 2016].

CHAPTER THREE

China's Spratly-KIG Maritime Dispute with the Philippines

———— * ————

MILITARY TENSIONS BETWEEN the Philippines and China have been increasing in recent years. In addition to their disagreement over the Spratly islands, the Philippines and China actively contest territorial sovereignty over Scarborough Shoal (called Bajo de Masinloc in the Philippines, and Huangyan Dao in Chinese), located in the northeastern part of the South China Sea. Scarborough Shoal was the focus of an on-again off-again Sino-Philippine naval standoff during April 2012. Some even referred to China's obstructionist tactics as a naval "blockade."[126]

Since opening relations with China in 1975, the Philippine's economic interaction with the PRC has become increasingly important, with China growing in 2013 to become the third highest trade partner (accounting for 12% of the Philippine's exports and 11% of its imports) after Japan and the United States.[127] In 2015, their bilateral trade hit $17.646 billion, with Manila importing almost twice ($11.471 billion) what it exported ($6.175 billion).[128] This growing trade relationship could be severely damaged by any SCS maritime disputes.

While China asserts territorial sovereignty over the majority of the SCS on historic grounds, the Philippines claims sovereignty

---

[126] Richard Javad Heydarian, "The US-Philippine-China Triangle: From Equibalancing to Counter-Balancing amid the South China Sea Disputes," in Enrico Fels and Trung-Minh Vu, eds., *Power Politics in Asia's Contested Waters: Territorial Disputes in the South China Sea* (New York: Springer, 2016), 349.

[127] Philippines Balance of Trade, see http://www.tradingeconomics.com/philippines/balance-of-trade [accessed 15 May 2013].

[128] Elizabeth Ruth Deyro, "In Numbers: Philippines-China relations," *Rappler.com*, 18 October 2016, http://www.rappler.com/newsbreak/iq/95744-in-numbers-philippines-china-relations [accessed 8 February 2017].

over many of the same islands. It refers to a number of the Spratly islands as the Kalayaan Island Group (KIG), basing its claim to the right of discovery. Even though the Philippines "won" the U.N. tribunal decision, rather than challenge China's presence in disputed waters – such as Scarborough Shoal – the current Philippine government and the PRC appear to have negotiated a separate compromise, but there are valid doubts that it will succeed. We will start with the Philippine claim.

THE PHILIPPINE CLAIM

The Philippine island province of Palawan is located less than 50 nm from the easternmost islands in the Spratly archipelago, well within the Philippine's 200 nm EEZ. This makes the Philippine Republic the closest nation geographically to the Spratlys, which helps explain the Philippine's extreme interest in the SCS. But no official territorial claim was made by the Philippine government until the late 1970s, which greatly weakens Manila's case when compared to either the PRC, ROC, or Vietnam.

Parts of the Spratly archipelago were explored by Philippine civilians shortly after World War II. On 23 July 1946, the Philippines announced "inclusion of the Spratly Islands into its national defense space," which was not a formal claim but indicated that it considered the Spratlys to be *terra nullius*.[129] But it was not until the withdrawal of Chinese military forces from Itu Aba in the early 1950s that a new claimant came forward. On 15 May 1956, a Filipino citizen named Tomas Cloma, director of the Maritime Institute of the Philippines, issued a proclamation claiming "ownership, by discovery and occupation, of all the territory, 33 islands, sand cays, sand bars, coral reefs and fishing grounds [in the Spratlys] of 64,976 square nautical miles," naming these islands "Freedomland."[130] The Philippine name for this area is Free Territory of Freedomland or Kalayaan Island Group (KIG). This incident was called the Cloma Affair.

The Philippine foreign secretary, Carlos Garcia, issued the so-called Garcia Declaration in December 1956, which stated that this part of the Spratlys were *terra nullius* when Tomas Cloma,

---

[129] Hara, *Cold War Frontiers in the Asia-Pacific*, 146, 221.
[130] Chiu and Park, "Legal Status of the Paracel and Spratly Islands," 9.

at that point a Filipino lawyer and private businessman, first discovered them during 1947.[131] Beginning in May 1956, Cloma was also the first Filipino citizen to live there and to take legal possession of these islands through occupation. Even though many of these islands are located almost 400 nautical miles southwest of Palawan, on 31 May 1956 Cloma declared that the Free Territory of Freedomland was founded, and on 6 July 1956 he established his government on Flat Island (called Patag Island by the Philippines).

Tomas Cloma's claim of discovery and annexation of the Spratlys prompted official protests from China, Taiwan, and Vietnam. His claim also did not initially receive Philippine government support. During July 1971, President Ferdinand Marcos announced that the "53-island group known as Kalayaan, exclusive of the Spratlys, which Philippine explorer Tomas Cloma explored and occupied from 1947 to 1959, was regarded as *res nullius* [nobody's property] and may be acquired according to the modes of acquisition of territory recognized under international law, among which are occupation and effective administration."[132]

In 1974, the Philippine government briefly argued that because Japan had not specified which country the islands should go to, "the islands are under the trusteeship of the victorious Allied Powers of World War II, and their status should be jointly decided by the Allied Powers of the United Nations."[133] Following international protests, however, this claim was dropped by the Philippines once it became clear that none of the other signatories to the San Francisco Peace Treaty would back it. Meanwhile, Manila's argument that all other competing SCS claims had lapsed by abandonment really only applied to the French position, and not to the other parties to the dispute.[134]

Seven years later, in 1978, Manila made an official territorial claim based on Cloma's supposed discovery. The Philippine claim extends 300 nm west to include the northern three-quarters of the Spratlys but stops just short of Spratly Island itself, which is not

---

[131] Roy, *The South China Sea Disputes*, 6.
[132] Chiu Hungdah, *China and the Taiwan Issue* (New York: Praeger Publishers, 1979), 359.
[133] Chao, "South China Sea: Boundary Problems Relating to the Nansha and Hsisha islands," 103.
[134] Haller-Trost, *The Spratly Islands*, 58–62.

included. Despite competing Chinese, Taiwanese, and Vietnamese claims to most of these islands, the Philippine rationale was best explained by Corazon Siddayao:[135]

> At the time Cloma staked his claim in 1956, the Philippine Department of Foreign Affairs stated that the Philippine government regarded the islands, islets, etc. within Freedomland as *res nullius*, that some of them were 'newly risen'; therefore, they were available for economic exploration and settlement by Philippine nationals under international law. It was also argued that the Spratlys (and the Paracels) had been turned over to the Allied Powers by Japan in the Peace Treaty signed in San Francisco on 8 September 1951, but disposition of the territories had remained unsettled.

The Philippines ignored all previous claims to the islands by other states, and three of the islands – Pag-asa, Nanshan, and Patag Island – were reportedly garrisoned by the Philippine military as early as 1968.[136] If true, this was three years prior to the 1971 Marcos statement on Kalayaan and ten years before their official annexation as part of the Philippines.

Since 1968, the Philippine government has used several different arguments to justify its territorial claim to KIG, including the rights acquired under the 1958 Geneva Convention on the Continental Shelf, Manila's economic and national defense interests, and proximity of the islands to the Philippines. For example, on 20 March 1968, Presidential Proclamation No. 370 proclaimed a continental shelf. On 11 June 1978, the Philippine government assumed Cloma's claim for one peso and President Marcos immediately issued Presidential Decree 1596 proclaiming Filipino sovereignty over the sea-bed, sub-soil, continental margin, and air space in a 200-mile exclusive economic zone that included KIG. This decree explained that since "these areas do not legally belong to any state or nation but, by reason of history, indispensable need, and effective occupation and control established in accordance

---

[135] Siddayao, *The Off-shore Petroleum Resources of Southeast Asia*, 89.
[136] Donald E. Weatherbee, "The South China Sea: From Zone of Conflict to Zone of Peace?" in Lawrence E. Grintner and Young Whan Kihl, eds., *East Asian Conflict Zones* (New York: St. Martin's Press, 1987), 128.

with the international law, such areas must now deemed to belong and subject to the sovereignty of the Philippines."[137]

The Philippines occupies 6 islands, two cays, and two reefs as part of the Municipality of Kalayaan, which it says is part of Palawan Province. These include: (1) North East Cay (Parola or Dao Song Tu Dong); (2) West York Island (Likas or Dao Dua or Ben Lac); (3) Thitu Island (Pag-asa or Dao Thi Tu); (4) Flat Island (Patag or Dao Binh Nguyen); (5) Nanshan Island (Lawak or Dao Vinh Vien); (6) Commodore Reef (Rizal or Dao Cong Do); (7) Lankiam Cay (Panata or Con San Ho Lan Can); (8) Loaita Island (Kota or Dao Loai Ta); (9) Irving Reef (Balagtas); and 10) Second Thomas Shoal (Ayungin Reef or Ren'ai Reef).

The breadth of the Philippine territorial sea is highly variable, defined by coordinates set forth in the Philippine Treaty Limits. On 2 February 2009, Manila enacted an archipelagic baselines law in its House of Representatives Bill 3216 that included KIG and Scarborough Shoal.[138] In 2009, the Philippine Congress passed Republic Act No. 9522 amending its old baselines law and defining archipelagic baselines for the Philippines. This act claimed sovereignty over KIG and asserted that baselines over the features shall be determined consistent with the "regime of islands" under the UNCLOS.[139] As of May 2014, KIG had 150 residents, most living in a small village on the island of Pag-asa, with "small bands of marines and soldiers living rough on tiny patches of rock, reef and sand so China can't occupy them."[140]

---

[137] PRESIDENTIAL DECREE NO. 1596, 11 June 1978, http://www.gov.ph/1978/06/11/presidential-decree-no-1596-s-1978/ [accessed 12 January 2017].

[138] Ramses Amer and Li Jianwei, "Recent developments in the South China Sea," in Wu Shicun and Hong Nong, eds., *Recent Developments in the South China Sea Dispute: The Prospect of a Joint Development Regime* (New York: Routledge, 2014), 35.

[139] Republic Act No. 9522, An Act to Amend Certain Provisions of Republic Act No. 3046, as amended by Republic Act No 5446, to define the Archipelagic Baseline of the Philippines and for other Purposes, 10 March 2009.

[140] "Spratly Islands: Foreign Correspondent Visits Remote Reef Flashpoint Where Filipino Marines Hold Out Against Chinese Navy," *Australian Broadcasting Corporation*, 14 May 2014, http://www.abc.net.au/news/2014-05-20/oil-key-in-spratly-islands-dispute-south-china-sea/5463080 [accessed 13 March 2017].

There are also potential disputes with China east of the Philippines. For example, the Philippine government submitted preliminary information on the limits of its continental shelf beyond 200 nm in respect to the Benham Rise region on 8 April 2009, and its application was approved by the United Nations in 2012. In March 2017 the Philippine President Rodrigo Duterte ordered the Philippine Navy to put up "structures" to claim this area after reports of a Chinese survey ship conducting tests were received by Manila.[141]

There are several other potential Sino-Philippine conflicts. One is just to the north of the Philippines, where an equidistant line could be drawn from Taiwan's easternmost island of Lanyu and run through Japanese waters near the Sakishima islands group and the Philippines waters close to Amianan Island before proceding through the Bashi Channel into the SCS. This line curtails Taiwan's border well before its 200 nm EEZ limit is reached. From the Bashi Channel proceeding to the south and west, however, the equidistant line falls within the Philippines Treaty Limits.[142]

The Philippines and Taiwan also have overlapping EEZ claims that involve the Pratas islands, 458 nm (850 km) southwest of Taipei and 184 nm (340 km) southeast of Hong Kong. Pratas Island (Dongsha) is a small island just above sea level which is about 1.7 miles (2.8 km) long and just over a half mile (0.865 km) wide. The Pratas islands consist of three islands made up of coral atolls and reefs. While they are currently governed by Taiwan, they are also claimed by the PRC. Given the small size of the Pratas islands, the Philippines might be accorded a reduced effect.

To sum up, if maritime boundary delimitation negotiations were ever initiated the Philippine claims to the KIG would rest mainly on proximity. This argument is not based on international law, however, since many states control territory close to another state; the British colony at Gibraltar, which is connected to Spain by a land bridge, is just one example. Therefore, the task of delimiting the

---

[141] "Duterte tells navy to build 'structures' east of Philippines," *Reuters*, 13 March 2017, http://timesofoman.com/article/104826/World/Asia/Wary-of-China-Duterte-tells-navy-to-build-'structures'--east-of-Philippines [accessed 13 March 2017].

[142] Victor Prescott and Clive Schofield, *The Maritime Political Boundaries of the World* (Leiden/Boston, Martinus Nijhoff, 2005), 434–435.

Philippine's maritime boundaries with China and Taiwan would be highly complex. Other than the KIG and Scarborough Shoal, however, which will be discussed in greater detail below, the other overlapping maritime boundaries between the Philippines and China could be negotiated and resolved without too much difficulty.

THE CHINESE CLAIM

The PRC claims territorial sovereignty over the entire SCS based on the principle of discovery, calling them historic waters. China also cites the 1887 treaty between France and China, which by creating a boundary line "105 degrees 43 minutes east of Paris" ceded to the China all territory east of this line. Beijing argues that since the Spratlys lie east of this line, they belong to China.[143] While this treaty can perhaps be applied against Vietnam's claim to the Spratlys, it does not necessarily apply to Manila's claim since the Philippines were a Spanish colony at the time and did not sign the treaty. The PRC also claims that its "nine-dashed line" map, also called the "U-shaped line" map, encloses the main island features of the SCS[144] (see Map 6 below). But Beijing has not defined the precise locations of the dashes by providing their exact coordinates, so it is unclear whether the nine-dashed lines pertain merely to the enclosed island features, over the entirety of the waters they enclose, or to both.

During the 1995 Mischief Reef incident, however, it appears to be the latter since China built a number of concrete structures on this disputed reef and reportedly told American officials that if the Philippines refused to discuss joint development then "it will have no choice but to take over the islands forcibly."[145] In response, the U.S. Secretary of State reminded the Chinese foreign minister that "the United States had treaty obligations with the Philippines."[146]

---

[143] Chiu and Park. "Legal Status of the Paracel and Spratly Islands," 11, citing the "Convention Respecting the Delimitation of the Frontier Between China and Tonkin (Vietnam)," signed on 26 June 1887.

[144] Li Jinming and Li Dexia, "The Dotted Line on the Chinese Map of the South China Sea: A Note," 34 *Ocean Development & International Law* 2003, 287–295.

[145] Chung, *Domestic Politics, International Bargaining and China's Territorial Disputes*, 137.

[146] Lai, *Asia-Pacific: A Strategic Assessment*, 63, 84n87.

This incident suggested to many that the nine-dashed line represents a depiction of the PRC's historic waters over the entire SCS. Since 2012, all PRC passports have included a map with the U-shape line.

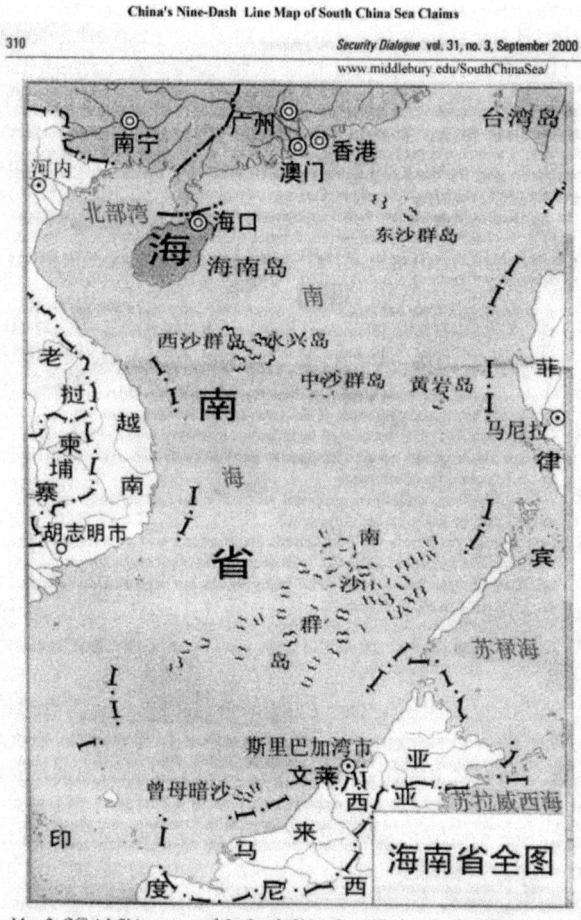

Map 2: *Official Chinese map of the South China Sea with the nine-dotted line*

Source: The Traffic and Tourist Map of Hainan, 1999.

Adapted from Stein Tonnesson, "China and the South China Sea: A Peace Proposal," *Security Dialogue*, vol. 31, no. 3, September 2000

Map 6: The PRC "nine-dash" Map of the SCS[147]

---
[147] SCS map courtesy of David Rosenberg www.southchinasea.org.

On 6 May 2009, Malaysia and Vietnam made a formal submission to the CLSC asking for recognition of their extended continental shelves (ECS) in the SCS. The next day, on 7 May 2009, the PRC protest included a copy of a map depicting the nine-dashed line that dated back to a Nationalist 11-dash map adopted in 1947. This was the first time China had officially submitted its dashed-line map to any international organization. While China used the *note verbale* and map to challenge the joint submission made by Malaysia and Vietnam, its claim also applied to the Philippines. On 4 August 2009, the Philippines filed a diplomatic protest over the submissions made by Vietnam and Malaysia, but then on 5 April 2011, the Philippines filed a separate diplomatic protest in response to China's 7 May 2009 protest.

This spate of diplomatic activity resulted in the Philippines submitting its case to the UN Permanent Court of Arbitration (PCA) in January 2013. On 12 July 2016, the UN tribunal announced that: "Having found that none of the features claimed by China was capable of generating an exclusive economic zone, the Tribunal found that it could – without delimiting a boundary – declare that certain sea areas are within the exclusive economic zone of the Philippines, because those areas are not overlapped by any possible entitlement of China."[148] What this means in practice is that the United Nations has now backed the validity of large sections of the Philippine's exclusive economic zone.

While not determining the exact maritime borders, the PCA did back Manila's general assertion that all of the SCS could not possibly be China's historic waters. It also determined that all of the features in the Spratlys were just rocks, not islands, and so could not generate their own EEZ. To date, however, Beijing has refused to respect the tribunal's decision, stating that the "tribunal has no jurisdiction over the case at all," and arguing that "China made a clear declaration in 2006 in accordance with UNCLOS to

---

[148] Matikas Santos, "Philippines wins arbitration case v. China over South China Sea, *Inquirer.net*, 12 July 2016, http://globalnation.inquirer.net/140358/philippines-arbitration-decision-maritime-dispute-south-china-sea-arbitral-tribunal-unclos-itlos [accessed 29 November 2016].

exclude maritime delimitation from compulsory arbitration."[149] China's Supreme Court even issued its own "counter-Hague ruling, threatening to arrest any intruders into its claimed South China Sea territories."[150] The PCA ruling calls into question the historical legitimacy of the nine-dash map, however, in particular regarding Scarborough Shoal.

OVERLAPPING MARITIME CLAIMS TO THE SCARBOROUGH SHOAL

Despite many positive trends in Sino-Philippine economic relations, additional conflicting maritime claims have produced friction over the Scarborough Shoal. Since the days of Spain's colonization, Filipino fishermen have used the area as a fishing ground and typhoon shelter. The Philippines refers to Scarborough Shoal as either Bajo de Masinloc or Panatag Shoal, while China calls it Huangyan Dao. It is located between the Macclesfield Bank and the Philippine island of Luzon. The Scarborough Shoal is claimed by China, Taiwan, and the Philippines.

Scarborough Shoal is triangular in shape, and comprised of a chain of reefs and island features with heights ranging from half a meter to three meters, which are mostly below water at high tide. The shoal has an area of around 44 nm^2 (150 km^2) and is considered especially valuable for its fishing resources. It is 189 nm (350 km) to the northeast of the Spratly islands and 119 nm (220 km) away from the nearest landmass, Palauig, Zambales, on the Philippine island of Luzon. The main problem is whether this feature can be classified as an island capable of generating EEZ and continental shelf claims or simply as rocks with 12 nm or submerged reefs incapable of making any maritime claims. If it were to be accorded full weight generating maritime claims, the maritime

---

[149] Liu Xiaoming, "Stop Playing with fire in the South China Sea," *Telegraph*, 10 June 2016, http://www.telegraph.co.uk/news/2016/06/09/stop-playing-with-fire-in-the-south-china-sea/ [accessed 9 March 2017].

[150] Robert A. Manning and James Przystup, "A Line in the Sea: How the Philippines Decision Could Settle the South China Sea," *Foreign Affairs*, 10 August 2016, https://www.foreignaffairs.com/articles/china/2016-08-10/line sea [accessed 5 April 2017].

spaces associated with Scarborough Shoal have been estimated at approximately 54,000 nm^2 (185,500 km^2).

The Philippine claim to this feature is based on the principles of discovery and proximity. The Philippines built and operated a lighthouse on Scarborough Shoal in 1965, which was registered with the IMO in 1992. Since the 1950s, the Philippines has repeatedly used the shoal as an impact range for defense purposes. It also conducted oceanographic surveys of the area with the U.S. Navy, then based in the U.S. Naval Base in Subic Bay, Zambales. On 2 February 2009, the Philippine Sea Baseline Bill reiterated Philippine sovereignty and jurisdiction over the Scarborough Shoal.[151]

Beijing and Taipei both agree that this feature is China's. They base their joint claim over Scarborough Shoal on historical evidence dating as far back as the Mongol empire's Yuan Dynasty. Early records mention the area as being used by Chinese fishermen. It was also reportedly used as a surveying point by the Chinese astronomer Guo Shoujing in his 1279 survey of the SCS for the Mongol ruler Kublai Khan. This led the PRC to conclude that "Huangyan Island was discovered by Chinese at least in the Yuan Dynasty (1271–1368)."[152] The shoal is regarded as part of the Chinese province of Hainan.

There have been constant disputes over these SCS fishing areas. The number of registered fishermen in the Philippines more than tripled from 1980–2002 to 1.8 million, even while average catches dropped by 90%. On 30 April 1997, Philippine naval vessels stopped three Chinese fishing boats from approaching the shoal. On 12 April 2012, the Philippine naval ship BRP *Gregorio Del Pilar* attempted to oust several Chinese fishing boats from the shoal. In response: "China deployed an armada of well-equipped para-military vessels, which practically placed the Filipino

---

[151] Nong Hong, "Arctic vs. South China Sea: How Coastal States and User States View the Navigation Regime and Security?" in Shicun Wu and Keyuan Zou, eds., *Non-Traditional Security Issues and the South China Sea: Shaping a New Framework for Cooperation* (Surrey: Ashgate, 2014), 112.

[152] "Backgrounder: Basic Facts on China's sovereignty over Huangyan Island," *Xinhuanet.com*, 14 April 2012, http://news.xinhuanet.com/english/2012-04/14/c_122980075.htm [accessed 29 November 2016].

warship under siege, threatening a potentially destructive military confrontation." When the Philippine ship retreated, the Chinese "blockaded" the area and would not allow Philippine ships to enter, thus effectively taking "control of the contested shoal, over which Manila has exercised varying degrees of jurisdiction since the Spanish colonial era."[153]

The lengthy naval blockade of a disputed fishing area is a new tactic for China. The Philippine government was particularly upset by Beijing's action, since "China had agreed previously to withdraw all ships from the sheltered lagoon following allegations that Chinese fishermen were poaching corals, exotic species of fish, sharks and turtles from the Shoal."[154] This Sino-Philippine standoff remained deadlocked for almost four years, which could not help but undermine attempts to start joint development of the area's natural resources.

RECENT SINO-PHILIPPINE RESOURCE DEVELOPMENT IN THE SPRATLYS

One major challenge in Sino-Philippine relations is how to share the SCS natural resources equitably. To date, all attempts to exploit resources jointly have failed. On 14 March 2005, the three national oil companies of the PRC, the Philippines, and Vietnam signed the *Tripartite Agreement for Joint Marine Seismic Undertaking in the Agreement Area in the South China Sea in Manila, Philippines* (JMSU). The three parties, including representatives from China National Offshore Oil Corporation (CNOOC), Vietnam Oil and Gas Corporation (PETROVIETNAM), and the Philippine National Oil Company (PNOC), acknowledged that the signing of the JMSU Tripartite Agreement did not undermine the territorial claims held by their respective governments. The tri-nation agreement covered 55,168 m^2 (142,886 km^2) and remained in effect for three years (see Map 7 below).

---

[153] Heydarian, "The US-Philippine-China Triangle," 349.
[154] Sigrido Burgos Caceres, *China's Strategic Interests in the South China Sea: Power and Resources* (New York: Routledge, 2014), 76.

On 28 April 2005, China and the Philippines issued a joint statement, right as Chinese President Hu Jintao concluded a two-day trip to the Philippines, calling the visit a "golden age of partnership" contributing "to peace, stability and prosperity in the region." Hu welcomed the signing of the JMSU Tripartite Agreement. In addition, the two countries agreed to continue efforts to safeguard peace and stability in the SCS and reaffirmed their commitments to the China-ASEAN strategic partnership for peace and prosperity, the China-ASEAN Free Trade Area, and the process of East Asian cooperation.[155] Philippine President Gloria Macapagal-Arroyo said the accord was a "breakthrough in implementing the provisions of the code of conduct in the South China Sea among Asean and China to turn the South China Sea into an area of cooperation rather than an area of conflict."[156]

This attempt to exploit the SCS jointly failed. The JMSU lapsed in June 2008, and was not renewed by any of the parties. Since that time, no other cooperative undertakings have been signed. On 2 March 2011, the Philippines reported that Chinese marine surveillance ships had interfered with the legitimate survey activities of the Forum Energy Philippine Corporation when it was exploring for oil and gas deposits near Reed Bank (in Chinese called Lile Tan), which is part of the KIG: "The Reed Bank, which is extremely close to the Filipino shores and may hold among the biggest hydrocarbon reserves in the South China Sea, is seen as a potential game-changer for the Philippines' energy-hungry economy in the coming decades, provided the Philippines can – without Chinese obstruction – proceed with exploration and drilling in the area. But Chinese para-military maneuvers in the area have dissuaded investors from chipping in."[157]

---

[155] "China, Philippines issue joint statement," *China View*, 25 April 2005, http://news.xinhuanet. com/english/2005-04/28/content_2890712.htm [accessed 8 February 2017].

[156] Aurea Calica and Donnabelle L. Gatdula, "RP inks oil search pact with China, Vietnam," *Philstar.com*, 15 March 2005, http://www.philstar.com/business/270404/rp-inks-oil-search-pact-china-vietnam [accessed 25 April 2017].

[157] Heydarian, "The US-Philippine-China Triangle," 348.

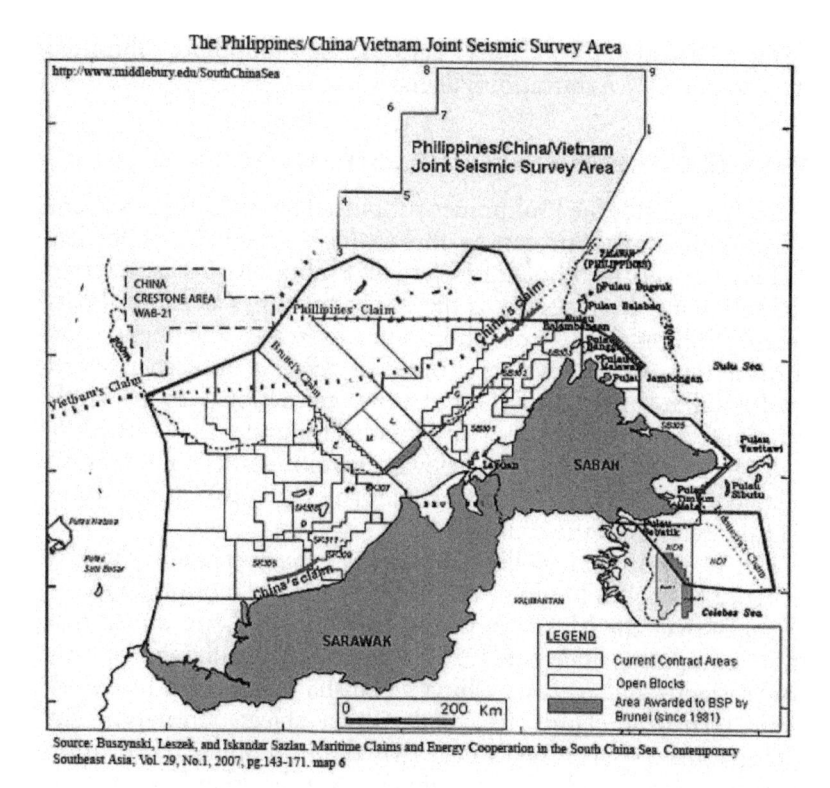

Map 7: The Joint Seismic Survey Area[158]

On 3 March 2011, the Philippines filed a diplomatic protest against China's action. The Reed Bank is located only about 85 nm from the Philippine island of Palawan and so is well within the Philippine 200 nm EEZ. The Philippines complained that Chinese patrol boats harassed the Philippine oil exploration ship. In response, two warplanes were deployed by the Philippine military, but the vessels had already departed when the aircraft reached the area. The Philippines announced that its oil exploration activity would resume soon at the Reed Bank, and ordered an unarmed Philippine Coast Guard patrol ship to protect the oil exploration

---

[158] SCS map courtesy of David Rosenberg www.southchinasea.org.

vessel.[159] Frustrated by China's actions, the Philippines submitted its case to a UN Arbitration Panel.

THE PHILIPPINES TURNS TO THE UNITED NATIONS

On 5 April 2011, the Philippines submitted to the United Nations CLCS a diplomatic protest against China's nine-dash line territorial claim over the whole of SCS. The Philippine protest asserted the following three points: 1) the KIG constitutes an integral part of the Philippines; 2) the Philippines exercises sovereignty and jurisdiction over the waters around or adjacent to each relevant geological feature in the KIG under the international law principle "the land dominates the sea," as provided for under the UNCLOS; and 3) the PRC's claim on "relevant waters, seabed and subsoil" related to the KIG has no basis under the UNCLOS as that jurisdiction belongs to the Philippines.[160]

On 14 April 2011, Beijing submitted a *note verbale* to the UN in reply to the Philippines, reiterating China's "indisputable sovereignty over the islands in the South China Sea." It argued that the Philippines, since the 1970s, "started to invade and occupy some islands and reefs of China's Nansha Islands and made relevant territorial claims, to which China objects strongly." The Chinese protest also mentioned that the Philippine "occupation of some islands and reefs of China's Nansha islands as well as other related acts constitutes infringement upon China's territorial sovereignty." The PRC's diplomatic notes refuted Philippine sovereignty over the KIG and argued that the Philippines cannot invoke illegal occupation to support its territorial claims under the legal doctrine "*ex injuria jus non oritur*," or "a right cannot rise from a wrong." In addition, China claimed that under the relevant UNCLOS provision, "as well as the Law of the People's Republic of China on Territorial Sea and Contiguous Zone (1992) and

---

[159] Lowell Bautista and Clive Schofield, "Philippine-China Border Relations: Cautions Engagement Amid Tensions," Elleman, et al., *Beijing's Power and China's Borders*, 244.
[160] Republic of the Philippines Note Verbale No. 000228, 5 April 2011, http://www.un.org/depts/los/clcs_new/submissions_files/mysvnm33_09/phl_re_chn_2011.pdf [accessed 3 April 2017].

the Law on the Exclusive Economic Zone and the Continental Shelf of the PRC (1998), China's Nansha Islands is fully entitled to Territorial Sea, EEZ, and Continental Shelf"[161] (see Documents 14 and 18).

The exchange of diplomatic protests between the PRC and the Philippines came at a bad time. Bilateral relations between the two countries were especially poor after three Filipinos convicted of drug-related offenses in China were executed on 30 March 2011. In addition, there were tensions over Second Thomas Shoal, also known as Ayungin Shoal (Ren'ai Reef in Chinese). In May 2013, President Aquino ordered the Philippine military to repair the BRP *Sierra Madre*, a small ship deliberately run aground at Ayungin Shoal in 1999 to serve as a marine base. When the Philippine Navy tried to reach *Sierra Madre*, two Chinese surveillance ships and a naval frigate blocked access to the ship. Manila protested this "provocative and illegal presence of Chinese government ships around Ayungin Shoal."[162]

The subsequent standoff lasted a month, and on 19 June 2013 the Chinese finally allowed the resupply ship to dock. In March 2014, a Chinese Coast Guard vessel again blocked two civilian ships bringing supplies to *Sierra Madre*, with a Chinese Foreign Ministry spokesman claiming that Manila had previously made an "unequivocal commitment" to remove the ship.[163] Nine marines were trapped for five months by the "Chinese Coast Guard blockade," before the Philippine Navy managed to evade the Chinese ships and deliver supplies.[164]

---

[161] Bautista and Schofield, "Philippine-China Border Relations," Elleman, et al., *Beijing's Power and China's Borders*, 245.

[162] Carlyle A. Thayer, "South China Sea Tensions: China, the Claimant States, ASEAN and the Major Powers," in Tran Truong Thuy and Le Thuy Trang, eds., *Power, Law, and Maritime Order in the South China Sea* (New York: Lexington Books, 2015), 7.

[163] "Ayungin Shoal Remains Part of PH Even if Troops Withdraw," *Inquirer*, 18 March 2014.

[164] "Troops fear 'miscalculation' in next mission to Ayungin," *Rappler*, 28 May 2014, http://www.rappler.com/nation/59149-ayungin-rotation-mission [accessed 13 March 2017].

Sick and tired of Beijing's provocations, Manila went to the United Nations to arbitrate the dispute. After four long years of hearings, when the PCA finally finished examining the Scarborough Shoal case, it concluded that these disputed features "in their natural condition, are rocks that cannot sustain human habitation or economic life of their own, within the meaning of Article 121(3) of the Convention and accordingly that Scarborough Shoal, Gaven Reef (North), McKennan Reef, Johnson Reef, Cuarteron Reef, and Fiery Cross Reef generate no entitlement to an exclusive economic zone or continental shelf." With regard to Chinese harassment: "Having found that certain areas are within the exclusive economic zone of the Philippines, the Tribunal found that China had violated the Philippines' sovereign rights in its exclusive economic zone by (a) interfering with Philippine fishing and petroleum exploration, (b) constructing artificial islands and (c) failing to prevent Chinese fishermen from fishing in the zone."[165]

The UN tribunal backed the Philippines, but China refused to accept it. During October 2016 President Rodrigo Duterte met with Xi Jinping in Beijing, and the two heads of state agreed to "fully recover" relations that had been damaged by their maritime dispute: "Both sides agree to continue discussions on confidence-building measures ... and to exercise self-restraint in the conduct of activities in the South China Sea that would complicate or escalate disputes."[166] No mention was made of the international court ruling, but in return for reports of from $13.5 to $24 billion in Chinese economic investment in the Philippines, Duterte stated: "I announce my separation from the United States. . . I've realigned myself in your ideological flow and maybe I will also go to Russia to talk to (President Vladimir) Putin and tell him that

---

[165] Matikas Santos, "Philippines wins arbitration case v. China over South China Sea," *Inquirer.net*, 12 July 2016, http://globalnation.inquirer.net/140358/philippines-arbitration-decision-maritime-dispute-south-china-sea-arbitral-tribunal-unclos-itlos [accessed 29 November 2016].

[166] "China, Philippines to set up negotiation mechanism to resolve South China Sea disputes," *South China Morning Post*, 21 October 2016, http://www.scmp.com/news/china/diplomacy-defence/article/2038993/china-philippines-agree-set-negotiation-mechanism [accessed 29 November 2016].

there are three of us against the world – China, Philippines and Russia. It's the only way."¹⁶⁷

Although Duterte vowed not to surrender Philippine sovereignty over the SCS to China, he agreed to the Chinese suggestion of putting the dispute to one side, which works to Beijing's long-term advantage. The UN tribunal also determined that "Chinese law enforcement vessels had unlawfully created a serious risk of collision when they physically obstructed Philippine vessels."¹⁶⁸ Philippine fishermen have been allowed by China to operate in disputed waters, including close to Scarborough Shoal, which had already undergone a four-year blockade by China.¹⁶⁹ While this change is in line with the UN Tribunal's finding that the blockade was illegal, the arrangement is unofficial.

When questioned during March 2017, Duterte said ties with China were in good shape and that diplomatic disputes would not resurface soon: "Let us not fight about ownership or sovereignty at this time, because things are going great for my country."¹⁷⁰ Just a few weeks later, however, Duterte told reporters that he was planning to build new barracks on Thitu island for Filipino servicemen defending the Philippine islands in the KIG, and that he was also planning during the "coming Independence Day," on 12 June 2017, to "go to Pagasa [Thitu] island to raise the flag there," a proposal that the *New York Times* concluded is "unlikely

---

[167] Ben Blanchard, "Duterte aligns Philippines with China, says U.S. has lost," *Reuters*, 20 October 2016, http://www.reuters.com/article/us-china-philippines-idUSKCN12K0AS [accessed 5 December 2016].

[168] Matikas Santos, "Philippines wins arbitration case v. China over South China Sea, Inquirer.net, 12 July 2016, http://globalnation.inquirer.net/140358/philippines-arbitration-decision-maritime-dispute-south-china-sea-arbitral-tribunal-unclos-itlos [accessed 29 November 2016].

[169] Jane Perlez, "Philippine's Deal with China Pokes a Hole in U.S. Strategy," *The New York Times*, 2 November 2016, http://www.nytimes.com/2016/11/03/world/asia/philippines-duterte-south-china-sea.html?_r=0 [accessed 5 December 2016].

[170] Manuel Mogato, "Looks like the Philippines may start building in the South China Sea as well," *Reuters*, 13 March 2017, http://www.businessinsider.com/looks-like-the-philippines-may-start-building-in-the-south-china-sea-as-well-2017-3 [accessed 13 March 2017].

to sit well with China, which lays claim to almost all the South China Sea."[171]

Expanding Sino-Philippine economic ties are good for everyone. Nobody denies that. But, this unofficial Sino-Philippine solution favor's China's long-term goal of asserting hegemony over the SCS. In particular, Manila has undercut American offers to assist. Professor Wang Hanling, a specialist on maritime issues and international law at the Chinese Academy of Social Sciences, even called it "a diplomatic victory for China, particularly over the US," although he then noted: "For the Philippines, it was also a win-win situation, because the South China Sea disputes could not be solved overnight, but having a good relationship with China could only benefit their economy."[172]

CONCLUSIONS

Although Manila does retain *de facto* control over ten of the islands, cays, and reefs in the SCS, and has established effective occupation of these features, Chinese island reclamation of 3,200 acres compared to the Philippines' much smaller 14 acres threatens access to these features. One estimate concludes "China has now 'reclaimed 17 times more land in 20 months than the other claimants combined over the past 40 years, accounting for approximately 95 percent of all reclaimed land in the Spratly Islands."[173] Due to the Chinese reclamation, a Philippine group called Kalayaan Atin Ito

---

[171] "Philippines' Duterte Says 'May' Visit Disputed South China Sea Island," *The New York Times*, 6 April 2017, https://mobile.nytimes.com/reuters/2017/04/06/world/asia/06reuters-southchinasea-philippines.html?rref=collection%2Fsectioncollection%2Freuters-news&_r=0&referer=https://www.nytimes.com/section/reuters [accessed 6 April 2017].

[172] "China, Philippines to set up negotiation mechanism to resolve South China Sea disputes," *South China Morning Post*, 21 October 2016, http://www.scmp.com/news/china/diplomacy-defence/article/2038993/china-philippines-agree-set-negotiation-mechanism [accessed 29 November 2016].

[173] Huxley and Schreer, "Standing up to China," 129; citing *Asia-Pacific Maritime Security Strategy: Achieving U.S. National Security Objectives in a Changing Environment* (Washington, DC: U.S. Department of Defense, August 2015), 10.

Movement recently warned that Pag-asa Island (Thitu) had already been lost: "We have lost to China the heart of the Kalayaan Island Group Municipality through their triangle militarized zone."[174]

To date, the Philippine government is the only party to the Spratly dispute that has submitted its claims to a UN arbitration panel, asserting that China's nine-dash line map was contrary to UNCLOS. The UN arbitration concluded that "there was no legal basis for China to claim historic rights to resources within the sea areas falling within the 'nine-dash line'."[175] Even though this decision backed the Philippines, Beijing and Manila have cut a separate deal that ignores this ruling and that split the Philippines away from the United States.[176] Meanwhile, a 28 January 2017 Pulse Asia Survey poll showed that the "majority of the Filipinos said they want the Philippine government to assert its right over the West Philippine Sea," but Presidential spokesman Ernesto Abella cautioned that asserting these rights is a "matter of timing and diplomatic relations."[177]

The Sino-Philippine dispute over the SCS remains unresolved to this day. The Philippine government could face severe challenges in resupplying and defending its garrisons on several of the other Spratlys. In hindsight, China appears to have obtained its primary objective, perhaps best stated by Deng Xiaoping on 16 April 1988 when he told President Aquino "after many years of

---

[174] "Kalayaan Protesters: We have lost Pag-asa Island to China," *GMA News Online*, 4 January 2016, http://www.gmanetwork.com/news/story/549895/news/nation/kalayaan-protesters-we-have-lost-pag-asa-island-to-china [accessed 29 November 2016].

[175] Matikas Santos, "Philippines wins arbitration case v. China over South China Sea, *Inquirer.net*, 12 July 2016, http://globalnation.inquirer.net/140358/philippines-arbitration-decision-maritime-dispute-south-china-sea-arbitral-tribunal-unclos-itlos [accessed 29 November 2016].

[176] Liu Zhen, "China, Philippines to set up negotiation mechanism to resolve South China Sea disputes," *South China Morning Post*, 22 October 2016, http://www.scmp.com/news/china/diplomacy-defence/article/2038993/china-philippines-agree-set-negotiation-mechanism [accessed 5 December 2016].

[177] "Palace welcomes survey results on deepening bilateral relations with China and Russia," 28 January 2017, http://pcoo.gov.ph/palace-welcomes-survey-results-on-deepening-bilateral-relations-with-china-and-russia-28-jan-2017/ [accessed 8 February 2017].

consideration, we think that to solve the issue [of Nansha/the Spratlys], all parties concerned could explore joint development under the premise of admitting China's sovereignty over them."[178] Even though the Philippines do not acknowledge China's sovereignty in public, in private they have agreed to Beijing's formula. In a situation that is very similar to the Philippines, Malaysia also occupies a number of disputed islands in the Spratly chain. Malaysia's claims will be discussed next.

---

[178] Ramses Amer and Li Jianwei, "Recent developments in the South China Sea," in Wu Shicun and Hong Nong, eds., *Recent Developments in the South China Sea Dispute*, 35.

CHAPTER FOUR

China's Continental Shelf Dispute with Malaysia

———— * ————

MALAYSIA WAS THE first Southeast Asian country to normalize relations with China in 1974. Since that time, Sino-Malaysian tensions have revolved mainly around maritime boundary delimitation of the continental shelf and the proper allocation of SCS resources. The Malaysian government is actively exploiting its oil resources on its own even while trying to enhance its claim over the area through occupation. To date, Malaysia has demonstrated a clear reluctance to develop the Spratly islands jointly with any other party, with the exception of Brunei, with which it has signed a joint agreement.

Since 1983, Malaysia has claimed a number of the southernmost Spratlys, and has occupied a number of them, because they are located within the self-proclaimed Malaysian Continental Shelf: Swallow Reef (1983) or Layang-Layang; Mariveles Reef (1986) or Mantanani; Ardasier Reef (1986) or Ubi; Erica Reef (1999) or Siput; and Investigator Shoal (1999) or Peninjau. Malaysia also claims James Shoal (called Beting Serupai in Malay, and Zengmu in Chinese), which is normally 20 meters under the water. The problem with Malaysia's case is that the legal justification for claiming territory just because it lies within a country's continental shelf reverses the normal method for creating maritime zones. According to international law, an island's title generates rights to surrounding waters and not vice versa.

During 2009, Malaysia and Vietnam made a joint continental shelf submission to the UN CLCS. This submission challenged China's nine-dashed map claiming ownership of the entire SCS (see Map 8 below). But Sino-Malaysian economic relations have recently improved. During late November 2016, Prime Minister Najib Razak signed 14 economic agreements totaling $34.4 billion with China. As part of this new deal, Najib reportedly promised to negotiate all SCS disputes bilaterally with Beijing.[179]

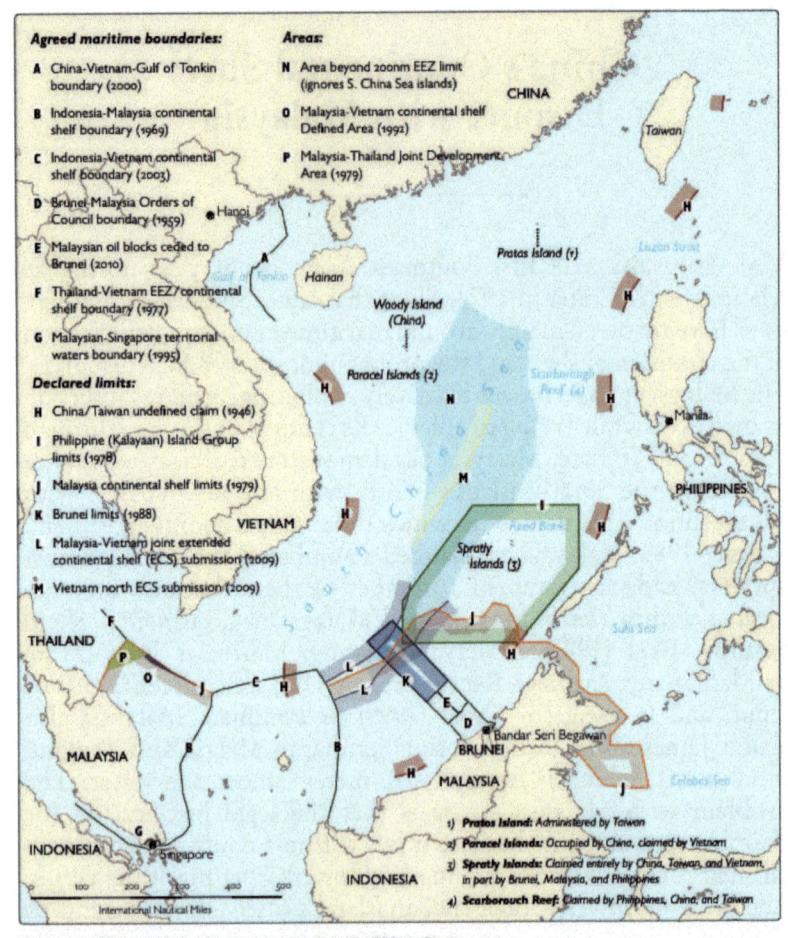

Figure 1: *Sovereignty Claims in the South China Sea.*

Map 8: Sovereignty Claims in the South China Sea[180]

---

[179] "Malaysia, China sign defense deal," *Philippine Daily Inquirer*, 3 November 2016, https://globalnation.inquirer.net/148589/malaysia-china-sign-defense-deal [accessed 5 December 2016].

[180] SCS map courtesy of David Rosenberg www.southchinasea.org.

THE MALAYSIAN CLAIM

Unlike the PRC, ROC, and Vietnam, the Malaysian government does not claim all of the Spratlys, but does control a number of the southernmost islands and currently occupies five of them. In December 1979, the Malaysian government adopted a map showing demarcation lines for its continental shelf based on Malaysia's Continental Shelf Act of 1966. This defined the continental shelf as the seabed and subsoil of submarine areas beyond its territorial waters but adjacent to the coast of Malaysia, but no greater than 200 meters below the ocean surface.

This continental shelf line enclosed several of the islands and reefs in the southern part of the Spratlys that were considered to be part of Malaysian territory. One of the most important was Amboyna Cay, which was at that point occupied by Vietnam. Jakarta is using a self-proclaimed maritime boundary to lay claim to territory, however, which is not considered to be a valid method of acquiring territory under international law, since it reverses the established procedure of using territory to establish maritime zones. Article 76 of the United Nations Law of the Sea, which defines the continental shelf, refers only to control over seabed and submarine resources, not to land which is above water level.

The incorrect use of UNCLOS to justify Malaysian territorial claims was reaffirmed by the Malaysian Deputy Foreign Minister after Chinese and Vietnamese forces clashed in the Spratlys in February 1988. He was quoted as saying:[181]

> The islands and atolls are under Malaysian sovereignty, and Malaysia has in the past reaffirmed its jurisdiction . . . They are within Malaysia's continental shelf area and Malaysia's sovereignty over them has been officially declared through the new Map of Malaysia, published on December 21st, 1979.

The irony is that if Malaysia's claims to these islands were to be upheld, they could then try to use the islands to claim a separate EEZ that would extend out even further into the SCS. This would expand its territorial baselines out to the Spratlys.

---

[181] Haller-Trost, *The Spratly Islands*, 65.

Beginning in May 1983, Malaysia's case was strengthened because Malaysian military forces occupied three of the islands inside its continental shelf boundaries. With an outpost well established on Swallow Reef, Malaysia can now say that it has effectively occupied these territories. To confirm its hold, Malaysia built a "five-star scuba diving resort."[182] In addition to building an airfield on Swallow Reef to promote tourism, in 1995 Prime Minister Mahathir visited the island to "reaffirm Malaysia's claim to this feature."[183] The Malaysian Foreign Ministry even issued a statement claiming that Swallow Reef "has always been and is part of the territory of Malaysia."[184]

Both China and Vietnam protested Malaysia's decision to occupy Swallow Reef. Malaysia's action spurred a strong Vietnamese response: "Vietnam further developed Amboyna Cay and fortified its infrastructure and increased its military capability there." This action then spurred Malaysia to occupy Mariveles Reef (Terumbu Mantanani in Malay) plus Ardasier Reef (Terumbu Ubi) in 1986. Vietnam protested these actions by Malaysia, and even "warned that it would not hesitate to use military force to enforce its claims to the 'islands'."[185] After the Chinese government adopted their new Law on the Territorial Sea in February 1992, which reiterated the Chinese claim to all of the SCS, the Malaysian government issued a statement on behalf of the Malaysian military: "The Commander of the Malaysian armed forces, Yacob Zain, reacted in March by saying that his country would defend the islands it claimed in the Spratly grouping 'until the last drop of blood'."[186]

---

[182] Yann-huei Song, "Okinotorishima: A 'Rock' or an "Island'? Recent Maritime Boundary Controversy between Japan and Taiwan/China," in Hong and Van Dyke, eds., *Maritime Boundary Disputes*, 176.

[183] Mark J. Valencia, Jon M. Van Dyke and Noel A. Ludwig, *Sharing the Resources of the South China Sea* (Honolulu: University of Hawai'i Press, 1997), 37.

[184] Liselotte Odgaard, *Maritime Security between China and Southeast Asia: Conflict and cooperation in the making of regional order* (Aldershot, UK: Ashgate, 2002), 70–71.

[185] Colonel Suleiman Bin Mahmud, *The South China Sea: Future Concern for Malaysia*, Research Report, Air War College, 1988, 31–32.

[186] "Spratlys Discussed With Malaysian Officials," Hong Kong AFP in English 18 August 1992 transcribed in *Daily Report: China*, 18 August 1992, 10.

In 1999, Malaysia continued its efforts to fortify its claims when it occupied Erica Reef (Terumbu Siput) and Investigator Shoal (Terumbu Peninjau). The Philippines opposed this action, and tried to convince ASEAN to discuss it at its annual meeting. Malaysian Foreign Minister Syed Hamid Albar vetoed this proposal, however, insisting that "bilateral problems should be discussed bilaterally," and he blocked an ASEAN communiqué demanding the halt to occupation and construction of disputed areas. During the same year, China and Malaysia cooperated at the ASEAN Regional Forum (ARF) meeting by insisting that it was not the appropriate forum "for a substantive discussion of the South China Sea dispute."[187] While helping Beijing to undermine multinational efforts to resolve the SCS dispute arguably helped Malaysia obtain its goals at that time, it also worked to China's long-term advantage.

CHINA'S CLAIM

Ever since the end of World War II, first the ROC and later the PRC have claimed all of the SCS as Chinese territory. The PRC and ROC have denounced Malaysia's maps showing a continental shelf line encompassing several of the southern Spratlys. China's and Taiwan's joint claim has been significantly impacted by UNCLOS. Legal specialists now consider that effective occupation is the most reliable mode of territorial acquisition. This is just another way of saying that possession is nine-tenths of the law. Even China, content for decades to let Taiwan's outpost on Itu Aba represent the Chinese presence in the Spratlys, has decided to establish its own island bases in the Spratlys.

Malaysia's claims have put it in direct conflict with several of the other countries, including Brunei, Vietnam, and the Philippines, but Malaysia has only discussed maritime boundary issues with these countries in bilateral negotiations. In 2012, PRC Premier Wen Jiabao appeared to support Malaysia's negotiating methods when he stated "territorial disputes and disputes over maritime rights and interests should be resolved between the countries

---

[187] Mak, "Maritime Security and the ARF," 196.

concerned . . . We disapprove of referring bilateral disputes to multilateral forums."[188]

Unfortunately, bilateral discussions, while possibly easing tensions and lessening the potential for armed clashes, can do little to resolve China's long-term tensions with Malaysia due to the conflicting claims of the other parties to the Spratly dispute. For example, on 23 March 2013, four PLAN ships visited James Shoal, which they call Zengmu Reef, which is just 43 nms (80 kms) from Malaysia. This feature is only 4 degrees north of the equator, and fully 810 nm (1,500 km) south of Woody Island in the Paracels. Chinese sailors on one of the ships, named *Jinggangshan*, reportedly pledged to "defend the South China Sea, maintain national sovereignty and strive towards the dream of a strong China," which resulted in an official protest.[189] A month later, other Chinese ships left steel markers on the shoal, claiming it as Chinese.

China is determined to defend its southernmost claim to James Shoal (Zengmu). During January 2014, three PLAN ships repeated the visit and again pledged to defend James Shoal as part of China's national territory. But James Shoal is completely underwater, so according to UNCLOS it cannot claim any ownership over surrounding waters; it is simply considered to be part of the seabed. Should China declare an Air Defense Identification Zone (ADIZ), as it previously did with the Diaoyu islands (called Senkakus in Japan), then defending this zone would require more local air bases, such as those being built on the Spratly islands.[190]

Sino-Malaysian tensions have remained at a relatively low level since 2014. Their ongoing talks relate to many other outstanding territorial and maritime boundary issues between the two countries, but the Spratly claims are also said to be included in these discussions and so they might set an example for future negotiations. Meanwhile, Malaysia and Brunei have signed

---

[188] Stuart Harris, *China's Foreign Policy* (Cambridge: Polity Press, 2014), 63.
[189] Prashanth Parameswaran, "Malaysia Walks Tightrope on China and the South China Sea," *Jamestown Foundation*, 20 March 2014.
[190] David Archibald, "China's 'Mobile National Territory'," *American Thinker*, 19 May 2014, http://www.americanthinker.com/2014/05/chinas_mobile_national_territory.html [accessed 9 March 2017].

several agreements on the SCS that have resolved their outstanding disputes with regard to each other, but not with regard to the PRC and ROC.

MALAYSIA, BRUNEI, AND THE SOUTH CHINA SEA DISPUTE

Malaysia-Brunei diplomacy has resulted in several bilateral agreements which may have a direct impact on the ongoing SCS dispute. In 1979, Malaysia published a map showing the Malaysia's territorial waters and continental shelf, usually referred to as the Peta Baru or New Map. It showed that Malaysia claimed 12 features in the Spratlys, including Louisa Reef. It has been suggested that Malaysia also occupied Louisa Reef sometime in the 1980s, but this assertion is probably not accurate.

In 1980, the UK, acting on behalf of Brunei, protested the Peta Baru on the basis that Louisa Reef fell within the 1958 delimitation of Brunei's continental shelf. In 1995, Malaysia and Brunei agreed to begin talks to resolve the dispute. In 2000, however, Brunei awarded oil exploration contracts to Blocks J and K in its EEZ to a consortium led by Shell and Total. In 2003, Malaysia retaliated by awarding concessions to its state-owned energy company Petronas plus its partner U.S.-based Murphy Oil. Its two blocks were in almost exactly the same area as Brunei's, but labeled Blocks L and M. In March 2003, however, all exploration work was halted when a Bruneian patrol boat intercepted a drilling ship owned by Murphy Oil, and in April two Malaysian warships prevented a Total chartered vessel from carrying out survey work in the concession. Both countries claimed the oil companies were working illegally in their respective EEZs.

Bilateral negotiations between Malaysi and Brunei took years. After 39 rounds of talks, on 16 March 2009 the Malaysian Prime Minister Abdullah Badawi and Brunei's Sultan Hassanal Bolkiah signed an Exchange of Letters (EoL). The exact contents of the EoL were kept secret. Contemporary press reports speculated, however, that the two countries had reached agreement on four key points: 1) the settlement of maritime boundaries; 2) joint development of offshore energy resources; 3) agreement on resolving their land frontiers; and 4) the right for Malaysian ships to navigate in Bruneian waters.

Controversy erupted when Prime Minister Abdullah later claimed that by signing the EoL Brunei had dropped its claim to the territory of Limbang, a slice of Brunei ceded in 1890 when the White Rajahs of Sarawak forced the Sultan of Brunei to hand it over. This accusation was quickly rejected by Brunei, which claimed that the agreement made no mention of the contested territory. Brunei did agree, however, that the Limbang Question could be settled once the mutual border was finally demarcated. This certainly suggested that Brunei might drop its claim to Limbang in return for Malaysian recognition of its EEZ.

On 21 April 2010, Murphy Oil issued a statement announcing the termination of its contracts for Blocks L and M because they were no longer part of Malaysia. On 29 April 2010, former Prime Minister Mahathir Mohamed accused Abdullah Badwi of forcing Malaysia to lose US$100 billion worth of oil and gas revenues. But in a statement to the media, Abdullah argued that the EoL was not a loss for Malaysia as both countries had agreed to develop jointly the energy resources through the establishment of a Commercial Arrangement Area. Abdullah also acknowledged for the first time that Brunei had "sovereign rights" to the two blocks and that Malaysia and Brunei had agreed to "establish a final and permanent sea boundary." Once the land demarcation process had been completed "there will be no longer any land boundary dispute between Malaysia and Brunei as a whole."[191]

A press statement issued by Malaysia's Ministry of Foreign Affairs a few days later confirmed Abdullah's press release: "Malaysia's oil concession Blocks L and M which coincided with Brunei's Blocks J and K are recognised under the Exchange of Letters as being situated within Brunei's maritime areas and over which Brunei is entitled to exercise sovereign rights under UNCLOS."[192] It

---

[191] Abdullah Ahmad Badawi, "The exchange of letters between Malaysia and Brunei," *The Malaysian Insider*, 1 May 2010.
[192] "Brunei has sovereign rights over 2 oil-rich areas: Wisma Putra," *The Star Online*, 3 May 2010, http://www.thestar.com.my/news/nation/2010/05/03/brunei-has-sovereign-rights-over-2-oilrich-areas-wisma-putra/ [accessed 25 April 2017].

was later revealed that Production Sharing Agreements between Malaysia and Brunei had been signed in September and December 2010 for Blocks CA1 and CA2 (the renamed Blocks J/L and K/M) by which Petronas would have a 10% interest in the former and Murphy Oil a 30% stake in the latter. Drilling in Block CA1 was slated to begin in the third quarter of 2011.

The Joint Malaysia-Brunei Darussalam Land Boundary Technical Committee was due to begin demarcation and survey activities in early 2011 and was expected to complete its work within 18 months. On 11 August 2015, it was reported that Prime Minister Datuk Seri Najib Abdul Razak and the Sultan of Brunei, Sultan Hassanal Bolkiah, expressed satisfaction over the progress of the joint demarcation and survey of the land boundary between Malaysia and Brunei Darussalam, and "urged officials of both countries to intensify their discussions with a view to establishing a memorandum of understanding or other appropriate framework to enable the early operationalisation of the Exchange of Letters' provision on maritime access," plus a "MoU in maritime cooperation."[193] However, reports from October 2016 show that the two countries have yet to reach an acceptable border agreement.[194]

CONCLUSIONS

Malaysia's legal claim to the Spratlys illustrate the importance of occupation as a means of demonstrating sovereignty. On 6 May 2009, Malaysia and Vietnam made a joint submission to the CLCS in respect to an area of seabed in the southern central SCS that did not recognize Brunei's EEZ claim. China protested the joint submission, but interestingly Brunei did not. While legal principles are obviously important in the Spratly dispute, the fact remains that each of the claimants has also felt it necessary to back up legal arguments with a physical presence in the islands.

---

[193] "Malaysia, Brunei reaffirm commitment for further cooperation," *The Sun Daily*, 11 August 2015, http://www.thesundaily.my/news/1516180 [accessed 3 April 2017].
[194] "Malaysia, Brunei to Initiate Discussions on Pan Borneo Highway Network," Bernama.com, 4 October 2016, http://www.bernama.com.my/bernama/v8/ge/newsgeneral.php?id=1288474 [accessed 12 December 2016].

The significance of this gradual expansion of island outposts in the Spratlys was discussed by Korean analyst Choon-Ho Park under the subheading of creeping jurisdiction, when he pointed out that "for purposes of sea boundary delineation in the future, an island will not be defined solely in terms of its physical size or usefulness, because even an obscure low-tide elevation can be reinforced with artificial construction on it."[195] The importance of retaining physical control over specific islands was further emphasized by Martin Katchen: "The Spratly Islands claims have the potential for extending the authority of the nations that hold them across the South China Sea, particularly under the rapid changes being made in the Law of the Sea."[196]

Malaysia is not the only state on the island of Borneo making claims to the SCS. As the next chapter will discuss in greater detail, although Brunei Darussalam has signed an agreement with Malaysia determining their maritime boundary, it has also made territorial claims to at least one island in the SCS called Louisa Reef. This feature was also claimed by Malaysia, but the 2009 EoL agreement ceded Brunei sovereignty to the two oil blocks located in the Louisa Reef, which suggests that Malaysia has also ceded Brunei sovereignty over this feature as well. Meanwhile, China, Taiwan, and Vietnam all have outstanding claims to Louisa Reef.

---

[195] Choon-Ho Park, "The South China Sea Disputes: Who Owns the Islands and the Natural Resources?" in *Ocean Development and International Law* 5 (1978): 45.
[196] Katchen, "The Spratly Islands and the Law of the Sea," 1181.

CHAPTER FIVE

China's Energy Resources Dispute with Brunei

———*———

BRUNEI DARUSSALAM IS a small, but extremely wealthy, Sultanate situated on the northern coast of the island of Borneo. Oil is at the heart of the Sino-Brunei dispute: "Hydrocarbon resources within its jurisdiction are estimated to run out in about 25 years, and Brunei is therefore keen to expand its sovereignty over oil rich areas."[197] Depending on exactly how the PRC's nine-dashed line map is portrayed, Beijing claims as much as 12,600 nm^2 (43,272 km^2) of territory in Brunei's EEZ. This overlap includes Louisa Reef and Rifleman Bank in the Spratly islands.

The Louisa Reef maritime area is the site of the majority of Brunei's offshore oil reserves. In September 1991, China and Brunei opened diplomatic relations after a long delay, in large part due to apprehensions among Brunei's leadership about Beijing's territorial intentions in Southeast Asia.[198] Politically and economically, Brunei's relations with China are less extensive than most of the other members of ASEAN. Bilateral trade between the two countries has increased quickly, despite the dispute over Brunei's oil resources, from about $300 million in 2008 to over a $1 billion in 2010.[199]

Since resolving its problems with Malaysia, Brunei's continuing SCS dispute is principally with the PRC, ROC, and Vietnam. China claims "indisputable sovereignty" over all of the

---

[197] Odgaard, *Maritime Security between China and Southeast Asia*, 80.
[198] Ian Storey, *Southeast Asia and the Rise of China: The Search for Security* (London and New York: Routledge, 2011), 268–273.
[199] "Brunei-China trade exceeds US$1b goal," *The Brunei Times*, 8 March 2011, http://www.bt.com.bn/business-national/2011/03/08/brunei-china-trade-exceeds-us-1b-goal [accessed 20 May 2013].

Spratlys, yet to date has not lodged a full submission with the United Nations CLCS, so its exact sovereignty claims remains unclear. This chapter will examine Brunei's claims in the South China Sea first.

BRUNEI'S SCS CLAIMS

During 1945, while still a British colony, the British government extended the boundaries of Borneo to include the continental shelf. Following independence, the Brunei government issued three maps in the late 1980s outlining the country's maritime claims: the Map Showing Territorial Waters of Brunei Darussalam (1987); Map Showing Continental Shelf of Brunei Darussalam (1988); and Map Showing Fishery Limits of Brunei Darussalam (1988).[200] These three maps together outlined a rectangular exclusive economic zone (EEZ) stretching 200 nautical miles from Brunei's coast, plus a continental shelf extending even further.

Contained within Brunei's EEZ and continental shelf claim are two features generally considered to be part of the Spratlys: 1) Louisa Reef (Terumbu Semarang Barat Kecil in Malay and Nan Tong Jiao in Chinese) and 2) Rifleman Bank (Bai Vung May in Vietnamese, Nanwei Tan in Chinese).[201] Louisa Reef lies 120 nm north of Brunei. The reef is only 1.24 miles long east to west and 0.6 miles wide from north to south. Since it is submerged at high tide, it is incapable of generating a maritime zone let alone a 200 nm EEZ. Moreover, under international law it remains unclear whether low-tide elevations can even be included within a state's sovereign waters. Nevertheless, Louisa Reef is also claimed by China, and Taiwan, and Vietnam.

Brunei has never formally lodged a claim to Louisa Reef. One scholar reports: "Brunei apparently does not consider this submerged feature as an island subject to territorial sovereignty claims."[202] In January 1992, *The Borneo Bulletin* reported that Foreign Minister Prince Mohamed Bolkiah had stated that Brunei

---

[200] Ian Storey, "Brunei's Contested Sea Border with China," in Elleman, et al., *Beijing's Power and China's Borders*, 38.
[201] Valencia, et al., *Sharing the Resources of the South China Sea*, 232.
[202] Odgaard, *Maritime Security between China and Southeast Asia*, 103.

was only claiming the seas surrounding Louisa Reef, and not the feature itself.[203] However, according to Ian Storey, officials from the Ministry of Foreign Affairs told him that Brunei does claim sovereignty over Louisa Reef.[204]

Brunei is the only South China Sea claimant not to have occupied or garrisoned any of the Spratly islands. Various observers have claimed that Malaysia "occupied" Louisa Reef in 1983 and constructed a lighthouse, and that in 1988 China planted a marker on the reef that was subsequently removed by Malaysia.[205] In fact, Malaysian troops have never been stationed on the reef and there is no hard evidence of a Malaysian-constructed lighthouse.

Brunei's claim to Rifleman Bank is also unclear. This feature lies at the edge of the country's continental shelf claim. According to Brunei's preliminary submission to the CLCS on 12 May 2009 the country's continental shelf extended beyond the 200 nm territorial sea. Exactly how far is still unclear, but Rifleman Bank is 242 nm (448 km) from Brunei's coastline.[206] To make the situation even more complicated, Rifleman Bank is also a low-tide elevation and thus not open to a sovereignty claim. Also, according to at least one source, Rifleman Bank was "occupied" by Vietnam in 1983.[207]

CHINA'S SCS CLAIM

China maintains that it has indisputable sovereignty over all the islands in the SCS and has historic rights to their adjacent waters. Attached to China's protest note in response to the joint

---

[203] "Brunei seeks security network," *The Borneo Bulletin*, 27 January 1992.
[204] Ian Storey interview with anonymous senior officials at the Ministry of Foreign Affairs, Brunei, 6–7 April 2011, Storey, "Brunei's Contested Sea Border with China," in Elleman, et al., *Beijing's Power and China's Borders*, 38.
[205] Greg Austin, *China's Ocean Frontier: International Law, Military Force and National Development* (St. Leonards, NSW: Allen & Unwin, 1998), 155.
[206] Brunei Darussalam's Preliminary Submission concerning the Outer Limits of its Continental Shelf, 12 May 2009, http://www.un.org/Depts/los/clcs_new/submissions_files/preliminary/brn2009preliminaryinformation.pdf [accessed 26 April 2017].
[207] Valencia et al., *Sharing the Resources of the South China Sea*, 232.

Vietnam-Malaysia submission to the CLCS in May 2009 was a map containing the nine-dotted line stretching from Taiwan to the Paracel Islands. China has yet to clarify what the nine segments mean or how they can be justified under UNCLOS. If the fifth and sixth segments are joined together, the line comes within approximately 40 miles of Brunei's coastline. This suggests that China does not recognize Brunei's EEZ claim and that it claims sovereignty over both Louisa Reef and Rifleman Bank.

Unlike China, Malaysia appears to have conceded its former claim to Louisa Reef to Brunei. By means of the above-mentioned 2009 EoL signed by Brunei and Malaysia, the Malaysian government recognized Brunei's EEZ and its sovereign rights to resources there. Although this pertains just to the water portion of Brunei's territory, it suggests that the Malaysian government has also dropped its demand for Louisa Reef. China did not protest the 2009 EoL. Vietnam, however, may still want Louisa Reef. Hanoi maintains indisputable sovereignty over all the Spratlys. However, Brunei's main concern is the joint PRC-ROC claim to the entire SCS. Malaysia and Brunei released a statement in September 2010 holding out the possibility of future cooperation beyond the two blocks with a "third country" but whether this meant China or not was unclear.[208]

In the past, China's leaders have raised the issue of shelving sovereignty claims and engaging in joint exploitation of maritime resources in the SCS with their Bruneian counterparts. On the sidelines of the 2006 ASEAN-China Summit in Nanning, for instance, Chinese Premier Wen Jiabao reiterated the utility of this formula to Sultan Hassanal Bolkiah.[209] Significantly, however, Brunei has remained silent on the possibility of joint exploration with the PRC in the disputed waters of the SCS.

---

[208] Joint Statement on the 14th Annual Leaders Consultation between Malaysia and Brunei Darussalam, 21 September 2010, http://bruneiembassy.be/joint-statement-on-the-14th-annual-leaders%E2%80%99-consultation-between-malaysia-and-brunei-darussalam/ [accessed 31 October 2011].

[209] "Brunei, China eye trade boost," *The Borneo Bulletin*, 1 November 2006.

RECENT DIPLOMACY

Not surprising, considering the small size of its military, Brunei's approach to the SCS territorial disputes puts a strong emphasis on diplomacy over military action. Brunei has sent representatives since the early 1990s to participate in the Indonesian sponsored workshops on the SCS. In 1992, Brunei supported the ASEAN Declaration on the SCS. In 1995 it sided with ASEAN when it issued a statement of "serious concern" following China's occupation of Philippine-claimed Mischief Reef.[210] In August 2002, Foreign Minister Tang Jiaxuan submitted a "New Security Concept" paper at the ARF meeting in Brunei that urged ASEAN nations to work together with China.[211] Brunei is also a signatory to the November 2002 ASEAN-China Declaration on the Conduct of Parties in the South China Sea (DoC), as well as a party to discussions on drawing up CoC guidelines to implement the DoC (see Document 19).

Economic relations between Brunei and the PRC are generally good. Chinese President Hu Jintao visited Brunei in April 2005, in part to sponsor continued purchases of oil. In November 2000, China agreed to purchase 10,000 barrels per day of "high-quality crude" from Brunei, and this doubled in 2004, which equalled 10% of Brunei's production. China has also expressed interest in investing in Brunei's oil industry.[212] Meanwhile, the Chinese Zhejiang Hengyi Group is constructing a new oil refinery in Brunei with a yearly capacity of 148,000 bbl/d; when completed in 2019, Brunei's trade with China is "expected to reach Japanese levels over the next few years."[213]

On 5 April 2013, the Sultan of Brunei Hassanal Bolkiah visited Beijing and met with President Xi Jinping. A joint statement was issued detailing their relations "on the basis of the principle

---

[210] "ASEAN ministers express concern over Spratlys," *Reuters News Service*, 18 March 1995.
[211] Bronson Percival, *The Dragon Looks South: China and Southeast Asia in the New Century* (Westport, CN: Praeger Security International 2007), 80.
[212] Percival, *The Dragon Looks South*, 73.
[213] MarEx, "Brunei: Asia's Newest Trade Hub," *The Maritime Executive*, 24 February 2016, http://www.maritime-executive.com/article/brunei-asias-newest-trade-hub [accessed 10 April 2017].

of mutual respect, equality and mutual benefit. It specified that cooperation will not affect the respective maritime rights and interests of the two countries." This led to a Joint Statement on 11 October 2013 saying the two sides "agreed to enhance maritime cooperation to promote joint development." Soon afterward, the China National Offshore Oil Company (CNOOC) and the Brunei National Petroleum Company Sendirian Berhad (Petroleum-BRUNEI) set up a joint venture whereby China would provide Brunei with various "oil field services."[214]

When compared to the Philippines and other SCS countries, Brunei appears to be getting preferential treatment from Beijing. This is due to Brunei's oil: "Though China displays a traditional tendency to pick on a militarily and economically weak rival, Brunei does not share the same unfortunate fate as the Philippines because China, driven by its insatiable thirst for energy resources, has actively sought to improve bilateral relations over the last decade." In this regard, Brunei has "benefitted from China's policy to enhance its energy security."[215]

BRUNEI DEFENSE POSTURE

Brunei has a very small military. But in the face of rapid military modernization programs by China, Brunei's 2007 White Paper highlighted the vital importance of the Royal Brunei Armed Forces' (RBAF) in defending the country's offshore maritime resources. Specifically, the defense policy noted the critical role in exercising control over the country's "border and adjacent maritime areas." The Royal Brunei Navy (RBN) commissioned three Darussalam-class offshore patrol boats and four Ijhtihad-class fast attack boats.[216] Over time, all maritime patrol craft would be replaced with new small and medium-sized patrol boats able

---

[214] Carlyle A. Thayer, "South China Sea Tensions," in Tran Truong Thuy and Le Thuy Trang, eds., *Power, Law, and Maritime Order in the South China Sea*, 26.
[215] Irene Chan and Li Mingjiang, "Political will and joint development in the South China Sea," in Wu Shicun and Hong Nong, eds., *Recent Developments in the South China Sea Dispute*, 192.
[216] Storey, "Brunei's Contested Sea Border with China," in Elleman, et al., *Beijing's Power and China's Borders*, 43.

to operate more effectively "out to the limits" of the country's EEZ.[217] This distinction certainly suggests that Brunei is prepared to defend Louisa Reef but not necessarily Rifleman Bank.

In April 2013, ASEAN leaders met again in Brunei for their annual summit. On 13 May 2013, Prime Minister Shinzo Abe met Sultan Hassanal Bolkiah during a summit in Tokyo, where they discussed ongoing disputes in the SCS. Abe urged the Sultan to cooperate in countering China's growing maritime ambitions, based on the "five principles of Japan's ASEAN diplomacy" released during his January 2013 visit to Indonesia. These principles advocate "protecting the free and open seas as common goods, which are governed by laws and rules and not by might."[218]

Brunei maintains close defense links with Singapore, the UK, Australia, and the United States, which provide the country with additional hedging options *vis-à-vis* the PRC. In 1994, an MOU on Defense Cooperation was signed with the United States, and the Brunei military holds annual exercises with U.S. military forces. In addition, three students from Brunei are studying in U.S. military institutions. But Brunei has been conspicuously silent about the recent UN ruling, which suggests that it is tacitly backing Beijing's position.

CONCLUSION

Brunei and China potentially have serious territorial and sovereignty tensions in the SCS. Both countries claim sovereignty over Louisa Reef and Rifleman Bank in the Spratlys. However, Brunei and China's maritime claims remain ambiguous and the two countries have sought to increase their bilateral economic relations, in particular with regard to oil purchases. Important Chinese leaders like Hu Jintao, Jia Qinling, Sun Jiazheng, and Yang Jiechi have

---

[217] *Shaping the Force Today: Defence White Paper Update 2007* (Brunei: Ministry of Defence, 2007) http://www.mindef.gov.bn/new_home/whitepaper2007/english.pdf.
[218] "Abe asks Brunei to help check China's influence," *The Asahi Shimbun*, 14 May 2013, http://ajw.asahi.com/article/asia/south_east_asia/AJ201305140076 [accessed 20 May 2013].

"kept up efforts to improve relations with Brunei . . . particularly in the energy sector."[219]

Brunei's most serious territorial dispute by far was with its near neighbor Malaysia. As the 2009 EoL between Brunei and Malaysia demonstrated, diplomatic resolution of these intricate SCS claims and counterclaims was possible. With this agreement with Malaysia as a possible example, Brunei might be willing to discuss joint development of offshore energy resources with a third party, which most likely refers to the PRC.

Unlike with its near neighbors the Philippines and Vietnam, the SCS dispute does not seem to be as important to Sino-Brunei relations. Within ASEAN, Brunei seldom takes the lead on matters pertaining to the SCS, and Brunei remains committed to diplomacy rather than force to resolve this SCS dispute. As the next chapter will discuss in greater detail, even though it has experienced fishing disputes with China the Indonesian government has not even agreed that negotiations with China are a possibility.

---

[219] Irene Chan and Li Mingjiang, "Political will and joint development in the South China Sea," in Wu Shicun and Hong Nong, eds., *Recent Developments in the South China Sea Dispute*, 192.

CHAPTER SIX

China's Natuna Island Fishing Dispute with Indonesia

———*———

INDONESIA CLAIMS THAT it does not border on China, but the PRC argues that the two countries overlap in the southwestern corner of the SCS where the Natuna Island Group (called Pulau Sekatung in Indonesia) is located. The maritime territory under dispute could be as great as 28,500 nm^2 (98,000 km^2).[220] While Indonesia has repeatedly rejected all Chinese invitations to engage in bilateral negotiations, a series of incidents regarding illegal Chinese fishing activities in the Natuna Sea may force Indonesia and China to open talks.

The Natuna islands are an archipelago of more than 200 islands located in Riau province about 800 miles north of Jakarta. It is unclear whether Indonesia actually shares a boundary with China. Indonesia officially recognizes ten neighbors, but not China. Indonesia shares land boundaries with three neighbors – Malaysia in Borneo, Timor-Leste in Timor Island, and Papua New Guinea on the island of New Guinea – and has seven maritime neighbors: from west to east they are India, Thailand, Singapore, Vietnam, the Philippines, Palau, and Australia.

Disputes over fishing are the main problems. But offshore oil fields adjacent to the Natuna islands may also become an important source of Sino-Indonesian conflict, since China and Indonesia have both claimed oil resources in the southern part of the SCS. The offshore fields near the Natuna islands are estimated to contain 46 trillion cubic feet of recoverable reserves of natural gas, and are of considerably economic importance to Indonesia.[221] Beijing

---

[220] I Made Andi Arsana and Clive Schofield, "Indonesia's 'Invisible' Border with China," in Elleman, et al., *Beijing's Power and China's Borders*, 61.
[221] Energy Information Administration, http://www.eia.gov/emeu/cabs/South_China_Sea/OilNaturalGas.html.

argues there is a maritime conflict that requires delimitation while Jakarta insists there is no overlap.

THE INDONESIAN CLAIM

Indonesia has more island borders than almost any other country. For this reason, it was closely involved with the drafting of the UNCLOS convention in 1982 so that it would include the concept of an archipelagic state. Indonesia signed the Convention in 1985 and ratified it in 1986.[222] Indonesia's maritime claims extend from baselines defined around the Natuna islands northward to the SCS. Jakarta has concluded maritime boundary agreements with Malaysia and Vietnam in the same areas that are potentially being claimed by China. To date, Indonesia has rejected all Chinese overtures to engage in bilateral negotiations.

The history of Indonesia's claim over maritime areas goes back to the late 1930s, when it was part of the Dutch East Indies. A Dutch claim was made in the *Territoriale Zee en Maritieme Kringen Ordonnantie 1939*, or Ordinance of Territorial Sea and Maritime Environment 1939. This was the last regulation produced by the Dutch East Indies concerning territorial seas prior to the 1945 independence of Indonesia. After independence, the Indonesian government was obliged by the Roundtable Conference involving Indonesia and the Netherlands in The Hague to recognize the legality of this ordinance, which is contained in the 1949 Agreement of the Transitional Measures.

As a result of this treaty, in 1949 Indonesia recognized a 3 nm territorial sea, measured from the low-water mark, which meant it could not contain the archipelago within a single jurisdiction. This fact led Indonesia to issue the Djuanda Declaration on 13 December 1957, named after Indonesian Prime Minister Ir. H Djuanda Kartawidjaja. It supported the concept known as an archipelagic state. Its official title was *Government Declaration concerning the Water Areas of the Republic of Indonesia*. This act

---

[222] Chronological lists of ratifications of, accessions, and successions to the Convention and the related Agreements as of 23 May 2017, http://www.un.org/Depts/los/reference_files/chronological_lists_of_ratifications.htm [accessed 20 September 2017].

defined archipelagic baselines for the whole archipelago, and claimed a 12 nm territorial sea measured from the archipelagic baseline. In 1960, Indonesia established its archipelagic baselines, which enclosed the Natuna islands. The latest version of Indonesia's archipelagic baselines was revised by Government Regulation number 37 of 2008, and deposited with the United Nations Secretary-General on 11 March 2009, accompanied by a map illustrating the baselines, consisting of 195 points.[223]

While continental shelf entitlements have been delimited with Malaysia and Vietnam, EEZs have yet to be determined and any potential overlap with China's claims on behalf of the Spratlys have not been addressed. Indonesia has made an unilateral EEZ claim in the SCS, as depicted in the official map of the Republic of Indonesia. Jakarta has also defined a Fisheries Management Area through the Ministry of Marine Affairs and Fisheries (MMAF), also known as *Wilayah Pengelolaan Perikanan* (WPP).[224] Indonesia's unilateral EEZ claim extends well to the north and east of its agreed continental shelf boundaries with Malaysia and Vietnam.

Indonesia does not claim any of the features among the Spratlys, but it has contested several other islands with neighboring states. When Indonesia and Malaysia disputed control over the islands of Sipadan and Ligitan, the International Court of Justice (ICJ) determined in 2002 that "Malaysia had better title and awarded the two islands to Malaysia."[225] Because Indonesia lost when it went to the ICJ before, in 2005 Indonesian and Malaysian warships engaged "in 'confrontational' manoeuvres in the contested Ambalat zone, off the eastern Sabah coast."[226] In May 2014, there was a reported violation – the building of an unauthorized lighthouse – by the Malaysian Navy in Indonesian claimed waters near

---

[223] http://www.un.org/Depts/los/LEGISLATIONANDTREATIES/STATEFILES/IDN.htm [accessed 20 September 2017].

[224] MMAF 2009. Ministry of Marine affairs and Fisheries' Regulation number 1 of 2009. At http://www.infohukum.kk go.id/files_permen/PER%2001%20 MEN%202009.pdf [accessed 22 March 2011].

[225] B. A. Hamzah, "US-Sino relations: impact on security in the South China Sea," in Wu Shicun and Nong Hong, eds., *Recent Developments in the South China Sea Dispute*, 23.

[226] Mak, "Maritime Security and the ARF," 196.

Tanjung Datak Island, located on the border between Indonesia's West Kalimantan and Malaysia's Sarawak.[227] Indonesia's archipelagic baselines conflict with China's 9-dash map. In a 8 July 2010 note submitted to the Secretary-General of the United Nations, Indonesia challenged this map: "Thus far, there is no clear explanation as to the legal basis, the method of drawing, and the status of those separated dotted-lines." It concluded, therefore, that the nine-dashed map "lacks international legal basis" under the 1982 UNCLOS agreement.[228] Jakarta refuses to acknowledge China's maritime claim in the SCS, and the recent decision of the UN Arbitration panel would appear to confirm Indonesia's position.

CHINESE CLAIMS IN THE SCS

Even though it is well over a thousand miles away, China now claims large portions of the SCS near the Natuna islands as historic waters. Its maritime borders in the SCS are defined by the "nine-dashed line" or "U-shape line." This map was first published in 1947 and was called *The Location Map of the South China Sea Islands* or *Nanhai zhudao weizhi tu* in Chinese.[229] In addition to claiming all islands, Beijing appears to be claiming all of the maritime area enclosed by the nine-dashed line, which is close to Indonesia's Natuna islands.

Since this map's publication, there have been hotly contested debates about the true meaning of the nine-dashed line on the Chinese map. While it is certain that China claims sovereignty over small island features in the region, including Pratas Island, the Paracel islands, the Spratly islands, Scarborough

---

[227] "Malaysia Allegedly Builds Lighthouse on Indonesian Island," *Jakarta Post*, 19 May 2014, http://www.thejakartapost.com/news/2014/05/19/malaysia-allegedly-builds-lighthouse-indonesian-island.html [accessed 13 March 2017].
[228] Note from the Permanent Mission of Indonesian to the United Nations to the Secretary-General of the United Nations, 8 July 2010, No. 840/POL-703/VII/10, http://www.un.org/Depts/los/clcs_new/submissions_files/mysvnm33_09/idn_2010re_mys_vnm_e.pdf [accessed 25 April 2017].
[229] Arsana and Schofield, "Indonesia's 'Invisible' Border with China," in Elleman, et al, *Beijing's Power and China's Borders*, 64.

Shoal, James Shoal, and Macclesfield Bank, one unanswered question is whether the line is also China's maritime border in the SCS. Some say that the line is only to the claimed land territory – that is, to the disputed islands – while others state that China is claiming the water column encompassed by the nine-dashed line. Chinese scholars have concluded that the nine-dashed line "had a dual nature" – to define Chinese sovereignty over the islands in the SCS and to serve as Chinese maritime boundary.[230]

Recent events have shed light on the Chinese claims. In response to an extended continental shelf (ECS) submission on the part of Vietnam, as well as one by Malaysia and Vietnam jointly, China issued protest notes to the United Nations' Secretary-General, stating that China held sovereignty over the disputed islands of the SCS and their "adjacent waters" and that China also "enjoys sovereign rights and jurisdiction over the relevant waters as well as the seabed and subsoil thereof."[231] This language appears to be consistent with a claim to sovereignty over both the disputed islands and to the entire sea area.

China says that its territory touches Indonesia, but the Indonesian government disagrees. Indonesia does not officially recognize China as its neighbor. In particular, if the PRC's claim over land territory in the SCS and its "nine-dashed line" were ever recognized internationally then this would require that maritime boundaries be negotiated. If Chinese sovereignty over the Spratlys were confirmed, its maritime entitlements measured from these features would also likely overlap with those of Indonesia.

MARITIME DELIMITATION IN THE SOUTHERN SOUTH CHINA SEA

Since 1960, Indonesia has concluded seventeen maritime boundary agreements with most of its neighbors. Indonesia has settled

---

[230] Li Jinming and Li Dexia, "The Dotted Line on the Chinese Map of the South China Sea: A Note," *Ocean Development & International Law*, 34 (2003), 287.
[231] Note from the Permanent Mission of the People's Republic of China to the United Nations to the Secretary-General of the United Nations, 7 May 2009, No. CML/17/2009. http://www.un.org/Depts/los/clcs_new/submissions_files/mysvnm33_09/chn_2009re_mys_vnm_e.pdf [accessed 3 April 2017].

maritime boundaries in the SCS in the vicinity of Natuna Sea with both Malaysia and Vietnam. Seabed boundary agreements have also been signed with Malaysia and Vietnam. Finally, in 2009, the MMAF's Regulation on Fisheries Management Area further confirmed Indonesia's position. Indonesia's official map depicting Indonesia's unilateral EEZ claim in the SCS has not been protested by its neighbors.

On 27 October 1969, Indonesia's first maritime boundary agreement on seabed boundary was signed with Malaysia. In 1971, this agreement was extended to serve as a three junction point of Indonesia-Thailand-Malaysia seabed boundaries. The 1969 agreement also defined a western line between peninsula Malaysia and the Natunas, and an eastern line between Malaysian territories on Borneo and Indonesian possessions, including the Natuna islands. The terminal points of these boundaries stop at two locations in the SCS. On 11 June 2003, these two boundary lines were connected to each other by a continental shelf boundary line between Indonesia and Vietnam just to the north of the Natuna islands. The Indonesia-Vietnam continental shelf boundary agreement was signed on 26 June 2003 and was ratified by Indonesia on 15 March 2007.

The 2003 Indonesia-Vietnam agreement applied only to the seabed. Even though these seabed delimitations involving Indonesia, Malaysia, and Vietnam took place within China's nine-dashed line, Beijing did not protest. In particular, Indonesia did not recognize China's claim over maritime area enclosed in the nine-dashed line in its official note of 8 July 2010.[232] Vietnam, for its part, has been absolutely clear that it will not recognize China's maritime claims in the SCS, and Hanoi calls China's map "null and void."[233] If one assumes that the nine-dashed line is intended to claim maritime areas, there are many potentially overlapping claim areas for

---

[232] Note from the Permanent Mission of Indonesian to the United Nations to the Secretary-General of the United Nations, 8 July 2010, No. 840/POL-703/VII/10, http://www.un.org/Depts/los/clcs_new/submissions_files/mysvnm33_09/idn_2010re_mys_vnm_e.pdf [accessed 3 April 2017].

[233] Note sent by the Permanent Mission of Vietnam to the United Nations to the Secretary General of the United Nations. http://www.un.org/Depts/los/clcs_new/submissions_files/mysvnm33_09/vnm_chn_2009re_mys_vnm_e.pdf [accessed 3 April 2017].

both continental shelf and EEZ in the SCS. Although the UN Arbitration panel has determined that China cannot make such claims, to date Beijing has ignored this ruling.

POLITICAL, ECONOMIC, AND MILITARY RELATIONS

Politically, Indonesia and China have had a rocky bilateral relationship after opening diplomatic ties on 13 April 1950. Relations were severed on 30 October 1967 due to concerns over the spread of Communism to Indonesia, and were only resumed 23 years later on 8 August 1990. This event was marked by a visit by the Foreign Minister of Indonesia, Ali Alatas, to China, and by the signing of a Memorandum of Understanding (MOU) on the Resumption of Diplomatic Relations. Since the reopening of diplomatic ties, the China-Indonesia relationship has included frequent high-level exchanges. The two countries even signed a "strategic partnership agreement" in 2005. This agreement was considered to be "the first such agreement between China and a Southeast Asian state."[234]

Oil exploration began during the 1960s around the Natuna islands. In October 1979, Pertamina, the Indonesian national oil company, announced that Gulf Oil had been awarded a contract to explore just northeast of the islands, and then in December 1979 Mobil Oil also purchased exploration rights. In 2004, the PRC imported $1.17 billion of Indonesian oil and natural gas. Long-term gas sales reportedly included an agreement to export 1 million tons of natural gas to Fujian province per year for twenty years.[235] This led to other types of agreements, including defense cooperation in 2007 and an extradition agreement in 2009.[236]

---

[234] Keith Loveard, "The Thinker: Caution Over Natuna," *The Jakarta Globe*, 2 July 2009, http://www.thejakartaglobe.com/columns/the-thinker-caution-over-natuna/315800

[235] Percival, *The Dragon Looks South*, 67.

[236] "South China Sea dispute a potential rift in RI-China ties: Envoy," *The Jakarta Post*, 25 May 2010, http://www.thejakartapost.com/news/2010/05/25/south-china-sea-dispute-a-potential-rift-richina-ties-envoy.html [accessed 3 April 2017].

Indonesia's foreign trade with China is very important. Indonesia is well aware that it would have much to lose if relations with China become tense:[237]

> China has pledged US$19 billion of investment credit and US$9 billion loans for infrastructure development in Indonesia. In defence, too, China and Indonesia have established cooperation, among other things, on joint naval missile development and production. Beijing also offered to build a coastal surveillance system in Indonesia worth US$158 million to supplement the existing systems provided by the U.S., worth only US$57 million. In addition, both countries agreed to establish the Indonesia-China Centre for Ocean and Climate (ICCOC) for oceanography and weather research, with the Natuna Islands as one of its locations. As discussed by Ristian Atriandi Supriyanto, Indonesia's cooperation with China is not exclusive: "Jakarta reckons its interests would be best served if it maintains a strategic independence by forging partnerships with multiple powers."

China exports manufactured goods to Indonesia, while Indonesia exports mainly natural resources, such as coal and nickel, to China. Many Chinese businesses have also opened manufacturing plants in Indonesia.

Since the resumption of relations, the volume of bilateral trade has risen significantly from $1.18 billion in 1990 to $7.464 billion in 2000. Due to the global economic slowdown at that time, the bilateral trade volume in 2001 decreased slightly to $6.725 billion, but increased again during the first half of 2002. After hitting a high of almost $23 Billion in exports to China in 2011, it has now leveled off at around $17 billion per year.[238] For Indonesia, in 2014 China was the 2nd largest trade partner after Japan for exports, at US$17 billion, and the first for imports at over US $30 billion.[239]

---

[237] Ristian Atriandi Supriyanto, "Indonesia's South China Sea Dilemma: Between Neutrality and Self-Interest," *RSIS Commentaries*, 12 July 2012, http://www.rsis.edu.sg/publications/Perspective/RSIS1262012.pdf [accessed 21 May 2013].
[238] Indonesia Exports to China, http://www.tradingeconomics.com/indonesia/exports-to-china [accessed 3 April 2017].
[239] World Bank, Country Snapshot. http://wits.worldbank.org/CountrySnapshot/en/IDN/textview [accessed 21 February 2017].

Contrary to Indonesia's official view, which is that there is no maritime dispute between Indonesia and China, a map produced by the Chinese delegation as early as at a Surabaya workshop in 1993 showed the country's historic waters overlapping with the Natuna islands' EEZ. Immediately after the Surabaya workshop, Foreign Minister Ali Alatas protested to Beijing, asking the Chinese government to clarify its position. Beijing supported negotiations to settle the problem, but Jakarta rejected China's offer to negotiate the issue, since this would imply that China might have a valid claim. As Alatas reiterated, "repetition of an untruth will eventually make it appear as truth."[240] In 1996, Indonesia conducted a major military exercise in the Natuna islands, apparently to send a message to China that it was committed to defending its sovereign rights there.

Indonesia refuses to acknowledge that China has a valid fishing claim. But on 20 June 2009, a dispute erupted when eight vessels and approximately 75 fishermen from China were detained by an Indonesian patrol vessel just north of the Natunas. According to Indonesia's description, the Chinese fishermen were caught fishing illegally in the Indonesian EEZ.[241] Beijing argued that the detainment of its fishermen took place in China's traditional fishing grounds, and "demanded the immediate release of the men and their boats."[242] The Indonesian Ambassador to Beijing insisted that Indonesia could punish the Chinese fishermen for illegal fishing. After talks were opened, however, Indonesia agreed to release 59 of the 75 fishermen on 10 July 2009. A total of 16 fishermen were detained, which was a compromise to maintain friendly relationship with Beijing. The absence of any further official reports on this incident suggests that it has been quietly dropped.

During 2010, other fishing incidents in the SCS involved Chinese fishermen. On 15 May 2010, two out of three Chinese

---

[240] Paul Jacob, "Alatas Downplays China's Claims in Natuna Islands Map," *Straits Times*, 4 June 1995, 2.
[241] "China protests arrest of fishermen," *The Jakarta Post*, 23 June 2009. According to Indonesia, the number of fishermen was 77 instead of 75.
[242] "China 'dissatisfied' with Indonesia over detention of fishermen," *Xinhua*, 25 June 2009, https://chineseindonesian.wordpress.com/2009/06/26/china-dissatisfied-with-indonesia-over-detention-of-fishermen/ [accessed 25 April 2017].

fishing boats operating in Indonesia's EEZ were seized, but an armed Chinese patrol vessel threatened the Indonesian patrol vessels, forcing their release. On 22 June 2010, Indonesia again seized Chinese fishing vessels, but a Chinese fishery administration vessel once again appeared and demanded their release. Out-gunned, the Indonesians decided to release the Chinese. In November 2012, the Department of Marine and Fisheries of West Kalimantan reportedly arrested six foreign ships fishing illegally in the Natuna islands.

On 29 January 2013, the Chinese government identified nine areas in Natuna's sovereign waters that it claims are traditional fishing areas. Indonesian National Army (TNI) Commander Admiral Agus Suhartono stated that "TNI is anticipating China's possible claim over the waters as their territory," but in response, the Admiral asserted that "TNI has been increasing the strength of its Navy and Army guarding the Natuna area."[243] During March 2016, when Beijing again declared that the waters around the Natunas were part of its "traditional fishing grounds," President Joko Widodo visited the area during June 2016 in an Indonesia warship, a trip that "appeared to many as a veiled response to Beijing's claim."[244]

The Indonesian military is too weak to oppose China alone. In 1992, Jakarta bought one-third of the former East German Navy, which included 39 ships, but these are all obsolete. Its total force of 65,000, which includes marines and aviation, is split up into two fleets. While boasting 2 submarines and 11 frigates, none of these assets can stand up against the PLAN. In recent years, Jakarta also has purchased four Dutch-built corvettes and five Korea-built amphibious landing vessels. By far the largest problem is the size of its coastline, which is third longest in the world after

---

[243] Francisco Rosarians, Aseanty Pahlevi, "TNI guards Natuna, fearing China's claim," AsiaViews, 30 January 2013, http://www.asiaviews.org/headlines/1-headlines/41724-tni-guards-natuna-fearing-chinas-claim [accessed 21 May 2013].

[244] Francis Chan, "Indonesia blows up and sinks another 81 fishing boats for poaching," *The Straits Times*, 2 April 2017, http://www.straitstimes.com/asia/se-asia/indonesia-blows-up-and-sinks-another-81-fishing-boats-for-poaching [accessed 3 April 2017].

Canada and Norway, at 54,716 km. In order to coordinate patrols, Indonesia has an integrated maritime surveillance system, paid for by the U.S. government to combat piracy. Although it is comparative weak militarily, the Indonesian government wants to avoid acknowledging the legitimacy of China's maritime claims. In 1995, Minister Alatas stated: "On Natuna, there is no claim from China and there has never been a problem between China and Indonesia. So there is no question to be discussed."[245] But in 2010, Indonesia's Navy Chief of Staff, Agus Suhartono, acknowledged that Indonesia and China should settle their maritime boundaries in the overlapping EEZ. This suggests that overlapping maritime claims do exist between Indonesia and China in the SCS.

CONCLUSIONS

Indonesia's determination is that it has only ten neighbors and China is not one of them. Indonesia has rejected the validity of China's maritime claim in the SCS since the 1990s. To date, Indonesia's seabed delimitation with Malaysia in 1969, and Vietnam in 2003, have not been protested by China. However, Chinese claims appear to impact not just sovereignty over land territory in the SCS but also over adjacent waters, seabed, and subsoil. Disputes over fishing grounds are particularly sharp. While it appears unlikely that Indonesia and China will enter into negotiations any time soon to delimit a maritime boundary, they must first clarify each other's maritime claim in the SCS.

For Jakarta, the presence of Chinese fishermen guarded by Chinese fisheries administration vessels around the Natuna islands clearly demonstrates Beijing's aggression. Halting illegal fishing activities in the Natuna islands is of great importance for Indonesia. On 1 April 2017, it was announced that Indonesia blew up and sank 81 fishing boats caught poaching in its waters, bringing the number of destroyed ships up to 317 since October 2014: Vietnam (142), the Philippines (76), Malaysia (49), and China (1). Maritime

---

[245] Simon Sinaga, "No Problem with China over Natuna Isles, Says Alatas," *Straits Times*, 27 June 1995, 15.

Affairs and Fisheries Minister Susi Pudjiastuti called it "a victory for Indonesia's war against illegal fishing," and said: "There was a time when thousands of foreign vessels came freely to steal our fish, but now they will know, Indonesia will overcome this crime."[246]

Indonesia has made its claims public, while Beijing has yet to explain the exact meaning of the nine-dash map, a map that has been consistently rejected by neighboring states. The UN tribunal's decision that China's map is invalid helps Indonesia. As noted by Nien-Tsu Alfred Hu about the SCS in general, it is primarily "political will" that is the key to turning the SCS from "troubled waters" into a "sea of opportunity."[247] The question of political will also applies to Taiwan's relations with the PRC.

---

[246] Francis Chan, "Indonesia blows up and sinks another 81 fishing boats for poaching," *The Straits Times*, 2 April 2017, http://www.straitstimes.com/asia/se-asia/indonesia-blows-up-and-sinks-another-81-fishing-boats-for-poaching [accessed 3 April 2017].

[247] Nien-Tsu Alfred Hu and Ted L. McDorman, *Maritime Issues in the South China Sea: Troubled Waters or A Sea of Opportunity* (New York: Routledge Press, 2013), 9. Thanks to I Made Andi Arsana and Clive Schofield for helping me locate this citation.

CHAPTER SEVEN

China's Sovereignty Disputes with Taiwan

———————*———————

CHINA AND TAIWAN'S maritime border conflicts are particularly complex. Taiwan has extensive territorial claims and exerts actual control over a number of islands in the SCS, including the Pratas islands and Itu Aba (called Taiping Island in Taiwan), the largest island in the Spratlys. In fact, it was the ROC that first published a map in 1947 that included the now infamous eleven-dashed line claiming the majority of the SCS, a claim that the PRC later adopted in the early 1950s in its nine-dashed map.

Taiwan is not a member of the UN and so has been unable to become a party to UNCLOS, but Taipei has defined straight baselines around not just its main islands but also to Pratas Island, Itu Aba, and the Macclesfield Bank.[248] In line with UNCLOS, Taiwan has claimed maritime zones, including a 12 nm territorial sea, a 200 nm EEZ, and continental shelf rights. In the case of the Macclesfield Bank, the feature is permanently submerged from 7 to 82 meters below sea level, so has no capacity to claim the surrounding water even if a structure has been built on them.[249]

Both the ROC and PRC claim that the SCS is Chinese territory, and so when promoting Chinese claims against other Asian nations the two governments tend to agree with each other and have cooperated in the past against other claimants. The PRC and ROC disagree, however, on which China should retain control

---

[248] US Department of State, "Taiwan's Maritime Claims," *Limits in the Seas No. 127,* Washington DC, 15 November 2005.
[249] Clive Schofield, "The Trouble with Islands: The Definition and Role of Islands and Rocks," in Hong and Van Dyke, eds., *Maritime Boundary Disputes,* 27.

in the SCS. In 1969, the United Nations published the results of a geological survey that first noted sizable petroleum deposits beneath the seabed of the SCS. Exploiting these deposits was bound to create greater ROC-PRC tensions. However, increasing levels of cross-strait investment and trade could give the two governments common ground to cooperate on exercising their joint claim to the SCS.

TAIWAN'S SCS CLAIMS

After World War II, China claimed all of the SCS. In this case China meant "Republic of China," or "Nationalist China" since it was under the sole authority of Chiang Kai-shek and his Nationalist party. However, the civil war was renewed in China right after World War II ended, and by 1949 the Chinese Communists under Mao Zedong were able to push southward into China proper from their base area in Manchuria. On 1 October 1949, the Communists created the PRC, while the Nationalist government retreated to the island security of Taiwan. Chiang Kai-shek and his advisors moved to Taiwan in early December 1949. For much of its post-1949 history, the ROC proclaimed all of mainland China as its territory. Gradually its claims diminished, but Taiwan still controls a number of small islands off the coast of China, plus the Pratas islands and Itu Aba in the SCS. Beijing incorporates Taipei's claim into its own because China does not recognize Taiwan as an independent state separate from the PRC. The PRC has warned Taiwan not to try to claim its independence (see Document 20).

The Taiwan Strait separates the ROC on Taiwan from the PRC on the mainland. Although the PRC has threatened to invade Taiwan on numerous occasions, the maritime security provided by the strait, which is about 80 miles at its narrowest point, has proved to be an even better security buffer than the much smaller English channel, which is only 21 miles wide at its narrowest point. To date, the Taiwan Strait has proven itself to be the most important physical barrier protecting the Nationalists from attack. It was arguably this geographic divide between continental China and Taiwan that precipitated the "two Chinas" problem, and which has allowed the political division to continue down to the present time.

Additional protection for Taiwan was provided by Nationalist domination of a large number of offshore islands, some of them right off the PRC's coast. There are about 3,000 offshore islands off the southeastern coast of the PRC, including 1,800 in Zhejiang province, 600 islands off Fujian province, and 550 islands off Guangdong province. Many are too small to support habitation, while others, such as the 60-square mile island of Jinmen (formerly Quemoy), had over 60,000 people living there in the 1950s, and it is now closer to 85,000, while the Mazu (Matsu) Islands have about 10,000. It would be these small offshore islands, not Taiwan proper, which would be at the heart of two Taiwan Strait crises during the 1950s and one in the early 1960s.

Taipei's claim to the SCS is based on the principles of discovery and occupation. In 1946, Taiwan was the first to establish its presence in the Spratlys following the Japanese withdrawal after World War II. Since at least 1956, it has physically occupied and exercised continuous sovereignty over Itu Aba, the largest island in the Spratlys chain. While Japan renounced its claim to the Spratlys in the 1951 Treaty of San Francisco, this agreement did not specify the country to which they were being returned. Subsequently, in a separate, bilateral peace treaty concluded between the ROC on Taiwan and Japan in 1952, the Spratly and Paracel islands were included with Taiwan and the Pescadores islands (a small group of islands off the west coast of Taiwan, known in Chinese as the Penghu islands) as territories to which Japan had renounced all claims.

Since the ROC was then occupying Taiwan and the Penghus, plus according to some accounts had troops during this entire period on Itu Aba, the largest island in the Spratlys, the Chinese consider that this act of cession implied that the Japanese claims to the other islands were also ceded to the ROC. This would appear to be indicated by Japan's precondition for negotiating with Taiwan, where Japan insisted that "only territorial issues related to the Republic of China should be subject to the treaty"[250] (see Document 5). When this treaty was signed, Japan recognized the Republic of China on Taiwan as the only legitimate government of China.

---

[250] Haller-Trost, *The Spratly Islands*, 50.

Chinese commentators from Taiwan have made it clear that the SCS claims of both the PRC and ROC are identical and that Beijing's claims "are essentially supplementary to those of Taipei."[251] A Taiwanese stamp contained a map of the SCS showing Taiwan's claim (see Map 9 below). Both governments have also been willing to use force to assert their claim. Open conflict erupted over these islands in 1974, when the Chinese PLAN drove South Vietnamese troops out of the Paracels, and again in 1988 when China fought with Vietnamese troops in the Spratlys. During this second conflict, the ROC reportedly offered to assist the PRC by providing fresh water from Itu Aba. But the PRC's official policy is that only mainland China has the right to claim sovereignty over the SCS.

PRC CLAIMS IN THE SCS

In 1988, the PRC incorporated the Paracels and the Spratlys into a new Chinese province called Hainan Province. Then, on 4 December 2007, China unilaterally announced it had created a new "city" in Hainan Province to administer the Paracels, Macclesfield Bank, and the Spratlys, even though China's sovereignty over these islands remains in dispute. Called Sansha, this huge new city overlaps islands occupied by the ROC. Meanwhile, negative reactions were strong among the countries throughout the region, in particular Vietnam and Indonesia, which both protested China's announcement.

In response to China's action, during February 2008 Taiwanese President Chen Shui-bian flew to Itu Aba for an official visit. Chen's trip not only proved that the recently lengthened runway could handle C-130 cargo planes, but was also perceived as reinforcing Taiwan's claim to these disputed territories. However, the 2008 election of the Nationalist candidate Ma Ying-jeou ushered in greater ROC-PRC cooperation in the SCS. This concerned Washington, fearful that the Taiwanese might inadvertently give away too much to Beijing. During April 2014, however, Taiwan

---

[251] Steven Kuan-Tsyh Yu, "Who Owns the Spratly Islands? – An Evaluation of the Nature and Legal Basis of the Conflicting Territorial Claims," in *International Academic Conference on Territorial Claims in the South China Sea* (Hong Kong: University of Hong Kong, 1991), 16.

responded to the PRC's continued encroachment by holding the largest military exercise ever on Itu Aba.

Map 9: A Taiwanese stamp showing the connected U-shaped line[252]

---
[252] SCS map courtesy of David Rosenberg www.southchinasea.org.

There is no conflict between the sovereignty claims of the Beijing and Taipei over the SCS with regard to other states, just between themselves. The PRC and the ROC insist that they are both representing Chinese claims, and that the Paracels and Spratlys belong to China. Other scholars disagree that they are of equal weight, however, arguing instead that the PRC's legal position on the islands, based on applicable international law, is not only weak *de jure*, but also *de facto*, principally because China had done nothing to exercise its jurisdiction in the Paracels before 1974 and the Spratlys before 1988. By contrast, Taiwan effectively held and developed Itu Aba. However, this does not mean Taiwan can claim the entire Spratly archipelago just because it occupies one feature of the group.

Beijing periodically asserts that it alone has the ability to settle the territorial disputes in the SCS, but this is debatable, in particular since complete resolution of sovereignty over disputed islands and delimitation of maritime boundaries hinges in many ways on the final resolution of the PRC-ROC political dispute. For example, their combined impact would be much greater if the PRC and Taiwan were jointly to dispute Vietnam's claim to sovereignty over the Paracels. As for the Spratlys, Beijing and Taipei claim the entire group, and at various times both the PRC and ROC have supported military actions against other claimants. Should there be a military dispute similar to those reported incidents during the 1990s then a combined PRC-ROC response would be much more effective.

Even though they dispute each other's claims, Taiwan's occupation of Itu Aba since the end of World War II, which is arguably the main island in the Spratlys group, could be considered as also underpinning the claims made by mainland China. Both governments insist that they are representing a single Chinese claim, and "historically, there is no question that the Paracels and Spratlys belong to China."[253] In the meantime, the two governments have often used offshore islands to exert military and economic pressure against the other.

THE PRC-ROC STRUGGLE OVER THE OFFSHORE ISLANDS

As a result of the Civil War, Taiwan pulled its troops out of the SCS. When the PLA halted its spring 1950 offensive, however, the

---

[253] Yu, *The Four Archipelagoes in the South China Sea*, 10–18.

Nationalists continued to retain approximately 30 offshore islands in the East China Sea and South China Sea. This gave the Nationalists the ability to dominate a 400-mile arc of coastal waters from the Dachen islands in the north off Zhejiang province, to Jinmen in the south off Fujian province, to the Pratas islands off Guangdong province. Taiwan's control over these islands helped stop a PRC cross-strait invasion, while also allowing the Nationalists to conduct a naval blockade of the mainland. The Nationalist blockade remained in effect in one form or another for a decade, through 1958.

Soon after retreating to Taiwan, the Nationalists lost control over the Miao Islands, north of Shandong Peninsula, which had formerly given them naval control over the Bo Hai Gulf that provided access to the PRC capital at Beijing. The Nationalists initially also controlled Hainan Island, right off of China's southern coast, in addition to the Paracels, Pratas, and Itu Aba. But from March-May 1950, Communist forces, despite naval and air inferiority, succeeded in pushing the Nationalist forces off of Hainan. Communist junks and troops overwhelmed the Nationalist air and surface units and their relatively small Nationalist island garrisons. As one report concluded: "The tremendous losses in men and boats sustained by the Communists attested to their stubborn determination to remove this threat to their security and their economy."[254] The PLA's fleets of small boats succeeded in crossing the Qiongzhou strait and taking Hainan Island, only 15 miles from the Chinese mainland. But naval historians speculated that such tactics "would be of no use against the primary target, Taiwan, which lay nearly 100 nautical miles from the coast."[255] In fact, for the PRC to invade Taiwan would require a major naval effort on its part, including the gathering of hundreds, perhaps thousands, of ships and the training of tens of thousands of troops.

After the PLA retook the northernmost and southernmost offshore islands held by the Nationalists during spring 1950, it stopped. To take the remaining Nationalist-controlled islands

---

[254] "The Southeast China Coast Today," *The ONI Review*, February 1953, 51-60.
[255] Muller, *China as a Maritime Power*, 16.

would have required more advanced naval technology, such as amphibious landing craft. This was beyond the PLAN's capabilities in the early 1950s. Since the PLAN could not successfully attack Taiwan, however, the U.S. Navy's Office of Naval Intelligence estimated Chinese forces would continue their "hit-and-run campaign against individual islands, without apparent plan."[256] To foil a PRC invasion, the Nationalists retained control over the Dachen islands further south off Zhejiang province, the large island bases of Mazu and Jinmen, right off the coast of Fujian Province, the Lema and Wan Shan islands near Guangzhou, the Penghu islands in the Taiwan Strait halfway between the mainland and Taiwan, and the Pratas islands in the SCS. By 1953, however, losses to the Communists meant that the Nationalists controlled only 25 offshore islands, most of them located in or near the Taiwan Straits.

On 30 July 1953, a U.S. Navy report entitled "Security of Offshore islands Presently Held by the Nationalist Government of the Republic of China," determined that only the four offshore islands off Fuzhou, including Mazu, and the four islands off Xiamen, including Jinmen, were worth defending since they "could be used to counter Chinese Communist invasion operations." No mention was made of Taiwan's islands in the SCS. As for the other offshore islands under Nationalist domination, U.S. Navy planners concluded they "are not now being utilized for important operations and are not considered worth the effort necessary to defend them against a determined attack." Still, as one U.S. Navy report was quick to point out, none of the offshore islands could be called "essential" to the defense of Taiwan and the Penghus in the sense of being "absolutely necessary" militarily. Their importance to the Nationalists was mainly for "psychological warfare purposes," as well as their "pre-invasion operations, commando raiding, intelligence gathering, maritime resistance development, sabotage, escape and evasion."[257]

---

[256] "The Struggle for the Coastal Islands of China," *The ONI Review Supplement*, December 1953, I-IX.
[257] Appendix to "Security of the Offshore Islands Presently Held by the Nationalist Government of the Republic of China," Memorandum from CNO, ADM Robert B. Carney, to Join Chiefs of Staff (Top Secret), 30 July 1953, Strategic Plans Division, NHHC Archives, Box 289.

During the early 1950s the Nationalist Navy could still dominate the majority of China's southeastern coastline, and both Communist and Nationalist forces fiercely defended their positions on numerous offshore islands, in the hopes of changing the strategic balance. Although according to Secretary-of-State John Foster Dulles "for the United States, the offshore islands were of no intrinsic importance except in the context of an attack on Formosa," they could be used as "stepping stones for such an attack."[258] Fear of Communist expansion into the First Island Chain was especially strong. It was mainly for this reason that the U.S. government supported Taipei during the two Taiwan Strait crises in 1954–1955 and 1958. Washington also felt obliged to sign security treaties supporting Chiang Kai-shek's efforts to defend a number of offshore islands from PRC attack (see Documents 6 and 7).

SINO-TAIWANESE PARALLEL CLAIMS IN THE SCS

From 1939 to 1945, the Japanese occupied Itu Aba, building a fuel depot, submarine base, and a radio station there. Near the end of the war, the Japanese were forced to withdraw. Beijing and Taipei both assert a single Chinese claim over the disputed territories in the SCS, arguing that China's historical use of these waters pre-dated Vietnam's and the Philippine's. This does not mean that the islands were never explored or used by Vietnamese or Filipino fishermen, but that the Chinese were the first to document their early presence. Soon after the end of World War II, two Nationalist ships, *Taiping* and *Zhongye*, formerly USS *Decker* and USS *LST 1056*, were sent during November-December 1946 to establish a garrison on Itu Aba, but this garrison appears to have left in 1950, and only returned following the successful conclusion of the first Taiwan Strait incident in 1954–1955.

In response to the "Cloma Incident," which appeared to be a Philippine attempt to claim the Spratlys, on 29 May 1956, the PRC Foreign Ministry issued a statement saying that Itu Aba and Spratly Island in the SCS, along with the small islands in their

---

[258] Telegram from UK Embassy, Washington, to Foreign Office (secret), 9 February 1955, The National Archives, Kew, PREM 11/867.

vicinity, had always been a part of Chinese territory. Therefore, the PRC had legitimate sovereignty over these islands. On 2 June 1956, the American Ambassador to Taipei assured the ROC Foreign Minister that the United States had no intention of getting involved in the Spratly dispute, and that the U.S. government's position was that ownership of the islands was unsettled. The ROC decided to re-establish its garrison on Itu Aba.

On 5 June 1956, the South Vietnamese (ROV) Minister Cao Bai stated that the Spratly and Paracel islands had been under the jurisdiction of the French colonial government and that Vietnam subsequently had jurisdiction by virtue of grant of sovereignty by France, and soon afterward South Vietnam landed naval units in the Spratlys. In reply, the Chinese insist that an 1887 treaty with France, the Sino-French Convention, ceded to China the Paracel and Spratly groups. However, other scholars have concluded that despite the historical claims of the Chinese and Vietnamese, only events that took place since the 1930s were relevant to the present dispute, which might make the 1887 treaty largely moot.[259] According to this view, only with the Japanese occupation of the islands in the late 1930s can valid claims of sovereignty through effective occupation be made. While Chinese historical claims to the islands could establish an inchoate or incipient right to sovereignty, therefore, such a right had be followed up with *de facto* occupation of the territory to establish legal sovereignty. This occupation was not attempted by China until after World War II.

The PRC's legal position on the SCS islands, therefore, especially when compared to Taiwan's, is weak. By contrast, Taiwan has by far the most valid claim to Itu Aba, in particularly since they have effectively held and developed it. However, the Taiwanese government cannot claim all the Spratlys, since almost thirty features in this island chain are occupied by other states. Plus, there is still significant uncertainty regarding the exact length of time that Chinese military forces occupied Itu Aba during this period. Most authorities agree that Chinese military forces left the Spratly islands in May 1950 due to the Civil War in China and only returned in July 1956, in response to

---

[259] Chiu and Park, "Legal Status of the Paracel and Spratly Islands," 19.

exploratory activity in the area by Philippine nationals. Either way, Taiwan's control of Itu Aba props up the PRC claim. During 1995–1996 the PRC tried and failed to put pressure on Taiwan to reunify. If it had succeeded, then Beijing would have assumed control over Itu Aba.

THE 1995–1996 TAIWAN STRAIT CRISIS

The U.S. Navy supported Taiwan during the two 1950s' strait crises, plus a smaller diplomatic dispute in the early 1960s. As a result of President Richard Nixon's 1972 trip to China, Sino-U.S. relations rapidly improved, leading to full recognition in 1979 (see Document 11). From 1979 to 1989, the U.S. and the PRC actively cooperated against the USSR, including Washington authorizing high-tech U.S. naval equipment sales to China. This period of Sino-U.S. Cold War cooperation against the USSR helped to limit tensions in the Taiwan Strait. But even after the U.S. government recognized the PRC, Washington maintained a strong interest in Taiwan's defense, including the continued sale of weapons[260] (see Document 13). During 1995–1996, as a result of provocative PRC missile testing off Taiwan, the U.S. Navy responded by sending USN aircraft carriers and destroyers into the region. This naval demonstration was similar to the USN's response to previous Taiwan Strait crises during the 1950s and early 1960s, and was called the fourth Taiwan Strait crisis.[261] The increasing power of the PLAN in turn helped create the rationale for the later strategic pivot by the U.S. Navy to Asia.

The delicate balance-of-power in the Taiwan Strait began to shift after the 1989 fall of the Berlin Wall, the 1990 end of the Cold War, and the 1991 collapse of the USSR. This situation left the PRC to fill the resulting power vacuum in Asia. Following the

---

[260] Michael S. Chase, "U.S.-Taiwan Security Cooperation: Enhancing an Unofficial Relationship," in Nancy Bernkopf Tucker, ed., *Dangerous Strait: The U.S.-Taiwan-China Crisis* (New York: Columbia University Press, 2005), 164.

[261] Wikipedia incorrectly refers to this event as the "Third Taiwan Strait Crisis." See http://en.wikipedia.org/wiki/Third_Taiwan_Strait_Crisis [accessed 21 September 2017].

collapse of the Soviet empire in Asia, the PRC rapidly expanded its naval forces, in part to fill the military vacuum following the USSR's retreat. With the help of Russia, mainly through sales of advanced naval equipment, the PLAN began a long period of reform.[262] The PRC also developed a large missile force, deployed mainly against Taiwan. This rapid military growth upset the delicate PRC-Taiwan military balance.

Beginning in July 1995, missile tests were conducted by the PRC. These tests are often portrayed as a response to the granting of an American visa to Taiwan's President Lee Teng-hui for an unofficial visit to Cornell University in early June 1995.[263] The more important underlying concern for the PRC, however, was over Taiwan's rapid democratization and the growing separatist claims by large numbers of Taiwanese. On 18 July 1995, China announced that ballistic missile tests would occur between 21 and 28 July. These dates corresponded with the fiftieth anniversary of the 1945 Potsdam treaty stating that China would regain all territories lost to Japan, including Taiwan, after the war ended (see Document 3).

The PRC missile tests created an exclusion zone, in this case a ten nautical mile circle, in which ships and planes could not safely enter. This zone was located about 85 miles north of Taiwan, which was outside Taipei's sovereign waters but actively interfered with international flight paths and shipping lanes. Six DF-15 (CSS-6/M-9) short-range ballistic missiles (SRBMs) were fired, two each on 21, 22, and 23 July 1995 (see Map 10 below). Beijing's announcement warned other states not to enter the impacted sea area and air space during the firing period. These PRC missile tests diverted hundreds of commercial flights heading for Taipei.[264]

---

[262] James C. Bussert and Bruce A. Elleman, *People's Liberation Army Navy (PLAN) Combat Systems Technology*, 14–15, 101, 175.
[263] Michael S. Chase, *Taiwan's Security Policy: External Threats and Domestic Politics* (Boulder: Lynne Rienner Publishers, 2008), 17.
[264] Richard D. Fisher, "China's Missiles over the Taiwan Strait: A Political and Military Assessment," in James R. Lilley and Chuck Downs, eds., *Crisis in the Taiwan Strait* (American Enterprise Institute for Public Policy Research, 1997), 170–171.

From 15 to 25 August 1995, PRC military exercises, including about 20 warships and 40 aircraft, were held in a large area to the northwest of the SRBM splash zone. The PRC also tested anti-ship missiles and anti-aircraft missiles. In November 1995, just prior to Taiwan's December parliamentary elections, the PLA staged further naval, amphibious, and air-assault operations near Dongshan Island. These exercises included conducting blockade operations, which made it appear that the PRC was planning to mount a naval blockade against Taiwan.[265]

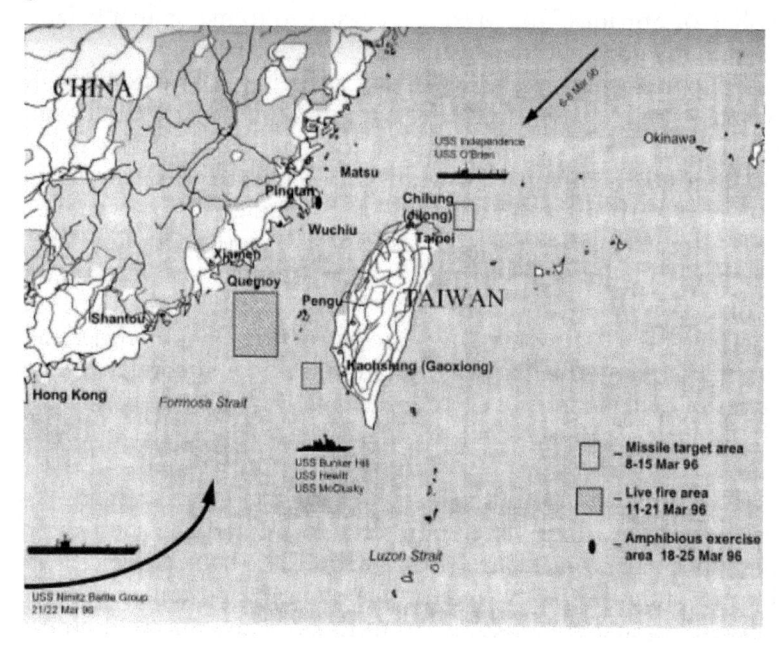

Map 10: Location of PRC Missiles Tests during 1995–1996

In response to these Chinese provocations, on 19 December 1995, the U.S. Navy sailed the USS *Nimitz* (CVN 68) through the Taiwan Strait on its way to the Indian Ocean. Poor weather was

---

[265] Chris Rahman, "Ballistic Missiles in China's Anti-Taiwan Blockade," in Bruce A. Elleman and S.C.M. Paine, eds., *Naval Blockade and Seapower: Strategies and Counter-strategies, 1805–2005* (London: Routledge, 2006), 215–224.

the stated reason for transiting the strait, rather than going east of Taiwan. The PRC did not publicly acknowledge this event, but on 27 January 1996, the *United Daily News* and *New York Times* both reported it. This was the first time an American aircraft carrier had publicly transited the Taiwan Strait since the late-1970s, which sent a sharp signal to Beijing not to interfere in Taiwan's domestic politics. This decision has been described as "a carefully controlled and minimally provocative use of military power which allowed the United States to reemphasize the 'ambiguous' policy of previous U.S. presidents designed to maintain a balance in U.S. relations with both sides of the strait."[266]

Following this U.S. show of force, Beijing told the Assistant Secretary of Defense, Chas Freeman, that the PRC would launch one missile per day against Taiwan for a period of 30 days if Taipei continued on its path towards independence. A Chinese official even warned Freeman that the U.S. should not intervene in a cross-Strait crisis, because U.S. leaders "care more about Los Angeles than they do about Taiwan," a direct threat that Washington should stop supporting Taiwan.[267] On 5 March 1996, the 43rd anniversary of the death of Stalin – one of the three major world leaders at Potsdam – Beijing announced that it would conduct a new series of ballistic missile exercises during 8–15 March, which was the runup to Taiwan's first presidential elections under universal suffrage.

This time the northern missile splash zone was a square just 30 miles from Jilong (Keelung), close to sea and air lanes servicing Japan and Korea. The southern zone, also square-shaped, was located about 47 miles west of Gaoxiong (Kaohsiung), and was close to air and sea lanes to Hong Kong. The tests were clearly intended to cut trade routes both from the north and the south, which accounted for about 70% of Taiwan's commerce. Between 8 and 13 March, four dummy missiles landed within the target areas. On 9 March, the PRC also warned ships and aircraft to avoid a live-fire exercise from 12 to 20 March in the southern part

---

[266] Rick M. Gallagher, *The Taiwan Strait Crisis*, Strategic Research Department, Research Report 10-97, U.S. Naval War College, October 1997, 2–3.
[267] Patrick E. Tyler, "As China Threatens Taiwan, It Makes Sure U.S. Listens," *The New York Times*, 24 January 1996.

of the Taiwan Strait. The rectangular zone for these exercises was just south of the Taiwanese outpost on Jinmen Island. A further exercise was announced on 15 March, to be carried out from 18 to 25 March, continuing the military pressure until after the presidential election. Although this zone was smaller, it was strategically located between the two small islands of Mazu and Wuchiu.

The PRC tests were timed to put pressure on Taiwan's presidential election, scheduled for 23 March 1996, so that the pro-independence candidates would not win. In reaction to this provocation, Congress backed Taiwan. The U.S. Navy dispatched the USS *Independence* (CV 62) aircraft carrier battle group to the area. Its aircraft were patrolling about 100 miles off of Taiwan. The USS *Nimitz* carrier group was also ordered to return from the Persian Gulf at high speed. Other naval assets included two Aegis guided-missile cruisers and U.S. Air Force RC-135 Rivet Joint electronic surveillance aircraft.

CinCPac Admiral Joseph Prueher decided to put *Independence* east of Taiwan, and to assign two Aegis cruisers north and south of Taiwan: We "got them there fast. Got them there quietly. But nobody knew that they were there, so we had to tell the media in Okinawa and Japan. Media switch is not vernier switch but on/off switch. Pictures in the press began to appear." As a result of sending *Independence*, and later recalling in *Nimitz* from the Persian Gulf, the Chinese only fired five missiles, three north and two south, instead of the much larger number that they had originally planned. As noted by Admiral Lyle Bien, Commander Carrier Group 7, "ordering *Nimitz* to sail all the way from the Gulf at flank speed was an unmistakable signal to the PRC that we were serious and it was noted by all onboard *Nimitz* that the missile firings stopped only when we approached on-station."[268]

The U.S. also sent official protests to the Chinese government, with Secretary of State Warren Christopher calling the PRC's actions "reckless" and a White House spokesman stating that

---

[268] Bruce A. Elleman, "The Right Skill Set: Joseph Wilson Prueher (1941-)," in John B. Hattendorf and Bruce A. Elleman, eds., *Nineteen Gun Salute: Case Studies of Operational, Strategic, and Diplomatic Naval Leadership during the 20th and Early 21st Centuries* (Newport, R.I.: NWC Press, 2010), 237.

Washington was "deeply disturbed by this provocative act."[269] The U.S. Congress resolved that consistent with the Taiwan Relations Act, it would continue to supply Taiwan with naval ships, aircraft, and air defense components to ensure the security of Taiwan (see Document 12). The Congressional resolution of 21 March 1996 further stated that the "United States is committed to the military stability of the Taiwan Straits and United States military forces should defend Taiwan in the event of invasion, missile attack, or blockade by the People's Republic of China"[270] (see Document 17).

The U.S. Navy's intervention gave the PRC pause. Washington's decision to send not one, but two, aircraft carriers to the Taiwan Strait constituted the largest demonstration of American naval diplomacy against China since the first two Taiwan Strait crises of the 1950s. The strategic rationale for sending ships to the Taiwan Strait, however, was much the same as in 1950: to neutralize this region so as to not allow a cross-strait invasion. Seen in this context, Washington's decision to send in *Independence* and *Nimitz* was a direct continuation in spirit of the earlier naval operation. After the PRC ended its missile blockade, Sino-U.S. tensions remained at a low simmer. Meanwhile, the PRC's relations with Taiwan continued to improve slowly, opening the possibility of further cooperation in the SCS.

PROSPECTS FOR ROC-PRC COOPERATION IN THE SCS

Although from 1949 onward the PRC and ROC were in an almost constant state of war, none of these tensions occurred in the SCS. The last Taiwan Strait crisis occurred over two decades ago. There is now a chance for greater ROC-PRC cooperation in the SCS. While there is still relatively little support on Taiwan for reunifying with the PRC, fully half of Taiwanese agree with continuing PRC-ROC economic integration. Since control of the SCS might

---

[269] Patrick E. Tyler, "China Signaling U.S. That It Will Not Invade Taiwan," *The New York Times*, 13 March 1996.
[270] 104th Congress (1995–1996), H.Con.Res. 148, 21 March 1996, https://www.congress.gov/bill/104th-congress/house-concurrent-resolution/148/text [accessed 27 March 2017].

include vast oil and natural gas resources, there are good economic reasons for the Taiwanese government to cooperate with the PRC.

Although the PRC-ROC military standoff has now lasted for almost 70 years, beginning in 1992 the PRC and ROC conducted a series of informal talks designed to clarify their positions on a wide range of issues, including Taiwan's support for the "one China" principle. The PRC's 1995–1996 "missile blockade" interfered with these talks. They then broke down for good in 1998, due to the increasing strength of the Taiwanese pro-independence movement, as indicated by Chen Shui-bian's presidential victories in 2000 and 2004, but finally resumed again during June 2008 following the Nationalist return to power. Since that time, PRC-ROC relations have included increased travel, cross-strait investment, and direct shipping. Taiwanese investment in the PRC rose sharply, hitting $13.3 billion in 2010 alone.[271] By 2016, cross-strait trade had grown to $100 billion, which was almost double Taiwan's second largest trade partner, the United States.[272] To date, 23 agreements promoting trade and cultural exchange have been signed, including the Cross-Straits Economic Cooperation Framework (see Document 21).

In 2014, the International Monetary Fund announced that China's purchasing power GDP hit $17.6 trillion, versus $17.4 trillion in the United States, making the PRC the largest economy in the world. The majority of China's and Taiwan's international trade is now conducted by sea. In 2010, Greater China – including China, Hong Kong, and Taiwan – accounted for 30% of container exports, and in 2011 the number of container units handled by Chinese ports hit 150 million. During the past five years alone, cargo and container throughput in Chinese ports has seen an annual growth rate of 35%. Between 2004 and 2013, China's percentage of the global bulk carrier fleet rose from 6.8% to almost 12%, from 3,821 to 6,532 Chinese-owned ships.

---

[271] "Taiwan investment in China Rises Sharply in 2010," *The Strait Times*, 31 December 2010.

[272] Bonnie S. Glaser, Matthew P. Funaiole, and Emily Jin, "Unpacking Tsai Ing-wen's New Southbound Policy: Can Taiwan's latest attempt to avoid economic dependence on China succeed?" *The Diplomat*, 1 April 2017, http://thediplomat.com/2017/04/unpacking-tsai-ing-wens-new-southbound-policy/ [accessed 3 April 2017].

Fishing is another sector where the PRC and ROC have overlapping interests. As of 2014, China's commercial fishing fleet included 695,555 fishing trawlers, more than double the next competitor. These fishing trawlers must compete with all of the other Asian nations, and on a number of occasions "navies from Indonesia, Vietnam, South Korea and the Philippines have used force to expel Chinese poachers." Taiwanese fishermen must face the same challenges as fishing trawlers from the PRC: "Acts of fishery patriotism like these often ignite territorial tensions, as many of the incidents occur in disputed waters."[273]

In the past, the PRC and ROC have shown a willingness to cooperate against other claimants in the SCS dispute, since the actions of both mainland China and Taiwan in the Spratlys are in support of a single Chinese claim. Taiwan's on-again off-again occupation since 1946 of what could arguably be called the "main island" in the Spratlys group must therefore also be considered to support the claims made by mainland China. When Sino-Vietnamese tensions led to conflict during 1988, Taiwan appears to have supported the PRC. Taiwan's Defense Minister Cheng Wei-yuan even stated that if Taiwan was asked, it would help defend PLA forces in the Spratlys against a third party. Although this did not happen, there have been credible claims that PRC garrisons perhaps received freshwater supplies from the ROC troops on Itu Aba during the conflict.

Cooperation asserting China's claims to the SCS is another example of warming relations. Most recently, a Taiwanese group called the Chinese (Taiwan) Society of International Law, which is linked to the previous president Ma Ying-jeou, petitioned the UN arbitration panel to let it present Taiwan's case. Remarkably, the judges allowed it to submit written evidence to the court. According to Ian Storey, this decision showed the tribunal was trying to be impartial, taking "into account the views of all the concerned parties, even China, which has refused to participate, and Taiwan, which isn't a member of the UN."[274] Even though the UN tribunal

---

[273] Holslag, *Trapped Giant: China's Military Rise*, 153.
[274] "Taiwan enters South China Sea legal fray, as group seeks to sway international court," *Thanhnien News*, 10 May 2016, www.thanniennews.com/print_v2.html [accessed 13 March 2013].

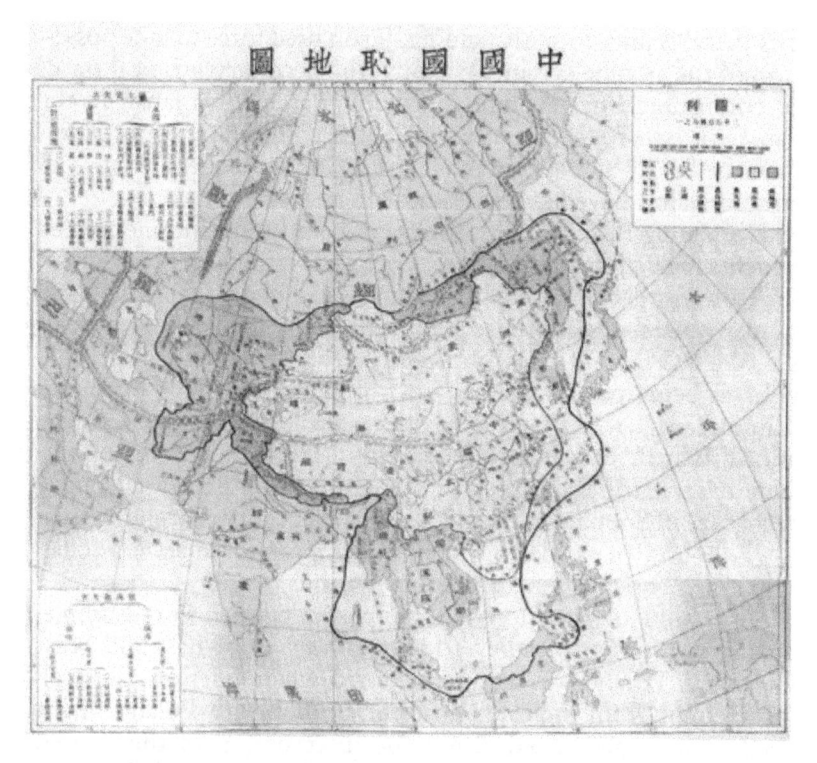

Map 11: Nationalist China's Territorial Claims in 1927

decided against China, the fact that Taipei argued its case suggests active cooperation with Beijing asserting joint territorial claims.

PRC-ROC JOINT TERRITORIAL CLAIMS

Since troops of the ROC were the first to occupy one of the Spratly islands after the Japanese withdrawal in 1945, Taipei's claim to the Spratlys is stronger than that of any other state. Taiwan's additional territorial claims throughout the region could also be huge. In 1927, the Nationalist government even published a map showing the largest extent of China's former borders[275] (see Map 11).

---

[275] "Zhonghua guochi ditu, zaiban" ("Map of China's National Humiliation, Reprint") (Shanghai:Zhonghua Shuju, 1927); reprinted with permission

Historical claims notwithstanding, Japan used force to take possession of the archipelago in 1939, but "the necessary juridical status of confirming the title internationally was lost by Japan in the San Francisco Peace Treaty [when] it had to renounce its claims over the Spratlys."[276] From that time on, all subsequent claims and counterclaims have not been simple to assess.

Deepening PRC-ROC cooperation could result in unexpected benefits for Beijing in the future, since the Nationalist government on Taiwan still claims territory from its neighbors that equals, and in many cases, exceeds those lands claimed by the PRC. For example, the ROC constitution for many years still listed all of Mongolia as being part of China, and perhaps all of Tuva (formerly Tannu Tuva), which was annexed by the USSR outright during World War II. Taiwan also potentially has a large number of outstanding territorial disputes with countries that do not currently recognize it. Should China and Taiwan ever unify peacefully, then a whole host of border disputes that appear to be settled today might be re-opened for further negotiations.

This kind of situation has happened before. For example, during negotiations leading to the unification of East and West Germany, Poland was very concerned when German Chancellor Helmut Kohl indicated that the border with Poland might need to be renegotiated. Only the intervention of the United States, France, Great Britain, and the USSR convinced Germany to declare that their borders would be maintained unchanged: "The treaty which finally came out of these talks, and paved the way for reuniting Germany, calls for the current borders to be maintained."[277] This is not the only outcome. Once Vietnam unified in 1976, the North appears to have adopted the SCS territorial claims of the South, not the other way around. Unlike Germany's decision to back down and respect the *status quo*, it is

---

from William A. Callahan, "The Cartography of National Humiliation and the Emergence of China's Geobody," in *Public Culture*, Vol. 21, No. 1 (2009), 154–155.

[276] Haller-Trost, *The Spratly Islands*, 59.
[277] David Petina, "Unified Germany: Friend or Foe?" *Res Publica*, Vol. 2, No. 1 (January 1991), http://www.ashbrook.org/publicat/respub/v2n1/petina1.html [accessed 21 September 2017].

more likely that a newly unified China would adopt Vietnam's expansionist tactics.

The PRC and Taiwan continue to dispute sovereign rights and actual control not only over the nearby offshore islands, therefore, but over many islands in the SCS. Based on the growth of its communications, intelligence gathering, and naval supply structure on its island bases in the SCS, China appears to be carrying out a gradual maritime strategy to exert control incrementally. By drawing enclosing baselines around the Paracel islands, Beijing has effectively removed these waters from their previous freedom-of-navigation and over-flight regimes. One scholar has warned: "Beijing could be intent on transferring large areas of the South China Sea from a regime in which warships have immunity from its jurisdiction, to one in which permission is required for entry. Of course, China cannot now enforce such a regime. But when it is strong enough, it may try to do so."[278]

CONCLUSIONS

Beijing's and Taipei's overlapping territorial claims make the PRC-ROC situation one of the most complex of any of the ongoing maritime and territorial disputes. Both governments agree on their territorial claims in the SCS against all the other claimants, with Taiwan currently occupying some of the largest islands there, including the Pratas islands and Itu Aba, even while the PRC occupies the Paracels and seven smaller islands in the Spratlys. In general, Taiwan supports the PLAN activities against all other SCS claimants, even though the PRC's official policy is that only Beijing has the right to claim sovereignty over the entire SCS, including all Taiwan-controlled islands.

To date, minimal progress has been made in the implementation of the confidence building measures outlined in the 2002 China-ASEAN Declaration on the Conduct of Parties in SCS. Beijing's submission of the infamous nine-dashed map of the SCS to the CLCS in May 2009 is based directly on Taiwan's claim to the

---

[278] Mark J. Valencia, "Tension Increasing In South China Sea," *Honolulu Advertiser*, 5 April 2001.

entire region as "historic waters." If Beijing succeeds, this could exempt all or part of the SCS from freedom of navigation and over-flight principles. Taking into account the historical examples of the PRC's maritime disputes, including over the Pratas, Paracel, and Spratly islands, repeated assertions by Beijing beginning in 2002 that it will work with the ASEAN countries to limit frictions over these islands and to resolve their differences peacefully should be met with healthy skepticism.

Taiwan's participation is imperative to negotiate any lasting solution to the SCS disputes. Even if Beijing were to resolve each and every one of its borders with its Southeast Asian neighbors, the ROC has its own outstanding claims on large territories in East Asia, including the SCS. Experts on this dispute have argued that if only the Kuomintang were to "de-escalate the historiographical conflict in the SCS, it would be much easier for the Beijing government to do the same."[279] Conversely, if the PRC and ROC were to one day unify or adopt a new United Front, then new border claims could perhaps be made based on Taiwanese maps; this might give Beijing a golden opportunity to renegotiate borders that it was already not completely satisfied with. This situation indicates just how important the United States' position is as an impartial maritime arbiter.

---

[279] Hayton, *The South China Sea*, 265.

CHAPTER EIGHT

The United States as the South China Sea Maritime Arbiter

———*———

OF ANY REGION surrounding China, the SCS is currently one of the most dangerous, with practically every single one of China's neighbors in that region experiencing outstanding maritime boundary disputes with Beijing of some type. This is a far cry from Washington's 19 December 1944 assessment in its CAC-301 study that these islands "will be of no vital interest, strategically or economically, to any single country or territory."[280] In fact, Washington does not really care which Southeast Asian nation controls the islands in the SCS, so long as trade, oil extraction, and navigation throughout the region is not negatively impacted.

During the past decade, numerous books have been published proclaiming China to be the world's newest superpower, destined to surpass the United States.[281] But few of these books discuss the geographic limits to China's great power ambitions, in particular the thousands of islands off its shores that constrain its exercise of sea power. While not a near neighbor of China, and also not a member of ASEAN, the United States is a Pacific nation and so is highly interested in continued global commerce and freedom of navigation. Its primary goal would be to act as a maritime arbiter to help keep the peace in the SCS.

---

[280] Hara, *Cold War Frontiers in the Asia-Pacific*, 147.
[281] Peter Navarro, *Crouching Tiger: What China's Militarism Means for the World* (New York: Prometheus Books, 2015); Michael Pillsbury, *The Hundred-year Marathon: China's Secret Strategy to Replace America as the Global Superpower* (New York: St. Martin's, 2016); Tom Miller, *China's Asian Dream: Empire Building along the New Silk Road* (New York: Zed Books, 2017).

In July 2010, Secretary of State Hillary Clinton announced at an ARF meeting in Hanoi that the United States would be "rebalancing" its military forces to Asia.[282] Later, this policy became known as the "pivot to Asia." In the past, the U.S. government has attempted to set itself up as a non-partisan arbiter in East Asia to help resolve outstanding problems between China and other Asian parties, such as Taiwan, but when it comes to the SCS Beijing has largely rejected U.S. efforts. As a result of these unresolved SCS disputes, the challenges facing the U.S. government, the U.S. military forces, and especially the U.S. Navy, are particularly complex, and could become even more so in the waters off China in the coming years.

THE STRATEGIC IMPORTANCE OF THE WATERS OFF CHINA

The division of China in 1949 was not as surprising as the dividing line along the Taiwan Strait. China's split largely fit within the framework of the Cold War, in which Germany was divided into a communist East and democratic West Germany, and both Korea and Vietnam were split into a communist North and a nominally democratic South. Whereas these other divided states were somewhat similar in territory and populations, the small size of the Nationalist island stronghold was greatly overshadowed by the enormous geographic dimensions and population of the PRC. To many outside observers it seemed certain that the PRC could overwhelm Taiwan at will. But the maritime security provided by the Taiwan Strait should not be overlooked. In fact, the much smaller English Channel, which is only 21 miles wide at its narrowest point, had proven itself to be a solid wall against Napoleon, Imperial Germany, and the Nazis. The Taiwan Strait proved to be an equally important barrier protecting the Nationalists from attack.

There were historical reasons why the Nationalists retreated to Taiwan. During the seventeenth century, Zheng Chenggong, known in the West as Koxinga, made Taiwan his base when attempting to defeat the invading Manchus from North China.

---

[282] Bernard D. Cole, *Asian Maritime Strategies: Navigating Troubled Waters* (Annapolis, MD: Naval Institute Press, 2013), 201.

Koxinga used a number of small offshore islands – including Jinmen Island – as stepping stones to cross the Taiwan Strait. In 1661, he based his forces on the Penghu islands to conduct naval operations to expel the Dutch colonizers from Taiwan. In 1683, Qing forces also used various offshore islands to defeat the Ming loyalists and retake Taiwan.

The Taiwan Strait is also an important strategic region in its own right, since it lies along the primary north-south sea lane in East Asia. Japanese, Korean, and northern and central Chinese produce and luxury goods flowing primarily from north-to-south must transit this strait to reach Southeast Asia, just as goods and raw materials flowing from south-to-north must travel through this region. The Taiwan Strait has long been a strategic chokepoint, and whichever country dominated both sides of the strait could close these waters to international shipping. Such an action would force commercial vessels to take the longer and more exposed route to the east of Taiwan.

Taiwan has been fought over many times, therefore, including in the seventeenth century by Ming loyalists, in the eighteenth century when the Manchus put down a local rebellion, and during the 1880s Sino-French War. As a result of the first Sino-Japanese War, China ceded Taiwan to Japan in perpetuity in the 1895 Treaty of Shimonoseki. Japan maintained control over Taiwan for fifty years, until Japan's surrender in 1945, at which point – according to the terms of the Cairo and Potsdam agreements – Taiwan was returned to Nationalist China, the internationally-recognized government of Chiang Kai-shek and his Nationalist Party. Chiang and his advisors officially moved the government to Taiwan on 8 December 1949, the eighth anniversary (Tokyo time) of the Japanese attack on Pearl Harbor, suggesting that for them the war had never ended.

Seen in a larger geographic context, Taiwan is also part of a chain of islands running from the Aleutians through Hokkaido to the Japanese main islands, and then on through Okinawa, Taiwan, and the Philippines, to Malaysia and finally Singapore. These islands would play an important role in any north-south invasion. Communist control over Taiwan could put both Japan and the Philippines at risk. U.S. Navy planners during World War II were keenly aware that Japan's successful invasion of the Philippines had been launched from Taiwan. Assuming Taiwan fell to the Chinese Communists, therefore, the PLA could use it as a base from which to invade other islands in the chain, as well as to interfere with international shipping.

For these reasons, keeping Taiwan out of Communist hands was vital.[283] In 1955, Australian Prime Minister Menzies put it succinctly: "From the point of view of Australia and, indeed, Malaya, it would be fatal to have an enemy installed in the island chain so that by a process of island hopping Indonesia might be reached and Malaya and Australia to that extent exposed to serious damage either in the rear or on the flank."[284] A year later, Foreign Minister Shigemitsu told the U.S. Ambassador in Tokyo that "Japan would consider the fall of Taiwan to the Communists as a threat to its interests and therefore supports the U.S. policy of preventing such an eventuality."[285] Finally, in 1958 British Foreign Secretary Selwyn Lloyd reaffirmed that the UK and U.S. shared the view that there was a "Communist menace in the Far East," and that the "containing line" had to be drawn to include Japan, South Korea, Okinawa, Taiwan, Hong Kong, South Vietnam, and Malaya.[286]

Due mainly to the strategic location of Taiwan and its offshore islands, therefore, it was not in the interest of the United States or its allies to see it fall to Communism. It was this geographic divide between the PRC and ROC that precipitated the "two Chinas" problem, and that has allowed this political division to continue down to the present time. Additional protection for Taiwan was provided by Nationalist domination of many offshore islands, some of them right off the PRC's coast. It would be these offshore

---

[283] "Meeting of Prime Ministers: The Strategic Importance of Formosa; Memorandum by the United Kingdom Chiefs of Staff (Top Secret)," signed by Fraser, P.S. Slessor, and W.J. Slim, 6 January 1951, TNA/UK, PREM 8/1408.

[284] "Formosa and Off-shore Islands, Note by the Prime Minister of Australia (Secret)," Meeting of Commonwealth Prime Ministers, 8 February 1955, TNA/UK, PREM 11/867.

[285] John Foster Dulles Papers, Princeton University, Reel 212/213, 2 December 1956, 94413.

[286] Letter from Selwyn Lloyd to John Foster Dulles (Top Secret), 11 September 1958, TNA/UK, CAB 21/3272.

islands, not Taiwan proper, which would be at the heart of two Taiwan Strait crises during the 1950s and one in the early 1960s.

An equally important U.S. military goal was to reassure America's East Asian allies, including Japan, South Korea, the Philippines, and Australia, that the PRC could not invade the so-called first island chain. The Japanese were especially worried about Chinese expansionism. During 1955, a Japanese official in Taipei clarified that it was the physical location of Taiwan, dominating the sea lanes from Japan to the south that mattered most to Tokyo: "for the future the real problem of Taiwan was the strategic value of the island itself and the importance of keeping it from the Chinese Communists."[287] While fear of Communist expansion has eased, regional tensions have escalated rapidly in large part due to competition to profit from the SCS's resource wealth in oil and natural gas.

THE IMPORTANCE OF SCS RESOURCE EXPLOITATION

Modern offshore oil technologies have made exploitation of oil reserves in the SCS area possible. The significant depths in much of the SCS, including waters measured at 2.5 miles deep around the Spratlys, made earlier oil exploration and drilling technologically impractical. But a United Nations task force reported during the early 1970s: "'more than half' of the China Basin is not that deep, and much of it is now or will soon be within the reach of drilling technology, including areas near the Paracels and the Spratly islands believed to contain petroleum deposits. In the long run, many geologists think that the petroleum and natural gas potential of the SCS is greater than that of the East China and Yellow Seas."[288] By the late 1970s, therefore, advances in offshore oil drilling technology for the first time made it technically feasible and cost effective to drill exploratory wells and establish producing wells throughout much of the SCS.

---

[287] John Foster Dulles Papers, Princeton University, Reel 212/213, 22 November 1955, 94355.
[288] Selig S. Harrison, *China, Oil and Asia: Conflict Ahead?* (New York: Columbia University Press, 1977), 54.

It is easy to blame China for trying to claim all of the SCS's maritime resources, but the United States government was one of the first major countries to claim extensive rights to undersea resources. Traditionally, most countries had recognized a 3 nm maritime border. In 1945, however, President Harry Truman asserted America's right to explore and exploit the oil and natural gas resources of its continental shelf outside of the 3 nm territorial sea. The U.S. Congress enacted legislation in 1953 granting greater control over the continental shelf, especially in the oil-rich Gulf of Mexico.

Thereafter, the 1958 Continental Shelf Convention in Geneva agreed that coastal states had sovereign rights to exploit natural resources on their continental shelf out to a water depth of 200 meters. This decision sparked a scramble by coastal states to stake out as much undersea territory as possible, which in turn led to rapid advances in technology to exploit the ocean floor. With remarkably little objection "coastal states naturally endowed with broad continental margins were conceded in principle to have exclusive rights to the resources of the continental shelf far beyond the seaward limits of their territorial sea. Legal debate focused on the formula to be applied to the definition of the shelf, rather than on the question of entitlement itself."[289]

In early 1976, a joint Swedish-Philippine consortium began conducting exploratory oil drilling in the Reed Bank area of the northeastern Spratlys, located about 140 nm (260 kms) west of the Philippine province of Palawan. The first of several exploratory wells, called Sampaguita No. 1, was drilled to a depth of over 4000 meters in a water depth of about 200 meters, and showed evidence of gas deposits.[290] This period also marked the first American involvement in the search for oil in the Spratlys, when the American-owned company Amoco became a partner to the consortium and drilled two additional exploratory wells using a U.S. registered drill ship. The drilling by the Swedish firm Salen Exploration Company at Sampaguita No. 1 failed, and Amoco resigned as an operator in 1978.

---

[289] Johnston and Valencia, *Pacific Ocean Boundary Problems*, 3.
[290] George Kent and Mark J. Valencia, *Marine Policy in Southeast Asia* (Berkeley: University of California Press, 1983), 173.

Three additional wells were drilled by Salen in 1978, 1979, and 1981, but none of these exploratory wells was converted to oil or gas production, in large part due to the protests by Vietnam and China.[291]

The results from these first exploratory wells confirmed the presence of petroleum-bearing deposits in the northeastern Spratlys. This discovery was substantiated by other offshore oil strikes made by the Philippines in January 1992. In the meantime, the presence of additional petroleum reserves in other areas of the Spratlys was also indicated by technical surveys conducted by mainland China: "In addition to the Reed Bank area, . . . the area claimed by both Malaysia and the Philippines includes some elongated sediment pods several kilometers thick and reefs such as Amboyna, Barque Canada, Mariveles, and Commodore, which are situated to be used as drilling platforms."[292] In 1985 alone, Brunei, Malaysia and Indonesia extracted 100 million tons of oil from these islands.[293]

On the basis of such information, Beijing contracted with an American oil exploration company, Crestone Energy Corporation, to conduct exploratory drilling in an area of the western Spratlys located some 125 nm off the coast of Vietnam and claimed by Hanoi as part of its Exclusive Economic Zone (EEZ). This zone was also located close to Vietnam's highly productive "White Tiger" offshore oil field. Changes in international law during the 1980s had a profound impact on oil and natural gas exploration and exploitation in the SCS.

CHANGES IN INTERNATIONAL LAW

During the early 1980s, UNCLOS codified coastal states' rights to extensive areas of undersea resources out to 200 nautical miles or more. This enclosure movement was a relatively new concept in international law, and China was initially optimistic that the Southeast Asian countries could cooperate to exploit the SCS's

---

[291] Siddayao, *The Off-shore Petroleum Resources of Southeast Asia*, 90–91.
[292] Kent and Valencia, *Marine Policy in Southeast Asia*, 175.
[293] You Ji and You Xu, "In Search of Blue Water Power: The PLA Navy's Maritime Strategy in the 1990s," *The Pacific Review*, Vol. 4 (1991), Issue 2, 137–138.

natural resources. Speaking before the Foreign Correspondents Association in Singapore on 24 July 1993, Chinese Vice Premier and Foreign Minister Qian Qichen stated: "Territorial disputes, border disputes as well as other disputes between Asian countries, should be settled peacefully through negotiations in accordance with relevant international conventions without resort to force or threat of force."[294]

Two decades later, however, when the UN tribunal did not back China's historic claim to all of the SCS during July 2016, Beijing ignored this ruling, even though the tribunal decided that "China's non-appearance in these proceedings does not deprive the Tribunal of jurisdiction."[295] While it was hoped that UNCLOS would lead to an increasingly open and cooperative use of the ocean's resources, national self-interest ultimately triumphed over cooperation. Rather than opening up large areas for joint exploitation, UNCLOS touched off intense competition by regional states to claim these resources as exclusive national assets. The changes to UNCLOS set "in motion the process of establishing vast national enclosures of offshore areas, especially those enclosures consonant with the new exclusive economic zone (EEZ) regime."[296] As a result, Beijing has conducted oceanographic surveys in the region, and has constructed its own outposts on the islands, manned and supported by naval forces.

The Chinese government undoubtedly felt that it was copying the U.S. government's own actions during the 1950s. Growing PLAN spending is intended to guarantee China access to these waters. Beijing's statements about being willing to shelve all problems of sovereignty, and being ready to cooperate with regional states for the development of the Spratly islands, no longer ring true. Assuming each island were able to claim a surrounding 200 nm EEZ around it, the resources of almost two thirds of the SCS would belong to the state exercising sovereignty over the Para-

---

[294] "China Ready to Take Part in Asian Security Dialogues," *Beijing Review* 39 (9–15 August 1993) : 9.
[295] *In the Matter of the South China Sea Arbitration*, 12 July 2016, https://pca-cpa.org/wp-content/uploads/sites/175/2016/07/PH-CN-20160712-Award.pdf [accessed 5 April 2017].
[296] Johnston and Valencia, *Pacific Ocean Boundary Problems*, 3–4.

cels and Spratlys, opening thousands of square miles to resource exploitation.

Beijing's interest in its maritime rights coincided exactly with the development and codification of an international legal regime ceding resource jurisdiction over large areas of ocean to coastal states. Thus, UNCLOS "is a triumph for China and other maritime and coastal powers, as some 40 percent of the area of the entire ocean and most of its resources have been placed under the jurisdiction of coastal states. China's expansive claims ... are congruent with the relevant provisions of the Convention, especially those on EEZs (Articles 55–75)."[297] Despite the apparent consensus of most of the Southeast Asian nations, the issue of oceanic sovereignty has little or no precedence in Chinese or Asian history. It has now become a driving force in future oil and natural gas exploration and exploitation.

FUTURE DEMAND FOR OIL AND NATURAL GAS

The SCS has enormous reserves of oil and natural gas, which American companies are eager to exploit. The demand for oil, both for domestic use and for foreign exports, has increased dramatically throughout Southeast Asia during the past two decades. Simultaneously, the need for ever greater oil and natural gas production is crucial for furthering economic development throughout the region, and particularly among the various claimants to the Spratly islands. Both Vietnam and the Philippines require increasing domestic oil production to support their own industrial development and to lessen their dependence on foreign oil imports, even while Brunei and Malaysia depend heavily on oil exports. A military conflict in the SCS could disrupt exploration and exploitation of oil and gas reserves.

The high rate of economic growth experienced by China in recent years has depended in large part on reliable supplies of petroleum. As early as the late 1980s, China experienced 10% per

---

[297] Samuel S. Kim, "Reviving International Law in China's Foreign Policy," in June Teufel Dreyer, ed., *Chinese Defense and Foreign Policy* (New York: Paragon House, 1989), 111–113.

year growth rates for oil, even while domestic consumption of light and middle distillates surged by 15–20% a year.[298] On average, consumption of refined oil in China rose by 7% a year between 1985 and 1992, and during the early 1990s, Chinese production increased to approximately 142 million tons of oil annually.[299] But by 1995, China had become a net importer of oil, since domestic energy production could not keep pace with the rising demand. While three-quarters of China's 1990's electricity production was from coal, and only 12% from oil and natural gas, internal shortages threatened to limit China's growth. One 1993 editorial succinctly described China's economic dilemma, warning that: "Most estimates see 120,000–140,000 b/d/year oil demand growth for at least several years."[300]

The seriousness of China's resource problem was outlined in a 1992 report to China's State Council by a research group of the Chinese Academy of Sciences, which concluded that "the country faces a crisis of shortages in key mineral resources and oil."[301] Only about 3 million tons of oil were being produced from offshore wells, so one major component of China's petroleum strategy was the expansion of offshore oil exploration and production. But China's offshore oil production was failing to meet expectations: "Of the total potential resource of more than 7 billion bbl identified by that effort, about 4 billion bbl is believed recoverable .... Disappointments aside, China continues to place heavy emphasis offshore, especially for offsetting onshore declines in order to boost total oil production slightly by the mid-1990s."[302]

---

[298] Kim Woodard and David Vernor, "Petroleum Exploration Update: China's Strategy into the '90s," *East Asian Executive Reports* 2 (15 March 1989): 9.
[299] "Final Frontier," *Far Eastern Economic Review*, 10 June 1993, 55 and "Oil Industry Fulfills Plan Ahead of Schedule," Beijing XINHUA in English 29 December 1992, transcribed in *Daily Report: China*, 31 December 1992, 41.
[300] "External Pressures Won't Change China," *Oil and Gas Journal*, 10 May 1993, 17.
[301] "Scientists Warn of Resource Shortages," *Beijing Review* 35 (18–24 May 1992): 7.
[302] "Foreign Firms to Figure More in Rebounding China E&B Scene," *Oil and Gas Journal*, 28 September 1992, 23.

In this context, the Chinese estimates of up to 70 billion barrels of oil in the Spratlys – equal to the output of the entire Tarim basin – are significant. China has supported an aggressive program of oil exploration, even while protesting the activities of the other claimants in the area. China's 1992 contract with the American oil exploration company Crestone Energy Corporation for exploratory drilling in an area designated as Wan'an Bei-21 was expected to find over one and a half billion barrels – $10–15 billion worth of oil – in this one contract area alone. China did not want to cede sovereignty over the increasingly valuable Spratly region (see Map 12 below).

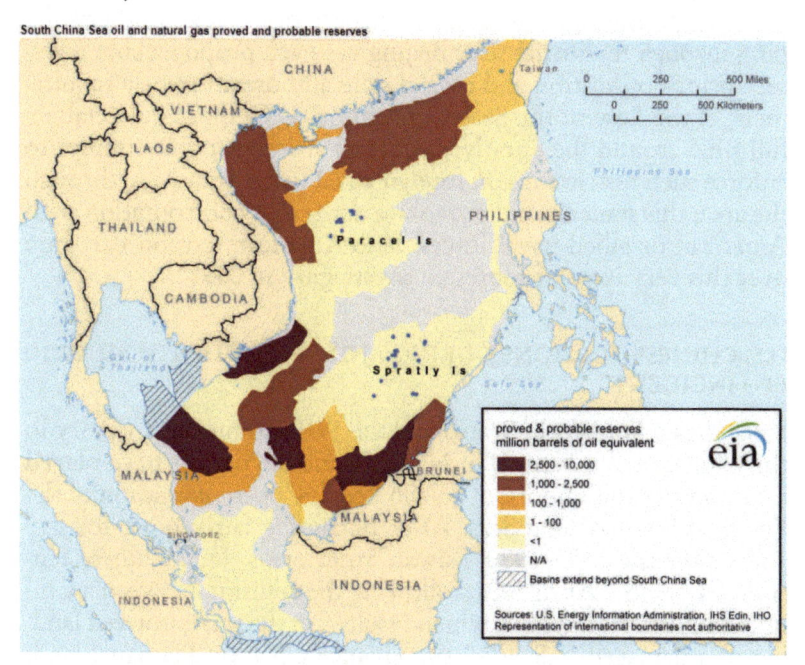

Map 12: SCS Oil and Natural Gas Proved and Probable Reserves

Beijing's ongoing claims to the SCS reflect its energy insecurity, therefore, and its attempts to take the entire SCS would lock in its oil supplies. Even though the SCS boasts a significant amount of oil reserves, it is estimated that they can only meet about three years' worth of China's oil imports of 335 million tons in 2015, and only about two years' of China's total oil demand of 541 million tons in 2015. The vast majority – 82% – of China's oil imports must travel though the Malacca Strait and the SCS. By 2030, if present trends continue, the PRC might have to import 80% of its petroleum and almost half of its natural gas.[303]

China has consistently maximized its strategic position *vis-à-vis* the other coastal states in the SCS, plus has continued to fortify its base on Woody Island in the Paracels. Although this base can pose a potential threat to commercial shipping, when the control of the Spratlys are added to the Paracels it is a different story. In reference to the right of innocent passage of naval and other shipping through territorial seas, Beijing has even proposed that a vessel's prior notification and coastal state authorization be a requirement of the Law of the Seas Convention. If China should claim a full EEZ around the Spratlys, and then at a later point attempt to enforce such restrictions on foreign naval forces transiting through the area, this stance could provoke a dangerous confrontation with American or allied naval forces. Sino-American tension flared up over this very issue of contested sovereignty in 2001.

U.S.-CHINESE TENSIONS DURING AND AFTER THE 1 APRIL 2001 EP-3 INCIDENT

Since the end of World War II and the 1949 Communist victory in the Chinese Civil War, U.S. Navy air and sea patrols have played a continuing and important role in keeping open navigation of the East and South China Seas. After remaining fairly quiet for five years after the 1995–1996 Taiwan Strait crisis, U.S.-Chinese tensions flared on 1 April 2001, following the collision between a Chinese and American plane, which resulted in the unauthorized landing of a damaged U.S. EP-3 surveillance plane on Hainan Island. The April 2001 standoff over the return of the EP-3 crew almost involved sending another U.S. aircraft carrier to China, which was seriously proposed in Washington as one possible response to

---

[303] Andrew B. Kennedy, "China's New Energy-Security Debate," *Survival*, Volume 52, Number 3 (June-July 2010), 138–139.

pressure Beijing to turn over the 24 crewmembers. But the U.S. Ambassador declined this suggestion, fearing that too strong a signal might backfire and lead to the prolongation of the incident.[304]

Rather than turning to the U.S. Navy, Ambassador Joseph Prueher urged the U.S. administration to focus on negotiations so as to ease tensions and resolve the impasse. Early in talks with China, Washington refused when Beijing tried to get Washington to agree that the EP-3's emergency landing on Hainan had invaded China's airspace: "We're not going to take that charge to the President, and we're not going to accept it." Prueher, however, in substantial upgrades from his first offer to use the term "regret," did agree to shift from using "sorry" for the airspace incursion to saying he was "very sorry."[305] This change made it seem to the Chinese public that the U.S. government was taking responsibility for the collision, even while in the English-language letter it was obvious that Prueher was simply expressing regrets for the unfortunate loss of the Chinese pilot. After his two sorrys letter was signed and delivered, the American crewmembers were released. China kept the plane to study it, however, and the disassembled aircraft was finally released over two months later on 3 July 2001 for transportation back to the United States on a Russian cargo plane.

After ten days of tense negotiations, it was Prueher's intentionally ambiguous apology that helped break the diplomatic impasse. Resolving the EP-3 crisis peacefully was largely due to Prueher's qualifications as an aircraft carrier pilot with actual combat experience in the region, as a test pilot cognizant of the capabilities of the airframes involved, and as a recent CinCPac with experience dealing with China. As Prueher later explained, the dispute was not really about the airplane or crew, but it was about "face," and China needed a "signal that it is taken seriously."[306] By writing a suitably polite apology that meant one thing in English and

---

[304] David E. Sanger and Steven Lee Myers, "How Bush Had To Calm Hawks In Devising A Response To China," *New York Times*, 13 April 2001.
[305] Johanna McGeary, "Safe Landing: A carefully engineered game plan helped Bush bring the U.S. flight crew home,"*Time*, 23 April 2001.
[306] Elisabeth Rosenthal, "China Gets White House's Attention, And Some Respect," *New York Times*, 12 April 2001.

another in Chinese, Prueher found a graceful way for Beijing to back down from its untenable negotiating position.

Even though a U.S. Navy aircraft carrier was not sent into the region during 2001, the possibility was seriously considered. During the next decade, Sino-U.S. naval relations remained outwardly calm, and there were few publicly acknowledged maritime disputes. This situation changed dramatically on 8 March 2009, however, when PRC ships confronted the USNS *Impeccable* (T-AGOS 23) while it was conducting operations in international waters in the SCS about 75 miles south of Hainan Island. Two Chinese vessels came within fifty feet, and sailors on-board were observed "waving Chinese flags and telling the U.S. ship to leave the area." In addition to lodging a protest with China officials, State Department spokesman Robert Wood later told reporters that "We felt that our vessel was inappropriately harassed."[307]

The U.S. Navy's reaction to these Chinese provocations was rapid. Within days a guided-missile destroyer, the USS *Chung-Hoon* (DDG 93), was sent to the SCS to accompany *Impeccable*. According to the *Washington Post*, the USS *Chung-Hoon*, "armed with torpedoes and missiles," was sent to "protect" the USNS *Impeccable*.[308] Commander of U.S. Pacific Command, Admiral Timothy Keating, said this incident was an "indicator that China, particularly in the South China Sea, is behaving in an aggressive and troublesome manner, and they're not willing to abide by acceptable standards of behavior or rules of the road."[309] But the Chinese government condemned this USN action as provocative. One Chinese scholar even acknowledged: "The '*Impeccable* Incident' constitutes the most serious friction between China and the United States since the collision of their military aircraft near Hainan Island in April 2001."[310]

---

[307] Tony Capaccio, "Chinese Vessels Harass U.S. Navy Ship, Pentagon Says," 9 March 2009, http://www.bloomberg.com/apps/news?pid=newsarchive&sid=aUMS9YLJ2OmM [accessed 24 March 2011].
[308] Ann Scott Tyson, "Destroyer to Protect Ship Near China," *Washington Post*, 13 March 2009.
[309] Sarah Raine, "Beijing's South China Sea Debate," *Survival*, Volume 53, Number 5 (October-November 2011), 71–72.
[310] Ji Guoxing, "The Legality of the '*Impeccable* Incident'," *China Security* Vol. 5 No. 2 Spring 2009.

Soon after the *Impeccable* incident, a second USN surveillance ship, the USNS *Victorious* (T-AGOS 19), operating 120 miles off China's northern coast in the Yellow Sea, was harassed several times on 4–5 March 2009 by Chinese patrol ships and aircraft. On 1 May 2009, U.S. defense officials announced that Chinese vessels had confronted the U.S. ship in the Yellow Sea. Two Chinese ships came within 30 yards of *Victorious*, which was forced to use water hoses to warn them off. Once again protesting China's actions, the U.S. government reiterated that it would not "end its surveillance activities in the region."[311]

Both incidents took place in international waters as part of the U.S. government's long-time support for freedom of the seas. U.S. Navy officials reiterated publicly that it should not be necessary to send armed ships to protect USNS survey ships.[312] There was even a "touch of irony" assigning *Chung-Hoon* to guard *Impeccable*, since this vessel was "named for a Chinese-American naval officer awarded the Navy Cross, the nation's second-highest combat decoration, for heroic action against Japanese kamikaze pilots during World War II."[313] Assigning this ship to patrol duty could not help but remind the PRC that the two countries were close allies in World War II against Japan. In addition to showing U.S. resolve not to cede freedom of the seas to the PRC, the decision to send a destroyer indicated renewed interest in SLOC security.

U.S. SUPPORT FOR FREEDOM OF NAVIGATION AND SLOC SECURITY

The United States and its allies have a long history of post–World War II freedom of navigation (FON) operations and SLOC protection. Chinese political hegemony in the region,

---

[311] "Pentagon Reports Naval Incident in Yellow Sea," 5 May 2009, http://www.voanews.com/english/2009-05-05-voa24.cfm [accessed 16 December 2010].
[312] Barbara Starr, "Chinese Boats Harassed U.S. Ships, Officials Say," 5 May 2009, http://articles.cnn.com/2009-05-05/world/china.maritime.harassment_1_chinese-ships-chinese-vessels-yellow-sea?_s=PM:WORLD [accessed 24 March 2011].
[313] Richard Halloran, "US-Chinese contacts are imperative for military," *Taipei Times*, 17 March 2009.

backed up by an ever larger number of SCS military bases, is not in either American or Asian interests. Over half of the world's top ten container ports are either in or near the SCS.[314] Due to its central geographic position, acknowledging Chinese sovereignty over the Spratlys could threaten international trade and regional economic interests. In addition, permanent Chinese naval bases throughout the SCS could provide a potential threat to navigation.

During the summer of 2006, CNO Admiral Mike Mullen stated at the Current Strategy Forum, in Newport, RI, that the U.S. Navy needed a new maritime strategy. According to Mullen, the U.S. Navy needed "to lay out a strategy that very broadly defines where the maritime services were going to go in the 21st century."[315] In October 2007, *A Cooperative Strategy for 21st Century Seapower* (CS-21 for short) was adopted based on the premise that: "The oceans connect the nations of the world, even those countries that are landlocked. Because the maritime domain – the world's oceans, seas, bays, estuaries, islands, coastal areas, littorals, and the airspace above them – supports 90% of the world's trade, it carries the lifeblood of a global system that links every country on earth."[316]

During the next five years, the PRC's aggressive actions in the SCS and elsewhere demanded a strategic reassessment. In 2012, the U.S.military released the Joint Operational Access Concept (JOAC) and the concept known as Air-Sea Combat, which are now at the heart of U.S. strategies in the SCS. In March 2015, a revised and expanded CS-21R took a more cautious attitude toward China:

> China's naval expansion also presents challenges when it employs force or intimidation against other sovereign nations to assert territorial claims. This behavior, along with a lack of transparency in its military intentions, contributes to tension and instability, potentially leading to miscalculation or even escalation. The U.S. Sea

---

[314] Roy, *The South China Sea Disputes*, 17.
[315] Mike Mullen, Telephone Interview, 24 January 2013.
[316] *A Cooperative Strategy for 21st Century Seapower*, October 2007, https://www.hsdl.org/?view&did=479900 [accessed 23 March 2017].

Services, through our continued forward presence and constructive interaction with Chinese maritime forces, reduce the potential for misunderstanding, discourage aggression, and preserve our commitment to peace and stability in the region.

In a not-so-discreet reference to China, CNO Jonathan W. Greenert also stated that the U.S. Navy had to be "able to project power despite threats to access."[317]

Unfortunately, if the PRC ever acquires absolute control of the Spratlys, Beijing could attempt to exercise its maximum rights under its interpretation of UNCLOS by bringing thousands of square miles of ocean area under Chinese control. If this happened, Beijing could determine which ships were allowed to use these waters. The SCS sea lanes are critically important for world trade, and especially for the East Asian economies. Japan, in particular, the United States' largest trading partner outside of North America, is almost totally dependent on oil that must be transported through these waters to meet its energy requirements.

Washington also stands up for American oil companies' rights to conduct exploration and drilling in the SCS. In July 2009, the U.S. State Department protested China's attempts to undermine ExxonMobil's ongoing negotiations with Vietnam: "Sovereignty disputes between nations should not be addressed by attempting to pressure companies that are not party to the dispute."[318] U.S. Secretary of State John Kerry, in remarks to students in New Delhi during fall 2016, cautioned "we are also interested in not fanning the flames of conflict but rather trying to encourage the parties to resolve their disputes and claims through the legal process and through diplomacy."[319] The top U.S. goal would be to generate profits for all of the countries surrounding the SCS.

---

[317] *A Cooperative Strategy for 21st Century Seapower: Forward, Engaged, Ready*, March 2015, 4, 7, https://www.uscg.mil/SENIORLEADERSHIP/DOCS/CS21R_Final.pdf [accessed 23 March 2017].

[318] Raine, "Beijing's South China Sea Debate," 75.

[319] Sara Hsu, "China's Energy Insecurity Glaring In South China Sea Dispute," *Forbes*, 2 September 2016, https://www.forbes.com/sites/sarahsu/2016/09/02/china-energy-insecurity-south-china-sea-dispute/#6d3c94a02eec [accessed 2 March 2017].

The sea lanes that pass through the SCS are essential to all of Asia, therefore, providing pathways for the imports and exports representing the foundation of Asian industrial development. Naval experts have warned: "Any interruption of shipping, even for a brief period, could be used to coerce or progressively to injure a nation sufficiently to cause it to lose vital political and economic strength."[320] As a sign of its concern, during March 2017 Tokyo announced that it would send its Izumo helicopter carrier, the largest ship in the Japanese Navy, on a three-month mission to the south, where "it will train with the U.S. Navy in the South China Sea."[321] These exercises are intended to send a warning to China's naval forces.

THE PLAN'S CHALLENGES IN THE SCS

The U.S. Navy faces a deadly regional competitor in the PLAN. China has experienced enormous military growth during the past two decades, especially of its navy. Paramount among the reasons for this rapid growth was China's concern about the encroachment in its territorial waters by other states. China lays claim to a coastline of 11,185 miles (18,000 km) and a vast expanse of ocean spanning some 1 million square nautical miles (3.6 million km^2). Securing and protecting these maritime interests is now seen as a "sacred duty" of the Chinese PLA. Discussing the achievements of the PLAN, one Chinese news broadcast concluded that China's Navy will certainly achieve great success in carrying out its sacred mission of "safeguarding the motherland's territorial waters and maritime rights and interests in the future."[322] Beginning in 1997,

---

[320] "Committee Statement: Security of the Asian-Pacific Sea Lanes," in Worth H. Bagley, *Committee on the Sea Lanes of Communication of Asia* (New York: International Security Council, 1988), 7.
[321] "Japan to Send Largest Warship to South China Sea: Reuters Sources," *Reuters*, 13 March 2017, http://www.nbcnews.com/news/world/japan-send-largest-warship-south-china-sea-reuters-sources-n732621 [accessed 13 March 2017].
[322] Huang Caihong, "PLA Navy Achieves '14 Firsts' in 14 Years," Beijing XINHUA in Chinese 3 Jan 1993. Translated and transcribed in *Daily Report: China*, 7 January 1993, 29.

China's president Jiang Zemin urged the Chinese navy to "build the nation's maritime great wall."[323]

Protecting Chinese maritime interests from foreign encroachment coincided with the strategic withdrawal of both the Soviet Union and the United States military forces from the SCS. China was ready for this shift, establishing the First Brigade of the Chinese Marine Corps on Hainan Island in December 1979. Beijing has also gradually transferred submarines, destroyers, and auxiliary ships from the North and East Sea Fleets to the South Sea Fleet. The construction of the Yulin submarine base, near Sanya on Hainan Island, gives the PRC a short logistics tail to either protect the nearby SLOC or to "threaten the same SLOCs on which Japan, Taiwan, and South Korea are dependent."[324] These reforms paralleled a gradual buildup and development of a military infrastructure in the South Sea Fleet homeport of Zhanjiang on China's southern coast and in the Paracels, both geared to support expanded operations to the south.[325]

This shift southward largely corresponded with China's gradual reclamation of island reefs to turn them into bases. Construction of habitable bases on reefs that are often submerged at high tide presented some unique technical problems for the Chinese. First, channels had to be blasted through the outer portion of the reef to allow ships to enter the lagoon. Then the channels and the interior of the lagoons were dredged, which also provided landfill needed to enlarge the land surface of the islands. Concrete buildings were then built on top of steel caissons driven into the coral reef. Larger buildings, housing communications equipment and barracks, were then built on the landfill. At this stage, a variety of defensive military systems, including anti-aircraft guns and perhaps even surface-to-air missiles, could be added. Recent reports

---

[323] Cha Chun-ming, "Chinese Navy Heads Toward Modernization," *Ta Kung Pao*, Hong Kong, 11 April 1999, cited by Bernard D. Cole, *The Great Wall at Sea* (Annapolis, MD: Naval Institute Press, 2001).

[324] Roy, *The South China Sea Disputes*, 21.

[325] Bruce A. Elleman, "Maritime Territorial Disputes and their Impact on Maritime Strategy – A Historical Perspective," in Sam Bateman and Ralf Emmers, eds., *Security and International Politics in the South China Sea: Towards a Co-operative Management Regime* (London: Routledge Press, 2009).

suggest that China has largely finished construction of its artificial islands in the SCS, and "can now deploy combat planes and other military hardware there at any time."[326]

These preparations suggest that China would not hesitate to use force to protect its interests in the Spratlys, a point not lost on other regional states. China's military growth has been rapid, with one scholar stating: "One reason for Beijing's greater assertiveness in recent years may be the increased confidence it derives from the growing asymmetry of military power between itself and its smaller neighbours, with the People's Liberation Army Navy now clearly the dominant navy among the littoral states of the South China Sea."[327]

Any prolonged conflict in the region could seriously curtail the shipment of goods and commodities through the region and would be potentially catastrophic for the world economy. The U.S. Navy has been tasked with the responsibility of keeping the SLOCs open to international traffic. To do so, Washington must walk a fine line to show its support for freedom of the seas but not accidently precipitate an incident with China. Most recently, the Trump administration has perhaps over-zealously suggested that China's access to its Spratly bases might be interdicted. In response, the *China Daily* stated: "Such remarks are not worth taking seriously because they are a mish-mash of naivety, shortsightedness, worn-out prejudices, and unrealistic political fantasies."[328] Donald Trump quickly reversed himself, but in recent years, the PLA's Central Military Commission has put a premium on exercising Chinese sovereignty over the SCS. This has led to large increases in the PLAN's budget. In fact, there is some evidence that China had been methodically preparing for a military clash in the SCS from mid-1990s onwards. Such concerns have prompted the U.S. "pivot to Asia."

---

[326] "China able to deploy warplanes on artificial islands any time: U.S. think tank," *Top News*, 28 March 2017, http://mobile.reuters.com/article/newsOne/idUSKBN16Z005 [accessed 28 March 2017].

[327] Christian Le Miere, "America's Pivot to East Asia: The Naval Dimension," *Survival*, Volume 54, Number 3 (June-July 2012), 92.

[328] Amitai Etzioni, "Tillerson, Trump and the South China Sea," *The Diplomat*, 28 January 2017, http://thediplomat.com/2017/01/tillerson-trump-and-the-south-china-sea/ [accessed 13 March 2017].

THE UNITED STATES' PIVOT TO ASIA

The SCS regional tensions are considered to be potentially dangerous to the free and open flow of world trade, much of which transits through these waters. On 16 November 2011, U.S. Secretary of State Hillary Clinton urged all the claimants not to resort to force: "The United States does not take a position on any territorial claim, because any nation with a claim has a right to assert it... But they do not have a right to pursue it through intimidation or coercion. They should be following international law, the rule of law, the U.N. Convention on Law of the Sea."[329] Clinton's warning was timed with President Barack Obama's announcement in Australia that 2,500 U.S. marines would be stationed in Darwin. Huang Jing, a visiting Chinese professor at the National University of Singapore, concluded that: "The US needs to show the Chinese that they still have the power to overwhelm them, that they still can prevail if something really wrong happens."[330]

From Washington's point of view, the most dangerous of the regional disputes is probably between China and Vietnam. The PLA's past aggression against Vietnamese forces includes the Paracel islands in 1974, the Sino-Vietnamese land war of 1979, and the Spratlys in 1988. Sino-Vietnamese border disputes have been a major preoccupation since full normalization of relations in 1991. During 2009–2011 tensions increased dramatically in the SCS. Despite these frictions, their 10 October 2011 Agreement, outlining six basic principles guiding the settlement of sea-related issues, including resolving disputes through friendly negotiation both "bilaterally" and through negotiations with other "concerned parties," which could indicate Taiwan since 10 October – double ten

---

[329] "Hillary Clinton warns against intimidation in South China Sea dispute," *The Economic Times*, 16 November 2011, http://economictimes.indiatimes.com/news /international-business/hillary-clinton-warns-against-intimidation-in-south-china-sea-dispute/articleshow/10757519.cms [accessed 20 November 2011].

[330] "Obama: Darwin, Australia, to host US marines: President Obama announces plans to send US marines to Darwin, Australia," *Global Post*, 16 November 2011, http://www.globalpost.com/dispatch/news/regions/asia-pacific/111116/darwin-australia-marines-obama [accessed 20 November 2011].

– is the founding anniverary of the ROC, most likely not by submitting their greviences to the UN tribunal.[331]

However, a clash at sea, especially if initiated by the Vietnamese, could provide a pretext for further Chinese military actions. On at least two previous occasions – in 1974 and 1988 – China has pointed to a Vietnamese incursion to justify the use of what it calls defensive military force. Following this pattern, a PLA air and sea attack against a few key Vietnamese outposts in the Spratlys could quickly neutralize opposition forces. While there might be temporary criticism against such an attack, Beijing would probably consider international censure a small price to pay for obtaining control over virtually all of the Spratly islands. In other words, Beijing appears willing to "absorb any short-term costs" so as to ensure China's rise "is not unduly, and – in its view – unfairly constrained by the U.S. and its partners."[332] Since the U.S. government has a mutual defense treaty with the Philippines, but not with Vietnam, there is also a real strategic "advantage for China in starting with Vietnam first."[333]

The use of force is not the only option. Other scenarios include bilateral discussions between China and Vietnam, with or without the participation and consent of other claimants, over the sharing of natural resources in the Spratlys. Beijing and Hanoi have already signed one agreement governing fishing zones in the Gulf of Tonkin. Although unlikely to be negotiated any time soon, any future bilateral agreement between Hanoi and Beijing might allow both states to move forward with oil and natural gas development. It could include a profit sharing scheme, or could perhaps detail separate geographical areas for Chinese and Vietnamese oil exploitation.

---

[331] "China and Vietnam agree principles for resolving maritime disputes," *IBRU: Centre for Borders Research*, 13 October 2011, https://www.dur.ac.uk/ibru/news/boundary_news/?itemno=12969 [accessed 11 April 2017].

[332] "Few barriers to China's Push in South China Sea," *Associated Press*, 21 May 2014, http://www.miningjournal.net/page/content.detail/id/508087/Few-barriers-to-China-s-push-in-South-China-Sea.html?isap=1&nav=5016 [accessed 13 March 2017].

[333] David Archibald, "China's 'Mobile National Territory'," *American Thinker*, 19 May 2014, http://www.americanthinker.com/2014/05/chinas_mobile_national_territory.html [accessed 9 March 2017].

If force is used, however, military victory could make China the dominant SCS power. Beijing would see no advantage in simply defeating Vietnamese forces and then withdrawing back to its bases in the Paracels or on Hainan. An overwhelming Chinese naval and military presence in the Spratlys, similar to the Chinese occupation of the Paracels after they drove South Vietnamese troops out of those islands in 1974, would almost certainly result in Chinese military forces occupying islands claimed by not just Vietnam, but probably also by the Philippines, Malaysia, and Brunei. However, Vietnam has a long history of prolonging wars, and a lengthy war would almost certainly interfere with nearby trade routes. The implications of such a protracted conflict, therefore, would be counter to U.S. government interests and those of its Asian allies.

From Washington's perspective, the second most dangerous situation is the possibility of a major maritime dispute between the Philippines and the PRC. The Philippines cannot fight China single-handedly. In 1995, Orlando Mercado, Chairman of the National Defence and Security Committee, said "We have an air force that can't fly and a navy that can't go out to sea."[334] The United States government must be directly concerned with the security of the Philippines through their Mutual Defense Treaty. While the Philippine's official claim to the islands post-date the 1951 treaty, Article V of this treaty does state: "An armed attack on either of the Parties is deemed to include an armed attack on the metropolitan territory of either of the Parties, or on the island territories under its jurisdiction in the Pacific or on its armed forces, public vessels and aircraft in the Pacific."[335]

The U.S. government is obliged to carry out its treaty with the Philippines. Therefore, any Chinese attack on one of the KIG fortified islands, a Philippine ship, or a Philippine aircraft could be construed as an attack on the Philippines itself, with the ultimate result that Manila could demand American assistance. In January 2016, the Philippine Supreme Court agreed that the 2014 Enhanced Defense

---

[334] Hayton, *The South China Sea*, 236.
[335] Department of State, "Mutual Defense Treaty Between the United States and the Republic of the Philippines," 30 August 1951, TIAS no. 2529, *United States Treaties and Other International Agreements* vol. 3, 3947–3952.

Cooperation Agreement (EDCA) was constitutional, which would allow for U.S. forces to be forward-deployed in the Philippines. Secretary of Defense Ash Carter has argued that the "U.S. commitment to the Philippines is ironclad."[336] Rather than retreating in the face of Chinese aggression, Philippine forces are well-entrenched on the islands that they occupy. Even though Duterte appears to be placating China now, the Philippine Defence Minister Delfin Lorenzana stated during March 2017 that the Philippine "military would strengthen its facilities in the Spratlys, building a new port, paving an existing rough airstrip and repairing other structures."[337]

Even if one were to argue that the Spratly islands are not covered by the mutual defense treaty, any clash between Chinese and Philippine forces over the Spratlys would almost certainly spill over onto Philippine military bases in nearby Palawan. This island is an integral part of the Philippines and well within its mutual defense treaty area. The issue of American support was previously raised by Philippine Foreign Secretary Roberto Romulo, who reportedly asked for a review of the United States-Philippine Defense Treaty to determine specifically "what Washington would do if hostilities broke out in the South China Sea."[338] From a Philippine perspective, therefore, the protection and defense of its sovereignty, territorial integrity, and the natural resources cannot be compromised.

The third most dangerous flashpoint would be a conflict between the PRC and Malaysia, which have extensive and overlapping SCS claims. Notwithstanding these outstanding Sino-Malaysian territorial disputes, past and present Malaysia government administrations have demonstrated great reluctance to sign joint

---

[336] Ash Carter, "The Rebalance and Asia-Pacific Security: Building a Principled Security Network," *Foreign Affairs*, November/December 2016, https://www.foreignaffairs.com/articles/united-states/2016-10-17/rebalance-and-asia-pacific-security [accessed 12 April 2017].

[337] "Philippines' Duterte Says 'May' Visit Disputed South China Sea Island," *The New York Times*, 6 April 2017, https://mobile.nytimes.com/reuters/2017/04/06/world/asia/06reuters-southchinasea-philippines.html?rref=collection%2Fsectioncollection%2Freuters-news&_r=0&referer=https://www.nytimes.com/section/reuters [accessed 6 April 2017].

[338] Jose Fernandez, "Manila Seeks US Pledge on Spratlys," *Asian Defence Journal* 16 (January 1993): 150.

development agreements. Instead, Malaysia is actively exploiting these resources on its own, even while trying to enhance its claim over the area through further military occupation and commercial development. Most importantly, Malaysia's 2009 decision to

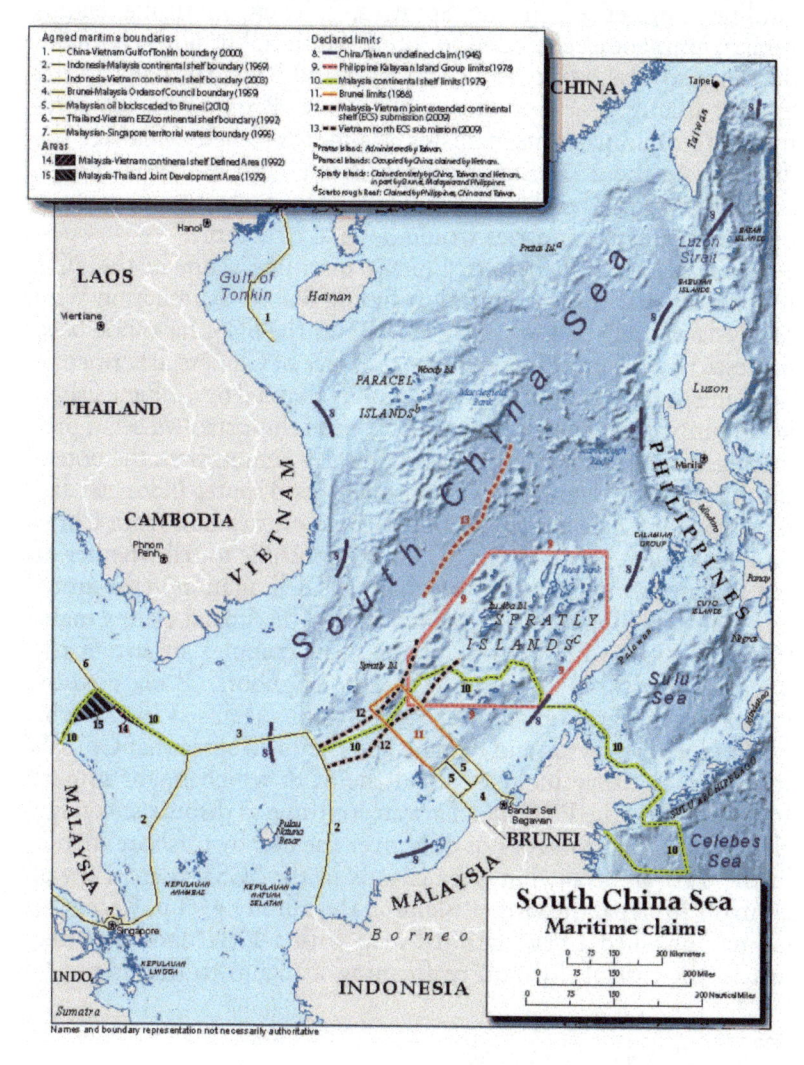

Map 13: The SCS Maritime Claims

submit with Vietnam a joint continental claim to the CLCS cannot help but conflict with China's claim to the entire SCS (see Map 13).

One of the least dangerous scenarios is probably between Brunei and China. To date, Brunei is the only claimant without a "military presence" in the Spratlys.[339] Their maritime claims remain ambiguous and open to interpretation, but both countries do claim sovereignty over Louisa Reef and Rifleman Bank in the Spratly islands. For the foreseeable future, Brunei remains committed to diplomatic mechanisms as a means to better manage the dispute. As the 2009 EoL between Brunei and Malaysia shows, such a diplomatic resolution is possible, despite the significant hurdles the claimant countries would have to overcome.

Indonesia officially rejects China's maritime claim in the SCS. Indonesia's maritime activities, including seabed delimitation with Malaysia in 1969 and Vietnam in 2003 in the SCS, have not been protested by Beijing. However, the presence of Chinese fishermen in maritime areas around the Natuna islands guarded by Chinese fisheries administration vessels, and the actions of this patrol vessel in provoking Indonesian maritime patrols, clearly demonstrate the potential for Chinese aggression. To resolve this dispute, Indonesia has largely made its claims public, but without clarification from China on its maritime claims in the SCS it is impossible to tell whether or not Indonesia and China require maritime delimitation in the area.

Finally, Beijing's and Taipei's differing territorial claims make the PRC-ROC situation one of the most complex of any of the ongoing territorial disputes between neighbors. Both governments largely agree on their territorial claims against Vietnam, the Philippines, Malaysia, and Brunei, and they also agree that China's sovereign territory includes all of the SCS, which might impact Indonesia. But the PRC and Taiwan continue to dispute sovereign rights and actual control not only over the nearby offshore islands in the Taiwan Strait, but over islands in the SCS, where Taiwan controls Itu Aba, the largest island in the Spratly group. Recently, China published a new national map with a 10th "dash" inserted just to the east of Taiwan, reaffirming its claim to that island.[340]

---

[339] Roy, *The South China Sea Disputes*, 18.
[340] Roy, *The South China Sea Disputes*, 14.

Taipei rejects this claim. When push comes to shove, however, Taiwan has generally supported the PLAN activities against all other SCS claimants, so if China goes to war with Vietnam or the Philippines then Taipei might decide to back Beijing.

To make matters even more complicated, China promises that it will work with the ASEAN countries to negotiate all differences peacefully, but it actively excludes Taiwan's participation from this process, which virtually guarantees that all negotiations will fail. If the PRC and Taiwan were to unify or sign some form of document, similar to the Nationalist-Communist United Fronts in the 1920s and 1930s, in which they agreed to cooperate on settling China's borders, then this could give Beijing increased leverage over the other claimants. The PRC's current borders could at some point in the future even be proclaimed null and void as it adopts Taiwan's larger claims, and a whole new round of negotiations might ensue. This situation would give Beijing a golden opportunity to renegotiate these borders.

China is playing a dangerous game in the SCS. As two China experts presciently warned in 2011: "China must tread carefully if it hopes to use the PLAN to obtain its national objectives, while avoiding a naval arms race."[341] Christian Le Miere, in the defense publication *Survival*, aptly called this era the "Return of Gunboat Diplomacy," as PLA Chief of Staff Chen Bingde cautioned that "preparations for potential military conflicts" in the South China Sea "must be . . . taken." Le Miere concluded that "China has become increasingly active in the naval sphere as its capabilities improve and its desire to either trial or showcase them expands."[342] Meanwhile, in 2011 *Global Times* aggressively warned that if the SCS claimants remain at loggerheads with Beijing they should "mentally prepare for the sounds of cannons."[343] This jingoistic attitude greatly increases the chance of a Sino-American clash.

---

[341] Bussert and Elleman, *People's Liberation Army Navy (PLAN) Combat Systems Technology*, 188.

[342] Christian Le Miere, "The Return of Gunboat Diplomacy," *Survival*, October-November 2011, Vol 53, No.5, 58.

[343] "China paper warns of "sound of cannons" in sea disputes," *Reuters*, 25 October 2011, http://www.reuters.com/article/2011/10/25/us-china-seas-idUSTRE79O1MV20111025 [accessed 20 November 2011].

THE POSSIBILITY OF A FUTURE SINO-U.S. MILITARY CLASH

During the past twenty years the PLAN has grown quickly with Russian equipment and training, but it continues to embody many of the special characteristics of past Chinese navies. Pertinent examples relating to face, an enduring belief in the Mandate of Heaven, and ethnic and regional differences can be seen over and over again. Whereas the Chinese tend to focus on size, and assume that the largest navy will win, size is not everything. Rather, it is efficient coordination of available naval assets that matters most. While today's PLAN looks large on paper, therefore, history suggests that smaller regional navies – such as the Japanese Maritime Self Defense Force (JMSDF) or even the Taiwanese Navy – could still prove more than a match for the Chinese Navy in an actual battle.

The Russians have tried hard to push China's attention to the south. In line with its long-time interests in East Asia, the Russian government wants to ensure the China does not look to the north to expand. Motivated by self-interest, therefore, Russia is actively pushing for a Sino-U.S. conflict in Asia. Not surprisingly, as early as 1920, Vladimir Lenin expressed his hope that there would be a major war in the Pacific: "America and Japan are on the eve of a war and there is no possibility of preventing this war, in which there will again be 10 million killed and 20 million mutilated."[344] It took two decades, but Stalin arguably made the biggest gains in East Asia for the least cost right as World War II was ending, securing Outer Mongolia's independence from Nationalist China and helping the Chinese Communists to secure all of Mainland China. In January 2017, one Russian news article even trumpeted that "China Prepares for a Military Conflict with the USA."[345]

To promote a war in the SCS, Russia is selling weapons to all sides. It has been estimated that between 1991 and 2010 "more

---

[344] David J. Dallin, *The Rise of Russia in Asia* (New Haven: Archon Books, 1971), 164–165.
[345] Владимир Скосырев, "Китай готовится к военному конфликту с США," 31 January 2017, http://www.ng.ru/armies/2017-01-30/2_6915_china.html [accessed 23 March 2017]; my thanks to Lyle Goldstein for pointing out this article.

than 90 per cent of China's imported major conventional weapons were supplied by Russia"[346] (see Graph 1 below). Effective use of this foreign equipment could pose a major problem for Chinese navies. British visitors to a Chinese naval ship recently noted that much of the hi-tech equipment appeared to have never been used, suggesting not just inadequate training but more importantly a possible reluctance to use valuable equipment for fear of breaking it.

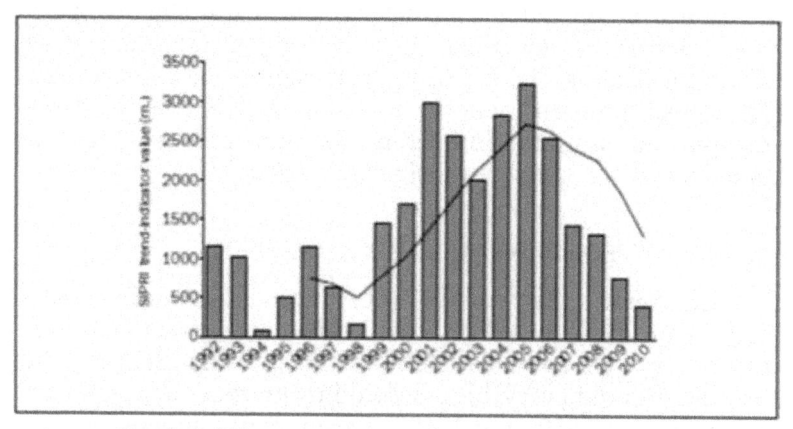

Graph 1: Chinese arms imports from Russia, 1992–2010[347]

Part and parcel of this problem is systems integration, as China attempts to merge its own equipment with imported technology from a large number of countries and suppliers. As technology experts have warned: "The real keys to the integration problem are naval training and documentation, which is difficult enough with a fully indigenous fleet, but almost impossibly complex when imported or copied foreign equipment is added to the mix."[348] In December 2013, the *Chinese People's Liberation Army Daily* admit-

---

[346] Linda Jakobson, Paul Holtom, Dean Knox and Jingchao Peng, "China's Energy and Security Relations with Russia," *SIPRI Policy Paper 29*, Ocotber 2011, 14.
[347] SIPRI Arms Transfers Database, http://www.sipri.org/databases/armstransfers [accessed 23 March 2017].
[348] Bussert and Elleman, *People's Liberation Army Navy*, 172.

ted that during a recent exercise sailors on four ships could hear each other, but could not transmit combat data.[349]

Not only is Russia selling weapons to many of the claimants in the SCS dispute, including to both China and Vietnam, but it is conducting combined operations with China's naval forces. To assist China, an eight-day joint naval exercise was held during September 2016 in the SCS in which Russian naval officers helped train the Chinese in "island and reef seizure maneuvers, as well as anti-submarine operations, air defense, and naval and air operations." During the most recent G-20 meeting in Hangzhou, Vladimir Putin said that the Russian government stood "in solidarity with China's position" of not recognizing the UN tribunal's decision, plus opposing the interference of third parties – read the United States – in the South China Sea dispute.[350]

AMERICAN EFFORTS TO AVOID AN ASIAN WAR

The only country that would profit from an Asian conflict, especially in the SCS, would be Russia. Moscow's attempt to promote a war to the south should not come as a surprise, since the United States did everything it could to promote a Sino-Soviet war during the 1950s and 1960s. Throughout Chinese modern history, foreign naval intervention in Chinese affairs has often been a determining factor. Naval blockade, strategic embargo, and economic sanctions have all been used to apply pressure on Beijing, with varying degrees of success. The most notable example was coordinating the Nationalist blockade and the U.S. strategic embargo during the 1950s to interdict the PRC's foreign trade. This policy had the long-term effect of pushing China and the USSR closer together, thereby increasing mutual economic and political tensions that ultimately resulted in a split. Other U.S. Navy interventions, such as to halt China's 1995–1996 "missile blockade" of Taiwan, have countered Chinese attempts

---

[349] Hayton, *The South China Sea*, 221.
[350] Elizabeth Wishnick, "Russia Wants to be a Contender: The New Problem in the South China Sea," *Foreign Affairs*, 19 September 2016, https://www.foreignaffairs.com/articles/russian-federation/2016-09-19/russia-wants-be-contender [accessed 4 April 2017].

to put pressure on Taiwan. In all such cases Beijing was forced to back down.

The U.S. Navy has the ability to blockade China at many different points. The December 2004-February 2005 humanitarian relief Operation Unified Assistance in northern Sumatra showed China that, without any prior warning, U.S. naval forces could travel to the western entrance to the Malacca Strait in less than a week and begin humanitarian operations there.[351] Not fully recognizing the global nature of China's trade, some commentators have falsely stated that for the U.S. Navy to lose access to the waters of the SCS would be "devastating" to America's foreign policy, and "If the United States loses access to those waters [SCS] it loses its global role and becomes just another power."[352] Beijing must be careful, therefore, that its attempts to assert regional dominance do not precipitate the far blockade it worries about.

Astute diplomacy can sometimes replace the need for foreign military intervention. During the aftermath of the EP-3 collision on 1 April 2001, and the plane's unauthorized landing on Hainan Island, Ambassador Prueher – born and raised in Tennessee, so no stranger to the importance of honor – gave China "face" by agreeing to express regret in his "two sorrys" letter. The clever use of vague terminology meant that the American version of the note did not accept responsibility for the collision, while in the Chinese-language note it appeared to do so. Negotiating with China involves creating ladders for Chinese officials to climb down from untenable positions.

Since 2001, there has often been an uneasy peace between the U.S. Navy and the PLAN, especially in waters bordering China. Rear Admiral James P. Wisecup, Captain of USS *Callaghan* (DDG 994) in 1996 and later the President of the U.S. Naval War College, said he could imagine – had the shoe been on the other foot – the type of meeting that might have occurred after Washington's intervention in 1995–1996, with China's leaders demanding of the PLAN: "I want to know what you are doing to make sure

---

[351] Bruce A. Elleman, *Waves of Hope: The U.S. Navy's Response to the Tsunami in Northern Indonesia*, Newport Paper No. 28 (Newport, RI: Naval War College Press, 2006).
[352] Hayton, *The South China Sea*, 208.

that never happens again."³⁵³ The PRC is currently conducting an overtly expansionist policy in the SCS by building island bases and fortifications. Experts have even argued that the PLAN is carrying out a "fleet-in-being" strategy in the SCS that would seek "to deny control of maritime areas at certain times to the rival through the fleet's presence and menace."³⁵⁴ Fearful of incurring Beijing's wrath, many of China's neighbors to the south might decide to increase cooperation with Beijing instead.

Perhaps the most ominous signal of Chinese naval designs on the Spratly islands stems from its domestic aircraft carrier program. The current Chinese carrier, *Liaoning*, is largely obsolete, since it does not have a catapult, but only a ski jump, meaning the J-15 jets cannot carry counter-measure pods or heavier missiles. China has just launched its first indigenous aircraft carrier, which it hopes will be operational by 2020. The PLAN will reportedly produce a total of six indigenously produced aircraft carriers. The two principal purposes of an aircraft carrier are to launch planes for sea-to-shore strikes and to provide air support for fleet operations at sea. Both of these capabilities would be critical in a major naval operation in the Spratlys. In this regard, even one carrier with 40 aircraft equals the military effectiveness of 200 to 800 land-based fighter planes. Furthermore, the "sea area under control of a convoy headed by a carrier is fifty times as large as that controlled by a convoy of destroyers. The navy only needs one such task force to control the entire sea and air space around the Nansha island."³⁵⁵ Added to this threat is China's recent announcement that it plans to increase the size of its marine corps from 20,000 to 100,000 personnel.³⁵⁶

China may be over-estimating its military abilities in the SCS. The lack of a unified naval command is potentially a major weakness. During September 2016, China held a rare joint naval drill in the Yellow and Bohai seas that included over a hundred ships

---

[353] Interview with RADM James P. Wisecup, 8 March 2011.
[354] Le Miere, "America's Pivot to East Asia: The Naval Dimension," 85.
[355] You and You, "In Search of Blue Water Power," 145.
[356] "Report: China Building 100,000-Strong Marine Corps," *Newsmax*, 27 March 2017, http://www.newsmax.com/Newsfront/China-marines-military-seas/2017/03/27/id/780869/ [accessed 27 March 2017].

from the North, East, and South Sea Fleets.[357] Such drills aside, however, during normal operations the three regional fleets tend to work independently of each other, and so the current division of the PLAN into three regional fleets might present divide-and-conquer opportunities. Similar to Japan in the 1930s, China today could face a potentially deadly combination of incomplete military institutions, a lethal international environment, a skewed civil and military balance, and a misunderstanding of geopolitics, which if not corrected in time could all too easily result in war.[358]

In a naval war between China and the United States, therefore, the currently-structured PLAN would almost certainly lose. However, the economic and political repercussions for all of East Asia could be devastating. Not surprising, the only country that might see a geopolitical advantage as a result of such a war would be Russia. Some Chinese commentators are aware of this risk, even warning that China's enemies – read Russia – want "to lure it into conflict in order to keep it weak."[359] The problem is that China continues to pursue the elusive Assassin's Mace (*Shashoujian*), like its 11 January 2007 anti-satellite (ASAT) test, which destroyed a defunct weather satellite, to guarantee the defeat of its primary enemy. Disaster might quickly ensue, however, once the Chinese military thinks it has actually found one.

CONCLUSIONS

The stage appears to be set for further U.S. Navy freedom of navigation (FON) operations to keep the SCS open to international commerce. While the political and strategic issues involved in this conflict are widely recognized and understood, China has steadfastly refused to subject its claim to the Spratlys to any foreign or

---

[357] "China Reveals it held secret combat drill with all its naval fleets in September," *The Times of India*, 29 November 2016, http://timesofindia.indiatimes.com/world/china/China-reveals-it-held-secret-combat-drill-with-all-its-naval-fleets-in-September/articleshow/55683944.cms [accessed 13 March 2017].

[358] S.C.M. Paine, *The Japanese Empire: Grand Strategy from the Meiji Restoration to the Pacific War* (New York: Cambridge University Press, 2017), 179–180.

[359] Hayton, *The South China Sea*, 223.

multinational arbitration, and so has stubbornly ignored the UN tribunal's decision. Beijing insists that the entire SCS is Chinese territory, based on both the historic waters argument and the fact that the PRC and Taiwan together occupy a number of the largest islands.

There is a hefty financial component to the SCS problem. Newly developed oil drilling technology can exploit the oil reserves in the Spratlys. Meanwhile, newly purchased military equipment can enforce territorial claims in the region. These two trends may become self-enforcing, setting up a vicious cycle that will be difficult to break. Both of these developments have made the potential value of the SCS, and the corresponding tensions over ownership, escalate. To make a complicated situation even more complex, while the U.S. government supports Taiwan against China in the Taiwan Strait, the two Chinas tend to agree on the ownership disputes in the SCS. If the PRC and ROC actively cooperate in the SCS, this might undercut American intervention.

This possibility makes determining an equitable solution to the SCS tensions particularly difficult. Without the PRC's and ROC's full participation, a "cooperative regime" for the Spratlys would ultimately be meaningless. Given appropriate incentives, however, China might consider such a cooperative regime to be in its long-term interests. The main difficulty is convincing China that compromise is in its national interests. Only China, among all the claimants, is financially capable of taking advantage of the latest military technology on a scale that can overwhelm all its smaller neighbors. This advantage will undoubtedly influence China's maritime strategy in the SCS.

CONCLUSIONS:

China's Contemporary and Future Maritime Strategy in the SCS

———*———

IN 2009, approximately half of the world's 259 unresolved boundary disputes (out of 427 total) involved disputed islands.[360] China has tense relations in the SCS with each maritime nation in the region, serious enough to be compared to the "ongoing tensions between Israel and Palestine."[361] At one point in May 2013, the Philippine Secretary of Defense even warned China that the Philippines will "fight for what is ours up to the last soldier standing."[362] Many battles in the SCS have already been fought over apparently insignificant reefs, rocks, and small islands. Relevant strategic lessons can be learned by examining the type and intensity of China's maritime conflicts with its neighbors, successful and unsuccessful efforts to delimit official borders, and possible areas where future maritime disputes might arise (see Map 14 below).

The most important question in the Spratly islands dispute concerns China's future strategy: Will China choose conflict or compromise? The determining factor is likely to be China's pragmatic calculation of the risks and gains involved in a military show-down with Vietnam, the Philippines, and other smaller Southeast Asian states over the SCS. Should war erupt, all of East Asia could well be impacted, since "close to 70% of

---

[360] Van Dyke, "Disputes Over Islands," in Hong and Van Dyke, eds., *Maritime Boundary Disputes*, 39; my thanks to Clive Schofield for this statistic.
[361] Caceres, *China's Strategic Interests in the South China Sea*, 75.
[362] Li Jianwei and Ramses Amer, "Managing Tensions in the South China Sea: Comparing the China-Philippines and the China-Vietnam Approaches," in Tran Truong Thuy and Le Thuy Trang, eds., *Power, Law, and Maritime order in the South China Sea* (New York: Lexington Books, 2015), 248.

South Korea's energy imports, approximately three-fifths of Japan's and Taiwan's oil shipments, and nearly four-fifths of China's energy supplies are brought from the Indian Ocean into the Straits of Malacca and pass directly to the South China Sea."[363]

The U.S. government, and in particular the U.S. Navy, has an important role in helping to resolve these outstanding problems, as it pivots to Asia. The U.S. government must be ready for China to choose among four alternative strategies discussed below: 1) an indirect strategy; 2) an unilateral maritime strategy; 3) a bilateral strategy; and 4) a multilateral strategy. Possible courses of action will be developed for each of these alternatives.

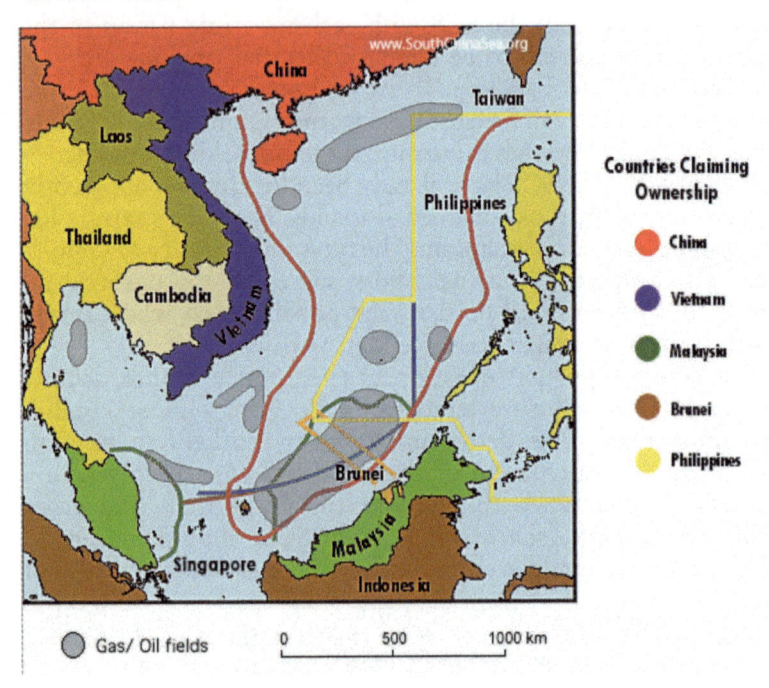

Map 14: Complex Nature of the SCS Claims[364]

---

[363] Caceres, *China's Strategic Interests in the South China Sea*, 88.
[364] SCS map courtesy of David Rosenberg www.southchinasea.org.

THE SCS VALUE AS A SLOC

Without a doubt, the SCS's greatest value is as an economic highway. Approximately 6% of the world's entire wealth, a quarter of its total trade, and almost a third of U.S. trade, relies on keeping this SLOC open and safe for commercial shipping. The Gross World Product in 2012 was estimated at almost $72 trillion, and a quarter of this is in goods and services, which hit an estimated world trade of almost $18 trillion in 2013. Over 80% of world trade in goods now moves by sea and, each year, over $5 trillion worth of that trade passes through the SCS. Of this $5 trillion, U.S. trade accounts for about one quarter, or about $1.2 trillion out of a total U.S. yearly trade in 2012 of $3.82 trillion.[365] The oil trade throughout the SCS is particularly important (see Map 15 below). While not a near neighbor of China, and also not a member of ASEAN, the United States is a Pacific nation and so is highly concerned by any threat to freedom of navigation. In other words, it is in the interest of the U.S. government to ensure that trade and other commercial activities in the SCS are not interrupted.

Like the United States, China also depends on this SLOC. In 2007, China became a net importer of food, and in 2013 it passed the U.S. to become the world's largest net oil importer. In 2012, the PRC passed America for the first time as the world's largest trading nation, achieving $3.87 trillion in total imports and exports.[366] As one Chinese website admitted: "The South China Sea region is one of the busiest sea lanes in the world, through which pass more than half of the world's merchant fleet tonnage, one third of

---

[365] "Gross World Product", http://en.wikipedia.org/wiki/Gross_world_product [accessed 24 September 2014]; Organisation for Economic Co-operation and Development, http://stats.oecd.org/index.aspx?queryid=167 [accessed 24 September 2014]; Bonnie S. Glaser, "Armed Clash in the South China Sea: Contingency Planning Memorandum No. 14," *Council on Foreign Relations*, April 2012, http://www.cfr.org/world/armed-clash-south-china-sea/p27883 [accessed 24 September 2014]; "China Eclipses U.S. as Biggest Trading Nation," *Bloomberg.com*, 10 February 2013, http://www.bloomberg.com/news/2013-02-09/china-passes-u-s-to-become-the-world-s-biggest-trading-nation.html [accessed 24 September 2014].

[366] "China Eclipses U.S. as Biggest Trading Nation," *Bloomberg.com*, 10 February 2013, http://www.bloomberg.com/news/2013-02-09/china-passes-u-s-to-become-the-world-s-biggest-trading-nation.html

global marine trade volume and half of energy supplies to Northeast Asia, including 80 percent of oil traffic to Japan, South Korea and China's Taiwan region."[367] Beijing also wants to protect its SLOCs, but on its terms, and to this end has been seeking ways to network its disparate maritime assets on Hainan, the Paracels, and the Spratly islands. These facilities, which range from airstrips, to submarine bases, to communications relays, to radar units, all demonstrate China's expanding regional reach.

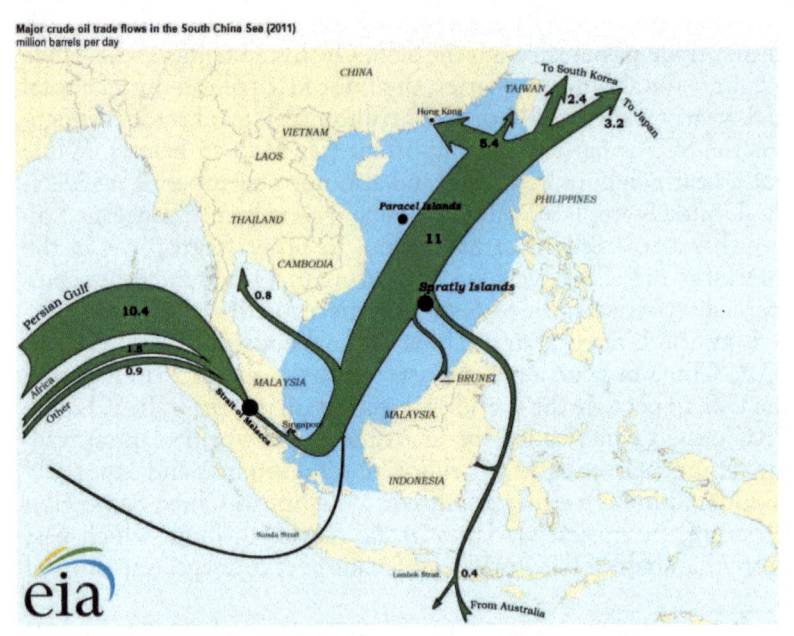

Map 15: Major Oil Deliveries through the SCS SLOC

Meanwhile, to help insure that it can protect its own trade from interference, or perhaps adopt a blockade policy against a potential enemy if necessary, the PLAN has developed a number of new sea control and sea denial capabilities. Using this military threat,

---

[367] "South China Sea islands dispute, issues explained," *Whatsonsanya.com*, 1 September 2012, http://www.whatsonsanya.com/sanya-info-948.html [accessed 26 September 2014].

Beijing has sought to open bilateral talks with each of the other claimants to the SCS, thereby pressuring them to accede sequentially to China's demands. Designed to cut the U.S. government out of the loop, these bilateral negotiations have so far failed to resolve the outstanding disputes, and tensions have been mounting.

China's growing naval capabilities are seen as an omnipresent threat by its neighbors and a potential challenge to the U.S. Navy. In the past, the U.S. government attempted to set itself up as a diplomatic arbiter helping to resolve outstanding problems among the various regional parties in East Asia. The U.S. government, the U.S. military forces, and especially the U.S. Navy have increasingly assumed greater responsibility to ensure that trade and other commercial activities in the SCS are not interrupted. This threat has forced America to "pivot" back to Asia to become the military arbiter in the SCS, a task that could become more challenging in coming years as the claimant nations continue to militarize, to develop their naval forces, and to reclaim more ocean territory. Some commentators have referred to this as the "flyspeck" option, since by controlling a multiple of SCS islands they are seeking to control it all.

SCS ISLANDS AS OWNERSHIP "FLYSPECKS"

Islands can be valuable territory of and by themselves. They can contain natural resources or perhaps have a strategic harbor that can protect warships. However, since the signing in 1982 of the UNCLOS convention, and its coming into force on 14 November 1994, islands can also be used to claim maritime territory, which can include water, the water column, seabed, and underground natural resources. Most importantly, some islands are capable of generating a maritime zone of their own, including a 12 nm territorial sea, 24 nm contiguous zone, a 200 nm exclusive economic zone (EEZ), and in certain circumstances an extended continental shelf (ECS) out to 350 nm or even more.

It is important to clarify that islands claim surrounding waters, not the other way around. Many SCS claimants have stated that because they have a 200 nm EEZ, or perhaps a bigger ECS, the islands within that zone must be theirs. In effect, this is attempting to use a maritime zone to claim territory, which is not considered to be a valid method under contemporary international law, and is also "difficult to justify under a continental shelf theory."[368] However, creating island bases to assert control over the surrounding waters and their natural resources is legal, and appears to be one of Beijing's primary goals motivating its recent island reclamation efforts in contested SCS waters.

The significance of using islands to support a gradual expansion of national sovereignty has been called "creeping jurisdiction," where an obscure low-tide elevation can be reinforced with artificial construction in order to increase their legal status as base points. In 1978, Choon-Ho Park even warned: "Some South China Sea coastal states might eventually be tempted to expand a few strategically situated islands in this way, in order to foreclose argument against their legal status as base points." Thus, it would appear that in order to claim ownership of the SCS and its resources, "a claimant has only to own the 'flyspecks'."[369] Using island flyspecks to control territory has a long and venerable history in East Asia, where England's minuscule – only 31 square miles – island of Hong Kong long dominated the China trade.

Control over strategic islands fits well with Asian traditions. In China, the 4,000 year-old game of "weiqi" (in Japan called "Go") seeks to take strategic territory so as to surround and starve out the enemy's bases, not to destroy them directly: "In other words, it is the seizure and maneuvering of strategic positions."[370] One of the biggest differences between weiqi and Western games like chess is that the white or dark pieces don't move around the board but are placed permanently anywhere on the board, with the goal of securing strategic territory for oneself or surrounding the enemy's territory. Unlike chess, the enemy's pieces are not attacked by a frontal assault, but are made ineffective once they are completely surrounded. Often, this means isolating an opponent's piece by surrounding it from the rear. The board pieces can be compared to islands surrounded by an expansive ocean (see Map 16 below).

---

[368] Valencia, et al., *Sharing the Resources of the South China Sea*, 37.
[369] Choon-Ho Park, "The South China Sea Disputes: Who Owns the Islands and the Natural Resources?" *Ocean Development and International Law* 5 (1978): 45.
[370] Roy, *The South China Sea Disputes*, 70.

By contrast, Western games like chess require that the pieces move. In 1911, Naval War College professor, Alfred Thayer Mahan, an avid chess player, first discussed jumping over an enemy's island forces. In three letters criticizing the NWC's 1910 "Strategic Plan" he proposed "island hopping" rather than taking all enemy islands during a campaign. On 4 March 1911 he argued some islands "may be even neglected, as immaterial, in favor of offensive action against the enemy's positions." On 17 March 1911, Mahan clarified that taking a certain island base could become "a stepping stone to a base in or near the Orange [Japanese] territory." Likewise, when discussing the importance of taking certain islands for sea denial operations, Mahan suggested bypassing a crucial enemy position in order to cut its lines of communication further down the line, thus undermining its logistical supply line and making its position more and more untenable. Mahan wisely cautioned that an enemy (in this case Japan) should not be made aware of this strategy, since once they occupied and fortified all of the Pacific islands then they would be "tied to supporting them" and so: "It might even be urged as a sound policy on the part of Blue [US], to induce Orange [Japan] to such distant effort, which would place it in the same position that Blue finds so difficult in trans-Pacific operations."[371]

Mahan may well have been the first Western strategist to suggest utilizing an "island hopping" strategy. According to Mahan, some islands can hold great strategic value that can be used to exert sea control or sea denial. But fortifying other islands can work against a nation's interests, trapping ones' forces in place. Mahan's clearly enunciated proposal that the U.S. should "deceive" the Japanese into building bases on as many Pacific Island bases as possible as one method of over-extending the Japanese forces would appear to have been adopted in practice, as Japan fortified many islands like Truk, which was never attacked directly by U.S. land forces but was surrounded, cut off from resupply, and was on the verge of collapsing due to starvation when Japan surrendered.

---

[371] These letters were addressed to Rear Admiral R. P. Rodgers, President of the Naval War College, and dated 22 February, 4 March, and 17 March 1911, Historical Collection, U.S. Naval War College.

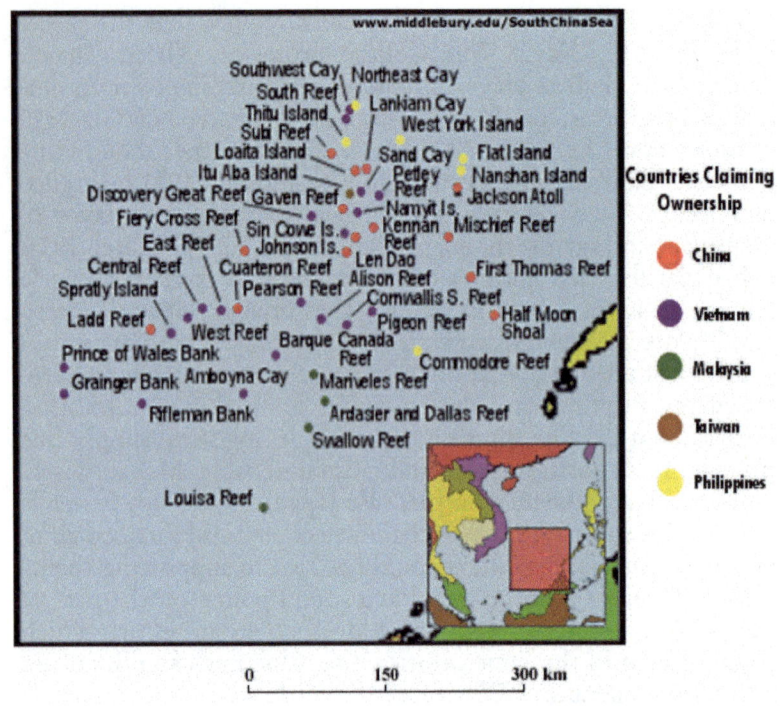

Map 16: The SCS resembles a "Weiqi" board[372]

China's reclaimed islands in the SCS could face a similar fate. Amitai Etzioni recently argued that the Chinese island bases in the SCS were of "little military value," since: "They are like broken-down aircraft carriers that are marooned and are sitting ducks which would be wiped out in a case of war in a matter of minutes."[373] As early as 1950, the British chiefs of staff concluded: "The Spratley [*sic.*] Islands are of no appreciable strategic value.... Enemy occupation in war would not, so long as we retain control of the [SLOC in the] South China Sea, be a serious strategic threat."[374] Like the infamous "Trojan Rabbit," which turns out to

---

[372] SCS map courtesy of David Rosenberg www.southchinasea.org.
[373] Amitai Etzioni, "Tillerson, Trump and the South China Sea," *The Diplomat*, 28 January 2017, http://thediplomat.com/2017/01/tillerson-trump-and-the-south-china-sea/ [accessed 13 March 2017].
[374] Hayton, *The South China Sea*, 237.

be empty of any threat, China may find itself similarly over-extended by its recently adopted island-reclamation activities in the SCS, which could negatively impact its attempts to assert sea control throughout the region.

SCS ISLANDS AS A MEANS TO ASSERT SEA CONTROL

China's rise as a sea power could include attempts to assert sea control. After World War II, "sea power emerged as the most potent force , . . . a phenomenon probably unparalleled in the entire course of world history."[375] If China seeks to alter the world order in its favor it must first face up to this challenge. In recent years, the Chinese government has invested heavily in the PLAN, apparently with the goal of building an ocean-going "blue water" navy. The rapid growth of the PLAN, in conjunction with Beijing's aggressive actions in the SCS, have raised the possibility that sea control throughout East Asia might soon be contested.

In peacetime, commercial traffic proceeds over an uncommanded and uncontested sea. The task of major sea powers is to ensure that nothing interferes with commerce. However, during wartime, according to Sir Julian S. Corbett (1854–1922): "The object of naval warfare must always be directly or indirectly either to secure the command of the sea or to prevent the enemy from securing it. . . . [T]he most common situation in naval war is that neither side has the command; that the normal position is not a commanded sea but an uncommanded sea."[376]

Sea control offers navies a greater range of strategic options. For example, during the early 1950s, immediately after losing the Chinese civil war, the Nationalist Navy used control over strategic offshore islands to blockade commerce. Passage through narrow channels amongst hundreds of small islands made merchant shipping near China's shores predictable, facilitating interception. Initially the Nationalist Navy covered most of the Chinese coastline, but by the mid-1950s it focused mainly on the southeast. Cut off from global

---

[375] Ludwig Dehio, *The Precarious Balance: Four Centuries of the European Power Balance* (New York: Vintage Books, 1962), 270.
[376] Sir Julian S. Corbett, *Some Principles of Maritime Strategy*, new edition (New York: Longmans, Green and Co., 1918), Part II, Chapter 1.

maritime trade by a U.S.-led strategic embargo plus Nationalist blockade, the PRC was forced to turn to inland commerce with the USSR, increasing Sino-Soviet trade from only 1% before World War II to over 50% by 1957. This over-dependence on Moscow then exacerbated pre-existing diplomatic tensions. The Nationalist blockade ended in 1958, just as the first signs of the Sino-Soviet split emerged.[377]

However, unlike the ROC in the 1950s, the PRC may not be in a position to adopt a maritime strategy based on sea control. Without clear egress to the sea, in wartime the PLAN must transit narrow seas in order to leave or reach home port. The existence of hundreds of islands, rocks, and reefs in the SCS make it a death-trap not so much for the U.S. Navy, which can choose not to deploy there, but for the PLAN, which cannot avoid these waters. Thus, the PRC is not geographically positioned to take advantage of its sea power, since it depends on numerous resources that can arrive only by sea. For example, as recently as 2013, 70–85% of the PRC's imported oil was transported "through Malacca from Venezuela and oil-rich nations in Africa and the Middle East," making these shipments vulnerable to interdiction at many different points along their route[378] (see Map 17 below).

Attempts to exert sea control can quickly lead to over-extension. If the PRC were not only to claim the SCS waters but also attempt to control them, for instance, by continuing to build island bases intended to exclude others, these actions could produce an opposing coalition, composed initially of those whose immediate territorial interests were most directly threatened, but eventually expanding to include nations deeply interested in the continuation of the present global order. The animating issues behind such a coalition would be freedom of navigation, territorial integrity, and sovereignty – all potentially valuable items in the current global order. Continuing PRC attempts to exert sea control in the SCS in defiance of its neighbors could easily produce a boomerang effect detrimental to its long-term interests.

---

[377] Bruce A. Elleman, "The Nationalists' blockade of the PRC," in Elleman and Paine, eds., *Naval Blockade and Seapower*, 142.
[378] "China's Reliance on Shipping Crude Oil Through the Straits of Malacca," February 2013, https://sites.tufts.edu/gis/files/2013/02/Brutlag_Daniel.pdf [accessed 21 February 2017].

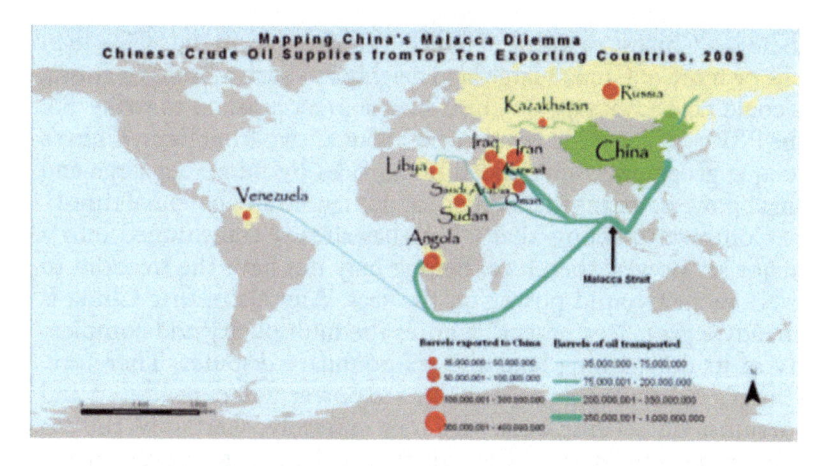

Map 17: China's Malacca Dilemma

There is enormous concern in the U.S. that China will try to use its sea power to exert sea control over the world's oceans. But Mahan pointed out that a country's geography and its political interactions can either help or impede a country becoming a sea power. Historians have since concluded that: "States with long land borders with multiple opportunities for attack, territorial expansion, and defense concerns are unlikely to develop successful sea power."[379] Those continental powers that do achieve status as sea powers – usually, in European history at least, for a relatively short period of time – must become regional hegemons first, only after which they can attempt to "acquire supremacy in the realm of intercontinental, maritime trade."[380]

Arguably, China is even now at the stage of trying to become a regional hegemon. But China's multi-front geography makes a conflict with one neighbor potentially risky, since it could give another neighbor an unexpected opportunity to attack. Even if all outstanding land and sea disputes are resolved, at any point in the future when

---

[379] William R. Thompson, "Some Mild and Radical Observations on Desiderata in Comparative Naval History," in John B. Hattendorf, ed., *Doing Naval History: Essays Toward Improvement* (Newport, RI: NWC Press, 1995), 107.
[380] Karen A. Rasler & William R. Thompson, *The Great Powers and Global Struggle, 1490–1990* (Lexington, KY: The University Press of Kentucky, 1994), 23.

there is a Chinese maritime conflict – for example, in the SCS – then one or more of China's large land neighbors – such as India or Russia – could take advantage of China's naval preoccupation to strike. So, the PRC will always have to worry about a "two front" war; China's unique geography, surrounded on all sides by numerous large and small powers, means that Beijing cannot ignore any potential threat.

Contrary to claims that China has already transitioned into a major sea power, therefore, Beijing may not have the freedom to exert its new-found power on the seas. Any claim that China is already a great "sea power" ignores the multiplicity and complexity of its outstanding land and sea boundary disputes. Therefore, China's rise to becoming a major sea power will depend first and foremost on settling these disputes amicably. Certainly the sea border dispute in the SCS, which involves seven governments including both the PRC and Taiwan, must be fully resolved prior to China taking upon itself the mantle of a full-fledged sea power. Furthermore, its actions on the sea will always have to be closely coordinated with those on the land. This fact cannot help but act as a major, and one might presume lasting, constraint on Beijing's "sea power" ambitions. Such concerns also impact the PRC's ability to use its bases in the SCS to exert sea denial.

SCS ISLANDS AS A MEANS TO EXERT SEA DENIAL

In the past ten years, China has not only expanded and fortified its island bases in the SCS, but is in the process of destroying and dredging up thousands of acres of pristine natural reefs to create brand new islands. The environmental devastation has been catastrophic, especially to the local fisheries. One recent report concluded that "increasing demands for food has led to over-exploitation, destructive fishing practices, and illegal, unreported, and unregulated (IUU) fishing activities that threaten fishery resources in the SCS."[381] In two decades from 1978 to 1998, China's catch

---

[381] Yao Huang and Pham Tran Vuong, "Fisheries Cooperation and Management Mechanisms in the South China Sea: Context, Limitations, and Prospects for the Future," *The Chinese Journal of Comparative Law*, Volume 4, Number 1 (March 2016), 128–148; 131.

grew fourfold, from 3 million to 12 million tons.[382] The PRC's extensive reclamation policy proves, however, that the PRC is developing the capacity to bar others from these waters. Sea denial entails closing down part of the maritime commons to the traffic of others, so unlike sea control – a positive objective – sea denial entails a negative objective.

One advantage of sea denial strategies is they usually go largely unseen. These strategies can force the target country to back down without its leaders bearing the public relations cost of having retreated, thus making it more politically feasible to get the target government to act in desired ways. In the past, many sea denial operations received little attention in the press because initially no one but those directly impacted knew what had happened. If all the ships involved were naval ships, their respective governments could simply decline to comment. Of course, political leaders can choose to go public and denounce sea denial strategies. During February 2014, Philippine President Benigno Aquino even compared China's sea denial actions in the SCS to 1938 Germany, emphasizing: "At what point do you say, 'Enough is enough'? Well, the world has to say it – remember that the Sudetenland was given in an attempt to appease Hitler to prevent World War 2."[383]

The feasibility of sea denial also depends on the geography of the theater. Sea denial from islands is particularly risky. World War II in the Pacific can be seen as a succession of battles with the operational goal of closing off the waters around island airbases in order to deny Japan key SLOCs. Following Mahan's advice, Allied forces simply hopped over fortified islands to occupy and build airbases on other less well-defended islands on the way to the Japanese home islands. This island hopping approach neutralized the utility of Japan's significant investments in these defenses and transformed the surrounding seas into a graveyard for Japanese ships. In the end, the Allies successfully denied Japan the use of the surrounding waters, which meant Japan could not resupply

---

[382] Hayton, *The South China Sea*, 241.
[383] Marex, "For South China Sea Claimants, a Legal Venue to Battle China," *The Maritime Executive*, 13 February 2014, http://www.maritime-executive.com/article/For-South-China-Sea-Claimants-a-Legal-Venue-to-Battle-China-2014-02-13/ [accessed 24 September 2014].

and defend its far-flung island bases, including Truk in particular, which eventually fell virtually without a fight due to lack of supplies.

Sea denial strategies do not necessarily have to sever all sea communications but can deny only certain types of traffic or can halt movement in one direction but not the other. This allows for fine-tuning maritime strategies. For example, in early 1953, the United States tried to put additional pressure on the PRC to end the Korean War by threatening to "unleash" Chiang Kai-shek's troops on Taiwan to invade the mainland. The U.S. Taiwan Patrol continued to stop any PRC sea invasion of Taiwan, but new instructions ordered U.S. Navy vessels not to halt a Nationalist attack on the PRC. As anticipated, Mao Zedong responded to this potential threat far to the south by diverting Chinese troops from Korea. Once Joseph Stalin died in March 1953, all remaining opposition to an armistice disappeared and a treaty was signed that summer.[384] Thus, rather than using its own troops to adopt an aggressive strategy of its own, Washington merely eased its sea denial strategy aimed at Taiwan to put additional military pressure on the PRC.

The control over key islands can also potentially position a country to deny passage to others. In January 1974, the PLAN wrested control of the Paracel islands in the SCS from the collapsing South Vietnamese government. The U.S. government decided not to intervene, perhaps preferring that China acquire the Paracels rather than a unified Vietnam allied with the USSR. Control of the Paracels positioned the PLA Navy to blockade the North Vietnamese port of Haiphong. This later became important during the 1979 Sino-Vietnamese War, when the Soviet Union declined to honor its mutual defense treaty with Vietnam and refused to ship weapons to Haiphong, in part because China could block the sea lanes.[385]

---

[384] Bruce A. Elleman, *High Sea's Buffer: The Taiwan Patrol Force, 1950–1979* (Newport, RI: NWC Press, 2012).

[385] Bruce A. Elleman, "China's 1974 expedition to the Paracel Islands," in Bruce A. Elleman and S.C.M. Paine, eds., *Naval Power and Expeditionary Warfare: Peripheral Campaigns and New Theatres of Naval Warfare* (London and New York: Routledge, 2011),149.

Thus, the geography of the impacted theater is perhaps the most important single factor in undertaking or withstanding sea denial. Countries hemmed in by islands can fortify these islands to close their own waters to others. Conversely, an enemy sea power can take advantage of such restricted geography to deny its opponent the use of its merchant marine and navy. For example, speaking of its Itu Aba (Taiping Island) naval base, Liang Kung-kai, head of Taiwan's Ministry of National Defense's Department of Strategic Planning, stated in 2006 that "if war broke out between Taiwan and China, Taiwan's submarines would definitely have the ability to make ambush attacks against China's oil tankers in the South China Sea."[386]

Dominating the SCS islands might allow the PLAN to interdict and destroy sea traffic, but other countries could equally retaliate by cutting off the PRC's commercial traffic through a combination of submarine attacks on merchant shipping and by blocking more distant chokepoints such as the Malacca Strait. Sea denial strategies are not one-sided therefore: "China can 'deny' the US the exercise of sea 'control' in the western Pacific; the US, and other countries such as Japan and India, however, have the advantage of sea 'denial' elsewhere, preventing China from projecting naval power in Asia or beyond, including for defence of sea lanes in the event of conflict."[387] For example, a recent RAND study has even suggested that the United States and its allies adopt a far-blockade strategy by encouraging the PRC's neighbors to position short-range (100–200 km), land-based, anti-ship missiles (ASMs) at a variety of chokepoints throughout East Asia, such as the Straits of Malacca, Sunda, and Lombok. According to RAND, this would "shut down China's naval movements," undermine its ability to project power, and vastly complicate its problems should Bijing initiate a conflict with its neighbors.[388]

Given the PRC's dependence on trade to maintain its economic growth, if Beijing decides to adopt a sea denial strategy it

---

[386] Edward Chung, "MND Says Spratly Airport Strategic," *Taipei Taiwan News* (Internet Version-WWW) in English, 6 January 2006, FBIS CPP20060106968041.
[387] Harris, *China's Foreign Policy*, 185.
[388] Wendell Minnick, "RAND Suggests Using Land-based ASMs Against China," *Defense News*, 7 November 2013.

could end up hurting itself more than any other country. Such strategies carry the additional risk of second-order effects such as skyrocketing insurance rates that might halt all commercial traffic through contested waters. Peter Dutton has warned: "The impact of a disruption for even a period of three weeks would be substantial," and for those shipping companies attempting "to pass through the area during a conflict – whether to access the resources there, or to cut transit times – the insurance costs 'would be prohibitive'."[389]

Any PLAN attempt to shut down access by sea, therefore, could undermine the very goals Beijing seeks. China's risks are principally economic and political, not military. They relate to the growing trade and economic ties between China and the regional states of Southeast Asia, and with Japan and the United States. A military move by China to enforce territorial claims in the Spratlys could threaten not just commerce, but the political independence of the regional states and the strategic interests of Japan and the United States. Rather than risk the probable backlash of adopting a sea denial policy, China may be seeking simply to exert limited sea control in the SCS.

In the long-run, the PRC leaders might decide that an offensive maritime strategy is self-defeating and, more importantly, that the PRC would profit more by becoming a full member of the global order on which its recent prosperity rests. China faces many military challenges, including a lack of jointness not just between services but among regional fleets, inadequate supply lines, and unreliable replenishment at sea. Finally, and perhaps most importantly, China's unique geographical position imposes limits on its naval power projection. In the meantime, it will be essential for the U.S. Navy to coordinate maritime cooperation among the PRC's many neighbors so that the accumulating precedents strengthen, rather than weaken, the security architecture of Asia. All of these issues will impact China's willingness to assume risk.

---

[389] Everett Rosenfeld, "Chinese naval push could affect global trade," *CNBC.com*, 29 August 2014, http://www.cnbc.com/id/101952236 [accessed 20 September 2014].

CHINA'S WILLINGNESS TO ASSUME RISK

A century ago Imperial Japan was a rising Pacific Ocean power, and so was in much the same position as China is today. The world's failure to introduce Japan peacefully into the international political order cost it dearly. Today, the amazingly short development time of new Chinese combat systems and missile systems, with help from the Russian government, show that the PRC is building a world-class Blue Water navy through foreign naval acquisitions, particularly of hi-tech ships and armaments from Russia, and from a robust indigenous shipbuilding program.

Similar to Japan during the 1930s, Beijing appears willing to risk much to obtain its military ambitions. China might be looking not just to reclaim Asian territories, lost to it during the so-called "century of humiliation" from the 1840s onward, but also to move out into the Pacific to challenge the United States to protect its interests. As noted China specialist Hugh White warned: "China seems to be prepared to run the risk so it can exploit these incidents to assert its claims . . . This is how wars start."[390] In particular, the PRC's decision to purchase Russian-made guided missile destroyers and diesel submarines, both of which are based mainly in the East and South Sea Fleets, will add greatly to China's rapidly growing capability to threaten Taiwan, on the one hand, and to challenge Southeast Asian countries for control of the SCS, on the other hand. All of these vessels offer superb "sea denial" capabilities, which will make it very difficult for foreign navies to intervene in China's littorals.

In the past, small-scale military clashes have characterized the SCS disputes, but this may change if the United States confronts China. Except for Brunei, at one time or another all these Southeast Asian nations have supported military actions, and there were numerous reported incidents during the 1990s alone (see Appendix A). However, of all the countries that have an interest in these waters, the PRC has arguably spent the most time and money building a multi-layered military support infrastructure in the SCS

---

[390] Roy, *The South China Sea Disputes*, 48; citing Peter Hartcher, "US finds unwilling partner in China to avert potential crisis in region," *Sydney Morning Herald*, 17 August 2011.

that might allow it to one day obtain its strategic goals through force. China's Southeast Asian neighbors fear Beijing's policy of militarizing the SCS. If the PRC secures its hold over crucial SCS islands it could adopt sea control strategies to pressure its smaller neighbors to back down even while adopting sea denial strategies to protect itself from an invasion.

Vietnam has already responded to PRC aggression by rapidly expanding its air and naval forces, including amphibious planes and Russian-made diesel *Kilo* submarines, presumably with sea denial plans of its own. During May 2014, when China stationed an oil rig in disputed waters off the west coast of the Paracel islands, anti-China riots in Vietnam damaged both PRC and ROC-run factories and resulted in 21 deaths of both PRC and ROC citizens.[391] In retaliation, China recalled over 7,000 workers from Vietnam, citing safety concerns, but really to punish Hanoi. One Vietnamese woman belonging to a Buddhist sect even "immolated herself to protest the Chinese incursions into Vietnamese waters."[392] Such public sacrifices are reminiscent of anti-American opposition during the height of the Vietnam War.

In sharp contrast to Vietnam, which has fought – and actually won – numerous wars with China during the past millennia, the Philippines appears more ready to throw in the towel. Not only did Philippine President Rodrigo Duterte announce his "separation" from the United States in October 2016, but he claimed the Philippines had realigned its foreign policy to form closer ties "with China as the two agreed to resolve their South China Sea dispute through talks." In early April 2017, Duterte said of China's reclamation efforts in the SCS: "We cannot stop them because they are building it with their mind fixed that they own the place.

---

[391] Ralph Jennings, "Vietnam Taking Long-Term Hard Line Toward China on Maritime Claims," *Asia*, 28 November 2016, http://www.voanews.com/a/vietnam-taking-long-term-hard-line-toward-china-on-maritime-claims/3614214.html [accessed 28 November 2016].

[392] T. T. Nhu, "Vietnam and China: Conflict over islands arouses Vietnamese patriotism," *San Jose Mercury News*, 23 September 2014, http://www.mercurynews.com/opinion/ci_26591028/vietnam-and-china-conflict-over-islands-arouses-vietnamese [accessed 21 September 2014].

China will go to war."[393] Most of the other countries in Southeast Asia are simply too weak to oppose China on their own.

Faced with this wide range of challenges, the PRC may hope to adopt a maritime strategy based on a robust navy that will allow it to claim the SCS and the so-called "first island chain," and then move beyond this area deeper into the Pacific. One author argues that "China's desire to assert itself in Asia is clear, as shown by the frequent outbreaks in tensions with neighbouring countries in the South China Sea."[394] China's growing submarine fleet is especially important. The number of active PLAN submarines is currently only about ten fewer than the U.S. Navy submarines, but China's new construction trends point to a future imbalance in China's favor, since it is outbuilding the U.S. in new submarines by 4:1 over the last 20 years, and by 8:1 over the last 15 years, a rapidly rising number that the diminished U.S. Navy ASW forces will be hard-put to handle.[395] As of 2016, the PLAN had four strategic submarines with nuclear propulsion, five conventional nuclear subs, and over 50 other types, including eight *Kilo*-class diesel submarines.[396]

Geography makes these growing numbers even more threatening from the U.S. perspective, since all of these PLAN submarines are in its coastal waters, and so face minimal transit distances. The deep waters of the SCS might allow China to adopt a bastion defense, similar to the Soviet defense of the Sea of Okhotsk during the Cold War, thereby cutting off all of the waters to outside warships and submarines. By contrast, until recently about half of the U.S. Navy submarines were based in the Atlantic. Even those based at Guam or Pearl Harbor are a long way from China. Therefore, any American submarines sent to Chinese waters could eas-

---

[393] "Philippines' Duterte Says 'May' Visit Disputed South China Sea Island," *The New York Times*, 6 April 2017, https://mobile.nytimes.com/reuters/2017/04/06/world/asia/06reuters-southchinasea-philippines.html?rref=collection%2Fsectioncollection%2Freuters-news&_r=0&referer=https://www.nytimes.com/section/reuters [accessed 6 April 2017].

[394] Christian Dargnat, "China's Shifting Geo-economic Strategy," *Survival*, Volume 58, Number 3 (June-July 2016), 63–64.

[395] Bussert and Elleman, *People's Liberation Army Navy*, 183.

[396] IISS, *The Military Balance* (Abingdon, UK: Routledge Press, 2016), 242.

ily be outnumbered, even while the PLAN diesel submarines are younger, which means that they are much quieter than the older Chinese vessels.

Viewed from this perspective, one of China's main strategic motivations behind building a strong navy is to be able to enforce its territorial claims. As early as 1977, Chinese Foreign Minister Huang Hua said of the Spratly islands "we will confiscate all of them in due time . . . When we will recover these islands depends upon opportunity."[397] According to John Pike, head of GlobalSecurity.org: "What is the next big problem the PLA navy could solve for the political leadership? The South China Sea. It has an incredible capability to grab everything down there. If I was in the PLA navy, that's a no-brainer."[398]

China's territorial and economic interests in this area arguably go hand-in-hand, since major shipping lanes, extensive fisheries, and a wide variety of energy sources are either located in these regions, or transit the all-important SLOCs that passes India, continues through the Malacca Strait, and reaches China via the SCS. But one scholar has asked Beijing if the SCS territory is "worth the risk of creating a conflict that could wreak havoc on the global economy and even involve nuclear weapons?"[399] Considering the size of Chinese trade through this region, for Beijing to want to hold the entire SCS hostage just to get what it wants would be like pointing a gun to its own head.

China has made some effort to improve bilateral negotiations regarding naval disputes, and as recently as 27 March 2017 a senior Chinese diplomat called for creating a new "cooperation mechanism" to "boost exchanges in such areas as disaster prevention, maritime rescue, environmental protection, biodiversity, scientific research and navigational safety."[400] Such a mechanism would be especially useful in the SCS, which suggests that China might

---

[397] Koo, *Island Disputes and Maritime Regime Building in East Asia*, 150.
[398] Chris O'Brien, "Beijing Hospital Ship Harbors Soft Power," *Washington Times*, 26 January 2009.
[399] Amitai Etzioni, "Accommodating China," *Survival*, Volume 55, Number 2 (April-May 2013), 54–55.
[400] "China Calls for Cooperation on South China Sea," *Reuters*, 27 March 2017, https://mobile.nytimes.com [accessed 27 March 2017].

be willing to utilize diplomatic means before adopting a military solution. After starting his research convinced there would be a war in the SCS, journalist Bill Hayton ended up concluding: "I became convinced that the Chinese leadership understands that it can only lose from a shooting war, although it views everything short of war as a useful policy tool."[401] Counter-balancing India, exerting limited sea control as far as the Malacca Strait, and insuring the continued viability of this invaluable SLOC are a high priority for China, so as to insure that it cannot be blockaded during periods of tension. Carrying out such a policy would be furthered by forming a new United Front with Taiwan.

A NEW PRC-ROC UNITED FRONT

For almost seven decades the two Chinas have opposed each other across the Taiwan Strait, with the U.S. Navy playing the role of maritime arbiter. At times, rising tensions appear to threaten war, such as in 1995–1996, when the PRC adopted a "missile blockade" against Taiwan. Since 1996, Sino-Taiwanese territorial tensions have remained at a low simmer. Conversely, Beijing and Taipei agree on many issues pertaining to their mutual sovereignty, including China's historic claim to the Diaoyu islands in the East China Sea, plus claims to the bulk of the sea territory and islands in the SCS. The situation in the SCS could radically change if leaders in Beijing and Taipei were to form a third United Front in order to promote a joint PRC-ROC foreign policy agenda.

The first and second United Fronts between the Nationalists and Communists proved disastrous, with Chiang Kai-shek purging the Communists in 1927, and the Communists returning the favor in 1949 when they defeated the Nationalists and put pressure on Taiwan to cede all disputed offshore islands. However, if the PRC and ROC should ever adopt a third United Front, and then work together to consolidate their joint territorial claims, they might be able to redraw their mutual borders with neighboring states. For example, new and expanded border claims in the SCS could be made based on Taiwanese maps. If adopted, such a policy

---

[401] Hayton, *The South China Sea*, 268.

could give Taipei and Beijing a golden opportunity to renegotiate maritime borders that neither government may be completely satisfied with.

The U.S. government also has a stake in these disputes. After the victory of the Chinese Communists in 1949, and following the beginning of the Korean War in 1950, Taiwan survived a number of international crises over the disputed offshore islands with U.S. assistance. During the 1950s, 1960s, and again during the 1990s, the PRC tried to put military pressure on Taiwan to reunify. Washington's decision to intervene in the Taiwan Straits by sending in the Seventh Fleet was crucial for halting any cross-strait war. During the most recent crisis in 1995-1996, a number of USN vessels, including the aircraft carriers *Nimitz* and *Independence*, conducted patrols near the Taiwan Strait in support of Taiwan.[402] China's attempts to coerce Taiwan backfired. It is widely acknowledged that U.S. intervention may have "closed out the option" of PLA escalation.[403]

The PRC's failure to halt American intervention arguably resulted in a shift away from military pressure and increasingly strong economic and diplomatic ties between Beijing and Taipei. With military invasion from either side of the strait ruled out, cooperation between the ROC and PRC has gradually increased. For example, CNOCC and Taiwan's state-owned oil refiner, CPC Corporation, have actively cooperated in conducting joint surveys in the SCS. Meanwhile, Vietnamese attacks, including firing on Taiwan's coast guard station on Itu Aba, have promoted a profound shift in loyalties: "Taiwan has started to view Vietnam as their enemy rather than China and thinks that the PLA would be capable of protecting them."[404] This attitude is perhaps not too surprising since their territorial claims in the SCS largely overlap each other.

Ever since 1949, U.S. intervention made PRC-ROC economic competition the main factor in line with the Open Door Policy.

---

[402] Nicholas D. Kristof, "Off Taiwan, U.S. Sailors Are Unworried," *The New York Times*, 19 March 1996.
[403] Douglas Porch, "The Taiwan Strait Crisis of 1996: Strategic Implications for the United States Navy," *Naval War College Review*, Vol. LII, No. 3 (Summer 1999), 21-23.
[404] Roy, *The South China Sea Disputes*, 62-63.

Maintaining the military balance between the PRC and Taiwan successfully kept the peace for the past seventy years, even while making the PRC and Taiwan's economic development their most important measure of success. But there has been a convergence of PRC and ROC commercial interests over the past three decades, with Taiwanese investors pouring billions of dollars into the mainland economy. To promote cross-strait communications and trade, in 1990 Taiwan created the Straits Exchange Foundation (SEF), while the PRC established the Association for Relations Across the Taiwan Straits (ARATS). PRC-ROC economic relations have improved dramatically since 2000, including increased travel, cross-strait investment, and direct shipping. Taiwanese investment in the PRC economy grew rapidly, outpacing all other foreign investors.

Although their military standoff has now lasted for almost seven decades, beginning in 1992 the PRC and ROC opened a series of informal talks designed to clarify their positions on a wide range of issues, including Taiwan's support for the "one China" principle, called the 1992 consensus. These talks broke down in 1998, due to the increasing strength of the Taiwanese pro-independence movement, as indicated by Chen Shui-bian's presidential victories in 2000 and 2004, but resumed again during June 2008 following the Nationalist return to power. With the January 2016 victory of Tsai Ing-wen, representing the Democratic Progressive Party (DPP), the future of this economic relationship may become even stronger.

Export trends are indictative. As mentioned above, in 2010, Greater China (including China, Hong Kong, and Taiwan) accounted for 30% of container exports, and in 2011 the number of container units handled by Chinese ports hit 150 million. During the past five years alone, cargo and container throughput in Chinese ports has seen an annual growth rate of 35%. By 2014, the International Monetary Fund announced that the PRC had the largest economy in the world. Continued economic integration among the members of Greater China appears to be inevitable. Assuming economic relations continue to improve, this could result in increased territorial cooperation.

There are also many cultural characteristics uniting both China and Taiwan. One of the most important characteristics is a firm belief in the inevitability of Chinese hegemony throughout East Asia. This trend has largely paralleled rising tensions with Japan over the Diaoyu islands, potentially creating a common cause with Taipei, which also claims these islands as Chinese territory. Taipei's March 2017 decision to name its two recently-purchased Perry-class frigates *Liu Ming-chuan* and the *Chiu Feng-jia*, two famous Taiwanese officials who opposed the Japanese during the early-to-mid 1890s, suggests that nationalist feeling may still run high.[405] This common ground is even more evident in the SCS, where the PRC and ROC are defending China's territorial claims against all of the other claimants. Vietnam has even opposed what it sees as a "China-Taiwan alliance" by sending patrols ships within six kilometers of Itu Aba over one hundred times in 2011 alone.[406] A political alliance between the two Chinas is not out-of-the-question, therefore, in particular if military tensions between the PRC and a number of other claimants – such as Vietnam and the Philippines – drive the PRC and ROC into working with each other to obtain their shared territorial objectives.

A PRC-ROC alliance would be in line with earlier periods when the two governments created temporary United Fronts. Territorial cooperation between Beijing and Taipei may increase, especially when one considers that the majority of their international trade is conducted by sea, and the volume of cross-strait trade is increasing every year. Deepening PRC-ROC ties could result in unexpected benefits for Beijing, since the Taiwanese government still claims territory from its neighbors that equals, and in many cases, exceeds those lands claimed by the PRC. Should a third United Front be established, this could result in many new challenges to the U.S. government and its many Pacific and Southeast Asian allies.

FOUR POSSIBLE SCENARIOS

This study has sought to outline the many complexities in the SCS dispute. After considering the major factors impacting the various claimants in the SCS, four possible scenarios are presented below discussing indirect, unilateral, bilateral, and multilateral scenarios. Although it is

---

[405] Chen Wei-han, "Taiwan takes possession of two US frigates," *Taipei Times*, 13 March 2017, http://www.taipeitimes.com/News/front/archives/2017/03/13/2003666662 [accessed 26 April 2017].
[406] Roy, *The South China Sea Disputes*, 62.

impossible to predict China's future actions with any certainty, these four scenarios are listed in order of most to least likelihood based on Beijing's current activities. To date, the PRC has made it very clear that multilateral solutions to the SCS disputes, the preferred methodology of the U.S. government, are out of the question.

Indirect Scenario

This scenario posits that China will maintain its current "flyspeck" policy of gradually expanding its Spratly bases even while conducting oil exploration and drilling new wells, but all without resorting to large-scale fighting. This is an incremental policy that depends on all of the other claimants acquiescing to China's gradual expansion and adopting a posture of watchful waiting. It is like slowly boiling the frog. This scenario would in some ways copy Japan's early 1930s' success in creating a "Greater East Asia Co-Prosperity Sphere," when it initially succeeded in establishing its economic dominance in Southeast Asia through mostly peaceful enterprise. Eric Posner, a law professor at the University of Chicago, refers to China's incrementalist policy as "Finlandization," and has advised: "As long as China allows its neighbors to govern themselves, and doesn't try to conquer them – and there is no reason to believe Beijing wants to go that far – the United States should leave it alone in the South China Sea."[407] But Beijing's so-called "Middle Kingdom mentality" is really just another word for bullying, which is something China promised never to do in its 1972 discussions with President Richard Nixon: "big nations should not bully the small and strong nations should not bully the weak. China will never be a superpower and it opposes hegemony and power politics of any kind" (see Document 10). Should China proceed too quickly with its reclamation projects, and attempt to assert hegemony too rapidly, then the chances go up that there will be violent conflicts with one or more neighbors. For the United

---

[407] Eric Possner, "China Can Sink All the Boats in the South China Sea: International law won't stop big countries from bullying littler ones," *Slate*, 28 May 2014, http://www.slate.com/articles/news_and_politics/view_from_chicago/2014/05/china_has_the_power_to_sink_vietnamese_boats_in_the_south_china_sea.html [accessed 13 March 2017].

States and its allies to "pre-emptively" cede a "sphere of influence to China in the East and Southeast Asian littoral would therefore risk sowing the seeds of a future geopolitical confrontation, to the ultimate disadvantage of all parties involved."[408]

Unilateral Scenario

This scenario assumes that China has the military power and the willingness to risk retaliation if it takes the Spratlys by military force. The Chinese ambassador to Great Britain compared the PRC's actions to "property owners" evicting "squatters."[409] This attitude is eerily reminiscent of the Cold War adage often applied to the Soviet Union: "What's mine is mine. What's yours is negotiable." On 28 August 2012, Air Force Colonel Dai Xu claimed in the *Global Times* that Japan, the Philippines, and Vietnam were the "three running dogs of the United States in Asia." "We only need to kill one, and it will immediately bring the others to heel."[410] Vietnam is the most likely candidate, since Washington and Hanoi have not yet signed a security treaty. In response to these jingoistic reports, a number of Western and Southeast Asian observers "worry about the region becoming a vassal of China," should Beijing promote a "Chinese Monroe Doctrine."[411] Others warn that Beijing is using its relations with the Southeast Asian nations to "dominate Asia," by setting up a "buffer against possible future U.S. pressure or containment of China," so as to "push the United States away from Chinese borders and nearby spheres of influence."[412] In October 1995, Jiang Zemin even asked Bill Clinton "Are you trying to contain China or not?" to which Clinton responded

---

[408] Huxley and Schreer, "Standing up to China," 139.
[409] Liu Xiaoming, "China is Not Trying to 'Rule the Waves'," *The World Post*, 23 June 2016, www.huffingtonpost.com/liu-xiaoming/china-not-trying-to-rule-the-waves_b_10635022.html [accessed 9 March 2017].
[410] Hayton, *The South China Sea*, 175.
[411] Amitav Acharya, *The Making of Southeast Asia: International Relations of a Region* (Ithaca: Cornell University Press, 2012), 269.
[412] Robert G. Sutter, *China's Rise in Asia: Promises and Perils* (New York: Rowman & Littlefield Publishers, 2005), 273–277.

"No, no, I am trying to engage, I don't want to contain you."[413] The UN tribunal's ruling was definitive, backing the Philippines "on almost every count," but has left Beijing with little wiggle room: "China's defeat was so crushing that it has left Beijing few ways to save face. Chinese officials may feel that the tribunal has backed them into a corner – and respond by lashing out."[414] China's rejection of the UNCLOS decision has arguably "increased tensions in the South China Sea and delayed both co-operation and progress towards an agreed Code of Conduct." As a result, "discussions over the past decade has shifted from co-operation to dispute resolution and zero-sum ("win-lose") outcomes driven largely by nationalistic assertions of sovereignty."[415] This scenario is one of the most realistic, albeit bleak, assessments of PRC intentions in the Spratlys, allowing Beijing to obtain control over all of the islands and waters in the SCS. This, plus "recovering Taiwan," would "signal a final dismantling of the imperial yoke of Japan and of traditional Western hegemons."[416] Concern over this option has led to a mini-arms race throughout Southeast Asia "to counter the perceived growing hegemony of China."[417] In 2012, the East Asian militaries for the first time ever had larger defense budgets than all of the NATO countries. If China adopts an unilateral scenario then Washington will almost certainly be required at some point in the future to send military forces to support its allies in the region, and war will be more likely.

---

[413] David Shambaugh, "Containment or Engagement of China? Calculating Beijing's Responses," in Michael E. Brown, Owen R. Cote, Jr., Sean M. Lynn-Jones, and Steven E. Miller, eds., *The Rise of China* (Cambridge: The MIT Press, 2000), 233.
[414] Mira Rapp-Hooper, "Parting the South China Sea: How to Uphold the Rule of Law," *Foreign Affairs*, September/October 2016, https://www.foreignaffairs.com/articles/china/2016-07-22/parting-south-china-sea [accessed 12 April 2017].
[415] Sam Bateman, "The Impact of the Arbitration Case on Regional Maritime Security," in Wu and Zou, *Arbitration Concerning the South China Sea: Philippines versus China*, 239.
[416] Caceres, *China's Strategic Interests in the South China Sea*, 79.
[417] Christian Le Miere, "The Spectre of an Asian Arms Race," *Survival*, Volume 56, Number 1 (February-March 2014), 139.

Bilateral Scenario

This scenario posits that China and other SCS claimants, most importantly Taiwan, Vietnam, or the Philippines given the size of their SCS bases, can establish a *modus vivendi* in the Spratlys by entering into joint ventures or agreeing to separate zones for exploitation. On the one hand this option would be positive for these two nations, since they would jointly cooperate for the economic benefit of both countries, but on the other hand this option might ignore the claims of neighboring states. Furthermore, if such pacts were created by two expansionist or militaristic governments, then there would be concern that the SLOCs running through the SCS could at any point be closed to outsiders. For example, a third United Front could presage greater ROC-PRC cooperation in the SCS, and perhaps over other disputed areas as well, such as over the Diaoyu islands. Hayton warns: "If the Taiwan government ever chose to merge with the People's Republic of China on the mainland this is one point [i.e. its stronger claims in the SCS] over which it would have considerable leverage."[418] While there is still relatively little support on Taiwan for reunifying with the PRC, fully half of Taiwanese agree with greater economic integration, including joint oil ventures. Such an option would not be reassuring to the world's great maritime powers, however, which would see such an alliance as potentially challenging freedom of navigation through the SCS.

Multilateral Scenario

Aggressive conquest is not inevitable, and China understands the risk of military aggression to its growing economic ties in Southeast Asia. China's economic dependence on Japan and the West as markets and sources of technology is a strong argument against aggression. Together, the ASEAN and South Asian nations represent a third of the world's population and have a combined GDP of $5.1 trillion, with an estimated annual economic growth rate

---

[418] Hayton, *The South China Sea*, 99.

for ASEAN and South Asian countries of "between 4.9 and 7.4 percent from 2017 and 2021."[419] In an almost exactly opposite scenario to the use of force, the Chinese government and all the other Spratly island claimants could decide to open negotiations based on the principle of shared rights to the islands, perhaps within the context of the creation of an Asian common market for free trade and economic cooperation. ASEAN states would warmly welcome a China willing to adopt a "world view" based on "transparency in its international dealings."[420] Some authors have argued that "China will be legally bound by the [UNCLOS] tribunal's decision."[421] If true, then the UN Security Council could theoretically sanction China if it does not follow it. Given China's current reclamation projects in the SCS, however, the multilateral option appears to be the least likely. Chinese Foreign Minister Yang Jiechi stated on 26 July 2010 that internationalizing the SCS conflict "will only make matters worse and the resolution more difficult."[422] Its "three no's strategy" has consistently included "no internationalization of the conflict," "no multilateral negotiations," and "no specification of China's territorial demands."[423] At the most, a "concert of Asian powers," parallel to the "Quintuple Alliance" in nineteenth century Europe, might sponsor "frequent informal meetings to identify major security challenges and coordinate solutions."[424]

---

[419] Bonnie S. Glaser, Matthew P. Funaiole, and Emily Jin, "Unpacking Tsai Ing-wen's New Southbound Policy: Can Taiwan's latest attempt to avoid economic dependence on China succeed?" *The Diplomat*, 1 April 2017, http://thediplomat.com/2017/04/unpacking-tsai-ing-wens-new-southbound-policy/ [accessed 3 April 2017].

[420] Chung, *Domestic Politics, International Bargaining and China's Territorial Disputes*, 171.

[421] Jerome A. Cohen, "Like it or not, UNCLOS arbitration is legally binding for China," Eastasiaforum.org, 11 July 2016, www.eastasiaforum.org/2016/07/11/like-it-or-not-unclos-arbitration-is-legally-binding-for-china [accessed 1 May 2017].

[422] Ian Jeffries, *Contemporary Vietnam: A guide to economic and political developments* (New York: Routledge Press, 2011), 57; citing the *International Herald Tribune*, 26 July 2010.

[423] Roy, *The South China Sea Disputes*, 98.

[424] Holslag, *Trapped Giant: China's Military Rise*, 138.

China seems determined to use it military leverage against it neighbors. Legal arguments have been used to rationalize the use of "blunt force." While each claimant has tried to maximize their legal case showing the validity of their SCS claims, the ongoing disputes over the Paracels and Spratlys cannot be solved solely on the basis of legal conventions. China seems to be following a time-honored tactic of "expanding Chinese territory firstly through cartographic aggression, then provoking border clashes by making incursions into the territories of the neighboring countries and finally asking for a peaceful settlement of the question of disputed areas' by maintaining *status quo* at the actual line of control."[425] While such tactics have worked against continental neighbors, like India, it is not clear whether they can win a maritime conflict.

Rather than a simple matchup between two opponents, the SCS dispute involves not just political sovereignty and economic growth, therefore, but a whole host of other factors: "Since 2007 tensions in the South China Sea have been on the upswing due to a combination of rising nationalism, increasing friction over access to energy and fishery resources, attempts by the disputants to bolster their respective jurisdictional claims, and the rapid modernization of the PLAN, which is shifting the military balance of power in China's favour."[426] Ever-growing energy requirements are particularly important, as new deep sea oil-drilling technology enables exploitation of areas that were previously inaccessible.

On the flip side, during the past two decades the linkage between resource access and energy security has weakened. In 2012 the Chinese-owned companies China National Offshore Oil Corporation and Sinopec together had a combined overseas production equivalent to 18% of China's oil imports, but the "percentage of this oil that was marketed in China is unknowable and, from a sup-

---

[425] Daljit Sen Adel, *China and her Neighbors: A Review of Chinese Foreign Policy* (New Delhi: Deep & Deep Publications, 1984), 197.

[426] Ian Storey, "Maritime Security in Southeast Asia and the United States," in Pavin Chachavalpongpun, ed., *ASEAN-U.S. Relations: What are the Talking Points?* (Sinagapore: Institute of Southeast Asian Studies Publishing, 2012), 43.

ply-security perspective, largely irrelevant."[427] The very anonymity of the global oil market could disengage territorial conquest from resource exploitation. Unfortunately, this change may have occurred too late, since "these specks of land, from which flow historical arguments and modern maritime zones, form the stage for an international chest-beating contest in which the status of a country, or rather the elite that runs that country, will be judged, abroad but more importantly at home, upon its public performance."[428]

CONCLUDING THOUGHTS AND RECOMMENDATIONS

The potential for a future SCS conflict is perhaps the most complicated challenge Washington has ever faced in East Asia. The U.S. government should continue to support economic integration and other similar multilateral approach as possible methods for convincing the Chinese government to open negotiations with its neighbors. The United States and its allies can also play key roles in bringing together the various claimants to the Spratlys in order to try to resolve this dispute by peaceful means. U.S. military assistance is critical, and America's annual intelligence collection budget of $50 billion is more than the total military spending of all ASEAN members combined in 2013.

The U.S. military does not have to work alone. Making use of "offshore balancing" might allow Washington to rely less on its own forces and more on "local powers to contain China."[429] In 1995, PACOM adopted the Cooperation Afloat Readiness And Training (CARAT) exercises, which conducts annual naval exercises with seven of the ten members of ASEAN. In 2012, seven countries contributed over 9,000 personnel to the annual Cobra Gold exercise, and in 2014 the Chinese participated in the humanitarian portion of the exercise. Concern over IUU fishing in the

---

[427] Pierre Noël, "Asia's Energy Supply and Maritime Security," *Survival*, Volume 56, Number 3 (June-July 2014), 210.
[428] Hayton, *The South China Sea*, 267.
[429] John J. Mearsheimer and Stephen M. Walt, "The Case for Offshore Balancing: A Superior U.S. Grand Strategy," *Foreign Affairs*, July/August 2016, http://www.cfr.org/united-states/case-offshore-balancing/p38068 [accessed 12 April 2017].

SCS could also offer "the ideal on-ramp for China and the United States to cooperate on a non-military issue."[430] If this SCS problem is not solved, it could threaten the food supply of half a billion people throughout Southeast Asia.

Diplomatic initiatives by the United States could also reassure China that its historic claims and territorial rights would not be threatened if Beijing agrees to negotiate this dispute peacefully. For example, China could be reminded that internationally-recognized sovereignty over a portion of the Spratly islands may be better in the long run than a disputed claim to them all that constantly threatens to erupt in conflict. On 4 February 2013, General Liu Yuan surprised readers of the ultra conservative *Global Times* when he argued: "China's economic development already has been shattered by war with Japan twice before," and "it absolutely must not be interrupted again by some accidental incident."[431] Unfortunately, China all too often perceives any type of multilateral solution as merely "a move towards joint containment."[432]

ASEAN can also contribute to finding a solution. Individually and collectively, these nations have a major stake in what takes place in the SCS. Economic relations between ASEAN and China will most likely continue to grow, and any aggressive actions in the Spratlys might put the future of these relations at risk. ASEAN must work together to oppose Chinese bullying, like it did in the 1990s when Beijing refused to continue talks with ASEAN about developing a new Code of Conduct agreement unless the Philippines was excluded, but "No international organization would of course shut out one of its members for such reasons."[433] By convincing China that they offer a forum that is unbiased by purely economic or strategic considerations of the western nations, ASEAN could become a credible venue for future negotiations.

Meanwhile, China, with its vast strengths but also many weaknesses, is not blind to the advantage of economic ties and global

---

[430] Lieutentant Nicholas Monacelli, "Opportunity for U.S.-Chinese Partnership?" *Proceedings*, July 2016, 48.
[431] Hayton, *The South China Sea*, 222.
[432] Hu and McDorman, *Maritime Issues in the South China Sea*, 162.
[433] Stein Tonnesson, "China's national interests and the law of the sea," in Wu and Nong, *Recent Developments in the South China Sea Dispute*, 210.

markets. But because of Beijing's reticence to adopt multilateral solutions to regional problems "Asians have been reluctant and incomplete globalists."[434] Ignoring the complexity of these relations, some authors have perhaps over optimistically concluded that "the likelihood of major conflict over the islands has already passed."[435] But others caution that even as Southeast Asia has become a "vital constituent of the same globalised sea-based trading system and an area in which even far-distant countries have strong interest," the various countries competing for the SCS must become more "proactive" in adopting national maritime policies that allow them to anticipate and prepare "for events before they occur rather than simply responding to them when they do."[436]

In seeking a peaceful resolution of the SCS dispute, it is in America's strategic interests to promote East Asian economic cooperation and perhaps even a common market. American policy since 1899 has supported the Open Door Policy, and Washington needs to renew its support for this policy of economic equal opportunity with regard to the contested waters of the SCS.[437] One looming problem could be if China were to "believe the American [jingoistic] rhetoric and embark upon an arms race and follow the Soviet Union to the same end."[438] To date, Washington's "confused approach toward China, combined with Beijing's own assertive behavior, has created a dangerous and deepening security dilemma in the Western Pacific."[439] Russia is actively seeking to exploit this security dilemma.

In an ever-increasing industrialized and globalized world, old and new trading partnerships, such as the European Common

---

[434] Amitav Acharya, "The new transregional security politics of the Asia-Pacific," in William T. Tow, ed., *Security Politics in the Asia-Pacific: A Regional-Global Nexus?* (New York: Cambridge University Press, 2009), 311.
[435] Womack, *China and Vietnam*, 29.
[436] Geoffrey Till, *Seapower: A Guide for the Twenty-First Century* (New York: Routledge, 2013), 335–336.
[437] Bruce A. Elleman, *International Competition in China, 1899–1991: The rise, fall, and restoration of the Open Door Policy* (New York: Routledge Press, 2015).
[438] Hayton, *The South China Sea*, 224.
[439] David A. Shalpak, "Towards a More Modest American Strategy," *Survival*, Volume 57, Number 2 (April-May 2015), 59.

Market (EU) and the North American Free Trade Agreement (NAFTA), would appear to be under threat. President Donald Trump's recent "bait and switch" tactic of announcing that the U.S. would be pulling out of the TPP agreement could let China step in as the major trade partner in ASEAN's Regional Comprehensive Economic Partnership (RCEP) – the RCEP is the Asia-centered counterpart to TPP that includes China – which may prove to be the first step in this direction. Such a regional arrangement would be of great potential value, both for the material benefits to China and all of its neighbors, and as a way to stabilize the region. By actively working to turn the SCS countries from nationalism and expansionism to resource-sharing, industry, and trade, the United States may find in such agreements the "catalyst that will change old antagonisms into new partnerships."[440]

***

In 2017, three major events occurred along China's periphery: 1) To the southwest, a Sino-Indian dispute erupted on 18 June; after a two month confrontation, this standoff ended on 28 August, when China apparently backed down so that Indian Prime Minister Narendra Modi would agree to attend the BRICs meeting in Xiamen in early September. 2) To China's northeast, on 23 June North Korea tested a new intercontinental ballistic missile engine, and then on 4 July successfully launched its first ICBM. 3) In early August, an IISS researcher named Michael Elleman (not a close relation of the author) announced that the rocket engine used in the North Korean ICBM came from the Ukraine, and was probably provided by Russia, which may reflect increased tensions to China's northwest as well.

On 6 August, reacting to these territorial crises to its southwest, northwest, and northeast, China and ASEAN adopted the basic framework for a regional Code of Conduct pertaining to the SCS. By late August, the 22nd meeting of the ASEAN-China Joint Working Group had convened to start hammering out a draft Code. Whether this long-anticipated development is just window dressing remains unclear. Some critics have argued China is using the crisis over North Korea to obscure a major geopolitical push into the South China Sea. But it seems equally likely that these three simultaneous threats along its borders have convinced Beijing to temper its aggressive policies, and so perhaps multilateral negotiations can finally move forward.

---

[440] Smith, "China, technology and the Spratly Islands: The Geopolitical impact of new technologies," 220.

APPENDIX A: TIMELINE

2nd century B.C.E — Early Chinese voyages through the South China Sea during Han Dynasty.

3rd century — SCS islands described in written documents of the Three Kingdom period, circa 220.

11th century — Song dynasty records describe and give names to many of the islands, reefs, and sand cays of the Spratly and Paracel island groups.

15th century — Ming Dynasty Indian Ocean voyages of Admiral Zheng He, who reportedly explored and left artifacts on several islands in the Spratly group.

29 March 1843 — British Captain Richard Spratly discovers Spratly Island.

1877 — British Crown formally claims Spratly Island and Amboyna Cay to allow for merchants in northern Borneo to exploit guano deposits.

1883 — German naval unit sent to Spratlys to conduct survey. Operation terminated due to Chinese protests.

1887 — Sino-French Convention on boundary between Annam (Vietnam) and China's Guangdong province states that the islands to the east of meridian of 105° 43' longitude belong to China.

1900 — Vietnam's Nguyễn Dynasty continued to assert that the state Bac Hai Company had exercised Vietnam's sovereignty in the Spratlys since the eighteenth century.

6 June 1909 — Admiral Li Xun raised a Chinese flag over Duncan Island in the Paracels.

September 1909 — Qing government renames the Naval Reorganization Council as the Ministry of the Navy.

1909 and 1910 — China formally annexed many of these islands to Guangdong province.

10 October 2011 — Chinese revolution leads to abdication of the Qing emperor and the creation of the Republic of China (ROC) in 1912.

1925–1927 — French Research ship *De Lanessan* sent on survey mission to Spratlys.

1930 — French ship *La Milicieuse* expedition to Spratlys; plants French flag on one island.

1932 — ROC sends the French government a memorandum contesting their sovereignty over the Paracels, stating that the Paracels were the extreme south of Chinese territories based on the Chinese interpretation of the 1887 treaty ending the Sino-French War.

1933 — Fourth French expedition of three ships to the Spratlys; on completion, France places six groups of islets under its control.

21 July 1933 — Decree No. 4762 attaching the Paracels to Baria Province in Vietnam.

1933 — French briefly occupy nine islands in Spratlys including Loaita Island; Paris claims jurisdiction on behalf of Vietnam.

1934–1935 — ROC's "Committee for the Examination of Land and Sea Maps," with representatives of the Foreign, Interior, and Naval ministries approve names of South China Sea Islands and print "Map of the South China Sea Islands," showing Spratlys and other island groups as Chinese territory.

March 1938 — Vietnam's Emperor Bao Dai issues ordinance to put Spratlys and Paracels under Vietnamese administration; move protested by France.

April 1939 — Japanese take control of Paracels and Spratlys, rename them "Shinnan Gunto" (New South Archipelago) and later put them under the administration of Takao-shu (Kaohsiung district), Taiwan.

1941 — Japanese construct submarine base on Itu Aba.

January 1945 — Japanese submarine base at Itu Aba shelled by USS *Hoe*.

August 1945 — Japanese garrison departs Itu Aba.

October 1946 — French battleship *Chevraud* lands crewmen on Itu Aba and Spratly Island to drop off stone markers.

Nov/Dec 1946 — Two Chinese destroyers, *Taiping* and *Zhongye*, dispatched to the Spratlys to establish garrison.

1947 — Philippine private citizen Tomas Cloma, founder of Philippine Maritime Academy, launches expedition to Spratlys.

1 December 1947 — Chinese Government promulgates names of all islands claimed in the South China Sea which includes Spratlys; China produces an 11-dashed map, and claims all of the islands within those lines.

1 October 1949 — People's Republic of China (PRC) established in Beijing; defeated political and military leaders of the Kuomintang reestablish ROC on the island of Taiwan.

May 1950 — ROC military garrison departs Itu Aba to assist in defense of Taiwan from expected Communist invasion.

15 August 1951 — PRC Foreign Minister Zhou Enlai declares that all islands in the South China Sea, including the Paracels and Spratlys, "have always been Chinese territory. Although they were occupied by Japan for some time during the war of aggression waged by Japanese imperialism, they were all taken over by the then Chinese government following Japan's surrender."

- September 1951 — Japan signs peace treaty in San Francisco. Article 2(f) states that "Japan renounces all right, title, and claim to the Spratly Islands and to the Paracel Islands," but it does not state to whom the islands should devolve.
- September 1951 — Vietnamese Prime Minister Tran Van Huu, delegate to San Francisco Peace conference, claims sovereignty of Spratly and Paracel Islands, "which have always belonged to Vietnam." No objection made by other delegates, since neither PRC nor ROC were represented at conference.
- 26 October 1955 — Republic of Vietnam (ROV) established, dividing Vietnam into two parts at the 17th parallel; North Vietnam or the Democratic Republic of Vietnam (DRV) in Hanoi and South Vietnam (ROV) in Saigon. South Vietnam controls the Paracel islands.
- 26 October 1955 — At International Civil Aviation Organization's Regional Conference in Manila, British delegate and delegation from International Aviation Transport Association submit official request for the Government of the Republic of China to establish a meteorological post in Spratly Islands, implying international recognition of Chinese sovereignty over the islands.
- 16 May 1956 — Tomas Cloma issues "A Proclamation to the Whole World" claiming that he has discovered an unoccupied group of islands (the Spratlys), names them Kalayaan (Freedomland) and seeks protectorate status from Philippine Government based on rights of discovery and occupation; Cloma's men occupy four islands; Philippine government ignores request.
- 23 May 1956 — ROC Ambassador in Manila files formal protest to Philippine Foreign Minister, claiming that islands "found" by Cloma belong to the Nansha Island group which is part of the territory of the China; ROC Ministry of Foreign Affairs presents documents to Philippine Embassy in Taipei which "proves" Chinese sovereignty over the islands.
- 24 May 1956 — ROV issues communiqué stating that the Nansha Islands "have always been part of Vietnam."
- 29 May 1956 — PRC Foreign Ministry issues statement that "Taiping [Itu Aba] and Nanwei [Storm/Spratly] Island in the South China Sea, together with the small islands in their vicinity, are known in aggregate as the Nansha Islands. These islands have always been a part of Chinese territory. The People's Republic of China has indisputable, legitimate sovereignty over these islands."
- 2 June 1956 — American Ambassador to Taipei assures ROC Foreign Minister that the United States has no intention of getting involved in the Spratly dispute between China and the Philippines.

5 June 1956 — ROV Minister Cao Bai states that the Spratlys and Paracels had been under the jurisdiction of the French colonial government and that Vietnam subsequently had jurisdiction by virtue of grant of sovereignty by France.

Early June 1956 — ROC reestablishes garrison on Itu Aba (Taiping); ROV lands naval unit in Spratlys.

8 June 1956 — South Vietnamese Foreign Minister reiterates claim to Spratly and Paracel Islands.

9 June 1956 — French Chargé in Manila informs Philippine Foreign Ministry that the Spratlys belongs to France by virtue of occupation effected in 1932–1933; states that while France had ceded the Paracel Islands to Vietnam, it had not ceded the Spratlys.

11 July 1956 — ROC naval force briefly lands on Spratly (Nanwei) Island located approximately 180 nautical miles southwest of Itu Aba.

27 August 1956 — ROV force occupies Spratly (Nanwei) Island and several others; protests filed by both PRC and ROC.

October 1956 — ROV assigns Spratly administratively to Phuoc Tuy Province.

4 September 1958 — PRC promulgates territorial sea claims in a "Declaration on Territorial Seas," which includes restatement of its claims to Spratly and Paracel island groups.

14 September 1958 — DRV Premier Pham Van Dong sends note to Zhou Enlai stating that "The Government of the Democratic Republic of Vietnam recognizes and supports the declaration of the Government of the People's Republic of China on its decision concerning China's territorial sea made on September 4, 1958."

October 1963 — ROC Ministry of National Defense inspection team visits several islands in the Spratlys.

October 1966 — ROC naval contingent sent to Spratlys to re-erect national boundary tablets on several islands.

1967 — Malaysia promulgates Continental Shelf Act of 1966, claiming "... the seabed and subsoil of submarine areas adjacent to the coast of Malaysia, but beyond the limits of the territorial waters of the States, the surface of which lies at a depth no greater than 200 meters below the surface of the sea ..."

1968 — The Philippines sends troops to three islands on the premise of protecting Kalayaan citizens.

July 1971 — Philippine President Marcos declares the islands known as Kalayaan in the Spratlys to be "derelict and disputed," claiming that henceforth "occupation and control" would be sufficient for a country to acquire legitimate claim to the islands; Malaysia issued claims to some of the Spratly Islands; A Philippine fishing trawler is fired on by Taiwanese forces stationed on Itu Aba.

26 September 1972 — ROC patrol boat boards and inspects a Japanese fishing vessel detected entering its territorial waters near Itu Aba.

September 1973 — ROV interior ministry announces the issuance of oil exploration permits to seven foreign companies and places eleven islands of the Spratlys under the jurisdiction of Phuoc Tuy Province.

11 January 1974 — PRC Foreign Ministry call South Vietnamese announcement "... a wanton infringement on China's territorial integrity and sovereignty."

19 January 1974 — PRC naval and air operation defeats South Vietnamese garrison and naval forces in the Paracels, sinking one ROV patrol boat and capturing 48 Vietnamese soldiers, 71 reported dead.

February 1974 — ROV occupies six islands in the Spratlys in retaliation for the Chinese defeat of Vietnamese forces in the Paracels.

June 1974 — PRC publishes map showing Chinese "territorial seas" extending to within 50 nm of the coastlines of Vietnam, Malaysia, and the Philippines.

August 1974 — During negotiations on the delineating of an ocean boundary in the Gulf of Tonkin, North Vietnam position is that the Gulf had already been divided by the Sino-French convention of 1887; China rejects this position on grounds that the line was not meant to determine the sea boundary and would give Vietnam the larger share of the Gulf.

February 1975 — ROV White Paper on the Hoang Sa and Truong Sa islands.

April 1975 — Hanoi sends troops to occupy the six Spratly islands seized by South Vietnam a year earlier.

May 1975 — United Vietnam (DRV) publishes map showing Spratly Islands as Vietnamese territory, begins negotiations with foreign oil companies for exploration in adjacent areas.

24 November 1975 — PRC's *Guangmin Daily* has lengthy article presenting historical claims to South China Sea islands.

Early 1976 — PLA August First Film Studio produces documentary entitled "Islands of the South China Sea" showing early Chinese presence in islands and archeological findings in area from Tang and Song Dynasties.

March 1976 — Philippine President Marcos establishes a Western Command on Palawan Island to defend Kalayaan "at all costs."

14 June 1976 — PRC Foreign Ministry issues warning to Vietnam: "The Nansha Islands, as well as the Xisha, Zhongsha, and Dongsha

islands, have always been part of the territory of China, which has indisputable sovereignty over them and the adjacent seas: any armed invasion and occupation, or exploration and exploitation of oil and other resources there by any foreign country constitutes encroachments on China's territorial integrity and sovereignty and are impermissible."

June 1976 — Joint Philippine-Swedish consortium begins drilling test well in Reed Bank area of Spratlys (Sampaguita No. 1) about 110 nm west of Philippine territorial sea; PRC Foreign ministry issues statement that "exploitation of oil and other resources in the Spratlys constitute encroachment on China's territorial integrity and sovereignty and are impermissible."

31 August 1976 — In response to Hanoi's suggestion about sharing the South China Sea islands, PRC spokesman reiterates Chinese claims to all the islands as "fully proven" by historical evidence. Islands called "sacred territory since ancient times."

12 May 1977 — Vietnam declares 12 nm territorial seas and 200 mile Exclusive Economic Zone (EEZ), which includes both the Paracels and Spratlys, stating that "... all the islands and archipelagos belonging to Vietnamese territory and situated outside the territorial seas mentioned ..." have their own territorial waters and EEZs.

June 1978 — Philippines claims 200 nm EEZ and sovereignty over Kalayaan to be administered by Palawan Province.

17 February 1979 — PRC attacks Vietnam across land border in response to Vietnamese actions against ethnic Chinese and escalating border problems and to "teach Vietnam a lesson"; PRC troops withdraw by mid-March.

18 April 1979 — Sino-Vietnamese peace and border talks begin.

30 July 1979 — Chinese delegation to 2nd round of peace talks in Beijing circulates pamphlet entitled "Some Documents and Materials Concerning the Vietnamese Government's Recognition of the Xisha and Nansha Islands as Chinese Territory"; includes copies of statements made by former Vietnamese President Pham Van Dong on 14 September 1958, Hanoi's endorsement of China's 9 May 1965 declaration, and Vietnamese maps showing Spratlys as Chinese territory.

August 1979 — Hanoi denounces Chinese statements, claiming that China had distorted the "letter and spirit" of the 1958 and 1965 statements and claimed that China had misused trust by printing a number of Vietnamese maps which showed Paracels and Spratlys as Chinese territory.

28 September 1979 — Vietnam issues White Book entitled "Vietnam's Sovereignty over the Hoang Sa and Truong Sa Archipelagoes" containing documents establishing Vietnam's historical claims.

September 1979 — ROC announces 200 nm EEZ.

December 1979 — Malaysia publishes map showing its 200 nm EEZ which encompasses several southern Spratly Islands.

30 January 1980 — China publishes document entitled "China's Indisputable Sovereignty over the Xisha and Nansha Islands" containing data showing that China had discovered the two archipelagos in the third century B.C.E. and had begun to inhabit them by the seventh century. Claimed that seizure by French in 1933 was an act of aggression that could not establish sovereign rights; that Vietnamese government itself had repeatedly recognized China's sovereignty prior to 1974; that China had named major islands in Spratlys and Paracels as early as the Song Dynasty (960–1297); and that the islands known as Hoang Sa and Truong Sa were actually the small island groups lying near the Vietnamese coast.

April 1980 — Malaysia claims 200 nm EEZ which encloses Swallow Reef, Amboyna Cay, Mariveles Reef, and Commodore Reef in Spratlys.

May 1980 — Vietnam awards USSR major rights to exploit offshore oil deposits in southern part of Vietnam's continental shelf.

July 1980 — Vietnam concludes formal agreement with USSR to cooperate in exploration for oil along Vietnam continental shelf; PRC protests Soviet-Vietnamese agreement for joint exploration and exploitation of petroleum: "It is illegal for any country to enter these areas (the so-called "continental shelf" of Vietnam) without China's permission ..."

28 July 1980 — The Philippines launch "Operation Polaris I" to occupy Commodore Reef in the southern Spratlys.

11 August 1980 — Vietnam sends a diplomatic protest denouncing the Philippine operation.

September 1980 — Ship from Taiwan Fisheries Research Institute studies area around Tizard Bank in Spratlys as fishing ground; concludes that area was not an economical fishing ground for Taiwan.

2 December 1980 — China publishes article stating that French-Chinese treaty of 1887 demarcation line at 108 West could not be considered to have delineated Gulf of Tonkin but merely established ownership of some coastal islands in the Gulf.

18 January 1982 — Vietnam's Foreign Ministry releases second white paper entitled "The Hoang Sa and Truong Sa Archipelagoes: Vietnamese Territories"; contains more historic documents and

states that Vietnam had exercised "long-standing and uninterrupted sovereignty" over the Paracels and Spratlys; Chinese occupation of Paracels by the PRC and Itu Aba by the ROC were acts of aggression and could not be used to establish sovereignty."

May 1982 — China opens bids for oil fields in southern part of the Gulf of Tonkin.

11 June 1982 — Xinhua commentary denounces Vietnam, stating that China's claims to the South China Sea islands had been repeatedly recognized by Vietnam itself as well as other nations before 1974; accuses Vietnam of distorting history and fabricating lies.

12 November 1982 — Vietnam's National Assembly promulgates territorial sea claims, premised on continued legal validity of 1887 French-Chinese Gulf of Tonkin territorial demarcation (108 degree W longitude line); 12 Soviet Naval ships based at Cam Ranh Bay.

April 1983 — Philippine Prime Minister states that "any offensive action against Kalayaan will be considered an assault against the Republic ..."

June 1983 — Malaysia occupies Swallow Reef (Terumbu Layang-Layang) with small military garrison in conjunction with military exercise in its claimed maritime zone; action protested by China and Vietnam.

1984 — Brunei established an exclusive fishing zone encompassing the Louisa Reef and neighboring areas in the southeastern Spratly Islands.

April 1984 — Joint Vietnam-Soviet amphibious exercise inside Gulf of Tonkin, just South of Haiphong.

May 1984 — Chinese Naval Task force circles Spratlys, returns to Chinese waters for large scale amphibious exercise around Hainan Island.

November/December 1985 — PRC Naval Task Force visits Indian Ocean; Conducts exercise at sea with American Naval units in South China Sea on return.

December 1985 — Chinese Communist Party chief Hu Yaobang visits Paracel Islands, signifying renewed interest in South China Sea islands.

June 1986 — PRC Naval exercises and patrols begin in Spratlys.

November 1986 — Malaysia occupies Mariveles Reef and Ardasier Bank (Matanani and Ubi).

April 1987 — PRC scientific expedition to Spratlys, surveying more than ten islands in 50 days; *New China News Agency* reports that Chinese Navy had completed comprehensive tour of Spratlys and conducted amphibious exercise on one of the islands; Vietnam occupies Barque Canada Reef (Thu Yen Chai).

June 1987 — Vietnam issues public protest regarding PRC naval patrols in Spratlys.

July 1987 — PRC announces that Spratly Islands constitute part of "strategic border" of newly established Hainan province.

October/November 1987 — PRC conducts series of naval exercises in Spratlys, operating as far south as James Shoal (Zengmu).

November 1987 — Bill drafted by Philippine Congress to redefine Philippine sea boundaries to include claimed islands in the Spratlys (Kalayaan).

December 1987 — PRC conference on Spratlys held in Guangdong Province.

February 1988 — PRC occupies six islands in Spratlys coincident with establishment of UNESCO-sponsored weather research station; Vietnam charges that PRC warships were hampering "circulation of Vietnamese vessels" and violating Vietnamese sovereignty.

February 1988 — ROC Minister of National Defense refutes Malaysia's claims in Spratlys.

14 March 1988 — PRC-Vietnam naval engagement in Spratlys at Johnson Reef (some sources say South Johnson Reef) results in 3 Vietnamese ships sunk, 72 Vietnamese killed (other sources say 64 killed) and 9 prisoners taken with limited Chinese casualties.

17 March 1988 — Manila warns Beijing and Hanoi not to interfere in Philippine-claimed islands; ROC conducts emergency supply mission to its garrison on Itu Aba, Defense Minister Hao tells Taiwan parliament that Taiwan would fight to the last man to defend Taiping island against any aggressor.

April 1988 — Vietnam occupies three additional islands; Vietnamese Defense Minister visits Spratlys to reaffirm determination to defend the islands.

May 1988 — PRC Foreign Ministry issues statement demanding that Hanoi immediately withdraw all "illegally occupied islands and reefs of China's Nansha Islands," declares Beijing's willingness to settle dispute through consultation if Vietnam withdraws from the Spratlys completely; PRC Navy conducts exercises in region; Philippines conducts scientific survey of sixty islands in Kalayaan.

June 1988 — Vietnam expands construction on Spratly (Nanwei) Island; PRC states that Chinese Marine corps is increasing its training "to defend the islands in the South China Sea"; senior naval officer reiterates vow to recover all the twenty-one islands held by Vietnam "at an appropriate time."

July 1988 — PRC completes permanent base at Fiery Cross Reef (Yongshu Jiao) to include oceanographic observation station, helicopter pad, 300 meter pier, postal and telecommunications links to mainland.

January 1990 — Workshop on Managing Potential Conflicts in the South China Sea held in Bali, Indonesia; attended by representatives of six ASEAN states.

December 1990 — International Academic Conference sponsored by Indonesia on Territorial Claims in the South China Sea in Hong Kong with international representatives; PRC and DRV did not attend, ROC not invited.

January 1991 — ROC interior ministry hosts conference on Spratlys; Admiral Liu Ta-Tsai says it is time for China to "drive foreign troops" out of the Spratlys.

May 1991 — Lingnan College in Hong Kong invites scholars from Taiwan, PRC, and Hong Kong to discuss the Spratlys issue.

July 1991 — Indonesia hosts 2nd Workshop on Managing Potential Conflicts in the South China Sea in Bandung; attended by ASEAN members as well as PRC and ROC, but not Vietnam; attendees agreed to seek "peaceful solutions" to Spratly issues.

25 February 1992 — PRC passes new law on territorial waters reiterating claims to all Spratly and Paracel Islands.

March 1992 — Commander of Malaysian Armed Forces Yacob Zain states that his country would defend the islands it claimed in the Spratlys "until the last drop of blood."

19 March 1992 — Chinese marines land on Da Ba Dau reef, close to the Vietnamese island of Sin Cowe East, which triggers a military clash; from June-September, China seizes almost 20 Vietnamese cargo ships transporting goods from Hong Kong.

8 May 1992 — PRC's China National Offshore Oil Corporation signs a petroleum contract with U.S. oil exploration firm, Crestone Energy Corporation, to explore for oil in a 10,000 square mile block in the southwestern Spratly Islands area, over 500 nm south of China's Hainan Island. This block is contiguous to a Vietnamese offshore oil block, about 100 nm from Vietnam's White Dragon oil field, and in waters claimed by both Vietnam and China; PRC assures Crestone that they will provide security for drilling operations; American Embassy official present at signing of contract in Beijing.

9 July 1992 — In response to DRV claim that PRC had landed troops on Da Lac Reef in Spratlys, PRC Foreign Ministry spokesman reiterates that Nansha archipelago, which includes Nanxun (Da Lac) reef, have been Chinese territory since ancient times.

21-26 July 1992 — ASEAN Foreign Ministers meeting attended by PRC; Spratly islands discussed; PRC Foreign Minister Qian Qichen quoted as saying that the Spratlys dispute has been exaggerated by outside observers and that Beijing has no interest in filling a perceived power vacuum in the region; PRC wants to pursue peaceful solution but in future, issues should be discussed in private; PRC spokesman said China has consistently advocated a peaceful settlement of territorial disputes over the Nansha Islands through negotiation and has been opposed to resorting to armed force.

August 1992 — PRC Defense Minister Qin Jiwei discussed Spratlys with Malaysian Defense Minister Razak in Beijing.

September 1992 — Vietnam accused China of drilling for oil in Vietnamese waters in the Gulf of Tonkin.

May 1993 — Vietnam accused a Chinese seismic survey ship of interfering with British Petroleum's exploration work in Vietnamese waters. The Chinese ship left Vietnamese block 06 following the appearance of 2 Vietnamese naval ships.

13-15 December 1993 — Crestone Energy Corporation President Randall Thompson meets with Vietnamese officials in Hanoi. Vietnam demanded that Crestone cancel offshore oil development in nearby waters. Thompson is upbraided for his company's illegal development deal with China in an area of the South China Sea that Vietnam says is within its territory.

July 1994 — Crestone joined with a Chinese partner to explore China's Wan' Bei-21 (WAB-21) block. China sends naval ships to blockade operations of a Vietnamese oil rig near Tu Chinh (Vanguard Bank) oil exploration blocks 133, 134, and 135, which are part of Vietnam's continental shelf claim, but which China says is its Wan' Bei-21 (WAB-21) exploration block. China offered to split Wan' Bei production with Vietnam, as long as China retained all sovereignty.

August 1994 — Vietnamese gunboats forced a Chinese exploration ship to leave an oilfield in a region claimed by the Vietnamese.

February 1995 — The Philippine government reveals Chinese military structure being built at the Mischief Reef. Philippine President Fidel Ramos ordered increased patrol of the Philippine-controlled areas, the incident leads to numerous arrests of Chinese fishermen and naval clashes with Chinese naval vessels that succeed in driving off the Philippine ships.

16 March 1995 — Malaysian navy boats fire on a Chinese trawler fishing in Malaysia's EEZ off Sarawak, reportedly injuring four crewmembers.

23 March 1995 — A Malaysian Navy vessel fires on a Chinese vessel, wounding four crewmembers.

25 March 1995 — Taiwanese artillery on Itu Aba fires on a Vietnamese supply ship, *Bien Dong 80*, which was approaching the island.

According to Vietnam's Ministry of Foreign Affairs, the Vietnamese ship was approaching Ban Than Reef where Taiwan was undertaking construction.

January 1996 — Chinese vessels engage in a 90-minute gun battle with a Philippine naval gunboat near the island of Capone, off the west coast of Luzon, just to the north of Manila.

April 1996 — Vietnam leased exploration blocks to U.S. firm Conoco, and ruled out cooperation with U.S. oil firms that signed Chinese exploration contracts in disputed waters. Vietnamese blocks 133 and 134 cover half the zone leased to Crestone by China. China protested, and reaffirmed a national law claiming the South China Sea as its own in May.

March 1997 — China sends three warships to survey the Philippine-occupied Lankiam Cay and Loaita island in the Spratly archipelago. Vietnamese issued a protest after the Chinese Kantan-3 oil rig drills near Spratlys in March. The drilling occurred offshore Da Nang, in an area Vietnam calls Block 113. The block is located 64 nautical miles off Chan May cape in Vietnam, and 71 nautical miles off China's Hainan Island. The diplomatic protests were followed by the departure of the Chinese rig.

April 1997 — The Philippine Navy orders a Chinese speedboat and two fishing boats to leave Scarborough Shoal; Philippine fishermen remove all Chinese markers and raise the Philippine flag; China sends three warships to survey the Philippine-occupied islands of Panata and Kota.

December 1997 — Vietnamese protested after the Exploration Ship No. 8 and two supply ships entered the Wan' Bei exploration block. All 3 vessels were escorted away by the Vietnamese navy.

January 1998 — The Philippine Navy arrests 22 Chinese fishermen close to Scarborough Shoal; Vietnamese soldiers fire on a Philippine trawler near the Vietnamese-controlled Tennent (Pigeon) Reef, injuring one Filipino fisherman.

September 1998 — Vietnamese protested after a Chinese report stated that Crestone and China were continuing their survey of the Spratly Islands and the Tu Chinh region (Wan' Bei in Chinese); The dispute over this area was resolved by an agreement between China and Vietnam concluded in December 2000.

1 May 1999 — Chinese naval ships are accused of harassing a Philippine naval ship after it ran aground near the Spratly Islands; A Chinese fishing boat is sunk after colliding with a Philippine warship off Scarborough Shoal.

July 1999 — One Chinese fishing boat was sunk in a collision with a Philippine warship.

October 1999 — Vietnamese troops fired upon a Philippine air force plane on reconnaissance in the Spratlys; two Philippine air force surveillance planes and two Malaysian fighter planes almost engage near a Malaysian-held reef in the Spratlys, but the Malaysian Defense Ministry says it is not a standoff.

May 2000 — Philippine troops open fire on Chinese fishermen, killing one and arresting seven.

January-March 2001 — The Philippine navy boards 14 Chinese-flagged boats, confiscates their catch, and ousts the ships from Philippine-claimed waters in the Spratlys.

March 2001 — The Philippines sends a gunboat to Scarborough Shoal to halt any Chinese attempt to build structures there.

1 April 2001 — EP-3 incident between U.S. and PRC; resolved ten days later through diplomacy.

August 2002 — Vietnamese troops fire warning shots at Philippine air force reconnaissance planes circling over the Spratlys.

May 2003 — A patrol boat from Brunei acted to prevent TotalFinaElf from undertaking exploration activities in an area offshore from Northern Borneo disputed by the two countries.

4 December 2007 — China announced that all of its claimed territory in the South China Sea would now be administered as a separate district within Hainan Province called Sansha.

2008 — Taiwan's President Ch'en Shui-bian became the first head of state from the claimant countries to visit Itu Aba. His visit sparks criticism from other claimants.

2009 — The Office of the Philippine President enacted the "Philippine Baselines Law of 2009" (RA 9522). The new law classifies the Kalayaan Island Group (KIG) and the Scarborough Shoal as a "regime of islands under the Republic of the Philippines." This means that the Philippines continues to lay claim over the disputed islands.

8 March 2009 — PRC ships confronted the USNS *Impeccable* (T-AGOS 23) while it was conducting operations in international waters in the SCS about 75 miles south of Hainan Island.

May 2009 — Two submissions to the Commission on the Limits of the Continental Shelf were made on May. A joint submission by Malaysia and Vietnam claims jurisdiction over their respective continental shelves out to 200 nautical miles. A lone submission by Vietnam claims jurisdiction over an extended shelf area. The PRC and the Philippines both protested the moves stating that they violated agreements made with regards to the islands.

23 July 2010 — U.S. Secretary of State Hillary Clinton announced at an ARF meeting in Hanoi that Washington had an interest in freedom of navigation in the SCS. This policy became known as the "pivot to Asia" whereby 60% of U.S. naval forces would be shifted to the Pacific region by 2020.

18 May 2011 — China Mobile announced that its mobile phone coverage has expanded to the Spratly Islands, under the rationale that it can allow soldiers stationed on the islands, fishermen and merchant vessels within the area to use mobile services, and can also provide assistance during storms and sea rescues. The deployment of China Mobile's support over the islands took roughly one year to fulfil.

May 2011 — Chinese patrol boats attacked and cut the cable of Vietnamese oil exploration ships near Spratly islands. The incident sparked several anti-China protests in Vietnam

June 2011 — Chinese navy conducted three days of exercises, including live fire drills, in the disputed waters. This was widely seen as a warning to Vietnam, which had also conducted live fire drills near the Spratly Islands. Chinese patrol boats fired repeated rounds at a target on an apparently uninhabited island, as twin fighter jets streaked in tandem overhead. 14 vessels participated in the maneuvers, staging antisubmarine and beach landing drills aimed at "defending atolls and protecting sea lanes."

July 2012 — China announced that it would station a special Sansha garrison in the disputed Paracel islands.

26 July 2012 — China announced that Senior Colonel Cai Xihong would command the Sansha garrison.

January 2013 — Philippines submits case to the UN Permanent Court of Arbitration.

May 2014 — Anti–China riots in Vietnam result in 21 PRC/ROC deaths.

12 July 2016 — UN Tribunal ruling backing the Philippines.

October 2016 — President Rodrigo Duterte meets with Xi Jinping in Beijing, and the two heads of state agree to "fully recover" relations that had been damaged by their maritime dispute: "Both sides agree to continue discussions on confidence-building measures ... and to exercise self-restraint in the conduct of activities in the South China Sea that would complicate or escalate disputes."

November 2016 — Prime Minister Najib Razak signed 14 economic agreements totaling $34.4 billion with China.

Sources: Esmond Douglas Smith, "China, technology and the Spratly Islands: The Geopolitical impact of new technologies," PhD dissertation (1994), Salve Regina University; Dhirendra K. Vajpeyi, "Shadow Dancing in the Indian and Pacific Oceans," in Adam Lowther, ed., *The Asia-Pacific Century: Challenges and Opportunities* (Maxwell Air Force Base, Alabama: Air University Press, 2013), 121–122; "South China Sea Tables and Maps-US EIA, http://www.southchinasea.org/south-china-sea-tables-and-maps-us-eia/; Nalanda Roy, *The South China Sea Disputes: Past, Present, and Future* (New York: Lexington Books, 2016).

SUPPORTING DOCUMENTS

Document 1
Convention Concerning the Delimitation of the Border Between China and Tonkin
(Signed at Beijing, June 26, 1887)

The commissioners named by the President of the French Republic and by His Majesty the Emperor of China, in execution of Article 3 of the Treaty of 9 June 1885, for the surveying of the border between China and Tonkin, have finished their work:

M. Ernest Constans, Deputy [of the National Assembly], former minister of the interior and of faiths, government commissioner, special envoy of the Republic of France, on the one hand;

And His Highness Prince Qing, Prince of the second rank, president of the Zongli Yamen, assisted by

His Excellency Sun Yuwen, member of the Zongli Yamen, first vice-president of the ministry of public works, on the other hand;

Acting in the name of their respective governments:

Have decided to record in the present act the following arrangements for the purpose of definitively settling the delimitation of the said border:—

1. The minutes and the maps annexed hereto, which have been drawn up and signed by the French and Chinese commissioners are and shall remain approved.
2. Those points in the accord on which the two commissions could not agree, and the corrections envisaged by the second paragraph of Article 3 of the Treaty of 9 June 1885, are settled as follows:

In Guangdong, it is agreed that the contested points situated to the east and northeast of Mangjie [Monkaï], beyond the border as was fixed by the delimitation commission, are assigned to China. The isles which are to the east of the meridian of 105° 43' longitude east of Paris, which is to say of the north-south line passing through the eastern point of the island of Chagu [Tch'a-Kou or Ouan-chan (Tra-co)] and forming the border, are similarly assigned to China. The Jiutou [Go-tho] islands and other islands which are to the west of this meridian belong to Annam.

Chinese guilty or accused of crimes or offences who seek refuge in these islands, shall, in conformity to the stipulations in Article XVII of the Treaty of 25 April 1886, be sought out, arrested and extradited by the French authorities.

On the border of Yunnan, it is agreed that the line of demarcation follow the following path:

From Goutouzhai [Keou-teou-tchai; Cao-dao-trai] on the left bank of the Xiaoduzhou River [Siao-tou-tcheou-ho; Tien-do-chu-ha], point M on the second section of the map, it heads for 50 *lis* (20 kilometers) directly from west to east, leaving to China the places of Jujiangshe [Tsui-kiang-cho] or Juyishe [Tsui-y-cho; Tu-nghia-xa], Jumeishe [Tsui-mei-cho; Tu-mi-xa], Jiangfeishe [Kiang-fei-cho] or Yifeishe [Nghia-fi-xa], which are to the north of this line, and to Annam, that of Youpengshe [Yeou-p'ong-cho; Hu-bang-xa] which is to the south, as far as the points marked P and Q on the annexed maps, where it cuts the two branches of the second tributary to the right of the Hei River [Heï-ho; Hac-ha] or Duzhou River [Tou-tcheou-ho; Do-chu-ha]. Leaving the point Q, the line veers to the southeast for about 15 *lis* [6 kilometers] to point R, leaving to China the territory of Nandan [Nan-tan; Nan-don] to the north of this point R; then, leaving this said point, the line climbs to the northeast to the point S, following the direction traced on the map as the line R-S, the course of the Nandeng River [Nan-teng-ho; Nam-dang-ha] and the territories of Manmei [Man-mei; Man-mi], Mengtongshangcun [Meng-tong-chan-ts'oun; Muong-dong-truong-thon], Mengtongshan [Meng-toung-chan; Muong-dong-son], Mengtongzhongcun [Meng-toung-tchoung-ts'oun; Muong-dong-truong-thon] and Mengtongxiacun [Meng-toung-chia-ts'oun; Muong-dong-ha-thon] staying with Annam.

Leaving point S (Mengtongxiacun or Muong-dong-ha-thon), the middle of the Qingshui River [Ts'ing-chouei-ho; Than-thuy-ha] represents, until it reaches its confluent, the adopted border.

From point T, its path follows the middle of the Clear River to the point X, at the level of Chuantou [Tch'ouan-teou; Thuyen-dan].

From point X, it climbs northward to the point Y, passing through Baishiya [Pai-che-yai; Bach-thach-giai] and Laoaikan [Lao-ai-k'an; Lao-hai-kan], with half of each of those places belonging to China and half to Annam, that to the east belonging to Annam and that to the west to China.

From point Y, it runs, in a northward direction, along the right bank of a small affluent to the left of the Clear River which receives it between

Bianbaoka [Pien-pao-kia; Bien-bao-kha] and Beibao [Pei-pao; Bac-bao], afterwards reaching Gaomabai [Kao-ma-pai; Cao-ma-bach], point Z, where it joins the line on the third section [of the map].

Leaving Longbozhai [Long-po-tchai] (fifth section), the common border of Yunnan and Annam climbs the course of the Longbo River [Long-po-ho] to the point of its confluence with the Qingshui River, marked A on the map; from point A, it follows the general direction northwest to southwest to the point indicated B on the map, the place where the Saijiang River [Saï-kiang-ho] receives the Mianshuiwan [Mien-chouei-ouan]; in doing so, the border leaves to China the course of the Qingshui River.

From point B, the border is in the direction east-west to the point C where it meets the Dengtiao River [Teng-tiao-tchiang] below Dashujiao [Ta-chou-tchio]. That which is south of this line belongs to Annam, that which is to the north to China.

From point C, it descends again to the south, following the middle of the Dengtiao River to its confluence, at point D, with the Jinzi River [Tsin-tse-ho].

It then follows the Jinzi River for about 30 *lis* and continues in an east-west direction to the point E, where it meets the little creek which flows into the Black River (Heijiang [Hei-tçiang or Hac-giang]) to the east of Lake Mengbang [Meng-pang]. The middle of this creek serves as the border from point E to point F.

Leaving point F, the middle of the Black River serves as the border to the west.

The Chinese local authorities and the agents designated by the Resident-General of the French Republic in Annam and Tonkin shall be charged with the marking out, in conformity with the maps prepared and signed by the delimitation commission, and the line therein.

Annexed to the present Act are three maps in two copies, signed and sealed by the two parties. On these maps, the new border is portrayed by a red line and indicated on the Yunnan maps by the letters of the French alphabet and the Chinese cyclical characters.

Made in Beijing, in duplicate, 26 June 1887.
(Signature and seal of the Chinese Plenipotentiary.)

Signed: CONSTANS.
(Seal of the French Legation at Beijing)

Art. 2.—The minister of foreign affairs is charged with carrying out the present decree.

Done at Rambouillet, October 19, 1896

FÉLIX FAURE.

For the President of the Republic:
the minister of foreign affairs,
G. HANOTAUX

Source: http://www.chinaforeignrelations.net/node/167

Document 2
Cairo Declaration, 1 December 1943

President Roosevelt, Generalissimo Chiang Kai-shek and Prime Minister Churchill, together with their respective military and diplomatic advisers, have completed a conference in North Africa.

The following general statement was issued:

"The several military missions have agreed upon future military operations against Japan. The Three Great Allies expressed their resolve to bring unrelenting pressure against their brutal enemies by sea, land, and air. This pressure is already rising.

"The Three Great Allies are fighting this war to restrain and punish the aggression of Japan. They covet no gain for themselves and have no thought of territorial expansion. It is their purpose that Japan shall be stripped of all the islands in the Pacific which she has seized or occupied since the beginning of the first World War in 1914, and that all the territories Japan has stolen from the Chinese, such as Manchuria, Formosa, and The Pescadores, shall be restored to the Republic of China. Japan will also be expelled from all other territories which she has taken by violence and greed. The aforesaid three great powers, mindful of the enslavement of the people of Korea, are determined that in due course Korea shall become free and independent.

"With these objects in view the three Allies, in harmony with those of the United Nations at war with Japan, will continue to persevere in the serious and prolonged operations necessary to procure the unconditional surrender of Japan."

Source:http://www.ndl.go.jp/constitution/e/shiryo/01/002_46/002_46tx.html

Document 3
Potsdam Proclamation, 26 July 1945

Proclamation Defining Terms for Japanese Surrender Issued, at Potsdam, July 26, 1945

1. We-the President of the United States, the President of the National Government of the Republic of China, and the Prime Minister of Great Britain, representing the hundreds of millions of our countrymen, have conferred and agree that Japan shall be given an opportunity to end this war.
2. The prodigious land, sea and air forces of the United States, the British Empire and of China, many times reinforced by their armies and air fleets from the west, are poised to strike the final blows upon Japan. This military power is sustained and inspired by the determination of all the Allied Nations to prosecute the war against Japan until she ceases to resist.
3. The result of the futile and senseless German resistance to the might of the aroused free peoples of the world stands forth in awful clarity as an example to the people of Japan. The might that now converges on Japan is immeasurably greater than that which, when applied to the resisting Nazis, necessarily laid waste to the lands, the industry and the method of life of the whole German people. The full application of our military power, backed by our resolve, will mean the inevitable and complete destruction of the Japanese armed forces and just as inevitably the utter devastation of the Japanese homeland.
4. The time has come for Japan to decide whether she will continue to be controlled by those self-willed militaristic advisers whose unintelligent calculations have brought the Empire of Japan to the threshold of annihilation, or whether she will follow the path of reason.
5. Following are our terms. We will not deviate from them. There are no alternatives. We shall brook no delay.
6. There must be eliminated for all time the authority and influence of those who have deceived and misled the people of Japan into embarking on world conquest, for we insist that

a new order of peace, security and justice will be impossible until irresponsible militarism is driven from the world.

7. Until such a new order is established and until there is convincing proof that Japan's war-making power is destroyed, points in Japanese territory to be designated by the Allies shall be occupied to secure the achievement of the basic objectives we are here setting forth.

8. The terms of the Cairo Declaration shall be carried out and Japanese sovereignty shall be limited to the islands of Honshu, Hokkaido, Kyushu, Shikoku and such minor islands as we determine.

9. The Japanese military forces, after being completely disarmed, shall be permitted to return to their homes with the opportunity to lead peaceful and productive lives.

10. We do not intend that the Japanese shall be enslaved as a race or destroyed as a nation, but stern justice shall be meted out to all war criminals, including those who have visited cruelties upon our prisoners. The Japanese Government shall remove all obstacles to the revival and strengthening of democratic tendencies among the Japanese people. Freedom of speech, of religion, and of thought, as well as respect for the fundamental human rights shall be established.

11. Japan shall be permitted to maintain such industries as will sustain her economy and permit the exaction of just reparations in kind, but not those which would enable her to re-arm for war. To this end, access to, as distinguished from control of, raw materials shall be permitted. Eventual Japanese participation in world trade relations shall be permitted.

12. The occupying forces of the Allies shall be withdrawn from Japan as soon as these objectives have been accomplished and there has been established in accordance with the freely expressed will of the Japanese people a peacefully inclined and responsible government.

13. We call upon the government of Japan to proclaim now the unconditional surrender of all Japanese armed forces, and to provide proper and adequate assurances of their good faith in such action. The alternative for Japan is prompt and utter destruction.

Source: http://www.ndl.go.jp/constitution/e/etc/c06.html

Document 4
Treaty of Peace with Japan, 8 September 1951

CHAPTER II
TERRITORY

Article 2

(a) Japan recognizing the independence of Korea, renounces all right, title and claim to Korea, including the islands of Quelpart, Port Hamilton and Dagelet.
(b) Japan renounces all right, title and claim to Formosa and the Pescadores.
(c) Japan renounces all right, title and claim to the Kurile Islands, and to that portion of Sakhalin and the islands adjacent to it over which Japan acquired sovereignty as a consequence of the Treaty of Portsmouth of 5 September 1905.
(d) Japan renounces all right, title and claim in connection with the League of Nations Mandate System, and accepts the action of the United Nations Security Council of 2 April 1947, extending the trusteeship system to the Pacific Islands formerly under mandate to Japan.
(e) Japan renounces all claim to any right or title to or interest in connection with any part of the Antarctic area, whether deriving from the activities of Japanese nationals or otherwise.
(f) Japan renounces all right, title and claim to the Spratly Islands and to the Paracel Islands.

Article 3

Japan will concur in any proposal of the United States to the United Nations to place under its trusteeship system, with the United States as the sole administering authority, Nansei Shoto south of 29 deg. north latitude (including the Ryukyu Islands and the Daito Islands), Nanpo Shoto south of Sofu Gan (including the Bonin Islands, Rosario Island and the Volcano Islands) and Parece Vela and Marcus Island. Pending the making of such a proposal and affirmative action thereon, the United States will have the right to exercise all and any powers of administration, legislation and jurisdiction over the territory and inhabitants of these islands, including their territorial waters.

Article 4

(a) Subject to the provisions of paragraph (b) of this Article, the disposition of property of Japan and of its nationals in the areas referred to in Article 2, and their claims, including debts, against the authorities presently administering such areas and the residents (including juridical persons) thereof, and the disposition in Japan of property of such authorities and residents, and of claims, including debts, of such authorities and residents against Japan and its nationals, shall be the subject of special arrangements between Japan and such authorities. The property of any of the Allied Powers or its nationals in the areas referred to in Article 2 shall, insofar as this has not already been done, be returned by the administering authority in the condition in which it now exists. (The term nationals whenever used in the present Treaty includes juridical persons.)

(b) Japan recognizes the validity of dispositions of property of Japan and Japanese nationals made by or pursuant to directives of the United States Military Government in any of the areas referred to in Articles 2 and 3.

(c) Japanese owned submarine cables connection Japan with territory removed from Japanese control pursuant to the present Treaty shall be equally divided, Japan retaining the Japanese terminal and adjoining half of the cable, and the detached territory the remainder of the cable and connecting terminal facilities.

Source: http://www.taiwandocuments.org/sanfrancisco01.htm

Document 5
Treaty of Peace between the Republic of China and Japan, 28 April 1952

TREATY OF PEACE

The Republic of China and Japan,
Considering their mutual desire for good neighbourliness in view of their historical and cultural ties and geographical proximity; Realising the importance of their close cooperation to the promotion of their common welfare and to the maintenance of international peace and security; Recognising the need for a settlement of problems that have arisen as a result of the existence of a state of war between them; Have resolved to conclude a Treaty of Peace and have accordingly appointed as their Plenipotentiaries,

His Excellency the President of the Republic of China: Mr. YEH KUNG-CHAO;

The Government of Japan: Mr. ISAO KAWADA

Who, having communicated to each other their full powers found to be in good and due form, have agreed upon the following Articles:—

Article 1

The state of war between the Republic of China and Japan is terminated as from the date on which the present Treaty enters into force.

Article 2

It is recognised that under Article 2 of the Treaty of Peace which Japan signed at the city of San Francisco on 8 September 1951 (hereinafter referred to as the San Francisco Treaty), Japan has renounced all right, title, and claim to Taiwan (Formosa) and Penghu (the Pescadores) as well as the Spratley Islands and the Paracel Islands.

Article 3

The disposition of property of Japan and its nationals in Taiwan (Formosa) and Penghu (the Pescadores), and their claims, including debts, against the authorities of the Republic of China in Taiwan (Formosa) and Penghu (the Pescadores) and the residents thereof, and the disposition in Japan of property of such authorities and residents and their claims, including debts, against Japan and its nationals, shall be the subject of special arrangements between the Government of the Republic of China and the Government of Japan. The terms nationals and residents include juridical persons.

Article 4

It is recognised that all treaties, conventions, and agreements concluded before 9 December 1941 between Japan and China have become null and void as a consequence of the war.

Article 5

It is recognised that under the provisions of Article 10 of the San Francisco Treaty, Japan has renounced all special rights and its interests in China, including all benefits and privileges resulting from the provisions of the final Protocol signed at Peking on 7 September 1901, and all annexes, notes, and documents supplementary thereto, and has agreed to the abrogation in respect to Japan of the said protocol, annexes, notes, and documents.

Article 6

(a) The Republic of China and Japan will be guided by the principles of Article 2 of the Charter of the United Nations in their mutual relations.
(b) The Republic of China and Japan will cooperate in accordance with the principles of the Charter of the United Nations and, in particular, will promote their common welfare through friendly cooperation in the economic field.

Article 7

The Republic of China and Japan will endeavour to conclude, as soon as possible, a treaty or agreement to place their trading, maritime, and other commercial relations, on a stable and friendly basis.

Article 8

The Republic of China and Japan will endeavour to conclude, as soon as possible, an agreement relating to civil air transport.

Article 9

The Republic of China and Japan will endeavour to conclude, as soon as possible, an agreement providing for the regulation or limitation of fishing and the conservation and development of fisheries on the high seas.

Article 10

For the purposes of the present Treaty, nationals of the Republic of China shall be deemed to include all the inhabitants and former inhabitants of Taiwan (Formosa) and Penghu (the Pescadores) and their descendents who are of the Chinese nationality in accordance with the laws and regulations which have been or may hereafter be enforced by the Republic of China in Taiwan (Formosa) and Penghu (the Pescadores); and juridical persons of the Republic of China shall be deemed to include all those registered under the laws and regulations which have been or may hereafter be enforced by the Republic of China in Taiwan (Formosa) and Penghu (the Pescadores).

Article 11

Unless otherwise provided for in the present Treaty and the documents supplementary thereto, any problem arising between the Republic of China and Japan as a result of the existence of a state of war shall be settled in accordance with the relevant provisions of the San Francisco Treaty.

Article 12

Any dispute that may arise out of the interpretation or application of the present Treaty shall be settled by negotiation or other pacific means.

Article 13

The present Treaty shall be ratified and the instruments of ratification shall be exchanged at Taipei as soon as possible. The present Treaty shall enter into force as from the date on which such instruments of ratification are exchanged.

Article 14

The present Treaty shall be in the Chinese, Japanese, and English languages. In case of any divergence of interpretation, the English text shall prevail.

In witness whereof the respective Plenipotentiaries have signed the present Treaty and have affixed thereto their seals.

Done in duplicate at Taipei, this Twenty Eighth day of the Fourth month of the Forty First year of the REPUBLIC OF CHINA, corresponding to the Twenty Eighth day of the Fourth month of the Twenty Seventh year of SHOWA of Japan and to the Twenty Eighth day of April in the year One Thousand Nine Hundred and Fifty Two.

YEH KUNG-CHAO, [L.S.]
*Minister of Foreign Affairs and
Plenipotentiary of the Republic of China*

ISAO KAWADA, [L.S.]
*Minister of Foreign Affairs and
Plenipotentiary of Japan*

Source: http://www.taiwandocuments.org/taipei01.htm

Document 6
U.S.-ROC Mutual Defense Treaty, 2 December 1954 (ratified 3 March 1955) (Terminated by the United States in 1980)

Mutual Defense Treaty between the United States of America and the Republic of China

The Parties to this Treaty,

Reaffirming their faith in the purposes and principles of the Charter of the United Nations and their desire to live in peace with all peoples and all Governments, and desiring to strengthen the fabric of peace in the West Pacific Area,

Recalling with mutual pride the relationship which brought their two peoples together in a common bond of sympathy and mutual ideals to fight side by side against irnperialist aggression during the last war,

Desiring to declare publicly and formally their sense of unity and their common determination to defend themselves against external armed attack, so that no potential aggressor could be under the illusion that either of them stands alone in the West Pacific Area, and Desiring further to strengthen their present efforts for collective defense for the preservation of peace and security pending the development of a more comprehensive system of regional security in the West Pacific Area,

Have agreed as follows:

Article 1

The Parties undertake, as set forth in the Charter of the United Nations, to settle any international dispute in which they may be involved by peaceful means in such a manner that international peace, security and justice are not endangered and to refrain in their international relations from the threat or use of force in any manner inconsistent with the purposes of the United Nations.

Article 2

In order more effectively to achieve the objective of this Treaty, the Parties separately and jointly by self-help and mutual aid will maintain and develop their individual and collective capacity to resist armed attack and communist subversive activities directed from without against their territorial integrity and political stability.

Article 3

The Parties undertake to strengthen their free institutions and to cooperate with each other in the development of economic progress and social well-being and to further their individual and collective efforts toward these ends.

Article 4

The Parties, through their Foreign Ministers or their deputies, will consult together from time to time regarding the implementation of this Treaty.

Article 5

Each Party recognizes that an armed attack in the West Pacific Area directed against the territories of either of the Parties would be dangerous to its own peace and safety and declares that it would act to meet the common danger in accordance with its constitutional processes. Any such armed attack and all measures taken as a result thereof shall be immediately reported to the Security Council of the United Nations. Such measures shall be terminated when the Security Council has taken the measures necessary to restore and maintain international peace and security.

Article 6

For the purposes of Articles 2 and 5, the terms "territorial" and "territories" shall mean in respect of the Republic of China, Taiwan and the Pescadores; and in respect of the United States of America, the island territories in the West Pacific under its jurisdiction. The provisions of Articles 2 and 5 will be applicable to such other territories as may be determined by mutual agreement.

Article 7

The Government of the Republic of China grants, and the Government of the United States of America accepts, the right to dispose such United States land, air, and sea forces in and about Taiwan and the Pescadores as may be required for their defense, as determined by mutual agreement.

Article 8

This Treaty does not affect and shall not be interpreted as affecting in any way the rights and obligations of the Parties under the Charter of the United Nations or the responsibility of the United Nations for the maintenance of international peace and security.

Article 9

This Treaty shall be ratified by the Republic of China and the United States of America in accordance with their respective constitutional processes and will come into force when instruments of ratification thereof have been exchanged by them at Taipei.

Article 10

This Treaty shall remain in force indefinitely. Either Party may terminate it one year after notice has been given to the other party.

IN WITNESS WHEREOF, The undersigned Plenipotentiaries have signed this Treaty.

DONE in duplicate, in the Chinese and English languages, at Washington on this Second day of the Twelfth month of the Forty-third Year of the Republic of China, corresponding to the Second day of December of the Year One Thousand Nine Hundred and Fifty-four.

For the Republic of China:
GEORGE K.C. YEH

For the United States of America:
JOHN FOSTER DULLES

Source: http://www.taiwandocuments.org/mutual01.htm

Document 7
The US Congress Formosa Resolution (1955)

(Approved by House vote 409–3 on January 25, 1955 and by Senate vote 85–3 on January 28, 1955)

1955

U.S. Congressional Authorization for the President to Employ the Armed Forces of the United States to Protect Formosa, the Pescadores, and Related Positions and Territories of That Area

Whereas the primary purpose of the United States, in its relations with all other nations, is to develop and sustain a just and enduring peace for all; and Whereas certain territories in the West Pacific under the jurisdiction of the Republic of China are now under armed attack, and threats and declarations have been and are being made by the Chinese Communists that such armed attack is in aid of and in preparation for armed attack on Formosa and the Pescadores,

Whereas such armed attack if continued would gravely endanger the peace and security of the West Pacific Area and particularly of Formosa and the Pescadores; and

Whereas the secure possession by friendly governments of the Western Pacific Island chain, of which Formosa is a part, is essential to the vital interests of the United States and all friendly nations in or bordering upon the Pacific Ocean; and

Whereas the President of the United States on January 6, 1955, submitted to the Senate for its advice and consent to ratification a Mutual Defense Treaty between the United States of America and the Republic of China, which recognizes that an armed attack in the West Pacific Area directed against territories, therein described, in the region of Formosa and the Pescadores, would be dangerous to the peace and safety of the parties to the treaty:

Therefore be it Resolved by the Senate and House of Representatives of the United States of America in Congress assembled, That the President of the United States be and he hereby is authorized to employ the Armed Forces of the United States as he deems necessary for the specific purpose of securing and protecting Formosa and the Pescadores against armed attack, this authority to include the securing and protection of such related positions and territories of that area now in friendly hands and the taking of such other measures as he judges to be required or appropriate in assuring the defense of Formosa and the Pescadores.

This resolution shall expire when the President shall determine that the peace and security of the area is reasonably assured by international conditions created by action of the United Nations or otherwise, and shall so report to the Congress.

United States Statutes At Large, Vol. 69 (1955), p. 7. The resolution was repealed on October 26, 1974, see Vol. 88, Part 2 (1974), p. 1439.

Source: www3.nccu.edu.tw/~lorenzo/Formosa%20Resolution.doc

Document 8
Declaration on China's Territorial Seas, 4 September 1958

On 4 September 1958, the PRC publicly claimed a 12-nautical mile territorial sea to be measured from straight baselines. The Peking Review text of September 9, 1958, states:

Declaration on China's Territorial Sea

The Government of the People's Republic of China on September 4 issued the following declaration on China's territorial sea:
The Government of the People's Republic of China declares:

1) The breadth of the territorial sea of the People's Republic of China shall be twelve nautical miles. This provision applies to all territories of the People's Republic of China, including the Chinese mainland and its coastal islands, as well as Taiwan and its surrounding islands, the Penghu Islands and all other islands belonging to China which are separated from the mainland and its coastal islands by the high seas.
2) China's territorial sea along the mainland and its coastal islands takes as its baseline the line composed of the straight lines connecting basepoints on the mainland coast and on the outermost of the coastal islands; the water area extending twelve nautical miles outward from this baseline is China's territorial sea. The water area inside the baseline, including Pohai Bay and Chiungchow Straits, are Chinese inland waters. The islands inside the baseline, including Tungyin Island, Kaoteng Island, the Matsu Islands, the Paichuan Islands, Wuchiu Island, the Greater and Lesser Quemoy Islands, Tatan Island, Erhtan Island and Tungting Island, are islands of the Chinese inland waters.
3) No foreign vessels for military use and no foreign aircraft may enter China's territorial sea and the air space above it without the permission of the Government of the People's Republic of China.

4) The principles provided in paragraphs 2) and 3) likewise apply to Taiwan and its surrounding islands, the Penghu Islands, the Tungsha Islands, and Hsisha Islands, the Chungsha Islands, the Nansha Islands, and all other islands belonging to China.

The Taiwan and Penghu areas are still occupied by the United States by armed force. This is unlawful encroachment on the territorial integrity and sovereignty of the People's Republic of China. Taiwan, Penghu and such other areas are yet to be recovered, and the Government of the People's Republic of China has the right to recover these areas by all suitable means at a suitable time. This is China's internal affair, in which no foreign interference is tolerated.

Source: http://www.state.gov/documents/organization/58832.pdf

Document 9
Prime Minister Pham Van Dong's Letter, 14 September 1958

On September 14, 1958, PM Pham Van Dong representing the Democratic Republic of Vietnam (North Vietnam) sent a Diplomatic Note to his Chinese counterpart, with the full text as follows:

"We would like to inform you that the Government of the Democratic Republic of Vietnam has noted and support the September 4, 1958 declaration by the People's Republic of China regarding territorial waters of China.

The government of the Democratic Republic of Vietnam respects this decision and will direct the proper government agencies to respect absolutely the 12 nautical mile territorial waters of China in all dealings with the People's Republic of China on the sea. We would like to send our sincere regards."

Source: http://english.vietnamnet.vn/fms/special-reports/10673/diplomatic-note-1958-with-vietnam-s-sovereignty-over-paracel--spratly-islands.html

Document 10
Shanghai Communiqué, 28 February 1972

Joint Communique between the People's Republic of China and the United States of America Issued in Shanghai, February 28, 1972

President Richard Nixon of the United States of America visited the People's Republic of China at the invitation of Premier Chou En-lai of the People's Republic of China from February 21 to February 28, 1972.

Accompanying the President were Mrs. Nixon, U.S. Secretary of State William Rogers, Assistant to the President Dr. Henry Kissinger, and other American officials.

President Nixon met with Chairman Mao Tsetung of the Communist Party of China on February 21. The two leaders had a serious and frank exchange of views on Sino-U.S. relations and world affairs.

During the visit, extensive, earnest and frank discussions were held between President Nixon and Premier Chou En-lai on the normalization of relations between the United States of America and the People's Republic of China, as well as on other matters of interest to both sides. In addition, Secretary of State William Rogers and Foreign Minister Chi Peng-fei held talks in the same spirit.

President Nixon and his party visited Peking and viewed cultural, industrial and agricultural sites, and they also toured Hangchow and Shanghai where, continuing discussions with Chinese leaders, they viewed similar places of interest.

The leaders of the People's Republic of China and the United States of America found it beneficial to have this opportunity, after so many years without contact, to present candidly to one another their views on a variety of issues. They reviewed the international situation in which important changes and great upheavals are taking place and expounded their respective positions and attitudes.

NOTE: Two versions of the Shanghai Communiqué were signed, one in English and one in Chinese. The American version had the USA position first, whereas the Chinese version had the Chinese position at top. The translated Chinese version is presented here.

The Chinese side stated: Wherever there is oppression there is resistance. Countries want independence, nations want liberation and the people want revolution — this has become the irresistible trend of history. All nations, big or small, should be equal; big nations should not bully the small and strong nations should not bully the weak. China will never be a superpower and it opposes hegemony and power politics of any kind. The Chinese side stated that it firmly supports the struggles of all the oppressed people and nations for freedom and liberation and that the people of all countries have the right to choose their social systems according to their own wishes and the right to safeguard the independence, sovereignty and territorial integrity of their own countries and oppose foreign aggression, interference, control and subversion. All foreign troops should be withdrawn to their own countries. The Chinese side expressed its firm support to the peoples of Viet Nam, Laos and Cambodia in their efforts for the attainment of their goal and its firm support to the seven-point proposal of the Provisional Revolutionary Government of the Republic of South Viet Nam and the elaboration of February this year on the two key problems in the proposal, and to the Joint Declaration of the Summit Conference of the Indochinese Peoples. It firmly supports the eight-point program for the peaceful unification of Korea put forward by the Government of the Democratic People's Republic of Korea on April 12, 1971, and the stand for the abolition of the "U.N. Commission for the Unification and Rehabilitation of Korea". It firmly opposes the revival and outward expansion of Japanese militarism and firmly supports the Japanese people's desire to build an independent, democratic, peaceful and neutral Japan. It firmly maintains that India and Pakistan should, in accordance with the United Nations resolutions on the India-Pakistan question, immediately withdraw all their forces to their respective territories and to their own sides of the ceasefire line in Jammu and Kashmir and firmly supports the Pakistan Government and people in their struggle to preserve their independence and sovereignty and the people of Jammu and Kashmir in their struggle for the right of self-determination.

The U.S. side stated: Peace in Asia and peace in the world requires efforts both to reduce immediate tensions and to eliminate the basic causes of conflict. The United States will work for a just and secure peace; just, because it fulfills the aspirations of peoples and nations for freedom and progress; secure, because it removes the danger of foreign aggression. The United States supports individual freedom and social progress for all the peoples of the world, free of outside pressure or intervention. The United States believes that the effort to reduce tensions is served by improving communication between countries that have different ideologies so as to lessen the risks of confrontation through accident, miscalculation or misunderstanding. Countries should treat each other with mutual respect and be willing to compete peacefully, letting performance be the ultimate judge. No country should claim infallibility and each country should be prepared to reexamine its own attitudes for the common good. The United States stressed that the peoples of Indochina should be allowed to determine their destiny without outside intervention; its constant primary objective has been a negotiated solution; the eight-point proposal put forward by the Republic of Viet Nam and the United States on January 27, 1972 represents a basis for the attainment of that objective; in the absence of a negotiated settlement, the United States envisages the ultimate withdrawal of all U.S. forces from the region consistent with the aim of self-determination for each country of Indochina. The United States will maintain its close ties with and support for the Republic of Korea; the United States will support efforts of the Republic of Korea to seek a relaxation of tension and increased communication in the Korean peninsula. The United States places the highest value on its friendly relations with Japan; it will continue to develop the existing close bonds. Consistent with the United Nations Security Council Resolution of December 21, 1971, the United States favors the continuation of the ceasefire between India and Pakistan and the withdrawal of all military forces to within their own territories and to their own sides of the ceasefire line in Jammu and Kashmir; the United States supports the right of the peoples of South Asia to shape their own future in peace, free of military threat, and without having the area become the subject of great power rivalry.

There are essential differences between China and the United States in their social systems and foreign policies. However, the two sides agreed that countries, regardless of their social systems, should conduct their relations on the principles of respect for the sovereignty and territorial integrity of all states, non-aggression against other states, non-interference in the internal affairs of other states, equality and mutual benefit, and peaceful coexistence. International disputes should be settled on this basis, without resorting to the use or threat of force. The United States and the People's Republic of China are prepared to apply these principles to their mutual relations.

With these principles of international relations in mind the two sides stated that:

- progress toward the normalization of relations between China and the United States is in the interests of all countries;
- both wish to reduce the danger of international military conflict;

-- neither should seek hegemony in the Asia-Pacific region and each is opposed to efforts by any other country or group of countries to establish such hegemony; and
-- neither is prepared to negotiate on behalf of any third party or to enter into agreements or understandings with the other directed at other states.

Both sides are of the view that it would be against the interests of the peoples of the world for any major country to collude with another against other countries, or for major countries to divide up the world into spheres of interest.

The two sides reviewed the long-standing serious disputes between China and the United States.

The **Chinese side reaffirmed its position:** The Taiwan question is the crucial question obstructing the normalization of relations between China and the United States; the Government of the People's Republic of China is the sole legal government of China; Taiwan is a province of China which has long been returned to the motherland; the liberation of Taiwan is China's internal affair in which no other country has the right to interfere; and all U.S. forces and military installations must be withdrawn from Taiwan. The Chinese Government firmly opposes any activities which aim at the creation of "one China, one Taiwan" "one China two governments", "two Chinas", an "independent Taiwan" or advocate that "the status of Taiwan remains to be determined".

The U.S. side declared: The United States acknowledges that all Chinese on either side of the Taiwan Strait maintain there is but one China and that Taiwan is a part of China. The United States Government does not challenge that position. It reaffirms its interest in a peaceful settlement of the Taiwan question by the Chinese themselves. With this prospect in mind, it affirms the ultimate objective of the withdrawal of all U.S. forces and military installations from Taiwan. In the meantime, it will progressively reduce its forces and military installations on Taiwan as the tension in the area diminishes.

The two sides agreed that it is desirable to broaden the understanding between the two peoples. To this end, they discussed specific areas in such fields as science, technology, culture, sports and journalism, in which people-to-people contacts and exchanges would be mutually beneficial. Each side undertakes to facilitate the further development of such contacts and exchanges.

Both sides view bilateral trade as another area from which mutual benefit can be derived, and agreed that economic relations based on equality and mutual benefit are in the interest of the peoples of the two countries. They agree to facilitate the progressive development of trade between their two countries.

The two sides agreed that they will stay in contact through various channels, including the sending of a senior U.S. representative to Peking from time to time for concrete consultations to further the normalization of relations between the two countries and continue to exchange views on issues of common interest.

The two sides expressed the hope that the gains achieved during this visit would open up new prospects for the relations between the two countries. They believe that the normalization of relations between the two countries is not only in the interest of the Chinese and American peoples but also contributes to the relaxation of tension in Asia and the world.

President Nixon, Mrs. Nixon and the American party expressed their appreciation for the gracious hospitality shown them by the Government and people of the People's Republic of China.

Source: http://www.sinomania.com/CHINANEWS/shanghai_communique_30th_anniversary.htm

Document 11
Joint Communiqué on the Establishment of Diplomatic Relations between the People's Republic of China and the United States of America, 16 December 1978

The People's Republic of China and the United States of America have agreed to recognize each other and to establish diplomatic relations as of January 1, 1979.

The United States of America recognizes the Government of the People's Republic of China as the sole legal Government of China. Within this context, the people of the United States will maintain cultural, commercial, and other unofficial relations with the people of Taiwan.

The People's Republic of China and the United States of America reaffirm the principles agreed on by the two sides in the Shanghai Communique and emphasize once again that:

- Both wish to reduce the danger of international military conflict.
- Neither should seek hegemony in the Asia-Pacific region or in any other region of the world and each is opposed to efforts by any other country or group of countries to establish such hegemony.

Neither is prepared to negotiate on behalf of any third party or to enter into agreements or understandings with the other directed at other states.

- The Government of the United States of America acknowledges the Chinese position that there is but one China and Taiwan is part of China.
- Both believe that normalization of Sino-American relations is not only in the interest of the Chinese and American peoples but also contributes to the cause of peace in Asia and the world.

The People's Republic of China and the United States of America will exchange Ambassadors and establish Embassies on March 1, 1979.

Source:http://www.china-embassy.org/eng/zmgx/doc/ctc/t36256.htm

Document 12
Taiwan Relations Act, 10 April 1979

Taiwan Relations Act
January 1, 1979

TAIWAN RELATIONS ACT
Public Law 96-8 96th Congress

An Act

To help maintain peace, security, and stability in the Western Pacific and to promote the foreign policy of the United States by authorizing the continuation of commercial, cultural, and other relations between the people of the United States and the people on Taiwan, and for other purposes.

Be it enacted by the Senate and House of Representatives of the United States of America in Congress assembled,

Short Title

SECTION 1. This Act may be cited as the "Taiwan Relations Act".

Findings and Declaration of Policy

Section. 2.
1. The President- having terminated governmental relations between the United States and the governing authorities on Taiwan recognized by the United States as the Republic of China prior to January 1, 1979, the Congress finds that the enactment of this Act is necessary--
   1. to help maintain peace, security, and stability in the Western Pacific; and
   2. to promote the foreign policy of the United States by authorizing the continuation of commercial, cultural, and other relations between the people of the United States and the people on Taiwan.

2. It is the policy of the United States--
    1. to preserve and promote extensive, close, and friendly commercial, cultural, and other relations between the people of the United States and the people on Taiwan, as well as the people on the China mainland and all other peoples of the Western Pacific area;
    2. to declare that peace and stability in the area are in the political, security, and economic interests of the United States, and are matters of international concern;
    3. to make clear that the United States decision to establish diplomatic relations with the People's Republic of China rests upon the expectation that the future of Taiwan will be determined by peaceful means;
    4. to consider any effort to determine the future of Taiwan by other than peaceful means, including by boycotts or embargoes, a threat to the peace and security of the Western Pacific area and of grave concern to the United States;
    5. to provide Taiwan with arms of a defensive character; and
    6. to maintain the capacity of the United States to resist any resort to force or other forms of coercion that would jeopardize the security, or the social or economic system, of the people on Taiwan.
3. Nothing contained in this Act shall contravene the interest of the United States in human rights, especially with respect to the human rights of all the approximately eighteen million inhabitants of Taiwan. The preservation and enhancement of the human rights of all the people on Taiwan are hereby reaffirmed as objectives of the United States.

Implementation of United States Policy with Regard to Taiwan

Section. 3.
1. In furtherance of the policy set forth in section 2 of this Act, the United States will make available to Taiwan such defense articles and defense services in such quantity as may be necessary to enable Taiwan to maintain a sufficient self-defense capability.
2. The President and the Congress shall determine the nature and quantity of such defense articles and services based solely

upon their judgment of the needs of Taiwan, in accordance with procedures established by law. Such determination of Taiwan's defense needs shall include review by United States military authorities in connection with recommendations to the President and the Congress.
3. The President is directed to inform the Congress promptly of any threat to the security or the social or economic system of the people on Taiwan and any danger to the interests of the United States arising therefrom. The President and the Congress shall determine, in accordance with constitutional processes, appropriate action by the United States in response to any such danger.

Application of Laws; International Agreements

Section. 4.
1. The absence of diplomatic relations or recognition shall not affect the application of the laws of the United States with respect to Taiwan, and the laws of the United States shall apply with respect to Taiwan in the manner that the laws of the United States applied with respect to Taiwan prior to January 1, 1979.
2. The application of subsection (a) of this section shall include, but shall not be limited to, the following:
    1. Whenever the laws of the United States refer or relate to foreign countries, nations, states, governments, or similar entities, such terms shall include and such laws shall apply with such respect to Taiwan.
    2. Whenever authorized by or pursuant to the laws of the United States to conduct or carry out programs, transactions, or other relations with respect to foreign countries, nations, states, governments, or similar entities, the President or any agency of the United States Government is authorized to conduct and carry out, in accordance with section 6 of this Act, such programs, transactions, and other relations with respect to Taiwan (including, but not limited to, the performance of services for the United States through contracts with commercial entities on Taiwan), in accordance with the applicable laws of the United States.

3.
1. The absence of diplomatic relations and recognition with respect to Taiwan shall not abrogate, infringe, modify, deny, or otherwise affect in any way any rights or obligations (including but not limited to those involving contracts, debts, or property interests of any kind) under the laws of the United States heretofore or hereafter acquired by or with respect to Taiwan.
2. For all purposes under the laws of the United States, including actions in any court in the United States, recognition of the People's Republic of China shall not affect in any way the ownership of or other rights or interests in properties, tangible and intangible, and other things of value, owned or held on or prior to December 31, 1978, or thereafter acquired or earned by the governing authorities on Taiwan.
4. Whenever the application of the laws of the United States depends upon the law that is or was applicable on Taiwan or compliance therewith, the law applied by the people on Taiwan shall be considered the applicable law for that purpose.
5. Nothing in this Act, nor the facts of the President's action in extending diplomatic recognition to the People's Republic of China, the absence of diplomatic relations between the people on Taiwan and the United States, or the lack of recognition by the United States, and attendant circumstances thereto, shall be construed in any administrative or judicial proceeding as a basis for any United States Government agency, commission, or department to make a finding of fact or determination of law, under the Atomic Energy Act of 1954 and the Nuclear Non-Proliferation Act of 1978, to deny an export license application or to revoke an existing export license for nuclear exports to Taiwan.
6. For purposes of the Immigration and Nationality Act, Taiwan may be treated in the manner specified in the first sentence of section 202(b) of that Act.
7. The capacity of Taiwan to sue and be sued in courts in the United States, in accordance with the laws of the United States, shall not be abrogated, infringed, modified, denied, or otherwise affected in any way by the absence of diplomatic relations or recognition.

8. No requirement, whether expressed or implied, under the laws of the United States with respect to maintenance of diplomatic relations or recognition shall be applicable with respect to Taiwan.
3. For all purposes, including actions in any court in the United States, the Congress approves the continuation in force of all treaties and other international agreements, including multilateral conventions, entered into by the United States and the governing authorities on Taiwan recognized by the United States as the Republic of China prior to January 1, 1979, and in force between them on December 31, 1978, unless and until terminated in accordance with law.
4. Nothing in this Act may be construed as a basis for supporting the exclusion or expulsion of Taiwan from continued membership in any international financial institution or any other international organization.

Overseas Private Investment Corporation

Section. 5.
1. During the three-year period beginning on the date of enactment of this Act, the $1,000 per capita income restriction in insurance, clause (2) of the second undesignated paragraph of section 231 of the reinsurance, Foreign Assistance Act of 1961 shall not restrict the activities of the Overseas Private Investment Corporation in determining whether to provide any insurance, reinsurance, loans, or guaranties with respect to investment projects on Taiwan.
2. Except as provided in subsection (a) of this section, in issuing insurance, reinsurance, loans, or guaranties with respect to investment projects on Taiwan, the Overseas Private Insurance Corporation shall apply the same criteria as those applicable in other parts of the world.

The American Institute of Taiwan

Section. 6.
1. Programs, transactions, and other relations conducted or carried out by the President or any agency of the United States Government with respect to Taiwan shall, in the manner and to the extent directed by the President, be conducted and carried out by or through--

1. The American Institute in Taiwan, a nonprofit corporation incorporated under the laws of the District of Columbia, or
2. such comparable successor nongovermental entity as the President may designate, (hereafter in this Act referred to as the "Institute").
2. Whenever the President or any agency of the United States Government is authorized or required by or pursuant to the laws of the United States to enter into, perform, enforce, or have in force an agreement or transaction relative to Taiwan, such agreement or transaction shall be entered into, performed, and enforced, in the manner and to the extent directed by the President, by or through the Institute.
3. To the extent that any law, rule, regulation, or ordinance of the District of Columbia, or of any State or political subdivision thereof in which the Institute is incorporated or doing business, impedes or otherwise interferes with the performance of the functions of the Institute pursuant to this Act; such law, rule, regulation, or ordinance shall be deemed to be preempted by this Act.

Services by the Institute to United States Citizens on Taiwan

Section. 7.
1. The Institute may authorize any of its employees on Taiwan--
    1. to administer to or take from any person an oath, affirmation, affidavit, or deposition, and to perform any notarial act which any notary public is required or authorized by law to perform within the United States;
    2. To act as provisional conservator of the personal estates of deceased United States citizens; and
    3. to assist and protect the interests of United States persons by performing other acts such as are authorized to be performed outside the United States for consular purposes by such laws of the United States as the President may specify.
2. Acts performed by authorized employees of the Institute under this section shall be valid, and of like force and effect within the United States, as if performed by any other person authorized under the laws of the United States to perform such acts.

Tax Exempt Status of the Institute

SECTION. 8.
1. The Institute, its property, and its income are exempt from all taxation now or hereafter imposed by the United States (except to the extent that section 11(a)(3) of this Act requires the imposition of taxes imposed under chapter 21 of the Internal Revenue Code of 1954, relating to the Federal Insurance Contributions Act) or by State or local taxing authority of the United States.
2. For purposes of the Internal Revenue Code of 1954, the Institute shall be treated as an organization described in sections 170(b)(1)(A), 170(c), 2055(a), 2106(a)(2)(A),, 2522(a), and 2522(b).

FURNISHING PROPERTY AND SERVICES TO AND OBTAINING SERVICES FROM THE INSTITUTE

Section. 9.
1. Any agency of the United States Government is authorized to sell, loan, or lease property (including interests therein) to, and to perform administrative and technical support functions and services for the operations of, the Institute upon such terms and conditions as the President may direct. Reimbursements to agencies under this subsection shall be credited to the current applicable appropriation of the agency concerned.
2. Any agency of the United States Government is authorized to acquire and accept services from the Institute upon such terms and conditions as the President may direct. Whenever the President determines it to be in furtherance of the purposes of this Act, the procurement of services by such agencies from the Institute may be effected without regard to such laws of the United States normally applicable to the acquisition of services by such agencies as the President may specify by Executive order.
3. Any agency of the United States Government making funds available to the Institute in accordance with this Act shall make arrangements with the Institute for the Comptroller General of the United States to have access to the; books and records of the Institute and the opportunity to audit the operations of the Institute.

Taiwan Instrumentality

Section. 10.
1. Whenever the President or any agency of the United States Government is authorized or required by or pursuant to the laws of the United States to render or provide to or to receive or accept from Taiwan, any performance, communication, assurance, undertaking, or other action, such action shall, in the manner and to the. extent directed by the President, be rendered or Provided to, or received or accepted from, an instrumentality established by Taiwan which the President determines has the necessary authority under the laws applied by the people on Taiwan to provide assurances and take other actions on behalf of Taiwan in accordance with this Act.
2. The President is requested to extend to the instrumentality established by Taiwan the same number of offices and complement of personnel as were previously operated in the United States by the governing authorities on Taiwan recognized as the Republic of China prior to January 1, 1979.
3. Upon the granting by Taiwan of comparable privileges and immunities with respect to the Institute and its appropriate personnel, the President is authorized to extend with respect to the Taiwan instrumentality and its appropriate; personnel, such privileges and immunities (subject to appropriate conditions and obligations) as may be necessary for the effective performance of their functions.

Separation of Government Personnel for Employment with the Institute

Section. 11.
1.
   1. Under such terms and conditions as the President may direct, any agency of the United States Government may separate from Government service for a specified period any officer or employee of that agency who accepts employment with the Institute.
   2. An officer or employee separated by an agency under paragraph (1) of this subsection for employment with the Institute shall be entitled upon termination of such employment to reemployment or reinstatement with such agency

(or a successor agency) in an appropriate position with the attendant rights, privileges, and benefits which the officer or employee would have had or acquired had he or she not been so separated, subject to such time period and other conditions as the President may prescribe.
3. An officer or employee entitled to reemployment or reinstatement rights under paragraph (2) of this subsection shall, while continuously employed by the Institute with no break in continuity of service, continue to participate in any benefit program in which such officer or employee was participating prior to employment by the Institute, including programs for compensation for job-related death, injury, or illness; programs for health and life insurance; programs for annual, sick, and other statutory leave; and programs for retirement under any system established by the laws of the United States; except that employment with the Institute shall be the basis for participation in such programs only to the extent that employee deductions and employer contributions, as required, in payment for such participation for the period of employment with the Institute, are currently deposited in the program's or system's fund or depository. Death or retirement of any such officer or employee during approved service with the Institute and prior to reemployment or reinstatement shall be considered a death in or retirement from Government service for purposes of any employee or survivor benefits acquired by reason of service with an agency of the United States Government.
4. Any officer or employee of an agency of the United States Government who entered into service with the Institute on approved leave of absence without pay prior to the enactment of this Act shall receive the benefits of this section for the period of such service.
2. Any agency of the United States Government employing alien personnel on Taiwan may transfer such personnel, with accrued allowances, benefits, and rights, to the Institute without a break in service for purposes of retirement and other benefits, including continued participation in any system established by the laws of the United States for the retirement of employees in which the alien was participating prior to the transfer to the Institute, except that employment with

the Institute shall be creditable for retirement purposes only to the extent that employee deductions and employer contributions, as required, in payment for such participation for the period of employment with the Institute, are currently deposited in the system's fund or depository.
3. Employees of the Institute shall not be employees of the United States and, in representing the Institute, shall be exempt from section 207 of title 18, United States Code.
   1. For purposes of sections 911 and 913 of the Internal Revenue Code of 1954, amounts paid by the Institute to its employees shall not be treated as earned income. Amounts received by employees of the Institute shall not be included in gross income, and shall be exempt from taxation, to the extent that they are equivalent to amounts received by civilian officers and employees of the Government of the United States as allowances and benefits which are exempt from taxation under section 912 of such Code.
   2. Except to the extent required by subsection (a)(3) of this section, service performed in the employ of the Institute shall not constitute employment for purposes of chapter 21 of such Code and title II of the Social Security Act.

Reporting Requirement

Section. 12.
1. The Secretary of State shall transmit to the Congress the text of any agreement to which the Institute is a party. However, any such agreement the immediate public disclosure of which would, in the opinion of the President, be prejudicial to the national security of the United States shall not be so transmitted to the Congress but shall be transmitted to the Committee on Foreign Relations of the Senate and the Committee on Foreign Affairs of the House of Representatives under an appropriate injunction of secrecy to be removed only upon due notice from the President.
2. For purposes of subsection (a), the term "agreement" includes-
   1. any agreement entered into between the Institute and the governing authorities on Taiwan or the instrumentality established by Taiwan; and

2. any agreement entered into between the Institute and an agency of the United States Government.
3. Agreements and transactions made or to be made by or through the Institute shall be subject to the same congressional notification, review, and approval requirements and procedures as if such agreements and transactions were made by or through the agency of the United States Government on behalf of which the Institute is acting.
4. During the two-year period beginning on the effective date of this Act, the Secretary of State shall transmit to the Speaker of the House and Senate House of Representatives and the Committee on Foreign Relations of Foreign Relations the Senate, every six months, a report describing and reviewing economic relations between the United States and Taiwan, noting any interference with normal commercial relations.

RULES AND REGULATIONS

Section. 13.
The President is authorized to prescribe such rules and regulations as he may deem appropriate to carry out the purposes of this Act. During the three-year period beginning on the effective date of this Act, such rules and regulations shall be transmitted promptly to the Speaker of the House of Representatives and to the Committee on Foreign Relations of the Senate. Such action shall not, however, relieve the Institute of the responsibilities placed upon it by this Act.

Congressional Oversight

Section. 14.
1. The Committee on Foreign Affairs of the House of Representatives, the Committee on Foreign Relations of the Senate, and other appropriate committees of the Congress shall monitor-
   1. the implementation of the provisions of this Act;
   2. the operation and procedures of the Institute;
   3. the legal and technical aspects of the continuing relationship between the United States and Taiwan; and
   4. the implementation of the policies of the United States concerning security and cooperation in East Asia.

2. Such committees shall report, as appropriate, to their respective Houses on the results of their monitoring.

Definitions

Section. 15. For purposes of this Act-
1. the term "laws of the United States" includes any statute, rule, regulation, ordinance, order, or judicial rule of decision of the United States or any political subdivision thereof; and
2. the term "Taiwan" includes, as the context may require, the islands of Taiwan and the Pescadores, the people on those islands, corporations and other entities and associations created or organized under the laws applied on those islands, and the governing authorities on Taiwan recognized by the United States as the Republic of China prior to January 1, 1979, and any successor governing authorities (including political subdivisions, agencies, and instrumentalities thereof).

Authorization of Appriations

Section. 16.
In addition to funds otherwise available to carry out the provisions of this Act, there are authorized to be appropriated to the Secretary of State for the fiscal year 1980 such funds as may be necessary to carry out such provisions. Such funds are authorized to remain available until expended.

Severability of Provisions

Section. 17.
If any provision of this Act or the application thereof to any person or circumstance is held invalid, the remainder of the Act and the application of such provision to any other person or circumstance shall not be affected thereby.

Effective Date

Section. 18.
This Act shall be effective as of January 1, 1979. Approved April 10, 1979.

Source: http://www.ait.org.tw/en/taiwan-relations-act.html

Document 13
Joint Communiqué of the United States of America and the People's Republic of China, 17 August 1982

In the Joint Communiqué on the Establishment of Diplomatic Relations on January 1, 1979, issued by the Government of the United States of America and the People's Republic of China, the United States of America recognized the Government of the People's Republic of China as the sole legal Government of China, and it acknowledged the Chinese position that there is but one China and Taiwan is part of China. Within that context, the two sides agreed that the people of the United States would continue to maintain cultural, commercial, and other unofficial relations with the people of Taiwan. On this basis, relations between the United States and China were normalized.

The question of United States arms sales to Taiwan was not settled in the course of negotiations between the two countries on establishing diplomatic relations. The two sides held differing positions, and the Chinese side stated that it would raise the issue again following normalization. Recognizing that this issue would seriously hamper the development of United States-China relations, they have held further discussions on it, during and since the meetings between President Ronald Reagan and Premier Zhao Ziyang and between Secretary of State Alexander M. Haig, Jr. and Vice Premier and Foreign Minister Huang Hua in October 1981.

Respect for each other's sovereignty and territorial integrity and non-interference in each other's internal affairs constitute the fundamental principles guiding United States-China relations. These principles were confirmed in the Shanghai Communiqué of February 28, 1972 and reaffirmed in the Joint Communiqué on the Establishment Of Diplomatic Relations which came into effect on January 1, 1979. Both sides emphatically state that these principles continue to govern all aspects of their relations.

The Chinese Government reiterates that the question of Taiwan is China's internal affair. The Message to Compatriots in Taiwan issued by China on January 1, 1979 promulgated a fundamental policy of striving for peaceful reunification of the motherland. The Nine-Point Proposal put forward by China on September 30, 1981 represented a further major effort under this fundamental policy to strive for a peaceful solution to the Taiwan question.

The United States Government attaches great importance to its relations with China, and reiterates that it has no intention of infringing on Chinese sovereignty and territorial integrity, or interfering in China's internal affairs, or pursuing a policy of "two Chinas" or "one China, one Taiwan." The United States Government understands and appreciates the Chinese policy of striving for a peaceful resolution of the Taiwan question as indicated in China's Message to Compatriots in Taiwan issued on January 1, 1979 and the Nine-Point Proposal put forward by China on September 30, 1981. The new situation which has emerged with regard to the Taiwan question also provides favorable conditions for the settlement of United States-China differences over United States arms sales to Taiwan.

Having in mind the foregoing statements of both sides, the United States Government states that it does not seek to carry out a long-term policy of arms sales to Taiwan, that its arms sales to Taiwan will not exceed, either in qualitative or in quantitative terms, the level of those supplied in recent years since the establishment of diplomatic relations between the United States and China, and that it intends gradually to reduce its sale of arms to Taiwan, leading, over a period of time, to a final resolution. In so stating, the United States acknowledges China's consistent position regarding the thorough settlement of this issue.

In order to bring about, over a period of time, a final settlement of the question of United States arms sales to Taiwan, which is an issue rooted in history, the two Governments will make every effort to adopt measures and create conditions conducive to the thorough settlement of this issue.

The development of United States-China relations is not only in the interests of the two peoples but also conducive to peace and stability in the world. The two sides are determined, on the principle of equality and mutual benefit, to strengthen their ties in the economic, cultural, educational, scientific, technological and other fields and make strong, joint efforts for the continued development of relations between the Governments and peoples of the United States and China.

In order to bring about the healthy development of United States-China relations, maintain world peace and oppose aggression and expansion, the two Governments reaffirm the principles agreed on by the two sides in the Shanghai Communiqué and the Joint Communiqué on the Establishment of Diplomatic Relations. The two sides will maintain contact and hold appropriate consultations on bilateral and international issues of common interest.

Source: http://www.fapa.org/generalinfo/shanghai1982.html

Document 14
Law on the Territorial Sea and the Contiguous Zone, 25 February 1992

The Law on the Territorial Sea and the Contiguous Zone of the People's Republic of China, adopted at the 24th meeting of the Standing Committee of the National People's Congress on 25 February 1992.

Article 1

This law is formulated in order to enable the People's Republic of China (PRC) to exercise its sovereignty over its territorial sea and its rights to exercise control over its contiguous zone, and to safeguard State security as well as its maritime rights and interests.

Article 2

The PRC's territorial sea refers to the waters adjacent to its territorial land.

The PRC's territorial land includes the mainland and its offshore islands, Taiwan and the various affiliated islands including Diaoyu Island, Penghu Islands, Dongsha Islands, Xisha Islands, Nansha (Spratly) Islands and other islands that belong to the People's Republic of China.

The PRC's internal waters refer to the waters along the baseline of the territorial sea facing the land.

Article 3

The extent of the PRC's territorial sea measures 12 nautical miles from the baseline of the territorial sea. The PRC's baseline of the territorial sea is designated with the method of straight baselines, formed by joining the various base points with straight lines.

The outer limit of the PRC's territorial sea refers to the line, every point of which is at a distance of 12 nautical miles from the nearest point of the baseline of the territorial sea.

Article 4

The PRC's contiguous zone refers to the waters that are outside of, but adjacent to, its territorial sea. The extent of the contiguous zone has a width of 12 nautical miles.

The outer limit of the PRC's contiguous zone is a line, every point of which has a nearest distance of 24 nautical miles from the baseline from which the territorial sea is measured.

Article 5

The People's Republic of China exercises sovereignty over its territorial sea and the airspace over the territorial sea, as well as its seabed and subsoil.

Article 6

Non-military foreign ships enjoy the right of innocent passage through the territorial sea of the People's Republic of China according to law.

To enter the territorial sea of the People's Republic of China, foreign military ships must obtain permission from the Government of the People's Republic of China.

Article 7

While passing through the territorial sea of the People's Republic of China, foreign submarines and other underwater vehicles shall navigate on the surface of the sea and show their flags.

Article 8

While passing through the territorial sea of the People's Republic of China, foreign ships shall abide by the laws and regulations of the People's Republic of China and shall not impair the peace, security and good order of the People's Republic of China.

Foreign nuclear-powered ships and other ships carrying nuclear, toxic or other dangerous substances must carry certain documents and observe special precautionary measures when they pass through the territorial sea of the People's Republic of China.

The Government of the People's Republic of China has the right to adopt all necessary measures to prevent and stop the passage of a ship which is not innocent through its territorial sea.

Foreign ships which violate the laws and regulations of the People's Republic of China shall be dealt with according to law by relevant departments of the People's Republic of China.

Article 9

To ensure the safety of navigation and satisfy other requirements, the Government of the People's Republic of China may require foreign ships passing through its territorial sea to use the designated sea lane or prescribed traffic separation scheme. Concrete methods should be issued by the Government of the People's Republic of China or its relevant responsible departments.

Article 10

The relevant responsible organs of the People's Republic of China shall have the right to order an immediate eviction of foreign military ships or ships owned by foreign Governments and operated for non-commercial purposes that violate the laws or regulations of the People's Republic of China while passing through the territorial sea of the People's Republic of China. Losses or damage caused shall be borne by the nations whose flag is being flown by the ship in question.

Article 11

Any international, foreign organization, or individual who intends to conduct activities connected with scientific research or marine survey shall first seek the consent of the People's Republic of China or its relevant responsible departments and abide by the laws and regulations of the People's Republic of China.

Whoever is found illegally entering the territorial sea of the People's Republic of China to conduct activities connected with scientific research or marine survey in violation of the preceding provisions shall be dealt with by the relevant organs of the People's Republic of China according to law.

Article 12

Foreign aircraft may not enter the air above the territorial sea of the People's Republic of China unless they do so in accordance with agreements or accords which the Governments of their countries have signed with the Government of the People's Republic of China, or they have been approved or accepted by the Government of the People's Republic of China or organs it has authorized.

Article 13

The People's Republic of China has the authority to exercise powers within its contiguous zone for the purpose of preventing or punishing infringement of its security, customs, fiscal sanitary laws and regulations or entry-exit control within its land territories, internal waters or territorial sea.

Article 14

When competent authorities of the People's Republic of China have good reasons to believe that a foreign ship has violated the laws and regulations of the People's Republic of China, they may exercise the right of hot pursuit.

The hot pursuit commences when the foreign ship, or one of its small boats, or other craft working as a team and using the ship pursued as a mother ship is within the limits of the internal waters, territorial sea or contiguous zone of the People's Republic of China.

If the foreign ships are in the contiguous zone of the People's Republic of China, the hot pursuit may proceed only when the rights of the relevant laws and regulations set forth in article 13 above have been violated.

As long as the hot pursuit is not interrupted, it may continue outside the territorial sea of the People's Republic of China or the contiguous zone. The hot pursuit ceases as soon as the ship pursued enters the territorial sea of its own country or of a third country.

The right of hot pursuit in this article is exercised by warships or military aircraft of the People's Republic of China, or by ships or aircraft authorized by the Government of the People's Republic of China to that effect.

Article 15

The baseline of the territorial sea of the People's Republic of China shall be established by the Government of the People's Republic of China.

Article 16

The Government of the People's Republic of China shall draw up relevant regulations in accordance with this law.

Article 17

This law becomes effective upon promulgation.

Source:http://www.un.org/depts/los/LEGISLATION-ANDTREATIES/PDFFILES/CHN_1992_Law.pdf

Document 15
1992 ASEAN Declaration on the South China Sea, 22 July 1992

WE, the Foreign Ministers of the member countries of the Association of Southeast Asian Nations;

RECALLING the historic, cultural and social ties that bind our peoples as states adjacent to the South China Sea;

WISHING to promote the spirit of kinship, friendship and harmony among our peoples who share similar Asian traditions and heritage;

DESIROUS of further promoting conditions essential to greater economic cooperation and growth;

RECOGNIZING that we are bound by similar ideals of mutual respect, freedom, sovereignty and jurisdiction of the parties directly concerned;

RECOGNIZING that South China Sea issues involve sensitive questions of sovereignty and jurisdiction of the parties directly concerned;

CONSCIOUS that any adverse developments in the South China Sea directly affect peace and stability in the region.

HEREBY

1. EMPHASIZE the necessity to resolve all sovereignty and jurisdictional issues pertaining to the South China Sea by peaceful means, without resort to force;
2. URGE all parties concerned to exercise restraint with the view to creating a positive climate for the eventual resolution of all disputes;
3. RESOLVE, without prejudicing the sovereignty and jurisdiction of countries having direct interests in the area, to explore the possibility of cooperation in the South China Sea relating to the safety of maritime navigation and communication, protection against pollution of the marine environment, coordination of search and rescue operations, efforts towards combatting piracy and armed robbery as well as collaboration in the campaign against illicit trafficking in drugs;
4. COMMEND all parties concerned to apply the principles contained in the Treaty of Amity and Cooperation in South-

east Asia as the basis for establishing a code of international conduct over the South China Sea;
5. INVITE all parties concerned to subscribe to this Declaration of principles.

Signed in Manila, Philippines, this 22nd day of July, nineteen hundred and ninety-two.

For Brunei Darussalam: HRH PRINCE MOHAMED BOLKIAH, Minister of Foreign Affairs

For the Republic of Indonesia: ALI ALATAS, Minister for Foreign Affairs

For Malaysia: DATUK ABDULLAH BIN HAJI AHMAD BADAWI, Minister of Foreign Affairs

For the Republic of Philippines: RAUL S. MANGLAPUS, Secretary of Foreign Affairs

For the Republic of Singapore: WONG KAN SENG, Minister for Foreign Affairs

For the Kingdom of Thailand: ARSA SARASIN, Minister of Foreign Affairs

Source: https://cil.nus.edu.sg/rp/pdf/1992%20ASEAN%20Declaration%20on%20the%20South%20China%20Sea-pdf.pdf

Document 16
United Nations Convention on the Law of the Sea, PART V, Exclusive Economic Zone, In force since 14 November 1994

Article 55

Specific legal regime of the exclusive economic zone
The exclusive economic zone is an area beyond and adjacent to the territorial sea, subject to the specific legal regime established in this Part, under which the rights and jurisdiction of the coastal State and the rights and freedoms of other States are governed by the relevant provisions of this Convention.

Article 56

Rights, jurisdiction and duties of the coastal State in the exclusive economic zone

1. In the exclusive economic zone, the coastal State has:
   (a) sovereign rights for the purpose of exploring and exploiting, conserving and managing the natural resources, whether living or non-living, of the waters superjacent to the seabed and of the seabed and its subsoil, and with regard to other activities for the economic exploitation and exploration of the zone, such as the production of energy from the water, currents and winds;
   (b) jurisdiction as provided for in the relevant provisions of this Convention with regard to:
      (i) the establishment and use of artificial islands, installations and structures;
      (ii) marine scientific research;
      (iii) the protection and preservation of the marine environment;
   (c) other rights and duties provided for in this Convention.

2. In exercising its rights and performing its duties under this Convention in the exclusive economic zone, the coastal State shall have due

regard to the rights and duties of other States and shall act in a manner compatible with the provisions of this Convention.
3. The rights set out in this article with respect to the seabed and subsoil shall be exercised in accordance with Part VI.

Article 57

Breadth of the exclusive economic zone
The exclusive economic zone shall not extend beyond 200 nautical miles from the baselines from which the breadth of the territorial sea is measured.

Article 58

Rights and duties of other States in the exclusive economic zone
1. In the exclusive economic zone, all States, whether coastal or land-locked, enjoy, subject to the relevant provisions of this Convention, the freedoms referred to in article 87 of navigation and overflight and of the laying of submarine cables and pipelines, and other internationally lawful uses of the sea related to these freedoms, such as those associated with the operation of ships, aircraft and submarine cables and pipelines, and compatible with the other provisions of this Convention.
2. Articles 88 to 115 and other pertinent rules of international law apply to the exclusive economic zone in so far as they are not incompatible with this Part.
3. In exercising their rights and performing their duties under this Convention in the exclusive economic zone, States shall have due regard to the rights and duties of the coastal State and shall comply with the laws and regulations adopted by the coastal State in accordance with the provisions of this Convention and other rules of international law in so far as they are not incompatible with this Part.

Article 59

Basis for the resolution of conflicts regarding the attribution of rights and jurisdiction in the exclusive economic zone
In cases where this Convention does not attribute rights or jurisdiction to the coastal State or to other States within the exclusive economic

zone, and a conflict arises between the interests of the coastal State and any other State or States, the conflict should be resolved on the basis of equity and in the light of all the relevant circumstances, taking into account the respective importance of the interests involved to the parties as well as to the international community as a whole.

Article 60

Artificial islands, installations and structures in the exclusive economic zone

1. In the exclusive economic zone, the coastal State shall have the exclusive right to construct and to authorize and regulate the construction, operation and use of:
   (a) artificial islands;
   (b) installations and structures for the purposes provided for in article 56 and other economic purposes;
   (c) installations and structures which may interfere with the exercise of the rights of the coastal State in the zone.
2. The coastal State shall have exclusive jurisdiction over such artificial islands, installations and structures, including jurisdiction with regard to customs, fiscal, health, safety and immigration laws and regulations.
3. Due notice must be given of the construction of such artificial islands, installations or structures, and permanent means for giving warning of their presence must be maintained. Any installations or structures which are abandoned or disused shall be removed to ensure safety of navigation, taking into account any generally accepted international standards established in this regard by the competent international organization. Such removal shall also have due regard to fishing, the protection of the marine environment and the rights and duties of other States. Appropriate publicity shall be given to the depth, position and dimensions of any installations or structures not entirely removed.
4. The coastal State may, where necessary, establish reasonable safety zones around such artificial islands, installations and structures in which it may take appropriate measures to ensure the safety both of navigation and of the artificial islands, installations and structures.
5. The breadth of the safety zones shall be determined by the coastal State, taking into account applicable international

standards. Such zones shall be designed to ensure that they are reasonably related to the nature and function of the artificial islands, installations or structures, and shall not exceed a distance of 500 metres around them, measured from each point of their outer edge, except as authorized by generally accepted international standards or as recommended by the competent international organization. Due notice shall be given of the extent of safety zones.
6. All ships must respect these safety zones and shall comply with generally accepted international standards regarding navigation in the vicinity of artificial islands, installations, structures and safety zones.
7. Artificial islands, installations and structures and the safety zones around them may not be established where interference may be caused to the use of recognized sea lanes essential to international navigation.
8. Artificial islands, installations and structures do not possess the status of islands. They have no territorial sea of their own, and their presence does not affect the delimitation of the territorial sea, the exclusive economic zone or the continental shelf.

Article 61

Conservation of the living resources
1. The coastal State shall determine the allowable catch of the living resources in its exclusive economic zone.
2. The coastal State, taking into account the best scientific evidence available to it, shall ensure through proper conservation and management measures that the maintenance of the living resources in the exclusive economic zone is not endangered by over-exploitation. As appropriate, the coastal State and competent international organizations, whether subregional, regional or global, shall cooperate to this end.
3. Such measures shall also be designed to maintain or restore populations of harvested species at levels which can produce the maximum sustainable yield, as qualified by relevant environmental and economic factors, including the economic needs of coastal fishing communities and the special requirements of developing States, and taking into account fishing patterns, the interdependence of stocks and any generally

recommended international minimum standards, whether subregional, regional or global.
4. In taking such measures the coastal State shall take into consideration the effects on species associated with or dependent upon harvested species with a view to maintaining or restoring populations of such associated or dependent species above levels at which their reproduction may become seriously threatened.
5. Available scientific information, catch and fishing effort statistics, and other data relevant to the conservation of fish stocks shall be contributed and exchanged on a regular basis through competent international organizations, whether subregional, regional or global, where appropriate and with participation by all States concerned, including States whose nationals are allowed to fish in the exclusive economic zone.

Article 62

Utilization of the living resources
1. The coastal State shall promote the objective of optimum utilization of the living resources in the exclusive economic zone without prejudice to article 61.
2. The coastal State shall determine its capacity to harvest the living resources of the exclusive economic zone. Where the coastal State does not have the capacity to harvest the entire allowable catch, it shall, through agreements or other arrangements and pursuant to the terms, conditions, laws and regulations referred to in paragraph 4, give other States access to the surplus of the allowable catch, having particular regard to the provisions of articles 69 and 70, especially in relation to the developing States mentioned therein.
3. In giving access to other States to its exclusive economic zone under this article, the coastal State shall take into account all relevant factors, including, *inter alia*, the significance of the living resources of the area to the economy of the coastal State concerned and its other national interests, the provisions of articles 69 and 70, the requirements of developing States in the subregion or region in harvesting part of the surplus and the need to minimize economic dislocation in States whose nationals have habitually fished in the zone or which have made substantial efforts in research and identification of stocks.

4. Nationals of other States fishing in the exclusive economic zone shall comply with the conservation measures and with the other terms and conditions established in the laws and regulations of the coastal State. These laws and regulations shall be consistent with this Convention and may relate, *inter alia*, to the following:
   (a) licensing of fishermen, fishing vessels and equipment, including payment of fees and other forms of remuneration, which, in the case of developing coastal States, may consist of adequate compensation in the field of financing, equipment and technology relating to the fishing industry;
   (b) determining the species which may be caught, and fixing quotas of catch, whether in relation to particular stocks or groups of stocks or catch per vessel over a period of time or to the catch by nationals of any State during a specified period;
   (c) regulating seasons and areas of fishing, the types, sizes and amount of gear, and the types, sizes and number of fishing vessels that may be used;
   (d) fixing the age and size of fish and other species that may be caught;
   (e) specifying information required of fishing vessels, including catch and effort statistics and vessel position reports;
   (f) requiring, under the authorization and control of the coastal State, the conduct of specified fisheries research programmes and regulating the conduct of such research, including the sampling of catches, disposition of samples and reporting of associated scientific data;
   (g) the placing of observers or trainees on board such vessels by the coastal State;
   (h) the landing of all or any part of the catch by such vessels in the ports of the coastal State;
   (i) terms and conditions relating to joint ventures or other cooperative arrangements;
   (j) requirements for the training of personnel and the transfer of fisheries technology, including enhancement of the coastal State's capability of undertaking fisheries research;
   (k) enforcement procedures.
5. Coastal States shall give due notice of conservation and management laws and regulations.

Article 63

Stocks occurring within the exclusive economic zones of two or more coastal States or both within the exclusive economic zone and in an area beyond and adjacent to it
1. Where the same stock or stocks of associated species occur within the exclusive economic zones of two or more coastal States, these States shall seek, either directly or through appropriate subregional or regional organizations, to agree upon the measures necessary to coordinate and ensure the conservation and development of such stocks without prejudice to the other provisions of this Part.
2. Where the same stock or stocks of associated species occur both within the exclusive economic zone and in an area beyond and adjacent to the zone, the coastal State and the States fishing for such stocks in the adjacent area shall seek, either directly or through appropriate subregional or regional organizations, to agree upon the measures necessary for the conservation of these stocks in the adjacent area.

Article 64

Highly migratory species
1. The coastal State and other States whose nationals fish in the region for the highly migratory species listed in Annex I shall cooperate directly or through appropriate international organizations with a view to ensuring conservation and promoting the objective of optimum utilization of such species throughout the region, both within and beyond the exclusive economic zone. In regions for which no appropriate international organization exists, the coastal State and other States whose nationals harvest these species in the region shall cooperate to establish such an organization and participate in its work.
2. The provisions of paragraph 1 apply in addition to the other provisions of this Part.

Article 65

Marine mammals
Nothing in this Part restricts the right of a coastal State or the competence of an international organization, as appropriate, to prohibit, limit

or regulate the exploitation of marine mammals more strictly than provided for in this Part. States shall cooperate with a view to the conservation of marine mammals and in the case of cetaceans shall in particular work through the appropriate international organizations for their conservation, management and study.

Article 66

Anadromous stocks
1. States in whose rivers anadromous stocks originate shall have the primary interest in and responsibility for such stocks.
2. The State of origin of anadromous stocks shall ensure their conservation by the establishment of appropriate regulatory measures for fishing in all waters landward of the outer limits of its exclusive economic zone and for fishing provided for in paragraph 3(b). The State of origin may, after consultations with the other States referred to in paragraphs 3 and 4 fishing these stocks, establish total allowable catches for stocks originating in its rivers.
3. (a) Fisheries for anadromous stocks shall be conducted only in waters landward of the outer limits of exclusive economic zones, except in cases where this provision would result in economic dislocation for a State other than the State of origin. With respect to such fishing beyond the outer limits of the exclusive economic zone, States concerned shall maintain consultations with a view to achieving agreement on terms and conditions of such fishing giving due regard to the conservation requirements and the needs of the State of origin in respect of these stocks.
   (b) The State of origin shall cooperate in minimizing economic dislocation in such other States fishing these stocks, taking into account the normal catch and the mode of operations of such States, and all the areas in which such fishing has occurred.
   (c) States referred to in subparagraph (b), participating by agreement with the State of origin in measures to renew anadromous stocks, particularly by expenditures for that purpose, shall be given special consideration by the State of origin in the harvesting of stocks originating in its rivers.
   (d) Enforcement of regulations regarding anadromous stocks beyond the exclusive economic zone shall be by

agreement between the State of origin and the other States concerned.
4. In cases where anadromous stocks migrate into or through the waters landward of the outer limits of the exclusive economic zone of a State other than the State of origin, such State shall cooperate with the State of origin with regard to the conservation and management of such stocks.
5. The State of origin of anadromous stocks and other States fishing these stocks shall make arrangements for the implementation of the provisions of this article, where appropriate, through regional organizations.

Article 67

Catadromous species
1. A coastal State in whose waters catadromous species spend the greater part of their life cycle shall have responsibility for the management of these species and shall ensure the ingress and egress of migrating fish.
2. Harvesting of catadromous species shall be conducted only in waters landward of the outer limits of exclusive economic zones. When conducted in exclusive economic zones, harvesting shall be subject to this article and the other provisions of this Convention concerning fishing in these zones.
3. In cases where catadromous fish migrate through the exclusive economic zone of another State, whether as juvenile or maturing fish, the management, including harvesting, of such fish shall be regulated by agreement between the State mentioned in paragraph 1 and the other State concerned. Such agreement shall ensure the rational management of the species and take into account the responsibilities of the State mentioned in paragraph 1 for the maintenance of these species.

Article 68

Sedentary species
This Part does not apply to sedentary species as defined in article 77, paragraph 4.

Article 69

Right of land-locked States
1. Land-locked States shall have the right to participate, on an equitable basis, in the exploitation of an appropriate part of the surplus of the living resources of the exclusive economic zones of coastal States of the same subregion or region, taking into account the relevant economic and geographical circumstances of all the States concerned and in conformity with the provisions of this article and of articles 61 and 62.
2. The terms and modalities of such participation shall be established by the States concerned through bilateral, subregional or regional agreements taking into account, *inter alia*:
   (a) the need to avoid effects detrimental to fishing communities or fishing industries of the coastal State;
   (b) the extent to which the land-locked State, in accordance with the provisions of this article, is participating or is entitled to participate under existing bilateral, subregional or regional agreements in the exploitation of living resources of the exclusive economic zones of other coastal States;
   (c) the extent to which other land-locked States and geographically disadvantaged States are participating in the exploitation of the living resources of the exclusive economic zone of the coastal State and the consequent need to avoid a particular burden for any single coastal State or a part of it;
   (d) the nutritional needs of the populations of the respective States.
3. When the harvesting capacity of a coastal State approaches a point which would enable it to harvest the entire allowable catch of the living resources in its exclusive economic zone, the coastal State and other States concerned shall cooperate in the establishment of equitable arrangements on a bilateral, subregional or regional basis to allow for participation of developing land-locked States of the same subregion or region in the exploitation of the living resources of the exclusive economic zones of coastal States of the subregion or region, as may be appropriate in the circumstances and on terms satisfactory to all parties. In the implementation of this provision the factors mentioned in paragraph 2 shall also be taken into account.

4. Developed land-locked States shall, under the provisions of this article, be entitled to participate in the exploitation of living resources only in the exclusive economic zones of developed coastal States of the same subregion or region having regard to the extent to which the coastal State, in giving access to other States to the living resources of its exclusive economic zone, has taken into account the need to minimize detrimental effects on fishing communities and economic dislocation in States whose nationals have habitually fished in the zone.
5. The above provisions are without prejudice to arrangements agreed upon in subregions or regions where the coastal States may grant to land-locked States of the same subregion or region equal or preferential rights for the exploitation of the living resources in the exclusive economic zones.

Article 70

Right of geographically disadvantaged States

1. Geographically disadvantaged States shall have the right to participate, on an equitable basis, in the exploitation of an appropriate part of the surplus of the living resources of the exclusive economic zones of coastal States of the same subregion or region, taking into account the relevant economic and geographical circumstances of all the States concerned and in conformity with the provisions of this article and of articles 61 and 62.
2. For the purposes of this Part, "geographically disadvantaged States" means coastal States, including States bordering enclosed or semi-enclosed seas, whose geographical situation makes them dependent upon the exploitation of the living resources of the exclusive economic zones of other States in the subregion or region for adequate supplies of fish for the nutritional purposes of their populations or parts thereof, and coastal States which can claim no exclusive economic zones of their own.
3. The terms and modalities of such participation shall be established by the States concerned through bilateral, subregional or regional agreements taking into account, *inter alia*:
   (a) the need to avoid effects detrimental to fishing communities or fishing industries of the coastal State;

- (b) the extent to which the geographically disadvantaged State, in accordance with the provisions of this article, is participating or is entitled to participate under existing bilateral, subregional or regional agreements in the exploitation of living resources of the exclusive economic zones of other coastal States;
- (c) the extent to which other geographically disadvantaged States and land-locked States are participating in the exploitation of the living resources of the exclusive economic zone of the coastal State and the consequent need to avoid a particular burden for any single coastal State or a part of it;
- (d) the nutritional needs of the populations of the respective States.

4. When the harvesting capacity of a coastal State approaches a point which would enable it to harvest the entire allowable catch of the living resources in its exclusive economic zone, the coastal State and other States concerned shall cooperate in the establishment of equitable arrangements on a bilateral, subregional or regional basis to allow for participation of developing geographically disadvantaged States of the same subregion or region in the exploitation of the living resources of the exclusive economic zones of coastal States of the subregion or region, as may be appropriate in the circumstances and on terms satisfactory to all parties. In the implementation of this provision the factors mentioned in paragraph 3 shall also be taken into account.

5. Developed geographically disadvantaged States shall, under the provisions of this article, be entitled to participate in the exploitation of living resources only in the exclusive economic zones of developed coastal States of the same subregion or region having regard to the extent to which the coastal State, in giving access to other States to the living resources of its exclusive economic zone, has taken into account the need to minimize detrimental effects on fishing communities and economic dislocation in States whose nationals have habitually fished in the zone.

6. The above provisions are without prejudice to arrangements agreed upon in subregions or regions where the coastal States may grant to geographically disadvantaged States of the same subregion or region equal or preferential rights for the exploitation of the living resources in the exclusive economic zones.

Article 71

Non-applicability of articles 69 and 70

The provisions of articles 69 and 70 do not apply in the case of a coastal State whose economy is overwhelmingly dependent on the exploitation of the living resources of its exclusive economic zone.

Article 72

Restrictions on transfer of rights
1. Rights provided under articles 69 and 70 to exploit living resources shall not be directly or indirectly transferred to third States or their nationals by lease or licence, by establishing joint ventures or in any other manner which has the effect of such transfer unless otherwise agreed by the States concerned.
2. The foregoing provision does not preclude the States concerned from obtaining technical or financial assistance from third States or international organizations in order to facilitate the exercise of the rights pursuant to articles 69 and 70, provided that it does not have the effect referred to in paragraph 1.

Article 73

Enforcement of laws and regulations of the coastal State
1. The coastal State may, in the exercise of its sovereign rights to explore, exploit, conserve and manage the living resources in the exclusive economic zone, take such measures, including boarding, inspection, arrest and judicial proceedings, as may be necessary to ensure compliance with the laws and regulations adopted by it in conformity with this Convention.
2. Arrested vessels and their crews shall be promptly released upon the posting of reasonable bond or other security.
3. Coastal State penalties for violations of fisheries laws and regulations in the exclusive economic zone may not include imprisonment, in the absence of agreements to the contrary by the States concerned, or any other form of corporal punishment.
4. In cases of arrest or detention of foreign vessels the coastal State shall promptly notify the flag State, through appropriate channels, of the action taken and of any penalties subsequently imposed.

Article 74

Delimitation of the exclusive economic zone between States with opposite or adjacent coasts
1. The delimitation of the exclusive economic zone between States with opposite or adjacent coasts shall be effected by agreement on the basis of international law, as referred to in Article 38 of the Statute of the International Court of Justice, in order to achieve an equitable solution.
2. If no agreement can be reached within a reasonable period of time, the States concerned shall resort to the procedures provided for in Part XV.
3. Pending agreement as provided for in paragraph 1, the States concerned, in a spirit of understanding and cooperation, shall make every effort to enter into provisional arrangements of a practical nature and, during this transitional period, not to jeopardize or hamper the reaching of the final agreement. Such arrangements shall be without prejudice to the final delimitation.
4. Where there is an agreement in force between the States concerned, questions relating to the delimitation of the exclusive economic zone shall be determined in accordance with the provisions of that agreement.

Article 75

Charts and lists of geographical coordinates
1. Subject to this Part, the outer limit lines of the exclusive economic zone and the lines of delimitation drawn in accordance with article 74 shall be shown on charts of a scale or scales adequate for ascertaining their position. Where appropriate, lists of geographical coordinates of points, specifying the geodetic datum, may be substituted for such outer limit lines or lines of delimitation.
2. The coastal State shall give due publicity to such charts or lists of geographical coordinates and shall deposit a copy of each such chart or list with the Secretary-General of the United Nations.

Source: http://www.un.org/depts/los/convention_agreements/texts/unclos/unclos_e.pdf

Document 17
A concurrent resolution expressing the sense of Congress regarding missile tests and military exercises by the People's Republic of China, 21 March 1996.

Whereas the People's Republic of China, in a clear attempt to intimidate the people and Government of Taiwan, has over the past 9 months conducted a series of military exercises, including missile tests, within alarmingly close proximity to Taiwan;

Whereas from March 8 through March 15, 1996, the People's Republic of China conducted a series of missile tests within 25 to 35 miles of the 2 principal northern and southern ports of Taiwan, Kaohsiung and Keelung;

Whereas on March 12, 1996, the People's Republic of China began an 8-day, live-ammunition, joint sea-and-air military exercise in a 2,390 square mile area in the southern Taiwan Strait;

Whereas on March 18, 1996, the People's Republic of China began a 7-day, live-ammunition, joint sea-and-air military exercise between Taiwan's islands of Matsu and Wuchu;

Whereas these tests and exercises are a clear escalation of the attempts by the People's Republic of China to intimidate Taiwan and influence the outcome of the upcoming democratic presidential election in Taiwan;

Whereas through the administrations of Presidents Nixon, Ford, Carter, Reagan, and Bush, the United States has adhered to a "One China" policy and, during the administration of President Clinton, the United States continues to adhere to the "One China" policy based on the Shanghai Communique of February 27, 1972, the Joint Communique on the Establishment of Diplomatic Relations Between the United States of America and the People's Republic of China of January 1, 1979, and the United States-China Joint Communique of August 17, 1982;

Whereas through the administrations of Presidents Carter, Reagan, and Bush, the United States has adhered to the provisions of the Taiwan Relations Act of 1979 (22 U.S.C. 3301 et seq.) as the basis for continuing commercial, cultural, and other relations between the people of the United States and the people of Taiwan and, during the administration of President Clinton, the United States continues to adhere to the provisions of the Taiwan Relations Act of 1979;

Whereas relations between the United States and the Peoples' Republic of China rest upon the expectation that the future of Taiwan will be settled solely by peaceful means;

Whereas the strong interest of the United States in the peaceful settlement of the Taiwan question is one of the central premises of the three United States-China Joint Communiques and was codified in the Taiwan Relations Act of 1979;

Whereas the Taiwan Relations Act of 1979 states that peace and stability in the western Pacific "are in the political, security, and economic interests of the United States, and are matters of international concern'";

Whereas the Taiwan Relations Act of 1979 states that the United States considers "any effort to determine the future of Taiwan by other than peaceful means, including by boycotts, or embargoes, a threat to the peace and security of the western Pacific area and of grave concern to the United States'";

Whereas the Taiwan Relations Act of 1979 directs the President to inform Congress promptly of any threat to the security or the social or economic system of the people on Taiwan and any danger to the interests of the United States arising therefrom";

Whereas the Taiwan Relations Act of 1979 further directs that "the President and the Congress shall determine, in accordance with constitutional process, appropriate action by the United States in response to any such danger'";

Whereas the United States, the People's Republic of China, and the Government of Taiwan have each previously expressed their commitment to the resolution of the Taiwan question through peaceful means; and

Whereas these missile tests and military exercises, and the accompanying statements made by the Government of the People's Republic of China, call into serious question the commitment of China to the peaceful resolution of the Taiwan question: Now, therefore, be it.

Resolved, That the resolution from the House of Representatives (H. Con. Res. 148) entitled "Concurrent resolution expressing the sense of the Congress that the United States is committed to military stability in the Taiwan Strait and the United States should assist in defending the Republic of China (also known as Taiwan) in the event of invasion, missile attack, or blockade by the People's Republic of China", do pass with the following

AMENDMENTS

Strike out all after the resolving clause, and insert:
That it is the sense of the Congress--
(1) to deplore the missile tests and military exercises that the People's Republic of China is conducting from March 8 through March 25, 1996, and view such tests and exercises as potentially serious threats to the peace, security, and stability of Taiwan and not in the spirit of the three United States-China Joint Communiques;
(2) to urge the Government of the People's Republic of China to cease its bellicose actions directed at Taiwan and enter instead into meaningful dialogue with the Government of Taiwan at the highest levels, such as through the Straits Exchange Foundation in Taiwan and the Association for Relations Across the Taiwan Strait in Beijing, with an eye towards decreasing tensions and resolving the issue of the future of Taiwan;
(3) that the President should, consistent with section 3(c) of the Taiwan Relations Act of 1979 (22 U.S.C. 3302(c)), immediately consult with Congress on an appropriate United States response to the tests and exercises should the tests or exercises pose an actual threat to the peace, security, and stability of Taiwan;
(4) that the President should, consistent with the Taiwan Relations Act of 1979 (22 U.S.C. 3301 et seq.), reexamine the nature and quantity of defense articles and services that may be necessary to enable Taiwan to maintain a sufficient self-defense capability in light of the heightened military threat; and
(5) that the Government of Taiwan should remain committed to the peaceful resolution of its future relations with the People's Republic of China by mutual decision.

Source:https://www.congress.gov/bill/104th-congress/house-concurrent-resolution/148/text

Document 18
Law on the Exclusive Economic Zone and the Continental Shelf of the PRC, 26 June 1998

(Adopted at the 3rd Meeting of the Standing Committee of the Ninth National People's Congress and promulgated and come into force on the date of June 26, 1998)

Article 1 This Law is enacted to ensure that the People's Republic of China shall exercise its sovereign rights and jurisdiction over its exclusive economic zone and its continental shelf and safeguard its national maritime rights and interests.

Article 2 The exclusive economic zone of the People's Republic of the China is the area beyond and adjacent to the territorial sea of the People's Republic of China, extending to 200 nautical miles from the baselines from which the breadth of the territorial sea is measured. The continental shelf of the People's Republic of China is the sea-bed and subsoil of the submarine area that extend beyond its territorial sea throughout the natural prolongation of its land territory to the outer edge of the continental margin, or to a distance of 200 nautical miles from the baselines from which the breadth of the territorial sea is measured where the outer edge of the continental margin does not extend up to that distance. The People's Republic of China shall determine the delimitation of the exclusive economic zone and the continental shelf in respect of the overlapping claims by agreement with the states with opposite or adjacent coasts in accordance with the equitable principle on the basis of international law.

Article 3 In the exclusive economic zone, the People's Republic of China exercises sovereign rights for the purposes in terms of exploring and exploiting, conserving and managing the natural resources of the waters superjacent to the sea-bed and of the sea-bed and its subsoil, and with regard to other activities for economic exploitation and exploration of the zone, such as the production of energy from the water, current and wind. The People's Republic of China has jurisdiction over the establishment and use of artificial islands, installations and structures, marine scientific research, the protection and preservation of the marine environment in the exclusive economic zone. The natural resources in the exclusive economic zone referred to in this law consist of living and non-living resources.

Article 4 The People's Republic of China exercises over the continental shelf sovereign rights for the purpose of exploring it and exploiting its natural resources. The People's Republic of China has jurisdiction over the establishment and use of artificial islands, installations and structures, marine scientific research, and the protection and preservation of the marine environment in the continental shelf. The People's Republic of China shall have the exclusive right to authorize and regulate drilling on the continental shelf for all purposes. The natural resources of the continental shelf referred to in this law consist of the mineral and other non-living resources of the sea-bed and subsoil together with living organisms belonging to sedentary species, that is to say, organisms which, at the harvestable stage, either are immobile on or under the seabed or are unable to move except in constant physical contact with the seabed or the subsoil.

Article 5 All international organizations, foreign organizations or individuals shall obtain approval from the competent authorities of the People's Republic of China for carrying out fishing activities in its exclusive economic zone, and shall comply with its law and regulations as well as its accords and agreements signed with the states concerned. The competent authorities of the People's Republic of China shall have the right to ensure through all necessary conservation and management measures that the living resources in the exclusive economic zone are not endangered by over-exploitation.

Article 6 The competent authorities of the People's Republic of China shall have the right to exercise conservation and management of straddling species, highly migratory species, marine mammals, anadromous stocks originating in the rivers of the People's Republic of China, catadromous species spending the greater part of their life cycle in the waters of the People's Republic of China in its exclusive economic zone. The People's Republic of China shall have the primary interest in anadromous stocks originating in its rivers.

Article 7 All international organizations, foreign organizations or individuals shall obtain approval from the competent authorities of the People's Republic of China for carrying out activities of exploring and exploiting natural resources in its exclusive economic zone and on its continental shelf or for any purposes drilling on its continental shelf and shall comply with the laws and regulations of the People's Republic of China.

Article 8 The People's Republic of China shall have the exclusive right to construct and to authorize and regulate the construction, operation and use of artificial islands, installations and structures in its exclusive economic zone and on its continental shelf. The People's Republic of

China shall have exclusive jurisdiction over the artificial islands, installations and structures in its exclusive economic zone and on its continental shelf, including jurisdiction with regard to customs, fiscal, health, safety and immigration laws and regulations. The competent authorities of the People's Republic of China shall have the right to establish safety zones around the artificial islands, installations and structures in its exclusive economic zone and on its continental shelf, and it may take appropriate measures to ensure the safety both of navigation and of the artificial islands, installations and structures.

Article 9 All international organizations, foreign organizations or individuals shall obtain approval from the competent authorities of the People's Republic of China for carrying out marine scientific research in its exclusive economic zone and on its continental shelf, and shall comply with the laws and regulations of the People's Republic of China.

Article 10 The competent authorities of the People's Republic of China shall have the right to take all necessary measures to prevent, reduce and control pollution of the marine environment for the protection and preservation of the marine environment in its exclusive economic zone and on its continental shelf.

Article 11 All states, subject to international laws and the laws and regulations of the People's Republic of China, enjoy the freedoms of navigation and over-flight in its exclusive economic zone and of the laying of submarine cables and pipelines, and other lawful uses of the sea related to these freedoms in the exclusive economic zone and on the continental shelf of the People's Republic of China. The routes for the submarine cables and pipelines shall be subject to the consent of its competent authorities.

Article 12 The People's Republic of China may, in the exercise of its sovereign rights to explore, exploit, conserve and manage the living resources in the exclusive economic zone, take such measures, including boarding, inspection, arrest, detention and judicial processes, as may be necessary to ensure compliance with the laws and regulations of the People's Republic of China. The People's Republic of China shall have the right to take necessary measures against violations of its laws and regulations in the exclusive economic zone and on the continental shelf, to pursue the legal responsibilities by law, and may exercise the right of hot pursuit.

Article 13 The People's Republic of China shall exercise the rights in its exclusive economic zone and on its continental shelf, if not provided in this law, in accordance with international laws and other relevant laws and regulations of the People's Republic of China.

Article 14 The provisions in this law shall not affect the historical right that the People's Republic of China enjoys.

Article 15 The Government of the People's Republic of China shall formulate the relevant regulations in accordance with this law.

Article 16 This Law shall come into force on the date of promulgation.

Source: http://library.uoregon.edu/ec/e-asia/read/ecozone.pdf

Document 19
2002 Declaration on the Conduct of Parties in the South China Sea, 4 November 2002

The Governments of the Member States of ASEAN and the Government of the People's Republic of China,

REAFFIRMING their determination to consolidate and develop the friendship and cooperation existing between their people and governments with the view to promoting a 21st century-oriented partnership of good neighbourliness and mutual trust;

COGNIZANT of the need to promote a peaceful, friendly and harmonious environment in the South China Sea between ASEAN and China for the enhancement of peace, stability, economic growth and prosperity in the region;

COMMITTED to enhancing the principles and objectives of the 1997 Joint Statement of the Meeting of the Heads of State/Government of the Member States of ASEAN and President of the People's Republic of China;

DESIRING to enhance favourable conditions for a peaceful and durable solution of differences and disputes among countries concerned;

HEREBY DECLARE the following:

1. The Parties reaffirm their commitment to the purposes and principles of the Charter of the United Nations, the 1982 UN Convention on the Law of the Sea, the Treaty of Amity and Cooperation in Southeast Asia, the Five Principles of Peaceful Coexistence, and other universally recognized principles of international law which shall serve as the basic norms governing state-to-state relations;
2. The Parties are committed to exploring ways for building trust and confidence in accordance with the above-mentioned principles and on the basis of equality and mutual respect;
3. The Parties reaffirm their respect for and commitment to the freedom of navigation in and overflight above the South China Sea as provided for by the universally recognized principles of international law, including the 1982 UN Convention on the Law of the Sea;

4. The Parties concerned undertake to resolve their territorial and jurisdictional disputes by peaceful means, without resorting to the threat or use of force, through friendly consultations and negotiations by sovereign states directly concerned, in accordance with universally recognized principles of international law, including the 1982 UN Convention on the Law of the Sea;
5. The Parties undertake to exercise self-restraint in the conduct of activities that would complicate or escalate disputes and affect peace and stability including, among others, refraining from action of inhabiting on the presently uninhabited islands, reefs, shoals, cays, and other features and to handle their differences in a constructive manner.

Pending the peaceful settlement of territorial and jurisdictional disputes, the Parties concerned undertake to intensify efforts to seek ways, in the spirit of cooperation and understanding, to build trust and confidence between and among them, including:

a. holding dialogues and exchange of views as appropriate between their defense and military officials;
b. ensuring just and humane treatment of all persons who are either in danger or in distress;
c. notifying, on a voluntary basis, other Parties concerned of any impending joint/combined military exercise; and
d. exchanging, on a voluntary basis, relevant information.
6. Pending a comprehensive and durable settlement of the disputes, the Parties concerned may explore or undertake cooperative activities. These may include the following:

a. marine environmental protection;
b. marine scientific research;
c. safety of navigation and communication at sea;
d. search and rescue operation; and
e. combating transnational crime, including but not limited to trafficking in illicit drugs, piracy and armed robbery at sea, and illegal traffic in arms.

The modalities, scope and locations, in respect of bilateral and multilateral cooperation should be agreed upon by the Parties concerned prior to their actual implementation.

7. The Parties concerned stand ready to continue their consultations and dialogues concerning relevant issues, through

modalities to be agreed by them, including regular consultations on the observance of this Declaration, for the purpose of promoting good neighbourliness and transparency, establishing harmony, mutual understanding and cooperation, and facilitating peaceful resolution of disputes among them;

8. The Parties undertake to respect the provisions of this Declaration and take actions consistent therewith;
9. The Parties encourage other countries to respect the principles contained in this Declaration;
10. The Parties concerned reaffirm that the adoption of a code of conduct in the South China Sea would further promote peace and stability in the region and agree to work, on the basis of consensus, towards the eventual attainment of this objective.

DONE on the Fourth Day of November in the Year Two Thousand and Two in Phnom Penh, the Kingdom of Cambodia.

For Brunei Darussalam: MOHAMED BOLKIAH, Minister of Foreign Affairs

For the Kingdom of Cambodia: HOR NAMHONG, Senior Minister and Minister of Foreign Affairs and International Cooperation

For the Republic of Indonesia: DR HASSAN WIRAYUDA, Minister for Foreign Affairs

For the Lao People's Democratic Republic: SOMSAVAT LENGSAVAD, Deputy Prime Minister and Minister for Foreign Affairs

For Malaysia: DATUK SERI SYED HAMID ALBAR, Minister of Foreign Affairs

For the Union of Myanmar: WIN AUNG, Minister for Foreign Affairs

For the Republic of the Philippines: BLAS F. OPLE, Secretary of Foreign Affairs

For the Republic of Singapore: PROF. S. JAYAKUMAR, Minister for Foreign Affairs

For the Kingdom of Thailand: DR. SURAKIART SATHIRATHAI, Minister of Foreign Affairs

For the Socialist Republic of Viet Nam: NGUYEN DY NIEN, Minister of Foreign Affairs

For the People's Republic of China: WANG YI, Special Envoy and Vice Minister of Foreign Affairs

Source: http://www.aseansec.org/13163.htm

Document 20
Anti-Secession Law adopted by NPC, 14 March 2005

Order of the President of the People's Republic of China
No. 34
The Anti-Secession Law, adopted at the Third Session of the Tenth National People's Congress of the People's Republic of China on March 14, 2005, is hereby promulgated and shall go into effect as of the date of promulgation.
Hu Jintao
President of the People's Republic of China
March 14, 2005

The following is the full text of the Anti-Secession Law adopted at the Third Session of the Tenth National People's Congress Monday:

Anti-Secession Law
(Adopted at the Third Session of the Tenth National People's Congress on March 14, 2005)

Article 1 This Law is formulated, in accordance with the Constitution, for the purpose of opposing and checking Taiwan's secession from China by secessionists in the name of "Taiwan independence", promoting peaceful national reunification, maintaining peace and stability in the Taiwan Straits, preserving China's sovereignty and territorial integrity, and safeguarding the fundamental interests of the Chinese nation.

Article 2 There is only one China in the world. Both the mainland and Taiwan belong to one China. China's sovereignty and territorial integrity brook no division. Safeguarding China's sovereignty and territorial integrity is the common obligation of all Chinese people, the Taiwan compatriots included.

Taiwan is part of China. The state shall never allow the "Taiwan independence" secessionist forces to make Taiwan secede from China under any name or by any means.

Article 3 The Taiwan question is one that is left over from China's civil war of the late 1940s.

Solving the Taiwan question and achieving national reunification is China's internal affair, which subjects to no interference by any outside forces.

Article 4 Accomplishing the great task of reunifying the motherland is the sacred duty of all Chinese people, the Taiwan compatriots included.

Article 5 Upholding the principle of one China is the basis of peaceful reunification of the country.

To reunify the country through peaceful means best serves the fundamental interests of the compatriots on both sides of the Taiwan Straits. The state shall do its utmost with maximum sincerity to achieve a peaceful reunification.

After the country is reunified peacefully, Taiwan may practice systems different from those on the mainland and enjoy a high degree of autonomy.

Article 6 The state shall take the following measures to maintain peace and stability in the Taiwan Straits and promote cross-Straits relations:

(1) to encourage and facilitate personnel exchanges across the Straits for greater mutual understanding and mutual trust;
(2) to encourage and facilitate economic exchanges and cooperation, realize direct links of trade, mail and air and shipping services, and bring about closer economic ties between the two sides of the Straits to their mutual benefit;
(3) to encourage and facilitate cross-Straits exchanges in education, science, technology, culture, health and sports, and work together to carry forward the proud Chinese cultural traditions;
(4) to encourage and facilitate cross-Straits cooperation in combating crimes; and
(5) to encourage and facilitate other activities that are conducive to peace and stability in the Taiwan Straits and stronger cross-Straits relations.

The state protects the rights and interests of the Taiwan compatriots in accordance with law.

Article 7 The state stands for the achievement of peaceful reunification through consultations and negotiations on an equal footing between the two sides of the Taiwan Straits. These consultations and negotiations may be conducted in steps and phases and with flexible and varied modalities.

The two sides of the Taiwan Straits may consult and negotiate on the following matters:

(1) officially ending the state of hostility between the two sides;
(2) mapping out the development of cross-Straits relations;
(3) steps and arrangements for peaceful national reunification;
(4) the political status of the Taiwan authorities;
(5) the Taiwan region's room of international operation that is compatible with its status; and
(6) other matters concerning the achievement of peaceful national reunification.

Article 8 In the event that the "Taiwan independence" secessionist forces should act under any name or by any means to cause the fact of Taiwan's secession from China, or that major incidents entailing Taiwan's secession from China should occur, or that possibilities for a peaceful reunification should be completely exhausted, the state shall employ non-peaceful means and other necessary measures to protect China's sovereignty and territorial integrity.

The State Council and the Central Military Commission shall decide on and execute the non-peaceful means and other necessary measures as provided for in the preceding paragraph and shall promptly report to the Standing Committee of the National People'sCongress.

Article 9 In the event of employing and executing non-peaceful means and other necessary measures as provided for in this Law, the state shall exert its utmost to protect the lives, property and other legitimate rights and interests of Taiwan civilians and foreign nationals in Taiwan, and to minimize losses. At the same time, the state shall protect the rights and interests of the Taiwan compatriots in other parts of China in accordance with law.

Article 10 This Law shall come into force on the day of its promulgation.

Source:http://www.chinadaily.com.cn/english/doc/2005-03/14/content_424643.htm

Document 21
Cross-Straits Economic Cooperation Framework Agreement, 29 June 2010

Cross-Straits Economic Cooperation Framework Agreement
Preamble

The Straits Exchange Foundation and the Association for Relations Across the Taiwan Straits, adhering to the principles of equality, reciprocity and progressiveness and with a view to strengthening cross-Straits trade and economic relations. Have agreed, in line with the basic principles of the World Trade Organization (WTO) and in consideration of the economic conditions of the two Parties, to gradually reduce or eliminate barriers to trade and investment for each other, create a fair trade and investment environment, further advance cross-Straits trade and investment relations by signing the Cross-Straits Economic Cooperation Framework Agreement (hereinafter referred to as this Agreement), and establish a cooperation mechanism beneficial to economic prosperity and development across the Straits.

The two Parties have agreed through consultations to the following:

Chapter 1 General Principles
Article 1 Objectives

The objectives of this Agreement are:
1. To strengthen and advance the economic, trade and investment cooperation between the two Parties;
2. To promote further liberalization of trade in goods and services between the two Parties and gradually establish fair, transparent and facilitative investment and investment protection mechanisms;
3. To expand areas of economic cooperation and establish a cooperation mechanism.

Article 2 Cooperation Measures

The two Parties have agreed, in consideration of their economic conditions, to take measures including but not limited to the following, in order to strengthen cross-Straits economic exchange and cooperation:
1. Gradually reducing or eliminating tariff and non-tariff barriers to trade in a substantial majority of goods between the two Parties;
2. Gradually reducing or eliminating restrictions on a large number of sectors in trade in services between the two Parties;
3. Providing investment protection and promoting two-way investment;
4. Promoting trade and investment facilitation and industry exchanges and cooperation.

Chapter 2 Trade and Investment

Article 3 Trade in Goods

1. The two Parties have agreed, on the basis of the Early Harvest for Trade in Goods as stipulated in Article 7 of this Agreement, to conduct consultations on an agreement on trade in goods no later than six months after the entry into force of this Agreement, and expeditiously conclude such consultations.
2. The consultations on the agreement on trade in goods shall include, but not be limited to:
   (1) modalities for tariff reduction or elimination;
   (2) rules of origin;
   (3) customs procedures;
   (4) non-tariff measures, including but not limited to technical barriers to trade (TBT) and sanitary and phytosanitary (SPS) measures;
   (5) trade remedy measures, including measures set forth in the Agreement on Implementation of Article VI of the General Agreement on Tariffs and Trade 1994, the Agreement on Subsidies and Countervailing Measures and the Agreement on Safeguards of the World Trade Organization, and the safeguard measures between the two Parties applicable to the trade in goods between the two Parties.

3. Goods included in the agreement on trade in goods pursuant to this Article shall be divided into three categories: goods subject to immediate tariff elimination, goods subject to phased tariff reduction, and exceptions or others.
4. Either Party may accelerate the implementation of tariff reduction at its discretion on the basis of the commitments to tariff concessions in the agreement on trade in goods.

Article 4 Trade in Services

1. The two Parties have agreed, on the basis of the Early Harvest for Trade in Services as stipulated in Article 8, to conduct consultations on an agreement on trade in services no later than six months after the entry into force of this Agreement, and expeditiously conclude such consultations.
2. The consultations on the agreement on trade in services shall seek to:
   (1) gradually reduce or eliminate restrictions on a large number of sectors in trade in services between the two Parties;
   (2) further increase the breadth and depth of trade in services;
   (3) enhance cooperation in trade in services between the two Parties.
3. Either Party may accelerate the liberalization or elimination of restrictive measures at its discretion on the basis of the commitments to liberalization in the agreement on trade in services.

Article 5 Investment

1. The two Parties have agreed to conduct consultations on the matters referred to in paragraph 2 of this Article within six months after the entry into force of this Agreement, and expeditiously reach an agreement.
2. Such an agreement shall include, but not be limited to, the following:
   (1) establishing an investment protection mechanism;
   (2) increasing transparency on investment-related regulations;
   (3) gradually reducing restrictions on mutual investments between the two Parties;
   (4) promoting investment facilitation.

Chapter 3 Economic Cooperation

Article 6 Economic Cooperation

1. To enhance and expand the benefits of this Agreement, the two Parties have agreed to strengthen cooperation in areas including, but not limited to, the following:
   (1) intellectual property rights protection and cooperation;
   (2) financial cooperation;
   (3) trade promotion and facilitation;
   (4) customs cooperation;
   (5) e-commerce cooperation;
   (6) discussion on the overall arrangements and key areas for industrial cooperation, promotion of cooperation in major projects, and coordination of the resolution of issues that may arise in the course of industrial cooperation between the two Parties;
   (7) promotion of small and medium-sized enterprises cooperation between the two Parties, and enhancement of the competitiveness of these enterprises;
   (8) promotion of the mutual establishment of offices by economic and trade bodies of the two Parties.
2. The two Parties shall expeditiously conduct consultations on the specific programs and contents of the cooperation matters listed in this Article.

Chapter 4 Early Harvest

Article 7 Early Harvest for Trade in Goods

1. To accelerate the realization of the objectives of this Agreement, the two Parties have agreed to implement the Early Harvest Program with respect to the goods listed in Annex I. The Early Harvest Program shall start to be implemented within six months after the entry into force of this Agreement.
2. The Early Harvest Program for trade in goods shall be implemented in accordance with the following rules:
   (1) the two Parties shall implement the tariff reductions in accordance with the product list and tariff reduction arrangements under the Early Harvest stipulated in Annex I, unless their respective non-interim tariff rates

generally applied on imports from all other WTO members are lower, in which case such rates shall apply;
(2) the products listed in Annex I of this Agreement shall be subject to the Provisional Rules of Origin stipulated in Annex II. Each Party shall accord preferential tariff treatment to the above-mentioned products that are determined, pursuant to such Rules, as originating in the other Party upon importation;
(3) the provisional trade remedy measures applicable to the products listed in Annex I of this Agreement refer to measures provided for in subparagraph (5) of paragraph 2 of Article 3 of this Agreement. The safeguard measures between the two Parties are specified in Annex III of this Agreement.

3. As of the date of the entry into force of the agreement on trade in goods to be reached by the two Parties pursuant to Article 3 of this Agreement, the Provisional Rules of Origin stipulated in Annex II and the provisional trade remedy measures provided for in subparagraph (3) of paragraph 2 of this Article shall cease to apply.

Article 8 Early Harvest for Trade in Services

1. To accelerate the realization of the objectives of this Agreement, the two Parties have agreed to implement the Early Harvest Program on the sectors and liberalization measures listed in Annex IV. The Early Harvest Program shall be implemented expeditiously after the entry into force of this Agreement.
2. The Early Harvest Program for Trade in Services shall be implemented in accordance with the following rules:
    (1) each Party shall, in accordance with the Sectors and Liberalization Measures Under the Early Harvest for Trade in Services in Annex IV, reduce or eliminate the restrictive measures in force affecting the services and service suppliers of the other Party;
    (2) the definition of service suppliers stipulated in Annex V applies to the sectors and liberalization measures with respect to trade in services in Annex IV of this Agreement;
    (3) as of the date of the entry into force of the agreement on trade in services to be reached by the two Parties

pursuant to Article 4 of this Agreement, the definitions of service suppliers stipulated in Annex V of this Agreement shall cease to apply;

(4) in the event that the implementation of the Early Harvest Program for Trade in Services has caused a material adverse impact on the services sectors of one Party, the affected Party may request consultations with the other Party to seek a solution.

Chapter 5 Other Provisions

Article 9 Exceptions

No provision in this Agreement shall be interpreted to prevent either Party from adopting or maintaining exception measures consistent with the rules of the World Trade Organization.

Article 10 Dispute Settlement

1. The two Parties shall engage in consultations on the establishment of appropriate dispute settlement procedures no later than six months after the entry into force of this Agreement, and expeditiously reach an agreement in order to settle any dispute arising from the interpretation, implementation and application of this Agreement.
2. Any dispute over the interpretation, implementation and application of this Agreement prior to the date the dispute settlement agreement mentioned in paragraph 1 of this Article enters into force shall be resolved through consultations by the two Parties or in an appropriate manner by the Cross-Straits Economic Cooperation Committee to be established in accordance with Article 11 of this Agreement.

Article 11 Institutional Arrangements

1. The two Parties shall establish a Cross-Straits Economic Cooperation Committee (hereinafter referred to as the Committee), which consists of representatives designated by the two Parties. The Committee shall be responsible for handling matters relating to this Agreement, including but not limited to:

(1) concluding consultations necessary for the attainment of the objectives of this Agreement;
(2) monitoring and evaluating the implementation of this Agreement;
(3) interpreting the provisions of this Agreement;
(4) notifying important economic and trade information;
(5) settling any dispute over the interpretation, implementation and application of this Agreement in accordance with Article 10 of this Agreement.
2. The Committee may set up working group(s) as needed to handle matters in specific areas pertaining to this Agreement, under the supervision of the Committee.
3. The Committee will convene a regular meeting on a semi-annual basis and may call ad hoc meeting(s) when necessary with consent of the two Parties.
4. Matters related to this Agreement shall be communicated through contact persons designated by the competent authorities of the two Parties.

Article 12 Documentation Formats

The two Parties shall use the agreed documentation formats for communication of matters arising from this Agreement.

Article 13 Annexes and Subsequent Agreements

All annexes to this Agreement and subsequent agreements signed in accordance with this Agreement shall be parts of this Agreement.

Article 14 Amendments

Amendments to this Agreement shall be subject to consent through consultations between, and confirmation in writing by, the two Parties.

Article 15 Entry into Force

After the signing of this Agreement, the two Parties shall complete the relevant procedures respectively and notify each other in writing. This Agreement shall enter into force as of the day following the date that both Parties have received such notification from each other.

Article 16 Termination

1. The Party terminating this Agreement shall notify the other Party in writing. The two Parties shall start consultations within 30 days from the date the termination notice is issued. In case the consultations fail to reach a consensus, this Agreement shall be terminated on the 180th day from the date the termination notice is issued by the notifying Party.
2. Within 30 days from the date of termination of this Agreement, the two Parties shall engage in consultations on issues arising from the termination.

This Agreement is signed in quadruplicate on this 29th day of June [2010] with each Party retaining two copies. The different wording of the corresponding text of this Agreement shall carry the same meaning, and all four copies are equally authentic.

Annex I: Product List and Tariff Reduction Arrangements Under the Early Harvest for Trade in Goods

Annex II: Provisional Rules of Origin Applicable to Products Under the Early Harvest for Trade in Goods

Annex III: Safeguard Measures Between the Two Parties Applicable to Products Under the Early Harvest for Trade in Goods

Annex IV: Sectors and Liberalization Measures Under the Early Harvest for Trade in Services

Annex V: Definitions of Service Suppliers Applicable to Sectors and Liberalization Measures Under the Early Harvest for Trade in Services

Chairman	President
Straits Exchange Foundation	Association for Relations Across the Taiwan Straits

Source:http://china.usc.edu/ShowArticle.aspx?articleID=2273&AspxAutoDetectCookieSupport=1

Document 22
In the Matter of the South China Sea Arbitration, 12 July 2016

X. DISPOSITIF

1202. The Tribunal recalls and incorporates the following findings reached unanimously in its Award on Jurisdiction and Admissibility of 29 October 2015:

A. that the Tribunal was properly constituted in accordance with Annex VII to the Convention.

B. that China's non-appearance in these proceedings does not deprive the Tribunal of jurisdiction.

C. that the Philippines' act of initiating this arbitration did not constitute an abuse of process.

D. that there is no indispensable third party whose absence deprives the Tribunal of jurisdiction.

E. that the 2002 China–ASEAN Declaration on Conduct of the Parties in the South China Sea, the joint statements of the Parties referred to in paragraphs 231 to 232 of the Tribunal's Award on Jurisdiction and Admissibility of 29 October 2015, the Treaty of Amity and Cooperation in Southeast Asia, and the Convention on Biological Diversity, do not preclude, under Articles 281 or 282 of the Convention, recourse to the compulsory dispute settlement procedures available under Section 2 of Part XV of the Convention.

F. that the Parties have exchanged views as required by Article 283 of the Convention.

G. that the Tribunal has jurisdiction to consider the Philippines' Submissions No. 3, 4, 6, 7, 10, 11, and 13, subject to the conditions noted in paragraphs 400, 401, 403, 404, 407, 408, and 410 of the Tribunal's Award on Jurisdiction and Admissibility of 29 October 2015.

1203. For the reasons set out in this Award, the Tribunal unanimously, and without prejudice to any questions of sovereignty or maritime boundary delimitation, decides as follows:

A. In relation to its jurisdiction, the Tribunal:

(1) FINDS that China's claims in the South China Sea do not include a claim to 'historic title', within the meaning of Article 298(1)(a)(i) of the Convention, over the waters of the South China Sea and that the Tribunal, therefore, has jurisdiction to consider the Philippines' Submissions No. 1 and 2;

(2) FINDS, with respect to the Philippines' Submission No. 5:

a. that no maritime feature claimed by China within 200 nautical miles of Mischief Reef or Second Thomas Shoal constitutes a fully entitled island for the purposes of Article 121 of the Convention and therefore that no maritime feature claimed by China within 200 nautical miles of Mischief Reef or Second Thomas Shoal has the capacity to generate an entitlement to an exclusive economic zone or continental shelf;

b. that Mischief Reef and Second Thomas Shoal are low-tide elevations and, as such, generate no entitlement to maritime zones of their own;

c. that there are no overlapping entitlements to an exclusive economic zone or continental shelf in the areas of Mischief Reef or Second Thomas Shoal; and

d. that the Tribunal has jurisdiction to consider the Philippines' Submission No. 5;

(3) FINDS, with respect to the Philippines' Submissions No. 8 and 9:

a. that no maritime feature claimed by China within 200 nautical miles of Mischief Reef or Second Thomas Shoal constitutes a fully entitled island for the purposes of Article 121 of the Convention and therefore that no maritime feature claimed by China within 200 nautical miles of Mischief Reef or Second Thomas Shoal has the capacity to generate an entitlement to an exclusive economic zone or continental shelf;

b. that Mischief Reef and Second Thomas Shoal are low-tide elevations and, as such, generate no entitlement to maritime zones of their own;

c. that Reed Bank is an entirely submerged reef formation that cannot give rise to maritime entitlements;

d. that there are no overlapping entitlements to an exclusive economic zone or continental shelf in the areas of Mischief Reef or Second Thomas Shoal or in the areas of the Philippines' GSEC101, Area 3, Area 4, or SC58 petroleum blocks;

e. that Article 297(3)(a) of the Convention and the law enforcement exception in Article 298(1)(b) of the Convention are not applicable to this dispute; and

f. that the Tribunal has jurisdiction to consider the Philippines' Submissions No. 8 and 9;

(4) FINDS that China's land reclamation and/or construction of artificial islands, installations, and structures at Cuarteron Reef, Fiery Cross Reef, Gaven Reef (North), Johnson Reef, Hughes Reef, Subi Reef, and Mischief Reef do not constitute "military activities", within the meaning of Article 298(1)(b) of the Convention, and that the Tribunal has jurisdiction to consider the Philippines' Submissions No. 11 and 12(b);

(5) FINDS, with respect to the Philippines' Submissions No. 12(a) and 12(c):

a. that no maritime feature claimed by China within 200 nautical miles of Mischief Reef or Second Thomas Shoal constitutes a fully entitled island for the purposes of Article 121 of the Convention and therefore that no maritime feature claimed by China within 200 nautical miles of Mischief Reef or Second Thomas Shoal has the capacity to generate an entitlement to an exclusive economic zone or continental shelf;

b. that Mischief Reef and Second Thomas Shoal are low-tide elevations and, as such, generate no entitlement to maritime zones of their own;

c. that there are no overlapping entitlements to an exclusive economic zone or continental shelf in the areas of Mischief Reef or Second Thomas Shoal; and

d. that the Tribunal has jurisdiction to consider the Philippines' Submissions No. 12(a) and 12(c);

(6) FINDS with respect to the Philippines' Submission No. 14:

a. that the dispute between China and the Philippines concerning the stand-off between the Philippines' marine detachment on Second Thomas Shoal and Chinese military and paramilitary vessels involves "military activities", within the meaning of Article 298(1)(b) of the Convention, and that the Tribunal has no jurisdiction to consider the Philippines' Submissions No. 14(a) to (c); and

b. that China's land reclamation and/or construction of artificial islands, installations, and structures at Cuarteron Reef, Fiery Cross Reef, Gaven Reef (North), Johnson Reef, Hughes Reef, Subi Reef, and Mischief Reef do not constitute "military activities", within the meaning of Article 298(1)(b) of the Convention, and that the Tribunal has jurisdiction to consider the Philippines' Submission No. 14(d);

(7) FINDS, with respect to the Philippines' Submission No. 15, that there is not a dispute between the Parties such as would call for the Tribunal to exercise jurisdiction; and

(8) DECLARES that it has jurisdiction to consider the matters raised in the Philippines' Submissions No. 1, 2, 3, 4, 5, 6, 7, 8, 9, 10, 11, 12, 13, and 14(d) and that such claims are admissible.

B. In relation to the merits of the Parties' disputes, the Tribunal:

(1) DECLARES that, as between the Philippines and China, the Convention defines the scope of maritime entitlements in the South China Sea, which may not extend beyond the limits imposed therein;

(2) DECLARES that, as between the Philippines and China, China's claims to historic rights, or other sovereign rights or jurisdiction, with respect to the maritime areas of the South China Sea encompassed by the relevant part of the 'nine-dash line' are contrary to the Convention and without lawful effect to the extent that they exceed the geographic and substantive limits of China's maritime entitlements under the Convention; and further DECLARES that the Convention superseded any historic rights, or other sovereign rights or jurisdiction, in excess of the limits imposed therein;

(3) FINDS, with respect to the status of features in the South China Sea:

a. that it has sufficient information concerning tidal conditions in the South China Sea such that the practical considerations concerning the selection of the vertical datum and tidal model referenced in paragraphs 401 and 403 of the Tribunal's Award on Jurisdiction and Admissibility of 29 October 2015 do not pose an impediment to the identification of the status of features;

b. that Scarborough Shoal, Gaven Reef (North), McKennan Reef, Johnson Reef, Cuarteron Reef, and Fiery Cross Reef include, or in their natural condition did include, naturally formed areas of land, surrounded by water, which are above water at high tide, within the meaning of Article 121(1) of the Convention;

c. that Subi Reef, Gaven Reef (South), Hughes Reef, Mischief Reef, and Second Thomas Shoal, are low-tide elevations, within the meaning of Article 13 of the Convention;

d. that Subi Reef lies within 12 nautical miles of the high-tide feature of Sandy Cay on the reefs to the west of Thitu;

e. that Gaven Reef (South) lies within 12 nautical miles of the high-tide features of Gaven Reef (North) and Namyit Island; and

f. that Hughes Reef lies within 12 nautical miles of the high-tide features of McKennan Reef and Sin Cowe Island;

(4) DECLARES that, as low-tide elevations, Mischief Reef and Second Thomas Shoal do not generate entitlements to a territorial sea, exclusive economic zone, or continental shelf and are not features that are capable of appropriation;

(5) DECLARES that, as low-tide elevations, Subi Reef, Gaven Reef (South), and Hughes Reef do not generate entitlements to a territorial sea, exclusive economic zone, or continental shelf and are not features that are capable of appropriation, but may be used as the baseline for measuring the breadth of the territorial sea of high-tide features situated at a distance not exceeding the breadth of the territorial sea;

(6) DECLARES that Scarborough Shoal, Gaven Reef (North), McKennan Reef, Johnson Reef, Cuarteron Reef, and Fiery Cross Reef, in their natural condition, are rocks that cannot sustain human habitation or economic life of their own, within the meaning of Article 121(3) of the Convention and accordingly that Scarborough Shoal, Gaven Reef (North), McKennan Reef, Johnson Reef, Cuarteron Reef, and Fiery Cross Reef generate no entitlement to an exclusive economic zone or continental shelf;

(7) FINDS with respect to the status of other features in the South China Sea:

a. that none of the high-tide features in the Spratly Islands, in their natural condition, are capable of sustaining human habitation or economic life of their own within the meaning of Article 121(3) of the Convention;

b. that none of the high-tide features in the Spratly Islands generate entitlements to an exclusive economic zone or continental shelf; and

c. that therefore there is no entitlement to an exclusive economic zone or continental shelf generated by any feature claimed by China that would overlap the entitlements of the Philippines in the area of Mischief Reef and Second Thomas Shoal; and DECLARES that Mischief Reef and Second Thomas Shoal are within the exclusive economic zone and continental shelf of the Philippines;

(8) DECLARES that China has, through the operation of its marine surveillance vessels in relation to M/V Veritas Voyager on 1 and 2 March 2011 breached its obligations under Article 77 of the Convention with respect to the Philippines' sovereign rights over the non-living resources of its continental shelf in the area of Reed Bank;

(9) DECLARES that China has, by promulgating its 2012 moratorium on fishing in the South China Sea, without exception for areas of the South China Sea falling within the exclusive economic zone of the Philippines and without limiting the moratorium to Chinese flagged vessels, breached its obligations under Article 56 of the Convention with respect to the Philippines' sovereign rights over the living resources of its exclusive economic zone;

(10) FINDS, with respect to fishing by Chinese vessels at Mischief Reef and Second Thomas Shoal:

a. that, in May 2013, fishermen from Chinese flagged vessels engaged in fishing within the Philippines' exclusive economic zone at Mischief Reef and Second Thomas Shoal; and

b. that China, through the operation of its marine surveillance vessels, was aware of, tolerated, and failed to exercise due diligence to prevent such fishing by Chinese flagged vessels; and

c. that therefore China has failed to exhibit due regard for the Philippines' sovereign rights with respect to fisheries in its exclusive economic zone; and DECLARES that China has breached its obligations under Article 58(3) of the Convention;

(11) FINDS that Scarborough Shoal has been a traditional fishing ground for fishermen of many nationalities and DECLARES that China has, through the operation of its official vessels at Scarborough Shoal from May 2012 onwards, unlawfully prevented fishermen from the Philippines from engaging in traditional fishing at Scarborough Shoal;

(12) FINDS, with respect to the protection and preservation of the marine environment in the South China Sea:

a. that fishermen from Chinese flagged vessels have engaged in the harvesting of endangered species on a significant scale;

b. that fishermen from Chinese flagged vessels have engaged in the harvesting of giant clams in a manner that is severely destructive of the coral reef ecosystem; and

c. that China was aware of, tolerated, protected, and failed to prevent the aforementioned harmful activities; and DECLARES that China has breached its obligations under Articles 192 and 194(5) of the Convention;

(13) FINDS further, with respect to the protection and preservation of the marine environment in the South China Sea:

a. that China's land reclamation and construction of artificial islands, installations, and structures at Cuarteron Reef, Fiery Cross Reef, Gaven Reef (North), Johnson Reef, Hughes Reef, Subi Reef, and Mischief Reef has caused severe, irreparable harm to the coral reef ecosystem;

b. that China has not cooperated or coordinated with the other States bordering the South China Sea concerning the protection and preservation of the marine environment concerning such activities; and

c. that China has failed to communicate an assessment of the potential effects of such activities on the marine environment, within the meaning of Article 206 of the Convention; and DECLARES that China has breached its obligations under Articles 123, 192, 194(1), 194(5), 197, and 206 of the Convention;

(14) With respect to China's construction of artificial islands, installations, and structures at Mischief Reef:

a. FINDS that China has engaged in the construction of artificial islands, installations, and structures at Mischief Reef without the authorisation of the Philippines;

b. RECALLS (i) its finding that Mischief Reef is a low-tide elevation, (ii) its declaration that low-tide elevations are not capable of appropriation, and

(iii) its declaration that Mischief Reef is within the exclusive economic zone and continental shelf of the Philippines; and

c. DECLARES that China has breached Articles 60 and 80 of the Convention with respect to the Philippines' sovereign rights in its exclusive economic zone and continental shelf;

(15) FINDS, with respect to the operation of Chinese law enforcement vessels in the vicinity of Scarborough Shoal:

a. that China's operation of its law enforcement vessels on 28 April 2012 and 26 May 2012 created serious risk of collision and danger to Philippine ships and personnel; and

b. that China's operation of its law enforcement vessels on 28 April 2012 and 26 May 2012 violated Rules 2, 6, 7, 8, 15, and 16 of the Convention on the International Regulations for Preventing Collisions at Sea, 1972; and DECLARES that China has breached its obligations under Article 94 of the Convention; and

(16) FINDS that, during the time in which these dispute resolution proceedings were ongoing, China:

a. has built a large artificial island on Mischief Reef, a low-tide elevation located in the exclusive economic zone of the Philippines;

b. has caused — through its land reclamation and construction of artificial islands, installations, and structures — severe, irreparable harm to the coral reef ecosystem at Mischief Reef, Cuarteron Reef, Fiery Cross Reef, Gaven Reef (North), Johnson Reef, Hughes Reef, and Subi Reef; and

c. has permanently destroyed — through its land reclamation and construction of artificial islands, installations, and structures — evidence of the natural condition of Mischief Reef, Cuarteron Reef, Fiery Cross Reef, Gaven Reef (North), Johnson Reef, Hughes Reef, and Subi Reef; and FINDS further that China:

d. has aggravated the Parties' dispute concerning their respective rights and entitlements in the area of Mischief Reef;

e. has aggravated the Parties' dispute concerning the protection and preservation of the marine environment at Mischief Reef;

f. has extended the scope of the Parties' dispute concerning the protection and preservation of the marine environment to Cuarteron Reef,

Fiery Cross Reef, Gaven Reef (North), Johnson Reef, Hughes Reef, and Subi Reef; and

g. has aggravated the Parties' dispute concerning the status of maritime features in the Spratly Islands and their capacity to generate entitlements to maritime zones; and DECLARES that China has breached its obligations pursuant to Articles 279, 296, and 300 of the Convention, as well as pursuant to general international law, to abstain from any measure capable of exercising a prejudicial effect in regard to the execution of the decisions to be given and in general, not to allow any step of any kind to be taken which might aggravate or extend the dispute during such time as dispute resolution proceedings were ongoing.

Done at The Hague, this 12th day of July 2016,

Judge Rudiger Wolfrum   Judge Stanislaw Pawlak

Source: https://pca-cpa.org/wp-content/uploads/sites/175/2016/07/PH-CN-20160712-Award.pdf

SELECTED BIBLIOGRAPHY

Accinelli, Robert, *Crisis and Commitment: United States Policy toward Taiwan, 1950-1955* (Chapel Hill: The University of North Carolina Press, 1996).

Acharya, Amitav, *The Making of Southeast Asia: International Relations of a Region* (Ithaca: Cornell University Press, 2012).

Adel, Daljit Sen, *China and her Neighbors: A Review of Chinese Foreign Policy* (New Delhi: Deep & Deep Publications, 1984).

Alagappa, Muthiah, ed., *Asian Security Practice: Material and Ideational Influences* (Stanford, California: Stanford University Press, 1998).

Ambekar, G.V., and Divekar, V.D., eds., *Documents on China's Relations with South and Southeast Asia, 1949-1962* (Bombay: Allied Publishers, 1964).

Amer, Ramses, *The Sino-Vietnamese Approach to Managing Boundary Disputes*, Maritime Briefing 3, no. 5 (Durham: International Boundaries Research Unit, University of Durham, 2002).

———, and Zou, Keyuan, eds., *Conflict Management and Dispute Settlement in East Asia* (Farnham and Burlington: Ashgate, 2011).

Austin, Greg, *China's Ocean Frontier: International Law, Military Force and National Development* (St. Leonards, NSW: Allen & Unwin, 1998).

Ballantine, Joseph W., *Formosa: A Problem for United States Foreign Policy* (Washington, DC: The Brookings Institution, 1952).

Balme, Stephanie and Sidel, Mark, eds., *Vietnam's New Order: International Perspectives on the State and Reform in Vietnam* (New York: Palgrave Macmillan, 2007).

Barlow, Jeffrey G., *From HOT WAR to COLD: The U.S. Navy and National Security Affairs, 1945-1955* (Stanford, CA: Stanford University Press, 2009).

Bate, H. Maclear, *Report From Formosa* (New York: E. P. Dutton & Co., Inc., 1952).

Bateman, Sam, and Emmers, Ralph, eds., *The South China Sea: Towards a Co-operative Management Regime*, (London: Routledge, 2009).

Black, Jeremy, ed., *The Seventy Great Battles of All Time* (London: Thames & Hudson, 2005).

Bouchard, Joseph F., *Command in Crisis: Four Case Studies* (New York: Columbia University Press, 1991).
Bouchat, Clarence J., *Dangerous Ground: The Spratly Island and U.S. Interests and Approaches* (Carlisle, PA: U.S. Army War College Press, 2013).
Bush, Richard C., *At Cross Purposes: U.S.-Taiwan Relations Since 1942* (Armonk, NY: M.E. Sharpe Press, 2004).
Bussert, James C., and Elleman, Bruce A., *People's Liberation Army Navy (PLAN) Combat Systems Technology 1949-2010* (Annapolis, MD: Naval Institute Press, 2011).
Caceres, Sigrido Burgos, *China's Strategic Interests in the South China Sea: Power and Resources* (New York: Routledge, 2014).
Carlson, Allen, *Unifying China, Integrating With the World: Securing Chinese Sovereignty in the Reform Era* (Ithaca, NY: Cornell University Press, 2004).
Chachavalpongpun, Pavin, *ASEAN-U.S. Relations: What are the Talking Points?* (Sinagapore: Institute of Southeast Asian Studies Publishing, 2012).
Chan, Steve, *East Asian Dynamism: Growth, Order and Security in the Pacific Region* (San Francisco: Westview Press, 1990).
Chang, Gordon H., *Friends and Enemies: The United States, China, and the Soviet Union, 1948-1972* (Stanford: Stanford University Press, 1990).
Chang, Jung, and Halliday, Jon, *Mao: The Unknown Story* (New York: Alfred A, Knopf, 2005).
Chang, L.T., *China's Boundary Treaties and Frontier Disputes* (New York: Oceana Publications, 1982).
Chang, Pao-Min, *Sino-Vietnamese Territorial Dispute* (New York: Praeger, 1986).
Chase, Michael S., *Taiwan's Security Policy: External Threats and Domestic Politics* (Boulder: Lynne Rienner Publishers, 2008).
Chen Jian, *Mao's China & the Cold War* (Chapel Hill, NC: The University of North Carolina Press, 2001).
Chen, King C., *China's War with Vietnam. 1979* (Stanford: Hoover Institution Press, 1987).
Chen Ming-tong, *The China Threat Crosses the Strait: Challenges and Strategies for Taiwan's National Security*, trans. Kiel Downey (Taipei: Dong Fan Color Printing Co., 2007).
Chiang Kai-shek, *China's Destiny* (1943; reprint, New York, 1947).
Chiu, Hungdah, *China and the Taiwan Issue* (New York: Praeger Publishers, 1979).
Christensen, Thomas J., *Useful Adversaries: Grand Strategy, Domestic Mobilization, and Sino-American Conflict, 1947-1958* (Princeton: Princeton University Press, 1996).

Chung, Chien-peng, *Domestic Politics, International Bargaining and China's Territorial Disputes* (New York: RoutledgeCurzon, 2004).
Cline, Ray S., and Carpenter, William M., eds., *Secure Passage at Sea* (Washington: United States Global Strategy Council, 1991).
Clough, Ralph N., *Island China* (Cambridge: Harvard University Press, 1978).
Cohen, J. A., and Chiu, H., *People's China and International Law: Documentary Study* (New Jersey: Princeton University Press, 1976).
Cohen, Warren I. ed., *New Frontiers in American-East Asian Relations* (New York: Columbia University Press, 1983).
Craig, Susan L., *Chinese Perceptions of Traditional and Nontraditional Security Threats* (Carlisle Barracks, PA: Strategic Studies Institute, US Army War College, 2007).
Cribb, Robert, and Ford, Michele, *Indonesia beyond the water's edge — Managing an archipelagic state* (Indonesian Update Series, RSPAS Australian National University, ISEAS, Singapore, 2009).
Curley, Melissa, and Wong, Siu-Lun, eds., *Security and Migration in Asia: the dynamics of securitisation* (Abingdon: Routledge, 2009).
Dallin, David J., *The Rise of Russia in Asia* (New Haven: Archon Books, 1971).
Daniels, Christopher L., *South China Sea: Energy and Security Conflicts* (Lanham: The Scarecrow Press, Inc., 2014).
Daugherty, Leo J., III, *The Marine Corps and the State Department: Enduring Partners in United States Foreign Policy, 1798-2007* (Jefferson, NC: Macfarland & Company Inc. Publishers, 2009).
Dikötter, Frank, *Mao's Great Famine: The History of China's Most Devastating Catastrophe, 1958-1962* (New York: Walker & Co., 2010).
Dreyer, June Teufel, ed., *Chinese Defense and Foreign Policy* (New York: Paragon House, 1989).
Dulles, Foster Rhea, *American Policy Toward Communist China, 1949-1969* (New York: Thomas Y. Crowell Company, 1972).
Durkin, Michael F., *Naval Quarantine: A New Addition to the Role of Sea Power*. Maxwell Air Force Base, AL: Air University: Air War College, 1964.
Dutton, Peter, *Scouting, Signaling, and Gatekeeping: Chinese Naval Operations in Japanese Waters and the International Law Implications* (U.S. Naval War College, China Maritime Studies No. 2, 2009).
Dzurek, Daniel J., *The Spratly Islands Dispute: Who's On First?* Maritime Briefing, 2, no. 1 (Durham: International Boundaries Research Unit, University of Durham, 1996).
Elleman, Bruce A., *Modern Chinese Warfare, 1795-1989* (London: Routledge Press, 2001).

_____. and Bell, Christopher, eds., *Naval Mutinies of the Twentieth Century: An International Perspective* (London: Frank Cass, 2003).

_____. and Paine, S.C.M., eds., *Naval Blockades and Seapower: Strategies and Counter-Strategies, 1805–2005* (London: Routledge Press, 2006).

_____. *Moscow and the Emergence of Communist Power in China, 1925–30: The Nanchang Uprising and the Birth of the Red Army* (London: Routledge, 2009).

_____. and Kotkin, Stephen, eds., *Manchurian Railways and the Opening of China, An International History* (Armonk NY: M.E. Sharpe, 2010).

_____. and Hattendorf, John B., eds., *Nineteen Gun Salute: Case Studies of Operational, Strategic, and Diplomatic Naval Leadership during the 20th and Early 21st Centuries* (Newport, R.I.: NWC Press, 2010).

_____. and Paine, S.C.M., *Modern China: Continuity and Change 1644 to the Present* (Boston: Prentice-Hall, 2010).

_____. and Paine, S.C.M., eds., *Naval Power and Expeditionary Warfare: Peripheral Campaigns and New Theatres of Naval Warfare* (London: Routledge Press, 2011).

_____. *High Sea's Buffer: The Taiwan Patrol Force, 1950–1979* (Newport, RI: NWC Press, 2012).

Elliott, David W. P., ed., *The Third Indochina Conflict* (Boulder, Colorado: Westview Press, 1981).

Erickson, Andrew, Goldstein, Lyle, Murray, William, and Wilson, Andrew, eds., *China's Future Nuclear Submarine Force* (Annapolis, MD: Naval Institute Press, 2007).

Fels, Enrico and Vu, Trung-Minh, eds., *Power Politics in Asia's Contested Waters: Territorial Disputes in the South China Sea* (New York: Springer, 2016).

Fravel, M. Taylor, *Strong Borders Secure Nation: Cooperation and Conflict in China's Territorial Disputes* (Princeton, NJ: Princeton University Press, 2008).

Gallagher, Rick M., *The Taiwan Strait Crisis* (Newport, RI: Strategic Research Department, Research Report, 1997).

Garthoff, Raymond L., ed., *Sino-Soviet Military Relations* (New York: Frederick A Praeger, 1966).

Garver, John W., *China's Decision for Rapprochement with the United States, 1968–1971* (Boulder, CO: Westview Press, 1982).

_____. *The Sino-American Alliance: Nationalist China and American Cold War Strategy in Asia* (Armonk, NY: M.E. Sharpe, 1997).

Gibert, Stephen P., and Carpenter, William M., *America and Island China: A Documentary History* (Lantham, MD: University Press of America, 1989).
Gill, Bates, *Rising Star: China's New Security Diplomacy* (Washington, D.C.: Brookings Institution Press, 2007).
Gilpin, Robert, *War and Change in World Politics* (New York: Cambridge University Press, 1981).
Gittings, John, *The Role of the Chinese Army* (New York: Oxford University Press, 1967).
Godwin, Paul H. B., *Development of the Chinese Armed Forces* (Maxwell: Air University Press, 1988).
Goodspeed, M. Hill, *U.S. Navy: A Complete History* (Washington, D.C.: Naval Historical Foundation, 2003).
Goscha, Christopher E., *Vietnam or Indochina? Contesting Concepts of Space in Vietnamese Nationalism, 1887-1954* (Copenhagen: Nordic Institute of Asia Studies, 1995).
Grintner, Lawrence E., and Kihl, Young Whan, *East Asian Conflict Zones* (New York: St. Martin's Press, 1987).
Gu, Weigun, *Conflicts of Divided Nations: The Case of China and Korea* (Westport, Conn.: Praeger, 1995).
Haacke, Jurgen and Morada, Noel M., eds., *Cooperative Security in the Asia-Pacific: The ASEAN Regional Forum* (New York: Routledge 2010).
Haller-Trost, R., *Occasional Paper No. 14 — The Spratly Islands: A Study on the Limitations of International Law* (Canterbury: University of Kent Centre of South-East Asian Studies, 1990).
Hancox, David, and Prescott, J.R. Victor, *A Geographical Description of the Spratly Islands and An Account of Hydrographic Surveys Amongst Those Islands*, Maritime Briefing, 1, 6 (Durham: International Boundaries Research Unit, 1995).
Hara, Kimie, *Cold War Frontiers in the Asia-Pacific: Divided Territories in the San Francisco System* (London: Routledge Press, 2007).
Harris, Stuart, *China's Foreign Policy* (Cambridge: Polity Press, 2014).
Harrison, Selig S., *China. Oil and Asia: Conflict Ahead?* (New York: Columbia University Press, 1977).
Hayton, Bill, *Vietnam: Rising Dragon* (New Haven: Yale University Press, 2010).
_____. *The South China Sea: The Struggle for Power in Asia* (New Haven: Yale University Press, 2014).
Heal, Geoffrey, and Chichilnisky, Graciela, *Oil and the International Economy* (Oxford: Clarendon Press, 1991).
Heinzig, Dieter, *Disputed Islands in the South China Sea* (Wies-baden: Otto Harrassowitz, 1976).

Herrmann, Wilfried A., *Asia's Security Challenges* (Commack, New York: Nova Science Publishers, 1998).
Hickey, Dennis Van Vranken, *United States-Taiwan Security Ties: From Cold War to Beyond Containment* (Westport, CT: Praeger, 1994).
Hinton, Harold C., *China's Relations with Burma and Vietnam: a brief survey* (NY: Institute of Pacific Relations, 1958).
_____. *China's Turbulent Quest* (New York: The Macmillan Company, 1972).
Ho, Khai Leong, ed., *Connecting and Distancing, Southeast Asia and China* (Singapore: Institute of Southeast Asian studies, 2009).
Holober, Frank, *Raiders of the China Coast: CIA Covert Operations during the Korean War* (Annapolis, MD: Naval Institute Press, 1999).
Holslag, Jonathan, *Trapped Giant: China's Military Rise* (Abingdon: Routledge, 2010).
Hong, Seoung-Yong, and Van Dyke, Jon M., eds., *Maritime Boundary Disputes, Settlement Processes, and the Law of the Sea* (Leiden: Martinus Nijhoff Publishers, 2009).
Hou, K.C., and Yeoh, K. K., eds., *Malaysia and Southeast Asia and the Emerging China: Political, Economic and Cultural Perspectives* (Kuala Lumpur: Institute of China Studies, 2005).
Hsu, Immanuel C. Y., *China without Mao: The Search for a New Order* (New York: Oxford University Press, 1983).
Hu, Nien-Tsu Alfred, and McDorman, Ted L., *Maritime Issues in the South China Sea: Troubled Waters or A Sea of Opportunity* (New York: Routledge Press, 2013).
Hugill, Paul D., *The Continuing Utility of Naval Blockades in the Twenty-first Century*. Fort Leavenworth, KS: U.S. Army Command and General Staff College, 1998.
Hyland, William, *The Cold War is Over* (New York, 1990).
Jeffries, Ian, *Vietnam: A guide to economic and political developments* (New York: Routledge Press, 2006).
_____. *Contemporary Vietnam: A guide to economic and political developments* (New York: Routledge Press, 2011).
Ji Guoxing, *SLOC Security in the Asia Pacific* (Honolulu, HI: Asia-Pacific Center for Security Studies.Center Occasional Paper, 2000).
Johnston, Douglas M., and Sanders, Phillip, eds., *Ocean Boundary Making: Regional Issues and Developments* (New York: Croom Held, 1988).
Johnston, Douglas M., and Valencia, Mark J., *Pacific Ocean Boundary Problems: Status and Solutions* (Boston: Martinus Nijhoff Publishers, 1991).

Jones, Rodney W. and Hildreth, Steven A., eds., *Emerging Powers Defense and Security in the Third World* (New York, Praeger Publishers, 1986).
Kao, Ting Tsz, *The Chinese Frontiers* (Aurora, Ill: Chinese Scholarly Publishing Company, 1980).
Keith, Ronald C., ed., *Energy, Security and Economic Development in East Asia* (New York: St. Martin's Press, 1986).
Kent, George, and Valencia, Mark J., eds. *Marine Policy in Southeast Asia*. Berkeley: University of California Press, 1985.
Kiang, Ying Cheng, *China's Boundaries* (Chicago: Institute of Chinese Studies, 1984).
Kim, Dalchoong, ed., *Resources, Maritime Transport and SLOC Security in the Asia-Pacific Region* (Seoul: Institute of East-West Studies, 1988).
Kissinger, Henry, *White House Years* (Boston: Little, Brown and Company, 1979).
Kondapalli, Srikanth, *China's Naval Power* (New Delhi: Knowledge World, 2001).
Koo, Min Gyo, *Island Disputes and Maritime Regime Building in East Asia: Between a Rock and a Hard Place* (New York: Springer, 2009).
Kynge, James, *China Shakes the World: A Titan's Rise and Troubled Future — and the Challenge for America* (Boston: Houghton Mifflin Harcourt, 2006).
Lai, David, *Asia-Pacific: A Strategic Assessment* (Carlisle: Army War College Press, 2013).
Lai Hongyi and Lim Tin Seng, eds., *Harmony and Development ASEAN-China Relations* (Singapore: World Scientific Publishing Co. Pte. Ltd., 2007).
Lamb, Alastair, *Asian Frontiers: studies in a continuing problem* (Melbourne: F.W. Cheshire for the Australian Institute of International Affairs, 1968).
Lasater, Martin L., ed., *Beijing's Blockade Threat to Taiwan: A Heritage Roundtable* (Washington, DC: Heritage Foundation, 1986).
Lee, Luke T., *China and International Agreements: a study of compliance* (Leyden & Durham NC: A.W. Sijthoff & Rule of Law Press, 1969).
Lilly, James R., and Downs, Chuck, eds., *Crisis in the Taiwan Strait* (American Enterprise Institute for Public Policy Research, 1997).
Lim, Joo-Jock, *Territorial Power Domains, Southeast Asia, and China* (Singapore: Institute of Southeast Asian Studies, 1984).
Liu, Ta Jen, *U.S.-China Relations, 1784–1992* (Lanham, MD: University Press of America, 1997).
Lo, Chi-kin, *China's Policy Towards Territorial Disputes: The Case of the South Sea Islands* (New York: Routledge, 1987).

Lowther, Adam, ed., *The Asia-Pacific Century: Challenges and Opportunities* (Maxwell Air Force Base, Alabama: Air University Press, 2013).
Lüthi, Lorenz M., *The Sino-Soviet Split: Cold War in the Communist World* (Princeton: Princeton University Press, 2008).
Mahmud, Colonel Suleiman Bin, *The South China Sea: Future Concern for Malaysia* (Research Report, Air War College, 1988).
Mancall, Mark, ed., *Formosa Today* (New York: Frederick A. Praeger, 1964).
Marolda, Edward J., "The U.S. Navy and the Chinese Civil War, 1945-1952," Ph.D. Dissertation, The George Washington University, 1990.
_____. *By Sea, Air, and Land: An Illustrated History of the U.S. Navy and the War in Southeast Asia* (Washington, DC: Government Printing Office, 1994).
_____. *The Approaching Storm: Conflict in Asia, 1945-1965* (Washington, DC: Government Printing Office, 2009).
McDonald, T. David, *The Technological Transformation of China* (Washington D.C.: National Defense University, 1989).
Miller, Tom, *China's Asian Dream: Empire Building along the New Silk Road* (New York: Zed Books 2017).
Morgan, Joseph R., and Valencia, Mark J., eds., *Atlas for Marine Policy in Southeast Asian Sea* (Berkeley: University of California Press, 1983).
Morris, Michael A., ed., *North-South Perspectives on Marine Policy* (Boulder: Westview Press, 1988).
Muller, David, *China as a Maritime Power* (Boulder: Westview Press, 1983).
Myer, Ramon H. and Zhang, Jianlin, *The Struggle Across the Taiwan Strait* (Stanford, CA: Hoover Institution Press, 2006).
Nadkarni, Vidya, *Strategic Partnerships in Asia: Balancing without alliances* (New York: Routledge, 2010).
Navarro, Peter, *Crouching Tiger: What China's Militarism Means for the World* (New York: Prometheus Books, 2015).
Neher, Clark D., *Southeast Asia in the New International Era* (San Francisco, Westview Press, 1991).
Odgaard, Liselotte, *Maritime Security between China and Southeast Asia: Conflict and cooperation in the making of regional order* (Aldershot, UK: Ashgate, 2002).
Paine, S.C.M., *Imperial Rivals: Russia, China and their disputed frontier* (Armonk, NY: M E Sharpe, 1996).
_____. *The Sino-Japanese War of 1894-1895: Perceptions, Power, and Primacy* (New York: Cambridge University Press, 2003).
_____. *The Japanese Empire: Grand Strategy from the Meiji Restoration to the Pacific War* (New York: Cambridge University Press, 2017).

Palmer, Norman D., *Westward Watch: The United States and the Changing Western Pacific* (New York: Pergamon-Brassey, 1987).

Park, Chang-Kwoun, "Consequences of U.S. Naval Shows of Force, 1946–1989," Ph.D. Dissertation, University of Missouri-Columbia, 1995.

Percival, Bronson, *The Dragon Looks South: China and Southeast Asia in the New Century* (Westport, CN: Praeger Security International 2007).

Pillsbury, Michael, *The Hundred-year Marathon: China's Secret Strategy to Replace America as the Global Superpower* (New York: St. Martin's, 2016).

Pipes, Richard, *The Formation of the Soviet Union Communism and Nationalism 1917–1923* (Cambridge, MA, 1964).

Porritt, V.L., *British Colonial Rule in Sarawak 1946–63* (Oxford: Oxford University Press, 1997).

Powell, Ralph L., *The Rise of Chinese Military Power, 1895–1912* (Princeton, NJ: Princeton University Press, 1955).

Prescott, J.R.Victor, *Map of Mainland Asia by Treaty* (Melbourne: University of Melbourne Press, 1975).

—————, and Schofield, Clive, *The Maritime Political Boundaries of the World* (Leiden/Boston, Martinus Nijhoff, 2005).

Rasler, Karen A., and Thompson, William R., eds., *The Great Powers and Global Struggle, 1490–1990* (Lexington: University Press of Kentucky, 1994).

Rawlinson, John L., *China's Struggle for Naval Development, 1839–1895* (Cambridge, MA: Harvard University Press, 1967).

Reardon, Lawrence C., *The Reluctant Dragon: Crisis Cycles in Chinese Foreign Economic Policy* (Seattle: University of Washington Press, 2002).

Ross, Robert S., ed., *After the Cold War: Domestic Factors and U.S.-China Relations* (Armonk, NY: M.E. Sharpe, 1998).

Roy, Nalanda, *The South China Sea Disputes: Past, Present, and Future* (New York: Lexington Books, 2016).

Ryan, Mark A., Finkelstein, David M., and McDevitt, Michael A., eds., *Chinese Warfighting: The PLA Experience Since 1949* (Armonk, NY: M.E. Sharpe Publishers, 2003).

Schell, Orville, *Mandate of Heaven* (NY: Simon & Schuster, 1994).

Samuels, Marwyn S., *Contest for the South China Sea* (New York: Methuen, 1982).

Schofield, C.H., Townsend-Gault, I., Djalal, H., Storey, I., Miller, M. and Cook, T., *From Disputed Waters to Seas of Opportunity: Overcoming Barriers to Maritime Cooperation in East and Southeast Asia* (National Bureau of Asian Research Special Report No.30, July 2011).

Schreadley, Commander R. L., USN (ret.), *From the Rivers to the Sea: The United States Navy in Vietnam* (Annapolis, MD: Naval Institute Press, 1992).
Shu Guang Zhang, *Economic Cold War: America's Embargo Against China and the Sino-Soviet Alliance, 1949–1963* (Stanford: Stanford University Press, 2001).
Singh, Swaran, *China-South Asia: Issues, Equations, Policies* (New Delhi: Lancer's Books, 2003).
Siddayo, C. M., *The Off-shore Petroleum Resources of Southeast Asia: Potential Conflict Situations and Related Economic Situations* (New York: Oxford University Press, 1978).
Smith, Esmond Douglas, "China, technology and the Spratly Islands: The Geopolitical impact of new technologies," PhD Dissertation, Salve Regina University, 1994.
Snyder, Edwin K., Gregor, A. James, and Chang, Maria Hsia, *The Taiwan Relations Act and the Defense of the Republic of China* (Berkeley, CA: University of California Press, 1980).
Storey, Ian, *Southeast Asia and the Rise of China: The Search for Security* (Abingdon, Oxon: Routledge, 2011).
Suryadinata, Leo, *China and the ASEAN States: The Ethnic Chinese Dimension* (Singapore: Singapore University Press, 1985).
Sutter, Robert G., *China's Rise in Asia: Promises and Perils* (New York: Rowman & Littlefield Publishers, 2005).
Swaine, Michael D., and Tellis, Ashley J., *Interpreting China's Grand Strategy: Past, Present, and Future* (Santa Monica CA., Rand Corporation, 2000).
Swanson, Bruce, *Eighth Voyage of the Dragon: A History of China's Quest for Seapower* (Annapolis, MD: Naval Institute Press, 1982).
Szonyi, Michael, *Cold War Island: Quemoy on the Front Line* (New York: Cambridge University Press, 2008).
Tang, Shiping, Li, Mingjiang, and Acharya, Amitav, eds., *Living with China: Regional States and China through Crises and Turning Points* (New York: Palgrave Macmillan, 2009).
Thayer, Carlyle A., and Amer, Ramses, eds., *Vietnamese Foreign Policy in Transition* (Singapore: Institute for Southeast Asian Studies; and, New York: St. Martin's Press, 1999).
Thuy, Tran Truong, ed., *The South China Sea: Cooperation For Regional Security and Developments, Proceedings of the International Workshop*, co-organized by the Diplomatic Academy of Vietnam and the Vietnam Lawyers' Association, 26–27 November 2009, Hanoi, Vietnam (Hanoi: The Gioi and Diplomatic Academy of Vietnam, 2010).
Thuy, Tran Truong and Le Thuy Trang, eds., *Power, Law, and Maritime Order in the South China Sea* (New York: Lexington Books, 2015).

Till, Geoffrey, *Seapower: A Guide for the Twenty-First Century* (New York: Routledge, 2013).
Tkacik, John J., Jr., ed., *Reshaping the Taiwan Strait* (Washington, DC: The Heritage Foundation, 2007).
Tsai, Shih-Shan Henry, *Maritime Taiwan: Historical Encounters with the East and the West* (Armonk, NY: M.E. Sharpe, 2009).
Tucker, Nancy Bernkopf, ed., *Dangerous Strait: The U.S.-Taiwan-China Crisis* (New York: Columbia University Press, 2005).
Valencia, Mark J., Van Dyke, Jon M., and Ludwig, Noel A., *Sharing the Resources of the South China Sea* (Honolulu: University of Hawai'i Press, 1997).
van Kemenade, Willem, *China, Hong Kong, Taiwan Inc: The Dynamics of a New Empire* (New York: Alfred A. Knopf, 1997).
Vo, Nghia M., *The Vietnamese Boat People, 1954 and 1975–1992* (London: McFarland & Company, Inc., 2006).
Vohra, Ranbir, *China's Path to Modernization: A Historical Review from 1800 to the Present* (Englewood Cliffs: Prentice-Hall, 1987).
Wang, Gabe T., *China and the Taiwan Issue: Impending War at Taiwan Strait* (Lanham, MD: University Press of America, 2006).
Winchester, Simon, *Pacific Rising: The Emergence of a New World Culture* (New York: Prentice Hall, 1991).
Womack, Brantly, *China and Vietnam: The Politics of Asymmetry* (New York: Cambridge University Press, 2006).
Woodward, Kim, *The International Energy Relations of China* (Stanford: Stanford University Press, 1980).
Wu Shicun and Hong Nong, eds., *Recent Developments in the South China Sea Dispute: The Prospect of a Joint Development Regime* (New York: Routledge, 2014).
_____. and Keyuan Zou, eds., *Non-Traditional Security Issues and the South China Sea: Shaping a New Framework for Cooperation* (Surrey: Ashgate, 2014).
_____. and Keyuan Zou, eds., *Arbitration Concerning the South China Sea: Philippines versus China* (Surrey: Ashgate, 2016).
Yang Zhiben [杨志本], ed., *China Navy Encyclopedia*, [中国海军百科全书], vol. 2 (Beijing: Sea Tide Press [海潮出版社], 1998).
Young, Marilyn, *The Vietnam Wars, 1945–1990* (New York: HarperCollins, 1991).
Yu, Peter Kien-hong, *The Four Archipelagoes in the South China Sea* (Taipei: Council for Advanced Policy Studies, 1991).
Zhao, Suisheng, ed., *Across the Taiwan Strait: Mainland China, Taiwan, and the 1995–1996 Crisis* (New York: Routledge Press, 1999)

Index

9-dash map, see Nine-dash Map
9-11 xviii
11-dash map, see Eleven-dash Map

A Bomb, see Nuclear Weapon
A Cooperative Strategy for 21st Century Seapower 142–143
Abdullah Badawi 81–82, 256
Abe, Shinzo 91
Accretion Principle 25, 27–28
Aegis Cruisers 119
Africa 170, 213
Agreement on Fishing Cooperation in the Gulf of Tonkin (2000) 51, 148
Air Control 111, 116, 118, 156, 158, 199
Air Defense Identification Zone (ADIZ) 80
Air-Sea Combat 142
Aircraft Carrier 115, 118–120, 138–140, 158, 168, 182
Alatas, Ali 99, 101, 103, 256
Aleutian Islands 129
Alliances 19, 184, 188, 189
Ambalat 95
Amboyna Cay 77, 78, 133, 195, 201
Amianan Island 59
Amoco 132–133
Amoy, see Xiamen
Amphibious 102, 112, 117, 178, 202
Amphitrite Island Group 8
Annam, see Vietnam
Anti-aircraft guns 18, 145
Anti-aircraft missiles 117
Anti-satellite (ASAT) missile 159
Anti-secession 281–283

Anti-ship missiles (ASM) 48, 117, 175
Antisubmarine Warfare (ASW) 156, 208
Aquino, Benigno 69, 73, 173
Ardasier Reef 75, 78, 202
Arthur, Stanley 21
Artificial Accretion Principle 27–28
Artillery 205
Association of Southeast Asian Nations (ASEAN) 1, 22, 23–24, 29, 31, 50, 66, 79, 85, 88, 89, 91, 92, 125–126, 127, 153, 163, 188–189, 191, 192, 194, 204, 255–256, 278–280, 292
ASEAN Declaration on the South China Sea (1992) 23, 24, 31, 89, 255–256
ASEAN Regional Forum (ARF) 79, 89, 128, 208–209
ASEAN Declaration on the Conduct of Parties in the South China Sea (DoC) 50, 125, 278–280, 292
Association for Relations Across the Taiwan Straits (ARATS) 183, 273, 284–291
Asymmetric Warfare 146
Australia xvii, 91, 93, 130, 131, 147
Ayungin Reef, see Second Thomas Shoal

Bac Bo Gulf, see Gulf of Tonkin
Bai Tu Chinh, see Vanguard Bank
Bai Vung May, see Rifleman Bank
Bajo de Masinloc, see Scarborough Shoal
Balagtas, see Irving Reef

Ballistic missile blockade 115, 116–120, 121, 156, 175, 181, 271–273
Bandung 204
Bao Dai 196
Baria Province 35, 196
Barque Canada Reef 133, 203
Bashi Channel 59
Beibu Gulf, see Gulf of Tonkin
Beijing 3, 6, 15, 17, 51, 70, 89, 111, 181, 200, 204, 205, 208, 209–212, 273
Ben Lac, see West York Island
Benham Rise 59
Berlin Wall 21, 115
Beting Serupai, see James Shoal
Bien, Lyle viii, 119
Bilateral negotiations xx, xxi, 23, 29, 49, 50, 76, 79–80, 81, 93, 94, 107, 147, 148, 162, 165, 180, 184, 188, 249, 266, 267, 268, 279
Bito-onon, Eugenio 13–14
Blockade 54, 65, 69, 71, 111, 115, 116–120, 121, 156–157, 164, 169, 170, 174, 175, 181, 205, 271–273
Bo Hai Gulf 111
Bohai Sea 158
Bojiao Island 19
Bolkiah, Hassanal 81, 83, 86–87, 88, 89, 91, 256, 280
Bonaparte Napoleon *see* Napoleon Bonaparte
Bonin Islands, see Ogasawara Islands
Borneo Bulletin 86
Borneo Island 84, 85, 86, 93, 98, 195, 207
Britain, see United Kingdom
British Petroleum 205
BRP *Gregorio del Pilar* 64
BRP *Sierra Madre* 69
Brunei vii, xvii, xxi, 1, 12, 29, 75, 79, 80, 81–83, 84, 85–92, 133, 135, 149, 152, 177, 202, 207, 256, 280

Brunei Darussalam, see Brunei
Brunei National Petroleum Company Sendrian Berhad (PetroluemBRUNEI) 90
Buddhism 178
Burma, see Myanmar
Bush, George H. W. 271

Ca Chau Vien, see Calderon Reef
CAC-301 Study 127
Cai Xihong 49, 208
Cairo Declaration (1943) 8, 129, 213, 215
Calderon Reef 49
Callaghan (DDG 994) 157
Cam Ranh Bay 17, 19, 45, 47, 202
Cambodia 1, 231, 280
Canada 103
Canton, see Guangzhou
Cao Bai 114, 198
Carter, Ash 150
Carter, Jimmy 271
Central Military Commission 146, 283
Cession Principle 25, 28–29, 36, 107
Chams 38
Chang, Pao-Min 4, 39, 40
Chen Shui-bian 108, 121, 183
Cheng Wei-yuan 122
Chiang Kai-shek 9, 106, 113, 129, 174, 181, 213
Chigua, see Johnson South Reef
China vii, xv–xxii, 1, 2, 3, 4, 5, 6, 7, 8–11, 12–14, 15–18, 19–24, 28, 29–30, 31–53, 54–74, 75–84, 85–92, 93–104, 105–126, 127–160, 161, 162, 163, 164–166, 168, 169, 171–175, 176, 177–181, 182, 183, 184–189, 190, 191, 192, 193, 194, 195–208, 209–212, 213, 214–215, 218–221, 225–226, 227–228, 229, 230–234, 235,

248–249, 250–254, 271–273,
274–277, 278–280, 281–283,
284–291, 292–299
Territorial disputes with Brunei
vii, xvii, xxi, 1, 12, 29, 75, 79,
80, 81–83, 84, 85–92, 133, 135,
149, 152, 177, 202, 207, 256,
280
India xvii, 93, 172, 175, 180, 181,
190, 231, 232
Indonesia vii, xvii, xxi, 1, 12,
23, 38, 48, 51, 77, 89, 91, 92,
93–104, 108, 122, 130, 133,
152, 204, 256, 280
Japan xvii, 1, 3, 6, 7–8, 10–11,
25, 28, 32, 35, 38, 41, 42, 54,
56, 57, 59, 80, 89, 91, 100,
107, 113, 114, 116, 118, 119,
123–124, 129–131, 141, 143,
144, 145, 154, 159, 162, 164,
166, 167–168, 173, 175, 176,
177, 183–184, 185, 186, 187,
188, 192, 196, 197, 199, 213,
214–215, 216–217, 218–221,
231, 232
Malaysia vii, xvii, xxi, 1, 12, 29,
38, 51, 62, 74, 75–84, 85, 87,
88, 92, 93, 94–96, 97–98, 103,
129, 133, 135, 149, 150–152,
198, 199, 201, 202, 203, 204,
205, 207, 256, 280
Philippines vii, xvii, xviii, xxi, 1,
2, 12, 13–14, 19, 21, 25, 26, 29,
34, 39, 47, 53, 54–74, 79, 89,
90, 92, 93, 103, 113, 115, 122,
129–130, 131, 132, 133, 135,
148, 149–150, 152, 153, 161,
173, 178, 184, 186, 187, 188,
192, 196, 197, 198, 199, 200,
201, 202, 203, 205, 206, 207,
208, 256, 280, 292, 293, 294,
295, 296, 297, 298

Taiwan vii, xvii, xxi, 1, 3, 6, 7, 9,
10, 11, 12, 13, 21, 22, 27, 28,
29, 32, 36, 37, 38, 39, 41, 42,
43, 50, 55, 56, 57, 59, 60, 63,
64, 77, 79, 81, 84, 85, 86, 88,
104, 105–126, 128–131, 138,
145, 147, 148, 152–153, 154,
156–157, 160, 162, 164, 170,
172, 174, 175, 177, 178, 181–
184, 187, 188, 195, 196, 197,
198, 199, 201, 202, 203, 204,
205, 206, 207, 213, 214–215,
216–217, 218–221, 222–224,
225–226, 227–228, 233, 235,
236–247, 248–249, 250,
271–273, 281–283, 284–291
United States xv, xvii, xviii, xx,
xxi, xxii, 1, 13, 17, 18, 19,
21, 29, 31, 45, 47, 54, 60, 64,
70, 72, 73, 81, 91, 100, 103,
108, 112, 113, 114, 115, 116,
117, 118, 120, 121, 124, 126,
127–160, 162, 163, 165, 167,
170, 171, 174, 175, 176, 177,
178, 179, 181, 182, 184, 185,
186, 187, 191, 192, 193, 194,
197, 202, 204, 206, 207–208,
214–215, 216–217, 222–224,
225–226, 227–228, 230–234,
235, 236–247, 248–249,
271–273
Vietnam vii, xvii–xviii, xxi, 1, 3, 5,
7, 10–12, 13, 15–19, 20–21, 22,
24, 27, 29, 30, 31–53, 55, 56,
57, 60, 62, 65, 75, 77, 78, 79,
83, 84, 85, 86, 87–88, 92, 93,
94, 95, 97, 98, 103, 108, 110,
113, 114, 122, 124, 125, 128,
130, 133, 135, 143, 147, 148,
149, 151, 152, 153, 156, 161,
174, 178, 182, 184, 186, 188,
195, 196, 197, 198, 199, 200,

201, 202, 203, 204, 205, 206, 207, 208, 229
China Basin 131
China Daily 146
China Mobile 208
China National Offshore Oil Company (CNOOC) 65, 90, 190, 204
China's Indisputable Sovereignty over Xisha and Nansha Islands (1980) 39, 201
China-ASEAN Free Trade Area 66
Chinese (Taiwan) Society of International Law 122
Chinese Academy of Social Sciences 72
Chinese Academy of Sciences 136
Chinese civil war, see Civil War, China
Chinese Communist Navy, see People's Liberation Army Navy (PLAN)
Chinese Communist Party (CCP) 10, 106, 112, 130, 131, 154, 182, 202, 225
Chinese Monroe Doctrine 186
Chinese People's Liberation Army Daily 155–156
Chokepoint 3, 129, 175
Chokepoint blockades 129, 175
Chongqing 7
Chou En lai, see Zhou Enlai
Christopher, Warren 119
Chung-Hoon (DDG 93) 140–141
CinCPac 119, 139
Civil War, China 6, 39, 41, 106, 110, 114, 138, 169, 281
Clinton, Bill 186–187, 271
Clinton, Hillary 128, 147, 207
Cloma Affair 55–57, 113, 197
Cloma, Tomas 34, 55–57, 196, 197
Coalitions, see Naval Coalitions
Coast Guards 67, 69, 182

Coastal defense 100, 107, 111, 112, 113, 130
Cobra Gold 191
Coconut 12
Code of Conduct (CoC) 50, 66, 187, 192, 256, 280
Cold War 18, 19, 21, 29, 31, 115, 128, 179, 186
Commission on the Limits of the Continental Shelf, UN (CLCS) 59, 68, 75, 83, 86, 87, 88, 125, 151
Commodore Reef 58, 133, 201
Communism 99, 128, 130–131
Communist 10, 11, 42, 43, 106, 111–113, 128, 129–131, 138, 153, 154, 181, 182, 196, 202, 223, 225, 230
Con San Ho Lan Can, see Lamkian Cay
Confidence building measures (CBM) 50, 70, 125, 208
Confucius 41
Conoco 206
Conquest Principle 25, 29, 35, 38, 188, 191, 214–215
Container traffic 121, 142, 183
Continental Shelf xxi, 19, 28, 32, 45, 51, 57, 59, 62, 63, 69, 70, 75–84, 86, 87, 95, 97, 98–99, 105, 132, 165–166, 198, 201, 205, 207, 260, 274–277, 293, 294, 295, 296, 297, 298
Convoy operations 158
Cooperation Afloat Readiness And Training (CARAT) 191
Corbett, Julian S. 169
Cornell University 116
Counterattack in Self-Defense in the Paracel Islands 16
Crescent Island Group 8
Crestone Energy Corporation 45, 133, 137, 204, 205, 206

Crimea 29
Cross-strait crises 111, 113, 118, 120, 182, 222–224, 225–226
Cuarteron Reef 53
Cultural Relations xix, 121, 183, 218, 230, 235, 236–237, 248, 249, 255, 271, 282

Da Chau Vien, see Cuarteron Reef
Da Chu Thap, see Fiery Cross Reef
Da Gac Ma, see Johnson South Reef
Da Gaven, see Gaven Reef
Da Hu-go, see Hughes Reef
Da Subi, see Subi Reef
Dachen Islands 111, 112
Dao Loai Ta, see Loaita Island
Dai Xu 186
Dao Binh Nguyen, see Flat Island
Dao Cong Do, see Commodore Reef
Dao Dua, see West York Island
Dao Loai Ta, see Loaita Island
Dao Song Tu Dong, see North East Cay
Dao Thi Tu, see Thitu Island
Dao Vinh Vien, see Nanshan Island
Darussalam-class Offshore Patrol Boat 90
Darwin 147
De Lanessan 195
Declaration of Conduct (DoC) 50, 89, 125, 278–280
Declaration on Territorial Seas (1958) 198, 227–228, 229
Del Rosario, Albert 26
Democratic People's Republic of Korea (DPRK) 231, also see Korea
Democratic Progressive Party (DPP) 183
Democratic Republic of Vietnam (DRV) 11, 36, 44, 197, 198, 229, also see Vietnam
Demonstrations, Anti-China 48–49

Deng Xiaoping 16, 73
DF-15 Missile 116
Diaoyu Islands 80, 181, 184, 188, 250
Disaster Prevention 180
Discovery Principle 5, 25–26, 38, 41, 43, 55, 56, 60, 64, 107, 197
Djuanda Declaration 94
Djuanda, Ir. H. Kartawidjaja 94
Dongment Jiao, see Hughes Reef
Dongsha, see Pratas Islands
Dongshan Island 117
Drugs 69, 255, 279
Dulles, John Foster 113, 222–224
Duncan Island 6, 12, 37, 195
Dutch 94, 102, 129, also see Netherlands, The
Dutch East Indies 94
Duterte, Rodrigo 59, 70–71, 150, 178, 208
Dutton, Peter 176

East Asia xviii, xxii, 19, 66, 126, 128, 129, 131, 143, 154, 159, 161, 165, 166, 169, 175, 183, 185, 191, 193, 246
East China Sea 40, 111, 181
East German Navy 102
Economic sanctions 156, 189
Eleven-dashed Map 8, 9, 62, 196, 105
Embargo, see Strategic Embargo
Encyclopedia of Public International Law 27
England, see United Kingdom
English Channel 106, 128
Enhanced Defense Cooperation Agreement (EDCA) 149–150
EP-3 Incident xviii, 138–141, 157, 207
Equidistance Principle 59
Erica Reef 75, 79
Eurasia 41
Europe 5, 171, 189

INDEX   317

European Common Market (EU) xx, 193–194
Exchange of Letters (EoL) 81–83, 84, 88, 92, 152
Exclusive Economic Zone (EEZ) xviii, 27, 28, 32, 47, 55, 57, 59, 62, 63, 67, 69, 70, 77, 81, 82, 83, 85, 86, 88, 91, 95, 98, 99, 101–102, 103, 105, 133, 134, 135, 138, 165–166, 200, 201, 205, 257–270, 274–277, 293, 294, 295, 296, 297, 298
Extended Continental Shelf (ECS) 62, 97, 165–166
ExxonMobil 143

Face 139, 154, 157, 187
Far East 130
Fiery Cross Reef 6, 20, 49, 53, 70, 203, 294, 295, 296, 297, 298, 299
Finlandization 185
First Island Chain 113, 131, 179
Fisheries Management Area 95, 98
Fishing xix, xxi, 3, 12, 15–16, 18, 37, 51, 52, 55, 63–65, 70–71, 86, 92, 93–104, 113, 122, 148, 152, 172–173, 180, 190, 191, 199, 201, 202, 205, 206, 207, 208, 220, 259, 260–270, 275, 296–297
Flat Island 56, 57, 58
Fleet-in-being Strategy 158
Flyspecks 165–166, 185
Foochow, see Fuzhou
Foreign policy 17, 157, 178, 181, 232, 236
Formosa 113, 213, 216–217, 218–221, 222–226, also see Taiwan
Formosa Patrol Force, see Taiwan Patrol Force
Formosa Resolution (1955) 225–226
Forum Energy Philippine Corporation 66

France 5, 7, 8, 10, 30, 34–36, 41, 50–51, 56, 60, 114, 124, 129, 195, 196, 198, 199, 201, 202, 209–212
Freedom of Navigation (FON) 21, 22, 125, 126, 127, 141–144, 146, 159, 163, 170, 188, 207–208, 258, 276, 278
Freeman, Charles W. "Chas," Jr. 118
French Indochina 7, 30, 232, also see Vietnam
Fu Nan Zhuan (*An Account of Fu Nan*) 40
Fujian Province 99, 107, 111, 112
Fuzhou 112

G-20 156
Gaoxiong 118
Garcia Declaration 55–56
Garcia, Carlos 55
Gaven Reef 49, 53, 70, 294, 295, 296, 297, 298, 299
Geneva Convention on the Continental Shelf (1958) 57, 132
Geopolitics xx, 17, 159, 186
Gepard frigates 48
Germany 102, 124–125, 128, 173, 195, 214
Gibraltar 59
Giving Face, see Face
Global Order 170–171, 176
Global Times 153, 186, 192
Global warming 28
Globalization 127, 142, 157, 164, 170–171, 176, 180, 191, 192–194
GlobalSecurity.org 180
Go, see Weiqi
Great Britain, see United Kingdom
Great Leap Forward 12
Great Wall 145
Greater China, see China
Greater East Asian Co-Prosperity Sphere 185

INDEX

Greenert, Jonathan W. 143
Gross National Product (GNP) xix
Gross World Product 163
Guam 21, 47, 179
Guangdong Province 6, 8, 9, 18, 34, 107, 111, 195, 203, 209
Guangmin Ribao 3, 199
Guangzhou 3, 112
Guano 6, 12, 195
Gulf Oil 99
Gulf of Mexico 132
Gulf of Thailand 51
Gulf of Tonkin xxi, 5, 18, 31, 32, 34, 45, 50, 51, 148, 199, 201, 202, 205, 209–212
Gunboat Diplomacy 153
Guomindang (GMD), see Nationalist Party

Hague, The 63, 94, 299
Haig, Alexander M. 248
Haikou 9, 10
Hainan Island 1, 8–10, 48, 49, 111, 138–140, 145, 149, 157, 164, 202, 204, 206, 207
Hainan Province 45, 48, 64, 108, 203, 207
Haiphong 174, 202
Han Dynasty 4, 39, 195
Hangzhou 156
Hanoi 48, 128, 197, 205, 207, also see Vietnam
Hayton, Bill 5, 181, 188
Hegemony 72, 141, 171, 183, 185, 187, 231, 233, 235
Hoang Sa, see Paracel Islands
Hoe 196
Hokkaido 129, 215
Holland, see Netherlands, The
Hong Kong 3, 59, 118, 121, 130, 166, 183, 204

Hong Kong Far Eastern Meteorological Conference 7
Hu Jintao 66, 89, 91, 281
Hu Yaobang 202
Hu, Nien-Tsu Alfred 104
Huang Hua 180, 248
Huang Jing 147
Huangyan Dao, see Scarborough Shoal
Huayang Jiao, see Cuarteron Reef
Hughes Reef 53, 294, 295, 296, 297, 298, 299
HY-2 antiship cruise missile 48

Ijhtihad-class Fast Attack Boat 90
Illegal, unreported, and unregulated fishing (IUU) 172, 191
Impeccable (T-AGOS 23) 140–141, 207
Independence (CV 62) 119–120, 182
India xvii, 93, 172, 175, 180, 181, 190, 231, 232
Indian Ocean xvii, 2, 3, 19, 117, 162, 180, 195, 202
Indochina, see French Indochina
Indonesia vii, xvii, xxi, 1, 12, 23, 38, 48, 51, 77, 89, 91, 92, 93–104, 108, 122, 130, 133, 152, 204, 256, 280
Indonesia-China Centre for Ocean and Climate (ICCOC) 100
Indonesian National Army (TNI) 102
International Aviation Transport Association 43, 197
International Court of Justice (ICJ) 42, 95, 270
International Law xx, xxi, 24–29, 35, 39, 45, 53, 56, 57–58, 59, 68, 72, 75, 77, 86, 110, 122, 133–135, 147, 166, 185, 258, 270, 274, 276, 278–279, 299
International Monetary Fund 121, 183
Investigator Shoal 75, 79
Irving Reef 58

INDEX

Itu Aba Island xvii, 3, 4. 8, 10, 21, 22, 27, 39, 41–42, 50, 55, 79, 105, 106–111, 113–115, 122, 125, 152, 175, 182, 184, 196, 197, 198–199, 202, 203, 205–206, 207
Izumo helicopter carrier 144

J-15 jets 158
Jakarta 77, 93–94, 95, 96, 100, 101, 102, 103
James Shoal 75, 80, 97, 203
Japan xvii, 1, 3, 6, 7–8, 10–11, 25, 28, 32, 35, 38, 41, 42, 54, 56, 57, 59, 80, 89, 91, 100, 107, 113, 114, 116, 118, 119, 123–124, 129–131, 141, 143, 144, 145, 154, 159, 162, 164, 166, 167–168, 173, 175, 176, 177, 183–184, 185, 186, 187, 188, 192, 196, 197, 199, 213, 214–215, 216–217, 218–221, 231, 232
Japanese Maritime Self Defense Force (JMSDF) 144, 154
Jia Qinling 91
Jiang Jieshi, see Chiang Kai-shek
Jiang Zemin 50, 145, 186
Jilong 118
Jinggangshan 80
Jinmen Island 107, 111, 112, 119, 129, 227
Johnson Reef 49, 70, 203, 294, 295, 296, 297, 298, 299
Johnson South Reef 20, 49, 53, 203
Joint Fishing Zone 51
Joint Marine Seismic Undertaking (JMSU) 65–66
Joint Malaysia-Brunei Darussalam Land Boundary Technical Committee 83
Joint Operational Access Concept (JOAC) 142
Journalists 181, 233, also see Media

Kagitinigan, see Fiery Cross Reef
Kalayaan Island Group (KIG) xxi, 2, 26, 55–58, 72, 73, 197, 198, 199, 200, 202, 203, 207
Kalayann Atin Ito Movement 72–73
Kamikaze 141
Kang Tai 40
Kaohsiung, see Gaoxiong
Katchen, Martin 35, 84
Katsuo Okazaki 42
Keating, Timothy 140
Keelung, see Jilong
Kennan Reef, see Johnson South Reef
Kerry, John 143
Kilo-class submarine 47, 178, 179
Kissinger, Henry 230
Kohl, Helmut 124
Korea xvii, 84, 102, 118, 128, 129, 174, 213, 216, 231, 232
Korean War 174, 182
Kosh, Gerald 17–18
Kota Island, see Loaita Island
Koxinga, see Zheng Chenggong
Kublai Khan 41, 64
Kuomintang (KMT), see Nationalist Party
Kurile Islands 216

L'Union d'Incochine, see French Indochina
La Milicieuse 195
Lankiam Cay 58, 206
Lanyu Island 59
Laos 1, 231, 280
Law on the Territorial Sea and Contiguous Zone (1992) 46, 78, 250–254
Lawak Island, see Nanshan Island
Layang-Layang, see Swallow Reef
Le Miere, Christian 153
Lee Teng-hui 116
Lenin, Vladimir 154

Li Xun 6, 195
Liang Kung-kai 175
Liaoning 158
Liberation Army Daily 156–157
Ligitan Island 95
Likas Island, see West York Island
Lile Tan, see Reed Bank
Limbang 82
Littoral 19, 21, 142, 146, 177, 186
Liu Ta-Tsai 39, 204
Liu Yuan 192
Lloyd, Selwyn 130
Loaita Island 58, 196, 206
Location Map of the South China Sea Islands, The 96
Lombok Strait 175
Lorenzana, Delfin 150
Los Angeles 118
Losing Face, see Face
Louisa Reef 81, 84, 85, 86–88, 91, 152, 202
Luzon 63, 206

Ma Ying-jeou 108, 122
Mabini, see Johnson Reef
Macapagal-Arroyo, Gloria 66
Macclesfield Bank xv, 48, 63, 97, 105, 108
Mahan, Alfred Thayer 167, 171, 173
Mahathir Mohamed 78, 82
Malacca 4, 170, 171
Malacca Strait 17, 40, 138, 157, 162, 170, 171, 175, 180, 181
Malaya 130, also see Malaysia
Malaysia vii, xvii, xxi, 1, 12, 29, 38, 51, 62, 74, 75–84, 85, 87, 88, 92, 93, 94–96, 97–98, 103, 129, 133, 135, 149, 150–152, 198, 199, 201, 202, 203, 204, 205, 207, 256, 280
Manchuria 106, 213
Mandate of Heaven 154
Manila 3, 65, 197, 198, 206, 256

Mantanani, see Mariveles Bank
Mao Tsetung, see Mao Zedong
Mao Zedong 106, 174, 230
Marcos, Ferdinand 56, 57, 198, 199
Maritime Institute of the Philippines 55
Mariveles Bank 75, 78, 133, 201, 202
Matsu Island, see Mazu Island
Mazu Island 107, 112, 119, 227, 271
McKennan Reef 70, 295, 296
Media 53, 82, 119, 181, 233
Meiji Jiao, see Mischief Reef
Memorandum of Understanding (MOU) 83, 99
Menzies, Robert G. 130
Mercado, Orlando 149
Miao Islands 111
Middle East xviii, 170
Ming Dynasty 4, 40, 195
Ministry of Marine Affairs and Fisheries (MMAF) 95
Mischief Reef 49, 53, 60, 89, 205, 293, 294, 295, 296, 297, 298
Missile Blockade 115–120, 121, 156, 181, 271–273
Mobil Oil 45, 99
Mongolian People's Republic (MPR), see Outer Mongolia
Mount Penatubo 21
Mullen, Michael viii, 142
Multilateral negotiations 30, 189
Murphy Oil Company 81, 82, 83
Myanmar 1, 280

Namyit Island 4, 295
Nan Tong Jiao, see Louisa Reef
Nan Zhou Yi Wu Zhi (Strange Things of the Southern Provinces) 40
Nanhai zhudao weizhi tu, see *Location Map of the South China Sea Islands, The*
Nansha Islands, see Spratly Islands

Nansha Qundao, see Spratly Islands
Nanshan Island 57, 58
Nanwei Island, see Spratly Islands
Nanwei Tan, see Rifleman Bank
Nanxun Jiao, see Gaven Reef
Napoleon Bonaparte 128
National Assembly of Vietnam 51, 202
National People's Congress of China 51, 250, 274, 281, 283
National Petroleum Board (South Vietnam) 15
National University of Singapore 147
Nationalism 190, 194
Nationalist Navy 6, 39, 113, 154, 169
Nationalist Party 106, 126, 129, 196
Nationalist blockade of PRC 111, 146, 169–170
Natuna Islands xxi, 12, 51, 93–104, 152
Natuna Sea 93–104
Natural Gas xix, xx, 12–14, 93, 99, 121, 131–133, 135–138, 148
Natural Prolongation Principle 274
Natural Resources xviii, xxii, 12–15, 65, 100, 132, 133–134, 148, 150, 165–166, 257, 274, 275
Naval Blockades 65, 111, 117, 146, 156, 169–170
Naval Coalitions 170
Naval Intelligence, see Office of Naval Intelligence
Naval War College, see United States Naval War College
Navy Cross 141
Navy, China, see People's Liberation Army Navy
Netherlands, The 94, 102, 129
New Delhi 143
New Guinea 93
New Security Concept 89
New York Times 71, 118
New Zealand 5
Newport, RI 142
Nguyen Minh Triet 50
Nimitz (CVN 68) 117–118, 119–120, 182
Nine-dashed Map 32, 60–63, 68, 73, 75, 85, 88, 96–97, 98, 104, 105, 109, 125–126, 295
Nixon, Richard 17, 115, 185, 230–234, 271
North America 143, 194
North American Free Trade Agreement (NAFTA) 194
North Atlantic Treaty Organization (NATO) 187
North Borneo 195, 207
North East Cay 58
North Vietnam 11–12, 15–18, 27, 36–37, 43–44, 174, 197, 199, 229, also see Vietnam
Northeast Asia 164
Norway 103
Nuclear Weapon 180, 239, 251

Obama, Barack 147
Occupation Principle xvi, 7, 10, 19, 25–29, 31, 35–36, 38, 41, 42, 43, 44, 45, 55, 56, 57–58, 68, 72, 75, 79, 83, 89, 107, 110, 114, 122, 149, 151, 168, 197, 198, 200, 202
Office of Naval Intelligence 112
Offshore-balancing 191–192
Offshore Islands xviii, xix, 3, 46, 107, 110–113, 125, 129, 130, 152, 169, 181, 182, 250
Ogasawara Islands 216
Okinawa 21, 119, 129, 130
Open Door Policy xxii, 183, 193
Operation Unified Assistance 157
Outer Mongolia 15, 17, 154

Pacific Ocean 2, 177, 225
Pacific War, see World War II

PACOM 191
Pag-asa Island, see Thitu Island
Pakistan 231, 232
Palau 93
Palauig, Zambales 63
Palawan Province 2, 55, 56, 58, 67, 132, 150, 199, 200
Panata Cay, see Lamkian Cay
Panatag Shoal, see Scarborough Shoal
Panganiban, see Mischief Reef
Papua New Guinea 93
Paracel Islands xv, xvii, xviii, xix, xx, xxi, 1, 2-3, 6-8, 10-12, 15-19, 27, 29-30, 31, 32, 34, 35, 36, 37, 39-40, 42, 43-45, 46, 48, 52, 57, 80, 88, 96-97, 107-108, 110-111, 114, 125, 126, 131, 138, 145, 147, 149, 164, 174, 178, 190, 195, 196, 197, 198, 199, 200, 201, 202, 204, 208, 216, 218, 229
Paris 5, 60, 209
Park, Choon-Ho 84, 166
Parola, see North East Cay
Patag Island, see Flat Island
Pattle Island 8
Pearl Harbor 129, 179
Penghu Islands 6, 107, 112, 129, 213, 216-217, 218-219, 220, 224, 225-226, 227-228, 247, 250
Peninjau, see Investigator Shoal
People's Liberation Army (PLA) 10, 16, 17, 53, 110-112, 117-120, 122, 130, 146, 147, 148, 182, 199
People's Liberation Army Air Force 10
People's Liberation Army Navy (PLAN) xvii, 10, 16, 18, 43, 47, 52, 80, 102, 108, 112, 115, 116, 125, 134, 144-146, 153, 154-156, 157-159, 164-165, 169-170, 174, 175, 176, 179-180, 190

People's Republic of China (PRC), see China
Permanent Court of Arbitration, see United Nations Permanent Court of Arbitration (PCA)
Persian Gulf 13, 119
Pescadores Islands, see Penghu Islands
Peta Baru 81
Petroleum vii, xix, 12-15, 19, 45, 46, 47, 51-52, 65, 66, 68, 70, 75, 81-83, 84, 85, 89-90, 91, 93, 99, 106, 121, 127, 131, 132, 133, 135-138, 143, 148, 160, 162, 163, 164, 170, 175, 178, 182, 185, 188, 190-191, 199, 200, 201, 202, 204, 205, 206, 208, 293
Petronas Oil Company 81, 83
Pham Van Dong 11, 36, 44, 198, 200, 229
Philippine Sea Baseline Bill (2009) 58, 64, 207
Philippine Coast Guard 68-69
Philippine National Oil Company (PNOC) 65
Philippine Treaty Limits 58, 59
Philippines vii, xvii, xviii, xxi, 1, 2, 12, 13-14, 19, 21, 25, 26, 29, 34, 39, 47, 53, 54-74, 79, 89, 90, 92, 93, 103, 113, 115, 122, 129-130, 131, 132, 133, 135, 148, 149-150, 152, 153, 161, 173, 178, 184, 186, 187, 188, 192, 196, 197, 198, 199, 200, 201, 202, 203, 205, 206, 207, 208, 256, 280, 292, 293, 294, 295, 296, 297, 298
Phuoc Tay Province 15, 36, 198, 199
Pike, John 180
Pivot to Asia 128, 146, 147-153, 208
Poaching 65, 103, 122
Poland 124
Posner, Eric 185
Potsdam 118, 214

Potsdam Declaration (1945) 8, 116, 129, 214–215
Pratas Islands xv, 3, 6, 7, 8, 10, 37, 59, 96, 105, 106, 111, 112, 125, 126, 119–200, 250
Prescription Principle 25, 27
Prueher, Joseph W. viii, 119–120, 139–140, 157
Pudjiastuti, Susi 104
Pulau Sekatung, see Natuna Islands
Pulse Asia Survey 73
Putin, Vladimir 70, 156

Qian Qichen 134, 204
Qin Jiwei 205
Qing Dynasty 4, 6, 129, 195
Qingshui River 210, 211
Qiongzhou Strait 111
Quan Dao Nham Dan 44
Quemoy Island, see Jinmen Island
Quintuple Alliance 189

Ramos, Fidel 205
RAND 175
Razak, Datuk Seri Najib Abdul 75–76, 83, 205, 208
RC-135 Rivet Joint 119
Reagan, Ronald 248, 271
Reclamation xxi, xxii, 32, 49, 53, 72, 145, 166, 169, 173, 178, 185, 189, 294, 297, 298
Reed Bank 13, 66, 67, 132, 133, 200, 293, 296
Regional Comprehensive Economic Partnership (RCEP) 194
Ren'ai Reef, see Second Thomas Shoal
Replenishment at sea 176
Republic of China (ROC) 9, 10, 21, 32, 37, 38, 39, 41, 42, 43, 55, 77, 79, 81, 85, 88, 105, 106, 107, 108, 110, 112, 114, 120–125, 126, 130, 148, 160, 170, 178, 181–184, 188, 195, 196, 197, 198, 199, 201, 202, 203, 204, 213, 214–215, 218–221, 222–224, 225–226, 236–247, 271–273, 281–283, also see Taiwan
Republic of Indonesia, see Indonesia
Republic of Korea (ROK), see South Korea
Republic of Vietnam (ROV), see South Vietnam
res nullius Principle 56, 57
Riau Province 93
Rifleman Bank 85, 86, 87, 88, 91, 152
Rizal Reef, see Commodore Reef
Romulo, Roberto 150
Royal Brunei Armed Forces (RBAF) 90
Royal Brunei Navy (RBN) 90
Russia xvii, xviii, 21, 29, 31, 44, 47, 48, 70–71, 116, 139, 154–156, 159, 172, 177, 178, 193, also see Union of Soviet Socialist Republics (USSR)

Sa Zhenbing 6
Sabah 95
Saigon 197, also see South Vietnam
Sakishima Islands 59
Salen Exploration Company 132–133
Sampaguita No. 1 132–133, 200
Samuels, Marwyn 37
San Francisco 10, 32, 42, 57, 218
San Francisco Peace Treaty (1951) 10, 11, 28, 32, 38, 41, 42, 56, 57, 107, 124, 149, 196–197, 216–217, 218–220
Sanctions 156, 189
Sand Cay 4
Sansha 32, 48–49, 108, 207, 208
Sanya 145
Sarawak 82, 96, 205
Saudi Arabia 14

Scarborough Shoal xv, 54–55, 58, 60, 63–64, 70, 71, 96, 206, 207, 295, 296, 297, 298
Sea Control 164, 167, 169–172, 173, 176, 178, 181
Sea Denial 164, 167, 172–176, 177, 178, 164, 167, 172–175
Sea Lanes xvii, 3, 18, 22, 40, 118, 129, 131, 143, 144, 163, 174–175, 208, 252, 260
Sea Lines of Communication (SLOC) vii, 2–3, 141, 145, 146, 163–164, 168, 173, 180, 181, 188
Sea of Okhotsk 179
Sea Power 127, 142, 169–170, 171–172, 175
Second Thomas Shoal 58, 69, 293, 294, 295, 296, 297
Senkaku Islands, see Diaoyu Islands
September 11, see 9–11
Seventh Fleet, see United States Navy
Shandong Peninsula 111
Shanghai 230
Shanghai Communiqué 17, 230–234, 235, 248–249, 271–273
Shell Oil Company 81
Shigemitsu Mamoru 130
Shinnan Gunto 7, 196
Short-Range Ballistic Missile (SRBM) 116–117
Siddayao, Corazon 57
Singapore xvii, 1, 3, 21, 91, 93, 129, 134, 147, 256, 280
Sino-centric 37
Sino-French Conflict (1884-1885) 5, 129, 196
Sino-French Convention (1887) 5, 34, 51, 60, 114, 195–196, 199, 201, 202, 209–212
Sino-Japanese War, First (1894-1895) 6, 129, 192
Sinopec 190

Sino-Vietnamese Agreement on Fishing Cooperation in the Gulf of Tonkin (2000) 51
Sino-Vietnamese Agreement on the Delimitation of Waters, EEZ and Continental Shelves in the Gulf of Tonkin (2000) 32, 50–51, 206
Sino-Vietnamese Land Border Treaty (1999) 31
Sino-Vietnamese Supplemental Protocol to the Fishing Agreement (2004) 51
Sipadan Island 95
Siput, see Erica Reef
Song Dynasty 40, 195, 199, 201
Song Tu Tay Dao, see Southwest Cay
South Asia 188–189, 232
South China Sea (SCS) vii, xv–xxii, 1, 2–8, 9, 11, 12–15, 17, 18, 19, 21, 22, 23–24, 25, 26, 27, 28, 29, 30, 31–53, 54–74, 75, 76, 77, 78, 79, 81–83, 84, 85, 86–88, 89, 90, 91, 92, 93, 94–99, 101, 103, 104, 105–126, 127–160, 161, 162, 163–168, 169–176, 177, 178, 179, 180, 181–184, 185, 187, 188, 189, 190, 191–194, 195–208, 255–256, 278–280, 292–299
  Accretion Principle 25, 27–28
  Artificial Accretion Principle 27–28
  Cession Principle 25, 28–29, 36, 107
  Conquest Principle 25, 29, 35, 38, 188, 191, 214–215
  Discovery Principle 5, 25–26, 38, 41, 43, 55, 56, 60, 64, 107, 197
  Equidistance Principle 59
  Natural Prolongation Principle 274
  Occupation Principle xvi, 7, 10, 19, 25–29, 31, 35–36, 38, 41,

42, 43, 44, 45, 55, 56, 57–58, 68, 72, 75, 79, 83, 89, 107, 110, 114, 122, 149, 151, 168, 197, 198, 200, 202
Prescription Principle 25, 27
Reclamation xxi, xxii, 32, 49, 53, 72, 145, 166, 169, 173, 178, 185, 189, 294, 297, 298
res nullius Principle 56, 57
terra communis Principle 25
terra nullius Principle 25, 26, 35, 55–56
South Korea xvii, 122, 130, 131, 145, 162, 164, also see Korea
South Sea Fleet 18, 145, 159, 177
South Vietnam xvii–xviii, 3, 10–12, 15–18, 27, 32–34, 36, 37, 43, 44, 52, 108, 114, 130, 149, 174, 197, 198, 199, 231, also see Vietnam
Southeast Asia xv, xvii, xviii, 1, 3, 5, 19, 21, 22, 23–24, 29, 31, 42, 47, 50, 66, 75, 79, 85, 88, 89, 91, 92, 99, 125, 126, 127, 129, 133, 135, 153, 161, 163, 176, 177, 178, 179, 184, 185, 186, 187, 188, 189, 192, 192, 193, 194, 204, 255–256, 278–280, 292
Southwest Cay 4, 53
Soviet Navy 19, 45, 47, 202
Soviet Union xvii, 17, 44, 47, 145, 174, 186, 193, also see Union of Soviet Socialist Republics (USSR)
Spain 59, 60, 63, 65
Spratly Islands xv, xvii, xviii, xix, xx, xxi, 1–30, 31–53, 54–74, 75–84, 85–92, 95, 96–97, 105, 107–108, 110, 113–114, 122, 123–124, 125–126, 131–133, 134–135, 137, 138, 142, 143, 146, 147, 148, 149, 150, 152, 158, 159, 160, 161, 164, 176, 180, 185, 186, 187, 188, 189, 190, 191, 192, 195, 196, 197, 198, 199, 200, 201, 202, 203, 204, 205, 206, 207, 208, 216, 229, 250–254, 296, 299
Spratly, Richard 5, 195
Stalin, Joseph 118, 154, 174
Stepping Stone 113, 129, 167
Storey, Ian 87, 122
Storm Island, see Spratly Islands
Straits Exchange Foundation (SEF) 183, 273, 284–291
Strategic embargo 156, 170
SU-27 Flanker 48
Su-30MK2 maritime bomber 47–48
Subi Reef 49, 53, 294, 295, 296, 297, 298, 299
Subic Bay 47, 64
Submarines 3, 8, 10, 18, 30, 44, 47, 77, 102, 113, 145, 156, 164, 175, 177, 178, 179–180, 196, 198, 208, 251
Suhartono, Agus 102, 103
Sumatra 157
Sun Jiazheng 91
Sun Yuwen 209
Sunda Strait 175
Supriyanto, Ristian Atriandi 100
Swallow Reef 75, 78, 201, 202
Sweden 132, 200

Taipei 39, 59, 116, 131, 224
Taiping 113, 196
Taiping Island 8, 39, 42, 105, 175, 197, 198, 203, also see Itu Aba Island
Taiwan vii, xvii, xxi, 1, 3, 6, 7, 9, 10, 11, 12, 13, 21, 22, 27, 28, 29, 32, 36, 37, 38, 39, 41, 42, 43, 50, 55, 56, 57, 59, 60, 63, 64, 77, 79, 81, 84, 85, 86, 88, 104, 105–126, 128–131, 138, 145, 147, 148, 152–153, 154, 156–157, 160, 162, 164, 170, 172, 174, 175, 177, 178, 181–184, 187, 188, 195, 196, 197, 198, 199, 201, 202, 203, 204, 205, 206, 207,

213, 214–215, 216–217, 218–221, 222–224, 225–226, 227–228, 233, 235, 236–247, 248–249, 250, 271–273, 281–283, 284–291
Taiwan Fisheries Research Institute 201
Taiwan Patrol Force 174
Taiwan Relations Act (1979) 120, 236–247, 271, 272, 273
Taiwan Strait 11, 106–107, 112, 113, 115–120, 128–129, 131, 138, 152, 160, 181, 182, 183, 222–224, 225–226, 233, 271, 272, 273, 281–283, 284, 291
Taiwan Strait Crisis (1954–1955) 107, 113, 120, 131, 222–224, 225–226
Taiwan Strait Crisis (1958) 11, 107, 113, 120, 131
Taiwan Strait Crisis (1995–1996) 115–120, 138, 182, 271–273
Takao-shu 7, 196
Tang Dynasty 199
Tang Jiaxuan 89
Tannu Tuva 15, 124
Tarim Basin 137
Tennent Reef 206
Tennessee 157
terra communis Principle 25
terra nullius Principle 25, 26, 35, 55–56
Territorial Sea 11, 27, 36, 46, 58, 68–69, 78, 87, 94, 95, 105, 132, 138, 165, 198, 199, 200, 202, 227–228, 250–254, 257–270, 274, 295, 296
Territoriale Zee en Maritime Kringen Ordonnantie 1939 94
Terumbu Layang, see Swallow Reef
Terumbu Mantanani, see Mariveles Reef
Terumbu Peninjau, see Investigator Shoal

Terumbu Semarang Barat Kecil, see Louisa Reef
Terumbu Siput, see Erica Reef
Terumbu Ubi, see Ardasier Reef
Thailand 1, 51, 93, 98, 256, 280
The Location Map of the South China Sea Islands 96
Thitu Island 4, 57, 58, 71, 73, 295
Thompson, Randall 205
Three Kingdoms 40, 195
Three No's Strategy 189
Timor Island 93
Timor-Leste 93
Tizard Bank 21, 201
Tokyo 91, 129, 130
TotalFinaElf 207
Total Oil Company 81
Tran Van Huu 197
Treaty of Portsmouth (1905) 216
Treaty of Shimonoseki (1895) 129
Tripartite Agreement for Joint Marine Seismic Undertaking in the Agreement Area in the South China Sea (JMSU Tripartite Agreement) 65, 66, 67
Truman, Harry S. 132
Trump, Donald 146, 194
Truong Sa, see Spratly Islands
Tuva, see Tannu Tuva
Two Chinas 106, 130, 160, 181, 184, 233, 249

Ubi, see Ardasier Reef
Union of Soviet Socialist Republics (USSR) xvii, xviii, 15, 17, 18, 19, 21, 43, 44–45, 47, 115–116, 124, 145, 156, 170, 174, 179, 186, 193, 201, 202
United Daily News 118
United Front 126, 153, 181–184, 188
United Kingdom 5, 106, 124, 128, 166, 186, 214

United Nations (UN) 29, 56, 59, 62, 68–72, 77, 86, 95, 96, 97, 106, 131, 213, 216, 219, 222–226, 231, 232, 257–270, 278
United Nations Commission on the Limits of the Continental Shelf (UNCLCS) 68, 75, 83, 86, 87–88, 125, 152
United Nations Committee for the Coordination of Joint Prospecting in Asian Off-shore Areas 13
United Nations Convention on the Law of the Seas (UNCLOS) xx, 4, 58, 62–63, 68, 73, 77, 79, 80, 82, 88, 94, 96, 105, 133–135, 143, 165, 187, 189, 257–270
United Nations Education, Scientific and Cultural Organization (UNESCO) 20, 203
United Nations Permanent Court of Arbitration (PCA) xv, xx, 4, 24, 26, 29, 55, 62–63, 68, 70, 71, 73, 96, 99, 104, 122, 134, 148, 156, 160, 187, 189, 208, 292–299
United States, see United States Government
United States Energy Information Administration 13
United States Government xv, xvii, xviii, xx, xxi, xxii, 1, 13, 17, 18, 19, 21, 29, 31, 45, 47, 54, 60, 64, 70, 72, 73, 81, 91, 100, 103, 108, 112, 113, 114, 115, 116, 117, 118, 120, 121, 124, 126, 127–160, 162, 163, 165, 167, 170, 171, 174, 175, 176, 177, 178, 179, 181, 182, 184, 185, 186, 187, 191, 192, 193, 194, 197, 202, 204, 206, 207–208, 214–215, 216–217, 222–224, 225–226, 227–228, 230–234, 235, 236–247, 248–249, 271–273
United States Marine Corps 147

United States Naval War College 157, 167
United States Navy 17, 18, 19, 21, 47, 64, 112, 115–120, 128, 129–130, 138–141, 142–144, 146, 156–157, 159, 162, 165, 170, 174, 176, 179, 181, 182, 196, 207
United States-Republic Of China Mutual Defense Treaty (1955) 222–224
United States Seventh Fleet 18, 21, 47, 182
United States Taiwan Straits Patrol, see Taiwan Patrol Force
United States-Philippine Mutual Defense Treaty (1951) 148, 149, 150
U-shape Line Map 60, 61, 96, 109, also see Nine-dashed Map
USNS *Impeccable* (T-AGOS 23) 140–141, 207
USNS *Victorious* (T-AGOS 19) 141
USS *Callaghan* (DDG 994) 157
USS *Chung-Hoon* (DDG 93) 140, 141
USS *Hoe* 196
USS *Independence* (CV 62) 119, 120, 182
USS *Nimitz* (CVN 68) 117–118, 119–120, 182

Vanguard Bank 53, 205
Victorious (T-AGOS 19) 141
Vietnam vii, xvii–xviii, xxi, 1, 3, 5, 7, 10–12, 13, 15–19, 20–21, 22, 24, 27, 29, 30, 31–53, 55, 56, 57, 60, 62, 65, 75, 77, 78, 79, 83, 84, 85, 86, 87–88, 92, 93, 94, 95, 97, 98, 103, 108, 110, 113, 114, 122, 124, 125, 128, 130, 133, 135, 143, 147, 148, 149, 151, 152, 153, 156, 161, 174, 178, 182, 184, 186, 188, 195, 196, 197, 198, 199, 200, 201,

202, 203, 204, 205, 206, 207, 208, 229
Vietnam Navy 206
Vietnam Oil and Gas Corporation (PETROVIETNAM) 65
Vietnam War 178

Wan Shan Islands 112
Wan Zhen 40
Wan'an Bei-21 137, 205
Wang Hanling 72
Wang Jingwei 10
Wang Yi 280
Washington 138, 224
Washington Post 140
Weapons of mass destruction (WMD) 180, 239
Weiqi 166, 168
Wen Jiabao 79, 88
West Germany 124, 128
West Kalimantan 96, 102
West York Island 4, 58
Western Pacific 47, 175, 193, 225, 236, 237, 272
White Dragon 204
White Rajahs 82
White Tiger 133
White, Hugh 177
Widodo, Joko 102
Wilayah Pengelolaan Perikanan (WPP) 95
Wisecup, James P. 157
Woody Island 8, 10, 11, 48–49, 80, 138
World Trade Organization (WTO) 284, 285, 288, 289
World War I 5, 213
World War II 3, 8–12, 15, 30, 35, 38, 42, 43, 55, 56, 79, 106, 107, 110,
113, 114, 124, 129–130, 138, 141, 154, 169, 170, 173
Wu Di 39
Wuchiu Island 119, 227, 271

Xi Jinping 70, 89, 208
Xiamen 112
Xinhua 23, 202
Xisha Islands, see Paracel Islands
Xisha Ziwei Fanjizhan, see Counterattack in Self-Defense in the Paracel Islands

Yang Jiechi 91–92, 189
Yeh, George Kung-chao 218–221, 222–224
Yellow Sea 131, 141, 158
Yongshu Jiao, see Fiery Cross Reef
Yu, Peter Kien-hong 43
Yuan Dynasty 40–41, 64
Yulin 10, 145

Zain, Yacob 78, 204
Zamora Reef, see Subi Reef
Zengmu, see James Shoal
Zhanjiang 145
Zhao Ziyang 248
Zhejiang Hengyi Group 89
Zhejiang Province 107, 111, 112
Zheng Chenggong 129–130
Zheng He 4, 195
Zhongsha, see Macclesfield Bank
Zhongye 113, 196
Zhongzhou, see Tizard Bank
Zhou Enlai 11, 36, 42, 196, 198, 230
Zhubi Jiao, see Subi Reef